THE RELIGIOUS POLEMICS OF AMOS

SUPPLEMENTS

TO

VETUS TESTAMENTUM

EDITED BY
THE BOARD OF THE QUARTERLY

J. A. EMERTON - W. L. HOLLADAY - A. LEMAIRE
R. E. MURPHY - E. NIELSEN - R. SMEND
J. A. SOGGIN - M. WEINFELD

VOLUME XXXIV

LEIDEN
E. J. BRILL
1984

THE RELIGIOUS POLEMICS OF AMOS

Studies in the Preaching of Am 2, 7B-8; 4,1-13; 5,1-27; 6, 4-7; 8, 14.

BY

HANS M. BARSTAD

LEIDEN
E. J. BRILL
1984

ISBN 90 04 07017 6

PRINTED IN THE NETHERLANDS

To the memory of my father, the Rev. Sverre I. Barstad, in grateful remembrance of my earliest lessons in the Old Testament.

TABLE OF CONTENTS

ACKNOWLEDGEMENTS

Sincere thanks are due to several persons who made the preparation of this book much easier. My particular thanks are due to Professor Benedikt Otzen, Aarhus, Professor Ebbe Egede Knudsen, Oslo, and Professor Magne Sæbø, Oslo, who read the manuscript of this book and made many valuable suggestions about the ways in which it might be improved; and further to Professor Eduard Nielsen, Copenhagen, who accepted the manuscript for inclusion in the series *Supplements to Vetus Testamentum.* Since I have not in all cases acted on the advice which either of these scholars has given, they should not in any way be held responsible for mistakes which occur in the text. The faults of this work are exclusively my own.

I have received much help from many people in the course of my work. I hope no one will fell offended when I single out Professor James Barr of Oxford. The many valuable conversations with this great scholar and fine person have, I hope, left much more ample traces in the work than one might guess from the few explicit references.

However, in spite of the rich contributions I received from each of the above-mentioned mentors, the present work would not have been done had it not been for the wise teaching, counsel and superb guidance through the vast area of prophetic research by my Old Testament teacher, Professor Arvid S. Kapelrud of the University of Oslo. I owe him more than I can express, and my debt to him will probably never be fully repaid.

Much of the research necessary for the present work was made possible through a research fellowship awarded by the Norwegian Research Council for Science and the Humanities in 1976 and 1978-79. I am deeply indebted to the Norwegian Research Council also for a substantial grant in support of publication. For assistance in bringing the present work to completion I am grateful to the Nordic Council of Ministers, the Secretariat for Nordic Cultural Cooperation. My manuscript was finished in May 1981, and I have been unable to take any notice of literature which has reached me after this time.

I further wish to thank the staff of the following libraries who have assisted me: the Library of the Pontifical Biblical Institute in Rome, the Bodleian Library and the Ashmolean Library, Oxford, the Royal Library, Copenhagen, the British Library and the library of the School of Oriental and African Studies, Cambridge University Library. Last but not least I wish to render a grateful word of appreciation to my colleagues at the Royal University Library, Oslo.

My chief thanks, however, must be given to my family for their continuous support; especially to my father, who encouraged me in this work in its early stages, but has, regrettably, not lived to see its completion, and to Wenche, Hans Petter and Kristine, for their love and patience during the long incubation period of this study.

Finally, I want to thank Mrs. Ann Franken-Battershill, who most willingly undertook the difficult task of correcting my ''foreign English'', and the Oriental Editor of E. J. Brill, Dr. F. Th. Dijkema, who provided professional counsel and assistance at every stage of the editing and publishing of this book.

Hokksund, February, 1983
Hans M. Barstad

ABBREVIATIONS

The abbreviations in the following list of literature quoted in the text are taken from S. Schwertner, *Internationales Abkürzungsverzeichnis für Theologie und Grenzgebiete. Zeitschriften, Serien, Lexika, Quellenwerke mit bibliographischen Angaben.* Berlin 1974.

Note: The references to the literature found in this book are often given in an abbreviated form. For full references one should always consult the bibliography.

The following abbreviations are not found in, or differ from, Schwertner:

AJBA	*Australian Journal of Biblical Archaeology*, Sydney.
ASORDS	*American Schools of Oriental Research. Dissertation Series*, Missoula, Mont., and Ann Arbor, MI.
AuS	See below Dalman, 1928-37.
BeitrAltTheol	*Beiträge zur Alttestamentlichen Theologie. Festschrift für Walther Zimmerli zum 70. Geburtstag.* Hg. v. H. Donner, R. Hanhart u. R. Smend. Göttingen 1977.
BRL[2]	See below Galling, 1977.
CRST	*The Claremont Ras Shamra Tablets.* Ed. by L. R. Fisher in Collaboration with M. C. Astour, M. Dahood, and P. D. Miller. Roma 1971 (*AnOr* 48).
DISO	See below Jean.
EAE	See below Avi-Yona.
GB	See below Frazer, 1915.
HAL	See below Köhler, 1967-.
HDR	*Harvard Dissertations in Religion*, Missoula, Mont.
IDBS	*The Interpreter's Dictionary of the Bible. An Illustrated Encyclopedia. General Editor K. Crim.* Supplementary Volume. Nashville, Tennessee 1976.
IGLS	See below Jalabert.
JANES	*The Journal of the Ancient Near Eastern Society of Columbia University*, New York.
JSOT	*Journal for the Study of the Old Testament*, Sheffield.
JSS	*Journal of Semitic Studies*, Manchester.
LÄ	*Lexikon der Ägyptologie.* Hg. v. W. Helck u. E. Otto. Wiesbaden 1975-.
OAC	*Orientis antiqui collectio*, Roma.
OECT	*Oxford Editions of Cuneiform Texts.*
PIBA	*Proceedings of the Irish Biblical Association*, Dublin.
ProblBiblTheol	*Probleme Biblischer Theologie. Gerhard von Rad zum 70. Geburtstag.* Hg. v. H. W. Wolff. München 1971.
PRU	See below *La Palais Royal d'Ugarit.*
PTMS	*Pittsburgh Theological Monograph Series*, Pittsburgh, PA.
RAO	See below Clermont-Ganneau.
RES	See below *Repértoire...*
RSF	*Rivista di Studi Fenici*, Roma.
Sacra Pagina	*Sacra Pagina. Miscellanea Biblica Congressus Internationalis Catholici de Re*

	Biblica (*Brux. et Louv. 1958*). Ed. J. Coppens, A. Dechamps, É. Massaux. Vol. I. Gembloux 1959 (*BEThL* 12).
Saglio	*Dictionnaire des antiquités grecques et romaines d'après les textes et les monuments.* Sous la direction de E. Saglio. Paris 1877-1919.
SaSe	*Samaria Sebaste. Reports of the Work of the Joint Expedition in 1931-33 and of the British Expedition in 1935.*
SBLDS	*Society of Biblical Literature. Dissertation Series* Missoula, Mont., and Chico, CA.
SVT	Supplements to Vetus Testamentum.
TA	*Tel Aviv. Journal of the Tel Aviv University Institute of Archaeology*, Tel Aviv.
THAT	See below Jenni 1971-76.
TWAT	See below Botterweck 1970-.
UT	See below Gordon 1965.

CHAPTER ONE

INTRODUCTION

1.1. *Preliminary Remarks*

One of the most fascinating phenomena within the history of religion of the Ancient Near East is undoubtedly the rise and development of prophecy in ancient Israel. Yet, despite the enormous influence of this religious movement on our western civilization, the modern, critical study of biblical prophecy is not much more than a hundred years old, constituting a part of the development commonly—even if somewhat inaptly—referred to as "the historical-critical method"[1].

Before these methods were used the prophets were almost exclusively regarded as harbingers of the coming of Christ, and their sayings were interpreted as "messianic", or "christological". Needless to say, many of the explanations of prophetic passages brought about by this kind of interpretation were rather speculative and fanciful.

However, after the introduction of modern critical methods into the study of the Old Testament, it could not be long before scientifically founded theories concerning the rise and development of ancient Israelite prophecy began to see the light of dawn.

Yet, a hundred years or so after the birth of the use of historical methods in Old Testament study, the scholarly world has been unable to reach a unanimous view concerning the role and nature of biblical prophecy. Despite the vast amount of literature which has increasingly flooded the market, and despite the many valuable insights which have undoubtedly been gained, one rather gets the impression that the study of biblical prophecy a hundred years after its inauguration can be said to be only in its very beginnings[2].

---

[1] A complete history of research into Israelite prophecy remains to be written. Much of the material is found scattered around in various "Introductions" and histories of research into Old Testament studies (see *e.g.* H. F. Hahn, *Old Testament in Modern Research* (1954), E. G. Kraeling, *The Old Testament since the Reformation* (1955), H.-J. Kraus, *Geschichte der historisch-kritischen Erforschung des Alten Testaments* (1969). A popular, yet illustrative account of the development of research on Old Testament prophecy is provided by R. E. Clements, *A Century of Old Testament Study* (1976) 51-75 (on books of an introductory character, see below n. 2.).

[2] A survey of the results of recent prophetic research is given by M. J. Buss, "Prophecy in Ancient Israel", *IDBS* (1976) 694-97. Cf. also J. Limburg, "The Prophets in Recent Study", *Interp* 32 (1978) 56-58. Rich in information is S. Herrmann, *Ursprung und Funktion der Prophetie im Alten Israel* (1976). Among the "Introductions" with good sections on

1.2. *The prophet Amos*

Among the so-called "classical" prophets of ancient Israel the prophet Amos is probably the one upon whom most of the attention of the scholarly world has focused. This is immediately evident when one contemplates the multitude of secondary literature that has been written on this prophet[3].

The reasons for this particular interest in the prophecies of Amos are various. Thus, Amos is the first prophet whose words went down to posterity. According to the heading of the book which bears his name, he delivered his message during the reign of King Jeroboam II of Israel (784/83-753/52) and the reign of King Uzziah of Judah (769/68-741/40[4]). Furthermore, the style of the prophet is easy to read, and the Hebrew text handed down is not encumbered with textual problems as is so often the case with biblical texts. In addition to this, there can be little doubt that the strong ethical elements in the preaching of this prophet, his severe criticisms of the social injustice prevailing in his country, etc. have greatly attracted the mind of the Christian scholar.

In the present book I do not aim at providing a general discussion of the whole of the message of Amos. Far from it! The work is in several respects an incomplete patchwork, centring, however, around one basic theme: interest in the religious polemics of the prophet and their background. Even if some research has been done on this over the years, it is a sadly neglected field. This, of course, is regrettable in itself; it is even more regrettable when it turns out that studies in the religious polemics of the prophet may yield results which are vital for a correct understanding of his message.

As a source for any attempt to reconstruct the development of early Israelite religion the prophetic achievement is of considerable importance. The prophets are the only surviving eye-witnesses of the

---

prophecy one may mention O. Kaiser, *Einleitung in das Alte Testament* (1969) 163-246, J. A. Soggin, *Introduction to the Old Testament* (1976) 211-359. A standard work on Israelite prophecy is J. Lindblom, *Prophecy in Ancient Israel* (1962). A recent book which is likely to become a classic is R. R. Wilson, *Prophecy and Society in Ancient Israel* (1980).

[3] A complete bibliography on Amos is still lacking. However, one may get an idea of the huge number of books on Amos by browsing through the yearly editions of *Elenchus Bibliographicus Biblicus* or the *Internationale Zeitschriftenschau für Bibelwissenschaft und Grenzgebiete.* The most comprehensive single bibliography on Amos is found in H. W. Wolff, *Dodekapropheton* 2 (1969) 139-44 and *passim.* Cf. also W. Rudolph, *Joel, Amos, Obadja, Jona* (1971) 103-08 and *passim.* Of general articles on Amos one may note J. L. Mays, "Words about the Words of Amos", *Interp* 12 (1959) 260-72, J. F. Craghan, "The Prophet Amos in Recent Research", *BTB* 2 (1972) 242-61.

[4] The present writer is not at all convinced that the chronological data currently accepted are correct. However, for the sake of convenience, they may retained for the present purpose.

ideological and cultural struggle between the two movements that formed the religion of ancient Israel, movements frequently, even if somewhat superficially, referred to as "Yahwism" and "Baᶜalism"[5]. In fact, they are more than mere eye-witnesses. They are themselves the foremost exponents of this struggle. True enough, the words of the prophets were handed down orally for a certain period. For how long we do not know. During this period the prophetic message undoubtedly underwent changes[6]. Thus, with regard to the book of the prophet Amos, no one today would assume that we really have the *ipsissima verba* of the prophet in this book. On the other hand, we have no means of deciding with any degree of certainty which words are genuinely Amos's and which words are not. In this respect Old Testament scholars have too often behaved in a very amateurish manner. My own work is concerned with *the book of Amos.* When I do assume that the message contained in this book *basically* corresponds to the message of the great religious mind known to us as the prophet Amos, my assumption is axiomatic. Many scholars will find an assumption like this unscientific. My only consolation in this matter is that many of the attempts one has seen to identify genuine and non-genuine Amos words, different layers, etc., according to every accepted standard of modern *Literaturwissenschaft*, must be judged as even more unscientific.

As an historical source[7] the prophetic literature takes easy precedence

---

[5] The literature within this field is enormous. Cf. *i.a.* N. C. Habel, *Yahweh versus Baal* (1964), E. F. Eakin, "Yahwism and Baalism before the Exile", *JBL* 84 (1965) 407-14, R. Rendtorff, "El, Baᶜal und Jahwe", *ZAW* 78 (1966) 277-92, W. F. Albright, *Yahweh and the Gods of Canaan* (1968), E. Zenger, "Jahwe und die Götter", *ThPh* 43 (1968) 338-59, H. D. Preuss, *Verspottung fremder Religionen im Alten Testament* (1971).

[6] One cannot any more share the optimistic view—in particular found among Scandinavian scholars—that the words of the prophets were handed down orally for generations without this process leaving its marks on the *traditum* (on the Scandinavian discussion on oral tradition, see D. A. Knight, *The Traditions of Israel* (1973) 215 ff). In view of the immense importance of the study of oral tradition for Old Testament studies it must be hoped that much more work will be put into oral tradition studies in the future. Old Testament scholars will here have to turn to modern research in other areas of oral tradition for help. Valuable insights in this field have recently been gained in the United States. However I cannot help feeling that the American debate, mostly concerned with poetry, has been somewhat over optimistic when regarding the possibility of using, *e.g.* the research of A. B. Lord and M. Parry on twentieth century Yugoslav oral traditions directly for the Old Testament material (an excellent introduction to the debate is found in *Oral Tradition and Old Testament Studies* (1976). In the future I believe that those interested in oral tradition and Old Testament traditions will have to take into consideration broader and much more varied research materials, as well as paying much more serious attention to the methodological implications of their task.

[7] The historical value of the prophetic literature is primarily of an indirect character; through the message of the prophets we may get an idea of the society in which they lived. Needless to say, the problem of historicity and the prophetic message is closely related to the problem of the reliability of oral tradition mentioned above and below.

over the so-called Deuteronomic history. For the latter is not at all a history, but basically represents an idyllizing, theologically biased rewriting of the traditions of the ancient Israelites and may be used as a source for historical reconstruction only with the utmost care[8].

The prophet Amos is regarded primarily as a preacher of social justice and moral invectives by the vast majority of the students of prophecy in ancient Israel. However, this interest in the social/ethical aspect of the preaching of the prophet has somewhat overshadowed the important fact that this prophet is as interested as his contemporary Hosea in proclaiming Yahweh the only god worth worshipping and, consequently, in the denunciation of deities other than Yahweh.

Thus, very few scholars seem to be of the opinion that Amos is engaged in any polemics against the deity Baᶜal. A scholar like A. S. Kapelrud, for instance, states in his monograph on the prophet: "In the case of Yahweh, as Amos saw it, the ethical motives dominated. It was first and foremost for ethical reasons that Yahweh wanted to destroy his own people[9]." And: "But he (Amos) is not concerned with Baal, who did not interest him... It is not the relationship to other gods which is the problem in the preaching of Amos"[10]. And H. W. Wolff: "Diese Einfachkeit entspricht es, dass neben Jahweh andere Gottheiten nicht ein einziges Mal erwähnt werden. Kein Baal macht ihm den Rang in Israel streitig, wie wir es bei Hosea finden[11]." Also H. D. Preuss shares this view: "Amos war in seiner Verkündigung mehr gegen das soziale Unrecht Israels gewendet, und so kennt er nur wenig explicite Polemik gegen fremde Gottheiten[12]."

The lack of interest in religious polemics in the preaching of the prophet Amos and the strong overemphasis on its social/ethical aspects are due to several circumstances. Many Old Testament scholars are of the opinion that the ethical teachings of the prophets—as opposed to the so-called "fertility-religion" of the Canaanites which they regard as more or less immoral—constitute the basic contents of the prophetic message.

However, this view is a gross misrepresentation of the prophetic message. True enough, the social/ethical aspect of the preaching of the

[8] A major problem in this connection is the fact that most of the work on oral texts has been done from the point of view of narration (a fairly representative survey is found in J. E. Grimes, "Narrative Studies in Oral Texts", *Current Trends in Textlinguistics* (1978) 123-32.). It is to be hoped that much more research in the future will be put into the question of the reliability of oral traditional history. A classic is the article by R. M. Dorson, "The Debate over the Trustworthiness of Oral Traditional History", *Volksüberlieferung* (1968) 19-35.

[9] A. S. Kapelrud, *Central Ideas in Amos* (1961) 67.

[10] *Op. cit.* p. 43.

[11] H. W. Wolff, *Dodekapropheton* 2 (1969) 122.

[12] H. D. Preuss, *Verspottung fremder Religionen im Alten Testament* (1971) 118.

prophets is pronounced[13]. But the Israelites and the Israelite prophets did not have a monopoly of high moral standards in the Ancient Near East, as some scholars seem to believe.

One representative of such a view is H. Donner, who believes that there was a particular "Israelite" and a particular "Canaanite" way of valuing possessions: whereas the Israelites were opposed to collecting riches, the Canaanites were in favour of doing so[14]. Donner's view, in this particular instance strongly influenced by A. Alt, which regards the Israelites as morally superior to the Canaanites (as well as to the whole of the *Umwelt*), very much seems to represent the *opinio communis* of scholars today[15].

A refreshing counterbalance to the attitude represented by Donner and others is provided by the Dane E. Hammershaimb who claims that the Israelites inherited their ethical teachings from the Canaanites so that the moral/social preaching of the prophets in fact represents Canaanite ethical traditions[16].

As is so often the case the truth is probably to be found on both sides. However, in all likelihood there have been rather similar moral and social codes in use all over the Ancient Near East, and there is little cause to assume that one particular culture should have been superior to another as regards moral and social behaviour. This fact is proved by the many legal texts that have been discovered by archaeologists, showing that the legislature of the Ancient Near Eastern nations must have been rather interdependent[17].

---

[13] This phenomenon has also had its share of books and articles devoted to it. I mention E. Hammershaimb, "On the Ethics of the Old Testament Prophets", *SVT* 7 (1960) 75-101, H. Donner, "Die soziale Botschaft der Propheten im Lichte der Gesellschaftsordnung in Israel", *OrAnt* 2 (1963) 230-45, K. Koch, "Die Enstehung der sozialen Kritik bei den Propheten", *ProblbiblTheol* (1971) 236-57, O. Loretz, "Die prophetische Kritik des Rentenkapitalismus", *UF* 7 (1975) 271-78, S. Holm-Nielsen, "Die Sozialkritik der Propheten", *Denkender Glaube* (1976) 7-23, S. Lindhagen, *Den profetiska samhällskritiken i Israel och Juda under 700-talet* (1978). Works dealing with the prophet Amos alone are L. Randellini, "Ricchi e poveri nel libro del profeta Amos", *SBFLA* (2 (1951-52) 5-86, G. J. Botterweck, "Sie verkaufen den Unschuldigen um Geld", *BiLe* 12 (1971) 215-31, M. Fendler, "Zur Sozialkritik des Amos", *EvTh* 33 (1973) 32-53.

[14] H. Donner, "Die soziale Botschaft der Propheten", *OrAnt* 2 (1963) 234.243.

[15] The reference *inter alia* to passages like Deut 5, 1 ff in support of this view is hardly convincing. What we find in this and similar texts is rather a reflection of what we might call a tribal mentality than of a universal ethical system.

[16] E. Hammershaimb, "On the Ethics of the Old Testament Prophets", *SVT* 7 (1960) 89 ff. Cf. also J. Gray, "Social Aspects of Canaanite Religion", *SVT* 15 (1969) 170-92.

[17] As an example one may think of the Old Testament stressing the rights of the widow, the orphan, and the poor (Ex 22, 21-24, Deut 24, 17.19.21, Is. 1, 17, Jer 5, 28, Ez 22, 7). The social rights of these low status groups were recognized also outside Israel (F. C. Fensham, "Widow, Orphan and the Poor in Ancient Near Eastern Legal and Wisdom Literature", *JNES* 21 (1962) 129-39).

With regard to the prophet Amos in particular attempts have been made to explain his concern for the social and moral behaviour of his fellow countrymen as being a reaction against the results of a prosperous economic development under the reign of King Jeroboam II. The favourable economic conditions of that period brought about a prosperous upper class. At the same time the lower classes did not benefit from the trade surplus and the newly gained riches.

It may well be that there was a flourishing period of foreign trade in Israel under Jeroboam II. On the other hand it is hardly likely that the social structure of Israelite society underwent any fundamental changes during the lifetime of Amos which would call for his particular concern with matters pertaining to the social and moral behaviour of his contemporaries. The social suppression and the economic exploitation of Israelite society was hardly much different in the times of the prophet Amos than fifty years before or fifty years after. Preaching social justice formed a part, and an important part for that matter, of the message of Amos in the same way as it formed an important part of the message of the prophets before and after him.

Scholarly preoccupation with the ethical aspects of the message of the prophet and the consistent lack of interest in the religious polemics of his preaching may further be due to a faulty interpretation of the role of the prophetic movement in relation to the development of ancient Israelite religion in general.

From the message of the prophets, from the Deuteronomic "history" and other biblical writings, and from archaeology it follows that the religious life in Israel at the time of the great prophets was manifold and complicated. The common notion that an orthodox, fully developed Yahwistic religious system existed before the time of the Exile has no base in history. What Yahwism there was must apparently have been rather syncretistic. As for the problem of the early history of Yahwism, all sources are silent. In this matter we are bound to accept the fact that the theories which have been presented represent nothing more than interesting working hypotheses. Thus, we may assume that a core of a early form of Yawhism survived among certain groups (prophets, Nazirites, etc.), and that this acted as a germinal cell for what was later to develop into such religious systems of orthodoxy as those known to us through late theological traditions like Deuteronomy and the Priestly Code. At this late stage Yahwism may legitimately present itself as *the* religion of Israel.

When it becomes clear that the notion so frequently found in the biblical traditions of the people who "have left" Yahweh and "followed other gods" is a purely theological construction inasmuch as the majority of the inhabitants of Canaan never were Yahweh followers according to the standards laid down by the theologians of later times, an important question arises: under what circumstances and within which circles were the foundations laid upon which the fully developed structure of orthodox Yahwism was later to be erected?[18]

In this connection the attention of the scholarly world has focused far too little on the role of the prophetic movement. It is the conviction of the present writer that this movement played a much more decisive role in the formation of ancient Israelite religion than is commonly accepted among scholars of today.

Consequently, in this respect pioneers like Wellhausen and Duhm were right, claiming that the prophets brought something new into Israel's religion. In fact, it is first and foremost to the prophetic achievement that we owe the picture of "classical" Israelite religion as it came to be.

Thus, the study of religious polemics in the message of the prophets becomes extremely important. Through the religious activity of the prophets we witness the very act of creation of classical Israelite religion.

A major problem in prophetic research has always been to what extent the prophets themselves created the "prophetic tradition" or to what extent did they inherit, modify or develop it. Much research has been put into the problem of prophecy and tradition, particularly in recent years[19].

With regard to the prophet Amos, everyone familiar with the research that has been done will know the work of the German H. W. Wolff on the so-called *Geistige Heimat* of this prophet. According to the thesis of Wolff, the "spiritual home" of Amos is to be found among the wisdom traditions of the clans[20].

In his work Wolff develops the theories of scholars who came before him. In particular he is dependent upon S. Terrien, probably the first scholar who systematically pointed to similarities between the message of Amos and wisdom traditions[21], and on E. Gerstenberger who had attempted to demonstrate that the woe-oracles in prophetic literature have their *Sitz im Leben* in the lament over the dead, ultimately stemming from the wisdom traditions of the clans[22].

When comparing details in the message of the prophet Amos to the wisdom literature of ancient Israel, it is above all upon the woe-oracles

---

[18] On the problem of *šwb*, see below pp. 65-66.

[19] A survey of the discussion up to 1974 is found in R. E. Clements, *Prophecy and Tradition* (1975).

[20] See in particular H. W. Wolff, *Amos' geistige Heimat* (1962). Cf. also by the same author *Dodekapropheton* 2 (1969).

[21] S. Terrien, "Amos and Wisdom", *Israel's Prophetic Heritage* (1962) 108-15.

[22] E. Gerstenberger, "The Woe-oracles of the Prophets", *JBL* 81 (1962) 249-63.

that the interest of scholars has focused. In addition to Am 5, 18-20 and 6, 1, also 2, 7; 5, 7, and 6, 13, following stylistic criteria, have been counted among the woe-oracles. Some scholars have even put in a conjectural "woe" *ipsissimum verbum* before the last-mentioned verses. Other features of the "wisdom approach" include the use of rhetorical questions, numerical pairs, the use of certain words known from wisdom literature, etc.[23]

The recent strong interest in the influence of wisdom traditions in Amos, as well as the solid success of the theories of H. H. Wolff is most easily explained as a reaction against the earlier assumed dependence of the prophet on cultic traditions and the belief that Amos (as well as other prophets) was a professional cultic prophet[24].

"The cultic trend" within prophetic research was initiated by S. Mowinckel, who, after the German H. Gunkel, was the foremost pioneer in pointing to stylistic similarities between the psalms of ancient Israel and the message of the prophets. Even if no one today would adhere to Mowinckel's early theories concerning, for example, the disciples of the prophet Isaiah[25], the fact remains that his discoveries concerning the many common stylistic features in this prophet and in the cultic language of Jerusalem initiated a new era in Old Testament scholarship.

Today, it seems, history repeats itself. In their enthusiasm over the discovery of stylistic and ideological similarities in the message of the prophet Amos and wisdom traditions, quite a few scholars have recently taken the position that the key to the understanding of the message of the prophet lies in the hotbed of ancient Israelite wisdom[26].

---

[23] For a survey, as well as a brief critical review of some of the arguments used by scholars who stress wisdom influence in Amos, see J. L. Crenshaw, "The Influence of the Wise upon Amos", *ZAW* 79 (1967) 42-52. See also by the same author "Methods for Determining Wisdom Influence upon "Historical" Literature", *JBL* 88 (1969) 129-42.

[24] The fact that some scholars hold the view that the prophets, or some of them, were "cultic prophets" does not imply that these scholars hold similar views concerning the character of the prophetic office, nor concerning the nature of the ancient Israelite cult. The designation "cultic prophet" is in itself a rather imprecise term. The most recent work to deal with the phenomenon is A. R. Johnson, *The Cultic Prophet and Israel's Psalmody* (1979).

[25] S. Mowinckel, *Jesajadisiplene* (1926).

[26] Inspired by the work of Wolff concerning the prophet Amos other scholars have applied similar theories to other prophets. It may indeed seem an irony of fate that the prophet Isaiah, according to the early work of Mowinckel mentioned above n. 25 the cultic prophet *par excellence*, is probably next to Amos the prophet who has been most radically interpreted in the light of the wisdom traditions of ancient Israel (cf. J. W. Whedbee, *Isaiah and Wisdom* (1971), J. Jensen, *The Use of tôrâ by Isaiah* (1973). More recently, Wolff has attempted to interpret the prophet Micah along the same lines ("Wie verstand Micha von Moreschet sein prophetisches Amt?", *SVT* 29 (1978) 403-17.

Obviously, no one could deny the importance of the discovery of wisdom influence on Amos[27]. Equally important is the establishment that the wisdom traditions—in contrast to what was normally believed—do not entirely belong to the post-exilic age. The event is parallelled by the establishment a few decades ago of the fact that Israelite psalmody could not be classified as post-exilic, pious poetry, but was seen to be ultimately stemming from the cultic life of ancient Israel, much of it with deep roots in Canaanite lore.

However, despite the great importance that has to be attached to the discovery of wisdom influence in the prophet Amos, the fact remains that much of the argumentation put forward by Wolff and his followers concerning the "spiritual home" of the prophet Amos appears to be rather speculative, some of it even fanciful. Also, it remains a fact that the newly discovered wisdom influence in the prophet Amos cannot deny the validity of some of the earlier discoveries concerning cultic influence. Consequently, if one chooses to regard the wisdom traditions of Israel as the "spiritual home" of the prophet, one is at the same time bound to admit that these traditions do not constitute his only *geistige Heimat.*

Obviously, any man is in his thinking dependent upon his cultural environment. If influences from the cult, from wisdom traditions, etc. could *not* be found in the message of the prophet Amos, *this* would indeed have been a remarkable thing. Even a religious genius like Amos was unable to detach himself from the influences of his own upbringing, or from the social and intellectual climate of his day when expressing his message. However, the discovery of cultic influence on his message makes Amos no more a "cultic prophet" than the discovery of wisdom influence makes him a "wise man".

The main problem in connection with the recent discussions concerning "prophecy and tradition" though, is not whether the key to the understanding of the prophetic message is to be found in cult or in wisdom. Unfortunately, it seems that scholarly preoccupation with the "spiritual home" of the prophet has somewhat overshadowed interest in the main intention of the prophetic message itself. It is regrettable, indeed, when the "discovery" that the prophets were dependent upon their cultural surroundings and did not live in a spiritual or intellectual vacuum diverts our attention from the greatness of the prophetic mind. And it is even more regrettable when the result of this is a more or less total negligence of the great importance of the role of Israelite prophecy in the formation of what was later to become the classical religion of Israel.

---

[27] On the other hand, I do agree with J. L. Crenshaw in his criticisms put forward concerning wisdom influence in the Book of Amos (above n. 23).

However, in their own lifetime the influence of the prophets on their contemporaries was indeed relative. If they did not conform to the rules laid down for them by society, or did not meet with the expectations of those of consequence in the country, they might fall into great difficulties (cf. Am 7, 10-13).

In their own lifetimes the prophets of Yahweh were not the "classical prophets of ancient Israel". They had to share their existence with other groups as influential as themselves. It is only in much later tradition—when Yahwism had won its complete victory, and the words of other prophets (the "false prophets", the "prophets of Baᶜal", etc.) had been lost to posterity—that the classical prophets became "classical". Among their contemporaries they had to fight hard for their existence.

It is mainly to that fight that we owe the picture of ancient Israelite orthodox Yahwistic religion as we know it today.

The fight fought by the Yahwistic prophets was primarily of a religious/polemical, if also of an ethical, character. Their main concern was to convince their fellow countrymen that Yahweh was the only god worth worshipping. He alone could help them in their daily life and with the provision of the fertility so vital to their existence.

Again and again we are shown in the Old Testament how the main concern of the worshipper is the fertility and the stability of people and animals, in cornfield and meadow, provision of rain, victory over enemies in war, absence of illness, etc. According to the prophets of Yahweh the only god that has the power to provide the people with all these benefits is Yahweh.

Consequently, it represents an over-simplification when scholars describe the ideological and cultural fight in ancient Israel which ended up with the victory of the Yahwistic religion as a fight between "Yahwism", on one side, and "Canaanite fertility religion", on the other. From a religio-phenomenological point of view Yahwism is as much a fertility religion as were the different Canaanite cults. In fact, the main purpose of prophetic activity in Israel was to demonstrate convincingly that Yahwism was *the* fertility religion[28]. This point, I believe, has never been fully accepted by the majority of Old Testament scholars. Nevertheless this is what the texts themselves tell us when we pay close attention to them.

---

[28] Cf. *e.g.* a text like Jer 14, 22, or Hos. 2, 8-9, or Am 4, 6 ff. See also the remarks by A. S. Kapelrud, "Israel's Prophets and their Confrontation with the Canaanite Religion", *Syncretism* (1969) 165.

CHAPTER TWO

"FILIUS AC PATER EIUS IERUNT AD PUELLAM". A STUDY IN AM 2, 7B-8

2.1. *Preliminary Remarks. The Context*

Being primarily concerned with religious polemics in the message of the prophet Amos, there is but little that may attract our interest in the first chapters of his book. The passage 2, 7b-8, however, constitutes an exception.

After the short, introductory remark in 1, 1, and the preliminary, more general utterance of doom in 1, 2, there follows the famous pronouncement against the nations[1]; Damascus 1, 3-5, Gaza 1, 6-8, Tyre 1, 9-10, Edom 1, 11-12, Ammon 1, 13-15, Moab 2, 1-3, and Judah 2, 4-5[2] (in order not to deal with the passage Am 2, 7B-8 in isolation, I quote extensively from the context):

1.1. Words of Amos, who was one of the Shepherds from Tekoa[3],
which he saw about Israel in the days of Uzziah, king
of Judah, and in the days of Jeroboam, son of Joash,
king of Israel, two years before the earthquake[4].
2. And he said:
Yahweh roars from Zion,
and lets his voice be heard from Jerusalem;
the pastures of the shepherds mourn,
and the top of Carmel withers.

---

[1] On the pronouncements against the nations in the prophetic books, see below p. 97 and pp. 103-108. Cf. also the literature given in n. 2 below.

[2] In addition to the current commentaries, the following literature may be noted: A. Bentzen, "The Ritual Background of Am 1, 2-2, 16", *OTS* 8 (1950) 85-99, M. Haran, "Observations on the Historical Background of Amos 1, 2-2, 6, *IEJ* 18 (1968) 201-12, W. Rudolph, "Die angefochtenen Völkersprüche in Am 1 und 2", *Schalom* (1971) 45-79, S. M. Paul, "Am 1, 3-2, 3", *JBL* 90 (1971) 397-403, Z. B. Luria, "The Prophecies Unto the Nations in the Book of Amos" (in Hebrew), *BetM* 54 (1973) 287-301, D. L. Christensen, "The Prosodic Structure of Am 1-2", *HTR* 67 (1974) 427-36, by the same author, *Transformations of the War Oracle* (1975) 57-72, G. Pfeifer, "Denkformenanalyse als exegetische Methode", *ZAW* 88 (1976) 56-71, J. Barton, *Amos's Oracles Against the Nations* (1980).

[3] The title of the Book of Amos is thoroughly discussed by W. Rudolph, *Joel, Amos, Obadja, Jona* (1971) 109-15.

[4] For an attempt to relate the earthquake mentioned in Am 1, 1 to history, see J. A. Soggin, "Das Erdbeben von Am 1, 1 und die Chronologie der Könige Ussia und Jotham von Juda", *ZAW* 82 (1970) 117-21.

3. Thus speaks Yahweh:
For three transgressions of Damascus, for four[5],
I will not be indulgent:
Because they have threshed Gilead with iron threshing-sledges,
4. I will send a fire upon the House of Hazael,
and it shall devour the palaces of Ben-hadad.
5. I will break the gatebars of Damascus,
and cut down the one who thrones at Bikath-aven,
and who holds the sceptre at Beth-eden,
and the people of Aram shall go into exile to Kir,
says Yahweh[6].
6. Thus speaks Yahweh:
For three transgressions of Gaza, for four,
I will not be indulgent:
Because they carried off a whole people[7],
and delivered them (as slaves) to Edom,
7. I will send a fire upon the walls of Gaza,
and it shall devour her palaces.
8. I will cut down the one who thrones at Ashdod,
and who holds the sceptre at Ashkelon,
and I will turn my hand against Ekron,
and the remnant of the Philistines shall perish,
says the lord Yahweh.
9. Thus speaks Yahweh:
For three transgressions of Tyre, for four,
I will not be indulgent:
Because they delivered a whole people (as slaves) to Edom,
and did not remember the covenant of brothers[8],
10. I will send a fire upon the walls of Tyre,
and it shall devour her palaces.

---

[5] On the numerical pattern in the oracles against the nations, see in addition to the literature mentioned above in n. 2 also B. Kingston Soper, "For Three Transgressions and for Four", *ET* 71 (1959) 86-87, M. Weiss, "The Pattern of Numerical Sequence in Am 1-2", *JBL* 86 (1967) 416-23. Further literature is found in D. L. Christensen, *Transformations of the War Oracle* (1975) 57-58, n. 105. A recent book in Hebrew, Y. Zakovitch, *For Three... and for Four* (1979) deals thoroughly with the phenomenon.

[6] There has been an attempt to relate this verse, too, to history (A. Malamat, "Am 1, 15 in the Light of the Barship Inscriptions", *BASOR* 129 (1953) 25-26). However, I do not believe that it is possible to relate any of the oracles against the foreign nations to particular historical events with any degree of certainty.

[7] The meaning of *šlmh* in this context is quite uncertain.

[8] On *bryt ʾḥym* cf. J. Priest, "The Covenant of Brothers", *JBL* 84 (1965) 400-06.

11. Thus speaks Yahweh:
For three transgressions of Edom, for four,
I will not be indulgent:
Because he persecuted his brother with the sword
and "spoiled his covenant mercy"[9],
and his rage tore to pieces always,
and he kept his wrath forever,
12. I will send a fire upon Teman,
and it shall devour the palaces of Bozrah.
13. Thus speaks Yahweh:
For three transgressions of the Ammonites, for four,
I will not be indulgent:
Because they ripped up the pregnant women of Gilead
in order to extend their borders,
14. I will send a fire upon the walls of Rabbah,
and it shall devour her palaces,
with war-cries on the day of battle,
with tempest on the day of the hurricane.
15. And their king shall go into exile,
he and his princes with him,
says Yahweh.
2.1. Thus speaks Yahweh:
For three transgressions of Moab, for four,
I will not be indulgent:
Because he burned the bones of the king of Edom
to lime,
2. I will send a fire upon Moab,
and it shall devour the palaces of Kerioth,
and Moab shall die in tumult, in war cries,
to the sound of the trumpet.
3. I will cut down the ruler[10] from her[11] midst,
and all her princes I will slaughter with him,
says Yahweh.

---

[9] The Hebrew phrase *wšḥt rḥmyw* is difficult. I have borrowed my rendering from R. B. Coote, "Amos 1, 11: *RḤMYW*", *JBL* 90 (1971) 206-08. For the recent discussion of the phrase see also M. Fishbane, "The Treaty Background of Am 1, 11 and Related Matters", *JBL* 89 (1970) 313-18, and, by the same author, "Additional Remarks of *rḥmyw*", *JBL* 91 (1972) 391-93.

[10] The word *šwpṭ*, most commonly translated by "judge", is here better rendered by "ruler".

[11] Inconsequences in the gender of the suffixes in Biblical Hebrew are not uncommon, and there is no reason for altering the text here (as suggested by H. W. Wolff, *Dodekapropheton* 2 (1969) 163, following Wellhausen).

4. Thus speaks Yahweh:
For three transgressions of Judah, for four,
I will not be indulgent:
Because they have rejected the laws of Yahweh
and have not kept his decrees; their lies—which
their fathers followed—led them astray;
5. I will send fire upon Judah,
and it shall devour the palaces of Jerusalem[12].

2.2. *Amos* 2, 6-8.

Closing the climactic list of words of judgement quoted above, there follows the equally famous pronouncement against Israel:

6. Thus speaks Yahweh:
For three transgressions of Israel, for four,
I will not be indulgent:[13]
because they sell the righteous for silver[14],
and the poor for a pair of sandals[15],
7. because they trample into the dust of the earth
the head of the poor[16],

[12] Several scholars hold the oracles against Tyre, Edom and Judah to be late additions to the Book of Amos (see *e.g.* W. H. Schmidt, "Die deuteronomistische Redaktion des Amosbuches", *ZAW* 77 (1965) 174-78). However, in recent research there seems to be a tendency towards regarding at least the oracles against Tyre and Edom as genuine (see *e.g.* D. L. Christensen, "The Prosodic Structure of Amos 1-2", *HTR* 67 (1974) 427ff., K. N. Schoville, "A Note on the Oracles of Amos against Gaza, Tyre and Edom", *SVT* 26 (1974) 55-63). The oracle against Judah, on the other hand, is regarded almost unanimously as non-genuine (among the exceptions I single out G. J. Botterweck, "Zur Authentizität des Buches Amos", *BZ* NF 2 (1958) 176-89). Altogether, I do not find any of the arguments against the genuineness of some of the oracles against the nations in the Book of Amos quite convincing.
On the relationship of the prophet Amos to Judah, see R. A. Carlson, "Profeten Amos och Davidriket", *RoB* 25 (1966) 57-78, H. Gottlieb, "Amos und Jerusalem", *VT* 17 (1967) 430-63, S. Wagner, "Überlegungen zur Frage nach den Beziehungen des Propheten Amos zum Südreich", *ThlZ* 96 (1971) 653-70.

[13] The Hebrew of Am 2, 6b-7a is in a rather bad condition and has caused trouble to commentators ever since the days of the LXX. In addition to the different commentaries, I mention the following article which has put much effort into the attempts to restore the text: M. A. Beek, "The Religious Background of Am 2, 6-8", *OTS* 5 (1948) 134ff. Despite being rather ingenious, Beek's attempt is not altogether convincing.

[14] Rather than a concrete reference to slave trade (thus S. Amsler, *Amos* (1965) 180-81), in this verse we probably have a general accusation of social and economic exploitation (cf. 5, 11ff.).

[15] The use of *nʿl* is illustrative, sandals being a typical oriental image for the base and inferior (cf. 8, 6, Ps 44, 13). "Eine grosse Erniedrung ist es, wenn man von Jemandem sagt: *mā yaswā madās* – er ist kein Schuh wert" (A. S. Yahuda, "Bagdadische Sprichwörter", *Orientalische Studien*, B.1 (1906) 409. Cf. also C. M. Carmichael, "A Ceremonial Crux", *JBL* 96 (1977) *passim.*

[16] Again a typical oriental token of disparagement: "*anāku epru ištu šupāl šēpē šarri* – I am

and turn aside the way of the humble.
A man and his father go to the maid,
profaning my holy name,
8. in front of every altar they lie down,
on garments seized in pledge[17],
and in the house of their[18] gods they drink the
wine given as rates[19].

The section starting in 2, 9 is relatively independent of 2, 6-8, and I therefore leave it out of the discussion.

---

the dust from under the sandals of the king" (J. A. Knudtzon, *Die El-Amarna-Tafeln* (1915) 149, 4-5 and *passim*). On *ʿpr*, see A. F. Rainey, "Dust and Ashes", *TA* 1 (1974) 77-83.

[17] *bgdym ḥblym* is normally rendered by "garments seized in pledge", or something similar. The translation is not entirely unproblematic, and depends to a certain degree upon how the context is to be understood. Essential to a correct reading of this passage is whether one chooses to see v.7b as belonging to vv.6-7a, or to the following v.8. (on this see below 17ff.). If the reference to the "maid" in 7b implies sexual activity of some sort, in accordance with what is assumed by the vast majority of the scholars that have commented upon the passage, it might be interesting to take *ḥblym* as a derivation from *ḥbl* IV, meaning "labour pains". MT would then have to be changed into a construct construction *bgdy ḥblym*, which might be translated by "garments of begetting", or something similar. If v.7b really had a sexual meaning, this would have given us a fine example of prophetic scorn. As I do not believe, however, that the reference to the maid implies any sexual activity, I have chosen to retain the traditional translation "garments seized in pledge". The prophet's reference must then be understood as directed towards the practice of taking pledges. In continuation with the description given by the prophet in v.6, the upper classes of Samaria are exploiting their fellow countrymen in this respect also. Thus, they do not conform to the rules concerning pledges which were laid down by society (cf. Ex 22, 25-26, Deut 24, 17), and the luxurious garments on which they stretch themselves in their palaces are not really their own (Am 3, 10!). (Cf. also the ingenious, but rather far-fetched solution offered by M. Dahood, "To Pawn One's Cloak", *Bib* 42(1961) 359-66.) That the verse in question is difficult and has caused problems in all periods may be seen from the ancient versions most of which are divergent.
I cannot at all accept the reasons given by H. W. Wolff for regarding *ʾsl kl-mzbḥ* and *byt ʾlhym* as late additions to the text (*Dodekapropheton* 2 (1969) 163).

[18] It is quite deliberately that Amos uses "their gods" here. The situation he is referring to is not the worship of Yahweh, at least not the way this deity is conceived of by the prophet.

[19] The expression *yyn ʿnwšym* is rendered in different ways: "...the wine of those who have been fined" (*RSV*), "... liquor got by the way of fines" (*NEB*), "... wine of the people they have fined" (*The Jerusalem Bible*), to cite only a few of the English translations. However, I cannot accept that "fine" in this context gives any sense. I have therefore chosen the translation "given as rates", which seems to fit the idea of the rich upper classes exploiting the poorer classes of society. Admittedly, *ʿnš* is not found with exactly this meaning in Biblical Hebrew. In the North-West Semitic languages, however, this meaning of *ʿnš* is richly attested. Based on the background to the context of Am 2, 8 I think this meaning of the word can be defended also here. After all, our translation represent only a nuance, rather than a completely different word (on *ʿnš* meaning "rates" in the West-Semitic languages, see J. T. Milik, *Recherches d'épigraphie proche-orientale* I (1972) 292-96. Cf. also *Syrie Centrale* (1868-77) nr. 124, 1.1 and 3, and p. 75).

The structure of the whole section 1, 3 - 2, 8 reveals an intentional composition, characterized by the particle *ʿl*, "because", giving the reason for the message of the prophet. A further stylistic feature is the stereotype formula "for three transgressions..., for four..."[20]

However, despite the marked stylistic similarities between 1, 3 - 2, 5 on the one hand and 2, 6-8 on the other, we note that the differences are far more conspicuous than the similarities, both with regard to style as well as contents. What strikes one in particular is the richness in details of 2, 7b-8 compared to the more stereotyped formulas of the preceding verses; the prophet has finally reached his audience.

As is the case in most of the words of the prophet Amos against Israel[21], the accusations of 2, 6-8 are divided in two parts: a moral and a religious.

In vv. 6-7a the prophet is concerned with the moral and social behaviour of the Israelites. He accuses the people of oppressing and exploiting the righteous (*ṣdyq*), the poor (*ʾbywn*), the destitute (*dlym*), and the humble (*ʿnwym*).

Most probably we have here accusations of a general character. It is very unlikely that we shall be able to get any closer to the specific character of the transgressions which the prophet has in mind. Also, the question whether the group of words *ṣdyq*, *ʾbywn*, *dlym* and *ʿnwym* refers to the social stratification of ancient Israelite society is very complicated[22].

A major problem of our text is constituted by the relationship between v.7b, "a man and his father go to the maid", and the following remarks in v.8 about lying down in front of every altar and drinking wine in the house of their gods. The reference in v.8 quite clearly has religious overtones. The situation depicted may be in a temple, or it may also be in the palace of a wealthy man where the religious rites or sacred meals took place.

It is my firm conviction that the verse concerning the father and son who visit the maid cannot be seen isolated from v.8. On the contrary, I believe it to constitute the very prelude of this verse. If this really is the case, it becomes obvious that the problem of "the maid" must be regarded as the key to the solution of the difficulties of the whole passage, 2, 7b-8. For this reason I shall deal with the problem of *hnʿrh* at some length.

---

20 On this formula, see above n. 5.

21 See below pp. 37, 76, 127, 143. Also the utterance against Judah, Am 2, 4-5, has this double composition.

22 On these different designations, see below p. 81.

2.2.1. *The Problem of the Maid* (*hnʿrh*).

A factor common to all scholars who have shown a special interest in the problem of the maid mentioned in Am 2, 7b is that they take the expression "a man and his father go to the maid" as a reference to some sexual activity[23]. Their problem then is whether Amos in this particular instance is referring to some moral or social offense (in which case the statement belongs with vv.6-7a), or, whether he is referring to some cultic "misbehaviour" (in which case the reference has to belong with v.8).[24]

As indeed any evaluation of the statement found in Am 2, 7b will have to depend upon one's understanding of the word *nʿrh*, it is of vital importance to have a close look at how this word is used in Old Testament literature. From the texts where *nʿrh* appears, it follows that the use of the word is not unambigous (I am not taking into consideration the male equivalent *nʿr*, which, more or less, seems to cover the same semantic range with regard to males).

Firstly, the word *nʿrh* may be used as a designation for a *virgo intacta* (Gen 24, 14ff.[25]). Despite the particular circumstances it is this meaning of the word we also have to assume in Gen 34, 3.12[26], and in Deut 22, 23-29[27]. The same meaning of *nʿrh* is further attested in Jud 21, 12, and probably implied also in 1 Kings 1, 2-4, as well as in Est 2, 2 ff.

Secondly, we find that *nʿrh* may also be used as a designation for a young married woman (Deut 22, 15ff., Jud 19, 3ff.).

Thirdly, we find the word used for a maid servant. With the exception of II Kings 5, 2, where *nʿrh*, with the determinative *qṭnh*, is used of a little

---

[23] The general arguments are found in A. Ehrlich, *Randglossen zur hebräischen Bibel.* B.5 (1912) 232.

[24] Among those who take the words of the prophet to refer to the moral aspect of the sexual behaviour of the Israelites we find L. Dürr, "Altorientalisches Recht", *BZ* 23 (1935-36) 150-57, M. A. Beek, "The Religious Background of Am 2, 6-8", *OTS* 5 (1948) 135-37, E. Würthwein, "Amos-Studien", *ZAW* 62 (1949-50) 45-46, R. Bach, "Gottesrecht und weltliches Recht", *Festschrift G. Dehn* (1957) 30-33, S. Amsler, *Amos* (1965) 181, J. L. Mays, *Amos* (1969) 46, H. W. Wolff, *Dodekapropheton* 2 (1969) 202-03, W. Rudolph, *Joel, Amos, Obadja, Jona* (1971) 142-43. Among those who consider the accusations of the prophet as directed against a cultic sacred marriage/prostitution rite are J. Wellhausen, *Die kleinen Propheten* (1963) 72-73, R. S. Cripps, *A Critical and Exegetical Commentary on the Book of Amos* (1929) 142, A. Weiser, *Die Prophetie des Amos* (1929) 91-93, (see also by the same author, *Das Buch der zwölf kleinen Propheten* (1956) 141-42), A. Neher, *Amos* (1950) 55 and 76, H.-J. Kraus, "Die prophetische Botschaft gegen das soziale Unrecht Israels", *EvTh* 15 (1955) 298, T. H. Robinson, *Die zwölf kleinen Propheten* (1964³) 79, E. Hammershaimb, *Amos* (1967) 44-5, M. Bič, *Das Buch Amos* (1969) 57-58, J. M. Ward, *Amos and Hosea* (1969) 135-37.

[25] *K* has *nʿr* (vv.14.16.28.55.57).

[26] *K* has *nʿr*.

[27] *K* has *nʿr*.

girl, the remaining passages in the Old Testament which contain the word *nʿrh* all refer to maid servants (Ex 2, 5, Ruth 2, 5.8.22-23; 3, 2, 1 Sam 25, 42, Est 2, 9; 4, 4.16, Prov 9, 3; 27, 27; 31, 15).

There is one thing in particular which it is worth noticing with regard to the use of Hebrew *nʿrh* as a designation for a maid servant. Automatically, there is a tendency to group servants together with the lower classes of society. With regard to the *nʿrh* it is important to be aware of the fact that her position in ancient Israelite society was among the most high-ranking. As the closest associate and assistant to the queen (1 Sam 25, 42, Est 2, 9; 4, 4.16) and the daughter of Pharaoh (Ex 2, 5), the *nʿrh* is more likely to rank with a high official than with a humble servant. It should further be noted than even if occurrences of *nʿrh* designating a high-ranking maid servant cannot always be found, further attestations of the word also bear witness to the fact that the word refers to someone employed by the wealthy in society, and with duties which cannot be compared to those of the lower servant classes and the slaves [28].

When dealing with the word *nʿrh* in connection with Am 2, 7b our first concern will have to be the assumption that the words of the prophet refer to some sexual, morally reprehensible behaviour. I can hardly believe that this assumption is correct, irrespective of whether the reference in our text should be to a *virgo intacta*, a young married woman, or a maid servant, the latter of a high social standing.

The first thing that strikes one when reading Am 2, 7b is that the rather general description "a man and his father" suggests that what the prophet is alluding to must have been a somewhat widespread phenomenon. If the matter referred to had been something which rarely occurred, it is unlikely that he would have mentioned it at all in a context as general as the present.

However, when the prophet is referring to a widespread practice among his fellow countrymen, and this practice involves sexual engagement of some sort, it is highly unlikely that he has in mind either the *virgo intacta* or the young married woman. The whole sentence "a man and his father go to the maid" [29] seems very strange indeed should this be the case.

---

[28] With regard to males designated by *nʿr*, this fact was clearly demonstrated by J. MacDonald, "The Status and Role of the *naʿar* in Israelite Society", *JNES* 35 (1976) 147-70. Cf. also Cutler, J. MacDonald, "Identification of the *naʿar* in the Ugaritic Texts", *UF* 8 (1976) 27-35.

[29] Several translations have "a man and his father visit the *same* maid". From a grammatical point of view there is nothing wrong with this translation (cf. W. Rudolph, *Joel, Amos, Obadja, Jona* (1971) 142-43). The rendering by "same" rather than "the", however, is probably prompted by the wish to aggravate the offence, seen as a sexual/moral one.

The legal and social regulations concerning sexual behaviour were so embedded in the patriarchal society of ancient Israel that it is unlikely that a general departure from them would be accepted at all[30]. The maintenance of these laws and regulations were of mutual interest to everyone and necessary for the balance of the society of that time.

If, on the other hand, the reference was to *nʿrh*/"maid servant", and the person in question was not a virgin or a married woman, the matter is quite different. In this case the regulations concerning adultery would not apply. But then sexual intercourse with a woman who was neither a virgin nor married was not an offense in ancient Irael. Whereas society took an extreme view of adultery, it did not object to the extra-marital relations of the man to a slave or an unmarried woman not being a virgin. According to the double standard of Israelite morality it was only the married woman to whom this was denied. In fact, the only case where an Old Testament law mentions intercourse with a slave woman as something offensive is in the case where the woman belongs to someone else. The act is then regarded as an offence against the right of ownership. The punishment, accordingly, is not the penalty of death as in the case of adultery (Lev 20, 10). All the transgressor has to do is to bring Yahweh a minor sacrifice (Lev 19, 20-22).

According to this view prostitution, as well, was a recognized social institution with few moral inhibitions attached to it despite its being looked upon with mixed feelings[31].

Consequently, there is no reason for regarding the statement in Am 2, 7b concerning the man and his father who visit the maid as a reference to the sexual/moral behaviour of the Israelites.

This fact becomes even more evident when we take a closer look at the very words with which the prophet Amos condemns the behaviour of his fellow countrymen. According to the prophet, Yahweh tells the people that they are not to behave the way they do because this is "profaning my holy name (*lmʿn ḥll ʾt-šm qdšy*)"[32]. This statement, which concerns the

---

[30] For a survey of the regulations concerning marriage and adultery, see W. Kornfeld, "L'adultère dans l'Orient antique", *RB* 57 (1960) 92-109, P. Trible, "Woman in the O.T.", *IDBS* (1976) 963-66, C. R. Taber, "Marriage", *ibid.* 573-76, C. R. Taber, "Sex, Sexual Behaviour", *ibid.* 817-20, R. de Vaux, *Ancient Israel* (1976) 24ff. Cf. also D. Marcus, "Civil Liberties under Israelite and Mesopotamian Kings", *JANES* 10 (1978) 58-60.

[31] Gen 38, 13ff, Jos 2, 1ff, Jud 1, 11; 16, 1, I Kings 3, 16ff. Cf. C. R. Taber, "Sex, Sexual Behaviour", *IDBS* (1976) 819. As far as I know, no systematic treatment of the Old Testament view of prostitution (similar to *e.g.* H. Herter, "Die Soziologie der antiken Prostitution", *JAC* 3 (1960) 70-111) has been written. The matter is complicated because of the tendency to view this institution through the eyes of our own culture.

[32] There is no reason to assume with H. W. Wolff (*Dodekapropheton* 2 (1969) 160.163) that this sentence represents a late addition to the words of Amos (cf. W. Rudolph, *Joel,*

accusation "a man and his father go to the maid" alone and does not apply to the preceding accusations concerning the oppression of the poor and needy is, by any standard, a very strong one. It is not likely that the prophet would have used such strong words when referring to extra-marital relations with a woman who did not come under the laws of adultery.

The word *ḥll* is fairly common in Biblical Hebrew and concerns the profanation of things sacred[33]. If we take a look at the passages in the Old Testament where the formula *piʿel* of *ḥll* + *šm* + reference to the deity occurs, we find that the formula is used frequently when non-Yahwistic deities or cults are being referred to.

Lev 18 is particularly illuminating. In this chapter there is a list of illicit sexual relationships. In the middle of the list there appears, somewhat unexpectedly, a reminder that the Israelites are not to give their children as a sacrifice to the deity Moloch[34], "and profane (*tḥll*) the name of your god" (v.21).

The remarkable thing here is that even if all the sexual irregularities mentioned in this context have been regarded, by *any* standard, as far more reprehensible than the visit of a man and his father to the maid mentioned in Am 2, 7b (*if* one chooses to take the accusation of the prophet as being directed against some sexual misbehaviour), it is only the participation in the Moloch rites which warrants the use of the severe term *tḥll*.

Consequently, in Lev 19, 12 we learn that to swear falsely by the name of Yahweh is a much more serious offence than stealing, lying, etc. Only the former offence is regarded as a profanation of Yahweh himself[35]. In Lev 20, 3 we find once more a reference to profanation of the name of Yahweh through Moloch worship. And in Lev 21, 6 the same set formula containing the word *ḥll* is used in the regulations concerning the

---

Amos, Obadja, Jona (1971) 143. Rudolph is wrong, however, when he takes the sentence to apply to *all* the accusations of the prophet in the context rather than to visiting the maid alone).

[33] F. Maass, "*ḥll*", THAT I (1975) 570-75, W. Dommershausen, "*ḥll*", *TWAT* II (1977) 972-81.

[34] When consulting current dictionaries, one gets the impression that the thesis, in particular maintained by O. Eissfeldt, not to regard *mlk* as the name of a deity, but as a sacrificial term in this and other Old Testament passages, has been commonly accepted by the scholarly world (see *e.g.* *WM* Abt.2.B.1 (1965) 299-300). This, however, is not in accordance with recent research concerning the term *mlk* in the Old Testament (see below 183-84).

[35] This must also be the reason why the prophet Jeremiah applies the formula in Jer 34, 16. The covenant breach concerning the release of the slaves represented in fact false swearing by the name of Yahweh (for this episode, see N. P. Lemche, "Manumission of Slaves", *VT* 26 (1976) 51-53).

behaviour of the priests; they are not to cut themselves, etc. As self-mutilation was a practice known from Canaanite religion[36], one must assume that this, as well as the other activities mentioned in the same context, represented a profanation of the name of Yahweh because they were connected with Canaanite cult practices. The ritual aspect is also the one stressed in Lev 22, where further instructions concerning the correct *ritus* are given. And in Ez 20, 39 non-Yahwistic cults are referred to as being a profanation of the name of Yahweh. References to the worshipping of gods other than Yahweh utilizing the same formula with *ḥll* are finally found in Ez 36, 20-23 (cf. v.25).

Obviously I do not assert that the word *ḥll* is used only in cultic/ritual contexts. However, it is a striking fact that the formula *piᶜel* of *ḥll* + *šm* + reference to the deity Yahweh almost exclusively appears in cultic contexts. For this reason, as well as for the reasons given above, I find it very unlikely that the accusation of the prophet Amos in Am 2, 7b concerning the man and his father who visit the maid has anything at all to do with morality. Consequently, we shall have to look elsewhere to find a solution to our problem.

2.2.1.1. Is the *nᶜrh* a Cult Prostitute?

As the accusation of the prophet Amos concerning the man and his father who visit the maid does not refer to any moral misbehaviour, the assumption that the accusation is of a cultic/religious character lies at hand. This assumption gains further support when we view the statement of the prophet in v.7b within its context, *i.e.* the following v.8:

> "... in front of every altar they lie down, on garments seized in pledge, and in the house of their gods they drink the wine given as rates".[37]

The question which now arises is whether, in accordance with what is assumed by the majority of the scholars who favour a cultic interpretation of v.7b, we may find the solution to our problem by interpreting the *nᶜrh* in our context as a designation for a cultic prostitute[38]. In fact, if our verse really alludes to some sexual activity and this activity is not offensive from a moral point of view, to take *nᶜrh* as a designation for a cultic prostitute may at first glance seem the only possible explanation. However, if we take a closer look at our knowledge of cultic prostitution in the Ancient Near East and in the Old Testament, it soon turns out that this solution too, causes great difficulties.

---

[36] Cf. *e.g.* I Kings 18, 28.

[37] For details concerning the interpretation of this verse, see above p. 15, notes 17, 18, and 19. See also below 33ff.

[38] See n. 24 above.

No one familiar with the problems of religious polemics and religious syncretism in Old Testament literature will be ignorant of the problems related to what is normally referred to as "cultic prostitution". Yet, this is a field where very little scholarly discussion has taken place. Cultic prostitution is something which always seems to have been taken for granted. However, even if everyone uses the expression "cultic prostitution", or something similar, one often gets the impression that very few know precisely what they mean when using the term. The apparent terminological confusion that seems to exist within these matters calls for a few remarks. It is my intention to inquire into the arguments which have been put forward in support of the existence of cultic prostitution in ancient Israel. However, as this problem is closely connected with the phenomenon cultic prostitution in the Ancient Near East, it seems unavoidable to start the discussion by having a look at the Ancient Near Eastern evidence relating to this institution.

2.2.1.2. Cultic Prostitution in the Ancient Near East

The larger context of cultic prostitution in the Ancient Near Eastern history of religion embraces the mythical/ritual sexual uniting of a god and a goddess, and sometimes of the deity and a human being. This event is commonly referred to as *hieròs gámos* (sacred marriage, *heilige Hochzeit*, *mariage sacré*, etc.). Originally, the term was reserved for the nuptial celebrations of the Greek deities Zeus and Hera[39]. From Greek religion the designation "sacred marriage" was passed on to be used for similar phenomena in other religions as well, including the Semitic pantheons[40]. Even though the Greek evidence undoubtedly contains much which may be of interest to us, I believe that the use of it for comparative purposes when evaluating the Ancient Near Eastern material is far too shaky to represent any real value. I shall therefore leave the Greek evidence out of consideration[41].

In Mesopotamian religion the sacred marriage is attested primarily in Sumerian religion[42]. However, after Frazer and the Pan-Babylonian

[39] For a survey of the Greek evidence, see A. Klinz, "*hieròs gámos*" *PRE*, Supplb. 6 (1935) 107-13.

[40] The first one to use the term in a wider sense was J. G. Frazer (cf. *The Golden Bough*, vol. 12 (1915) index 440 and 361-62.

[41] Despite the great attraction one may feel towards the theories developed by such scholars as C. H. Gordon (*Homer and the Bible* (1967)) and M. C. Astour (*Hellenosemitica* (1967)), the average scholar is far more restrictive in making comparisons between the two cultures. As for the late Hellenistic evidence, see my remarks below pp. 24-26.

[42] S. N. Kramer, "Cuneiform Studies and the History of Literature", *PAPS* 107 (1963) 485-516, *id.* "The Sacred Marriage", *Proc. 26. Int. Congr. of Orientalists*, vol. 2 (1968) 28-32, *id.*, *The Sacred Marriage Rite* (1969). Cf. also T. Jacobsen, *The Treasures of Darkness* (1976) *passim.*

school, elaborate theories concerning the sacred marriage rite within Assyrian-Babylonian religion and its influence through diffusion to the cultures of ancient Syria/Palestine developed. A tendency to overestimate the role of the sacred marriage rite in ancient Mesopotamia was soon apparent. A representative of this development is van Buren who considers the phenomenon to be altogether the most important factor in Assyrian-Babylonian religion[43].

However, in more recent times, there has been a change in the attitude of Assyriologists towards the rite of sacred marriage in Mesopotamian religion. Several of the views that were held earlier have had to be abandoned as a result of the lack of basis for them in the texts themselves. An excellent survey of the different arguments and the debate up till to-day is provided by J. Renger, and rather than going into details in this matter I shall be content to refer to this work[44].

According to Renger, one of the more remarkable facts in the discussion concerning the sacred marriage rite in ancient Mesopotamia is that even now a critical work dealing with the different theories, and taking as its starting point the Akkadian texts themselves, still remains to be written[45]. Renger claims further, making a distinction in terminology between *inter alia* theogamies—nuptial celebrations between gods and goddesses celebrated in the cult—and cosmogonic marriages—marriages related to creation and the provoking of fertility—that concerning the former, we have no certain knowledge of the *meaning* of this cultic celebration, and concerning the latter, we have no textual evidence supporting the theory that this mythical event was imitated in the cult[46]. Renger also claims that the commonly recognized relationship between the sacred marriage rite and the New Year Festival remains uncertain. There is no textual evidence supporting the theory that the sacred marriage rite was celebrated annually[47]. It is further remarkable that the neo-Assyrian and

---

[43] E. D. van Buren, "The Sacred Marriage", *Or* 13 (1944) 1: "The very ancient rite of the sacred marriage was of the utmost importance, if not the essential and pivotal element of Babylonian religion. The principal rôle was played by the god of the city-state, and the sacred marriage was celebrated in order that, by a species of sympathetic magic, the resulting fruitfulness might be extended to the people of the whole land; that is to say, that fertility and abundance might be bestowed upon the head of every family, his flocks and herds, and the land he cultivated". I quote this introductory passage by van Buren because it seems very much to represent the *opinio communis* of both the average Old Testament scholar and the historian of religion working on the Ancient Near East. It is, consequently, of a certain importance to be aware of the fact that this view expressed by van Buren and others does not correspond to more recent views expressed by Assyriologists.

[44] J. Renger, "Heilige Hochzeit", *RLA* B.4 (1972-75) 251-59.

[45] *Ibid.* 253ff.

[46] *Ibid.* 255.

[47] *Ibid.* 257.

Neo-Babylonian royal inscriptions, as well as other texts, give no reference to the ritual of the sacred marriage. This must be taken as an indication that the ritual did not play any important role in later Mesopotamian times[48].

Regarding this evidence in the light of the generally accepted idea of the all-important celebrations of the sacred marriage rite in ancient Mesopotamia, it becomes evident that the importance of this ritual has been widely over-estimated. In all likelihood, future research in this area will change the well known picture of this aspect of ancient Mesopotamian religion completely. That this has implications also for the view of the sacred marriage rite within other Ancient Near Eastern cultures goes without saying.

Of the Ugaritic texts there are only a few which one might regard as depicting a *hieros gamos* scene[49]. Here again we meet with great difficulties with regard to the relationship of the myths to the cult. There is no evidence to be found in the texts themselves that they have been used as cultic texts. And even if at least some of the descriptions of divine copulation found in these texts have the provocation of fertility as a main motif[50], there is absolutely no evidence whatsoever pointing in the direction that these acts were dramatically imitated in the cult.

If we return to the commonly accepted theory concerning a widespread institution of cultic prostitution in the Ancient Near East, we notice that the theory is based upon two fundamental assumptions: 1. a main function of the sacred marriage rite is to provoke fertility, and 2. in order to secure fertility the divine act of sacred marriage was imitated among the worshippers in the cult[51]. Needless to say, when these two main suppositions turn out to have no support whatever in the texts themselves, the theory of a widespread phenomenon "cultic prostitution" in the Ancient Near East cannot any longer be maintained.

Finally a few words should be said about the late Greek and Hellenistic evidence concerning cultic prostitution in the Ancient Near East. As everyone will know, this evidence has played an important role in the debate.

In his "Babylonian history" Herodotus recalls a custom among the Babylonians where every woman in the country once in her lifetime has

[48] *Ibid.* 258.

[49] The most prominent of these being *CTA* 23 (on this myth, see in particular P. Xella, *Il mito di šḥr e šlm* (1973)).

[50] *E.g. CTA* 5, V, 18-22.

[51] I admit that this may represent an over-simplification of the average scholarly view, especially as I have omitted the discussion on the particular nature of the assumed cultic prostitution, its relationship to the sometimes assumed sexual initiation rite, etc. Nevertheless, the description is sufficiently accurate to serve the present purpose.

to sit in the temple of Aphrodite and have intercourse with a stranger[52]. The custom, according to Herodotus, is regarded as a duty to the goddess, and cannot be denied. A similar custom among the Babylonians is recorded in the geography of Strabo[53]. Even more famous is probably the account in Lucian's treatise on the Syrian Goddess, where he describes how the cult in the temple of Aphrodite in Byblos is performed[54]. According to Lucian, the women who participate in the celebrations in connection with the death of Adonis and who on this occasion refuse to shave their heads, have to offer themselves to strangers in the market. Their pay is considered a sacrifice to Aphrodite[55].

The main problem in connection with the Greek authors is whether they can be trusted as historical sources[56]. On the whole, however, I believe that they are important to us in our attempt to reconstruct the history of religion of the Ancient Near East. But this is not the same as to say that we can use these sources uncritically. Thus, it is obvious that a text like that of Herodotus cannot be correct in every detail. If it really was the case in ancient Babylonia that every woman of the country once in her life-time had to perform the religious duty of a cultic prostitute, we should undoubtedly have expected to find traces of this fact in the vast legal and religious Akkadian literature. However, *all* the relevant literature remains completely silent on the matter.

On the other hand, if something of the kind described by Herodotus had not been going on in Babylonia—possibly very locally, and possibly on a small scale—it is not likely that he would have mentioned it at all. This kind of story is not likely to have been invented. Besides, it is supported by the account of Strabo, as well as by other authors[57].

In the case of Lucian, whose words we should not doubt, the matter is more complicated. We have no means of knowing whether here we have to do with a Greek/Hellenistic custom, or whether the description is of an originally Semitic rite.

Altogether, our late Greek and Hellenistic evidence is not of such a nature that it may change anything regarding the general view concerning cultic prostitution in the Ancient Near East presented above. If the

---

52 *Herodotus.* [Ed.] K. Abicht. B.1 (1884) 218-20.

53 *Strabonis Geographica.* Rec. A. Meineke. Vol. 3 (1877) 1039.

54 *Luciani Samosatensis opera.* Ex. rec. C. Jacobitz. Vol. 3 (1872) 342.

55 Cf. further on this C. Clemen, *Lukians Schrift über die syrische Göttin* (1938) 32-33.

56 On Herodotus, see W. Baumgartner, "Herodots babylonische und assyrische Nachrichten", *ArOr* 18 (1950) 69-72, on Lucian, see H. M. Barstad, "Der rasende Zeus", *Tem* 12 (1976) 163.

57 For further details, see W. Baumgartner, *op. cit.* 81-83. I do not share the scepticism of E. J. Fisher ("Cultic Prostitution in the Ancient Near East?" *BTB* 6 (1976) 225-36) concerning the validity of sources like Herodotus and Lucian.

late Greek and Hellenistic evidence had had any support from contemporary documents, the matter would have been quite different. However, all texts are silent in this matter. Consequently, if a institution of cultic prostitution did exist, there is nothing to indicate that it was "common", "pivotal", or "widespread". On the contrary, *if* it existed, it must certainly have been a fringe phenomenon[58].

One last aspect of the discussion which does not seem to have played any important role, but which nevertheless must be taken into consideration is whether the sources of Herodotus and other ancient writers do not simply give evidence of *profane* prostitution. That the name of the goddess of love, as well as terminology seemingly belonging to her cult should be connected to this *métier* also, should not at all surprise us. At least this is something at which future research in this area should take a closer look.

In any case, it must be quite clear that the late Greek and Hellenistic evidence concerning sacred prostitution in Mesopotamia and Syria has no bearing on the Old Testament as long as it is not supported by interior evidence in the Old Testament itself. As we shall see, this is not the case[59].

2.2.1.3. The Old Testament Evidence concerning Cultic Prostitution

From the above it follows that the belief in wide-spread cultic prostitution in the Ancient Near East can no longer be maintained. As the belief in the existence of such an institution within the ancient Canaanite/Israelite religion presupposes its widespread existence in the surrounding cultures, there should be good reasons for viewing the frequently assumed existence of cultic prostitution in the Old Testament in a more critical light than has hitherto been the case.

---

[58] The main problem with regard to all late information concerning the phenomenon "cultic prostitution" in the Ancient Near East is, of course, that we have hardly any means of sorting out what is original and what is due to later influence. Needless to say, not even the strictest survivalist would lay any stress on information stemming from the last centuries (I am thinking of books like S. I. Curtiss, *Primitive Semitic Religion* (1902) *passim*).

[59] The late Greek and Hellenistic evidence has been utilized by Old Testament scholars on several occasions. Suffice to mention one example. H. W. Wolff (*Dodekapropheton* I (1961)) attempts to explain the problem of Hosea's marriage by regarding Gomer as an ordinary Israelite woman who has participated in a Canaanite sexual initiation rite. Wolff builds his thesis on ancient sources like Herodotus and Lucian, as well as on modern authors (L. Rost, "Erwägungen zu Hos 4, 13f", *Festschrift A. Bertholet* (1950) 456). Wolff's assumption about Gomer is purely hypothetical, and there is no textual evidence which might support his view. This was rightly seen by W. Rudolph, "Präparierte Jungfrauen?", *ZAW* 75 (1963) 65-73. Rudolph, however, is too negative in his view on the validity of some of the extra-biblical evidence as a source for the reconstruction of the history of religion of the Ancient Near East. It is much more a question of *how* we read these authors than not reading them at all.

When one reads through the literature dealing with the institution cultic prostitution in the Old Testament, it strikes one that the phenomenon is always referred to axiomatically; the idea seems to be so widely accepted that no one has to prove it by means of textual evidence. Some scholars in their over-eagerness even place the common prostitute, the *znh*, in the service of the "Canaanite fertility religion"[60]. It should be unnecessary to state that this assumption is pure phantasy without any base in the texts. Not surprisingly, the belief in wide-spread cultic prostitution as a means of provoking fertility in ancient Israel seems to be particularly prevalent among Scandinavian scholars[61].

In what follows I intend to take a closer look at the main arguments and texts which have been put forward in favour of the existence of an institutional cultic prostitution in ancient Israel. For practical reasons I shall restrict myself to only a few texts. It may seem appropriate to concentrate on the passages Deut 23, 18-19, I Kings 14, 23-24, I Kings 15, 12, I Kings 22, 46, II Kings 23, 6-7, a group of texts referred to by one scholar as "clear references to cultic prostitution", as well as on the passages Num 25, 1-3, 1 Sam 2, 22, Jer 13, 27, Ez 16; 23, 37-41, a group of texts to which the same scholar referred as possible allusions to the same[62].

In Deut 23, 18-19, a text which gives rules concerning the participation in public worship, legal purity etc., we read:

> "There shall be no *qdšh* among the women of Israel (*mbnwt yśr'l*) and there shall be no *qdš* among the men of Israel (*mbny yśr'l*). 19. You shall not bring the pay of a whore (*'tnn zwnh*) or the wages of a "dog" (*mḥyr klb*) to the house of Yahweh your god (to pay for) any vow, for both these are an abomination to Yahweh your god."

A common feature among those scholars who take these two verses as a reference to the institution of cultic prostitution in ancient Israel is that they treat the two verses as a unit. However, there is no reason why we should assume that these two verses are dealing with the one and the same matter. In the same way as the verse preceding v.18 and the verse

---

60 B. A. Brooks, "Fertility Cult Functionaries in the Old Testament", *JBL* 60 (1941) 236-39, W. Kornfeld, "Fruchtbarkeitskulte im Alten Testament", *WBTh* 10 (1965) 11. That the prophets use the word *znh*, "to whore", as a designation for the Israelite people worshipping deities other than Yahweh, is quite another matter (see n. 86 below).

61 G. Widengren, "Hieros gamos och underjordsvistelse", *RoB* 7 (1948) 17-46, H. Ringgren, "Hieros gamos i Egypten, Sumer och Israel", *RoB* 18 (1959) 23-51, J. P. Asmussen, "Bemerkungen zur sakralen Prostitution im Alten Testament", *StTh* 11 (1957-58) 167-92.

62 E. M. Yamauchi, "Cultic Prostitution", *Orient and Occident* (1973) 218. The view of Yamauchi may be regarded as representative of the average scholar who has commented on the problem of cultic prostitution in the Old Testament.

following v.19 are dealing with quite separate matters, v.18 and v.19 give regulations concerning two, quite different matters.

The two terms *qdšh* and *qdš* of v.18 are normally taken to be references to female and male cultic prostitutes respectively. As we do not get any help from the context (v.19 is dealing with quite another matter), it is only on etymological grounds that one may draw the conclusion that the words *qdšh* and *qdš* are technical terms for cult prostitutes. However, on etymological grounds we may not draw this conclusion at all.

As a designation for a person, the root *qdš* occurs in the West-Semitic languages (excluding Qumran) only in Biblical Hebrew, in Ugaritic[63], and once in epigraphical Hebrew[64].

The background for rendering Biblical Hebrew *qdšh/qdš* by "cultic prositute" stems ultimately from the widespread, but unfounded[65] belief in the great importance of the sacred marriage rite in Mesopotamian religion, as well as from the belief that the institution of cultic prostitution was spread through diffusion from Mesopotamia to the surrounding cultures.

In this connection the Akkadian cultic title *qadištum* was widely thought to be the technical term for a cultic prostitute[66]. However, the view that the *qadištum* in ancient Mesopotamian religion was a cultic prostitute can no longer be maintained[67].

The incorrect assumption that *qadištum* in Akkadian is a term for a cultic prostitute was not only transferred to *qdšh/qdš* in Biblical Hebrew, but to the occurrences of this word in Ugaritic as well[68]. That *qdš* in Ugaritic does not mean a cultic prostitute, but is a designation for a male member of the lower ranks of priests, was correctly seen by von Soden[69].

Consequently, if one wants to make up one's mind concerning the meaning of Biblical Hebrew *qdšh/qdš* on the basis of comparative philology, it follows from the above that the words *qdšh/qdš* in ancient Canaan/Israel were titles of members, female and male, of the cult per-

---

[63] *UT* 63, 3; 81, 2; 113, 73; 114, 1; 169, 7.

[64] The inscription was published by N. Avigad, "Excavations at Beth Sheʿarim", *IEJ* 7 (1957) 241ff. In this inscription, probably dating from the 2nd or 3rd century, *qdš* has, according to Avigad, the meaning "chaste", "pure", and is consequently an honourable one (cf. *DISO* 253-54).

[65] See above pp. 22-24.

[66] It is only fair to mention that this view was always more fervently adhered to by biblical scholars than by Assyriologists.

[67] A survey of the meaning and function of the *qadištum* in Mesopotamian religion is given by J. Renger, "Untersuchungen zum Priestertum in der altbabylonischen Zeit", *ZA* 58 (1967) 179-84.

[68] N. 63 above.

[69] W. von Soden, "Zur Stellung des 'Geweihten' (*qdš*) in Ugarit," *UF* 2 (1970) 329-30.

sonnel. From the strongly negative view of this cult personnel that we meet with in Old Testament literature, we may assume that they formed a part of the non-Yahwistic cult.

In ancient Mesopotamia, the importance of the *qadištum* varied from time to time. In ancient Ugarit the *qdš* was apparently to be found among the low-ranking members of the priests. However, in Canaan it seems that the *qdšh* and the *qdš* must have belonged to the most high-ranking members of the cult personnel. Only if this was the case can we understand that their occupation could not be tolerated by the Yahwistic prophets and theologians. And, when we see the very strong objections that the occupations of these cultic persons were met with (Deut 23, 18), it may also be assumed that they were closely connected with the carrying out of certain rites which could not be tolerated by the Yahwistic religion. However, to assume that these cult servants or priests were engaged in any cultic prostitution is totally unfounded. It is moreover with interest that we note that Deut 23, 18 does not itself speak against the occupation of the *qdšh* and the *qdš* in general, but states particularly that no *Israelite* must occupy these positions.

The following verse 19 has nothing to do with the regulation in v.18 at all. V.19 is simply stating that money earned through prostitution cannot be accepted in the cult. Most probably this has to do with the purity of the cultic place (cf. the regulations in Lev 27). Even if prostitution was accepted in ancient Israel[70], it was certainly not regarded as praiseworthy. It is along the same lines that the priest was forbidden to take a prostitute as his wife[71].

As for the worb *klb*, most probably a designation for a male prostitute[72], the prohibition against this occupation at the same time concerns the regulations concerning homosexuality, a practice of which the Old Testament takes a strongly negative view[73]. Again it should be stressed that v.19 makes perfectly good sense in itself, and that there are no reasons why there should be any ideological connection between vv.18 and 19.

After having attempted to demonstrate that Deut 23, 18-19 do not concern cultic prostitution, we may proceed to other pasages in the Old

---

[70] N. 31 above.

[71] Lev 21, 7.

[72] The word *klb* was thoroughly discussed by D. Winton Thomas, "KELEBH 'Dog'", *VT* 10 (1960) 410-27. However, this scholar takes *klb* in our verse to be a designation for a male cultic prostitute (p. 425). This is not necessary. The use of *klb* as a designation for a male prostitute is probably caused by the sexual promiscuity which is characteristic of dogs (*ibid.* n. 3).

[73] Lev 18, 22; 20, 13.

Testament commonly regarded as evidence in support of the existence of such an institution in ancient Israel.

In I Kings 14, 23-24 we read:

> "And they built themselves high-places[74], stone monuments[75], and pillars[76] on every high hill and under every green tree[77]. 24. And there was even *qdš*[78] in the country, and they performed all the abominations of the nations (*htwʿbt hgwym*) which Yahweh had driven away from the Israelites."

And in I Kings 15, 12, in a context which describes the abolition of certain forms of non-Yahwistic rites:

> "And he (King Asa) drove out *hqdšym* from the country, and he removed all the *gllym*[79] which his forefathers had made."

Further, we read in I Kings 22, 47 of King Jehoshaphat of Judah:

> "And he swept out *hqdš*[80] who had remained from the days of Asa, his father, of the country."

The final passage which has been regarded as a certain reference to cultic prostitution in ancient Israel is II Kings 23, 7, which forms a part of the description of the religious reform of King Josiah. In this reform Josiah attempts to purify the Yahwistic religion and to remove all non-Yahwistic cultic influence within it:

> "And he broke down the houses of the *qdšym* in the temple of Yahweh where the women wove clothes[81] for Ashera[82]."

When viewing this evidence in the light of the context—the attack on non-Yahwistic or Yahwistic/syncretistic cults—and in the light of what we have written above concerning the meaning of the word *qdš* for a person in Biblical Hebrew, Ugaritic and Akkadian, we see that the most plausible explanation for the meaning of the word *qdš*/*qdšh* in the biblical

---

[74] On *bmwt*, see K.-D. Schunck, "*bmh*", *TWAT* I (1973) 662-67.

[75] On *msbwt*, see A. Reichert, "Massebe", *BRL*² (1977) 206-09.

[76] On *ʾšrym*, see J. C. de Moor, "*ʾšrh*", *TWAT* I (1973) 473-81.

[77] On this stereotyped Deuteronomic phrase, see W. L. Holladay, "On Every High Hill and under Every Green Tree", *VT* 11 (1961) 170-76. Students of ancient Greek religion will no doubt notice that this represents also the circumstances under which the Greek gods celebrated their sacred marriage (A. Klinz, "*hieròs gámos*", *PRE* Suppl. B.6 (1935) 109: 60). This fact may have influenced Old Testament scholars in their evaluation of this Deuteronomistic phrase.

[78] The singular may reflect the group, meaning both *hqdšwt* and *hqdšym*.

[79] On this designation of non-Yahwistic deities, see H. D. Preuss, "*glwlym*", *TWAT* 2 (1977) 1-5.

[80] Cf. n. 78 above.

[81] The meaning of Hebrew *btym* is uncertain.

[82] For *ʾšrh*, see above n. 76. Whether the reference in this verse is to the goddess Ashera or to a (her?) cult symbol, is uncertain.

passages which we have quoted above is to take the word as a designation for members of the non-Yahwistic or Yahwistic/syncretistic priesthood. Nowhere in the Old Testament do we find a shred of evidence which might point towards the possibility that the *qdšh*/*qdš* might be designations for cultic prostitutes. Nor do we find any traces which might point towards the existence of any such institution in ancient Israel in the texts. Consequently, as long as the texts themselves remain silent on this point, the sound scholarly attitude should be to regard cultic prostitution in Israel as non-existent.

However, when dealing with the problem of cultic prostitution in the Old Testament there are still a few texts which have to be mentioned as they have played a certain role in the discussion.

In the story of Tamar and Judah in Gen 38, 12-30 we find that there is an interchange between the words *znh* (in v.15) and *qdšh* (in vv.21-22). Apparently this provides us with some evidence for the identification of the two occupations. I cannot fully explain this circumstance. It may be, of course, that *qdšh* is a late addition to the text, in which case the problem solves itself. However, this is not very probable. It may also be, if we choose to take the words as they stand, that a *qdšh* might occasionally prostitute herself. If Tamar could do so, there is no reason why a priestess should not too[83]. The most important point, however, must be that we completely lack a *cultic* context in this story. From this fact alone it follows that we cannot take this text as evidence for the existence of cultic prostitution in ancient Israel.

In Hos 4, 14 the prophet is accusing the people because they "go apart with whores (*znwt*) and sacrifice with *hqdšwt*". The context is cultic/polemical and the prophet is accusing the people of participating in non-Yahwistic or Yahwistic/syncretistic rites. Admittedly, the text is complicated. However, it is easily understood without any necessity of connecting it with cultic prostitution. The most probable explanation of the verse is found when viewing it in the light of Deut 23, 18-19, discussed above. The reference to sacrificing with the *qdšwt* is the same as to say that the people are partaking in the rites of non-Yahwistic or Yahwistic/syncretistic cults. With regard to the *znwt*, this group was not, according to the purity regulations of Deut 23, 19, accepted into the cult. Another possibility is that the *znwt* mentioned in Hos 4, 14 is a metaphoric allusion to the worship of gods other than Yahweh[84]. However, this is difficult to decide.

---

[83] The explanation of E. A. Speiser (*Genesis* (1964) 300) that Hirah asks for the local *qdšh* rather than the *znh* in order to place the affair on a higher social level, is ingenious. Speiser too, however, believes that the *qdšh* is a cult prostitute.

[84] See the references below n. 86.

One of the most quoted passages which has been regarded as a possible reference to cultic prostitution in the Old Testament is Num 25, 1-3:

> "Israel stayed at Shittim. And the people were weakened into whoring with the daughters of Moab. 2. They invited the people to the sacrifices of their gods, and the people ate and prostrated before their gods. 3. And Israel served Baᶜal Peᶜor..."

Those who see a reference to cultic prostitution in this passage have misunderstood the contents of the text. Staying in a foreign country, the Israelites participated in the local cult. However, "the daughters of Moab" (*bnwt mwʾb*) have nothing to do with the female inhabitants of that country, but the phrase is rather a reference to the inhabitants of Moab in general. Similar geographic metaphors are well known from the Old Testament[85]. That the worship of gods other than Yahweh is referred to as "whoring" is also a well known biblical phenomenon[86].

Also 1 Sam 2, 22 has been interpreted as referring to cultic prostitution:

> "Eli was very old and he heard all the things which his sons were doing to all Israel, and that they slept with the women who served at the entrance of the tent of meeting."

However, the reason for Eli's worries is not connected with cultic prostitution at all. The group of women referred to in this passage is mentioned elsewhere as a quite respectable class of cult servants[87] and there are no reasons why they should be classed as cultic prostitutes. Eli is worried because of the general behaviour of his sons. As priests their conduct was supposed to be praiseworthy and in accordance with the purity laws which regulated the life of the priests[88].

Finally, still another passage much referred to by those who believe that cultic prostitution was a wide-spread phenomenon in ancient Israel, is Jer 13, 27. The verse appears in a harangue against Jerusalem:

> "Your adulteries (*nʾpyk*) and your neighings (*mṣhlwtyk*), the outrage of your harlotry (*zmt znwtk*) on the hills in the field—I have seen your abominations. Woe to you, O Jerusalem, not yet clean. How long will it still be?"

Again the verse in question has nothing to do with cultic prostitution. The verse may be regarded as a classic among the prophetic descriptions of the participation of the people in non-Yahwistic or Yahwistic/syncretistic cults. The metaphor of harlotry in the prophetic polemics against

---

[85] *E.g. bt ṣywn* (Is 1, 8 et al.), *bt ᶜdwm* (Lam 4, 21-22), *bt mṣrym* (Jer 46, 24).

[86] *E.g.* Hos 1, 2; 4, 12; 9, 1, Jer 2, 20; 3, 1-8. The most pointed use of this metaphor is found in the prophet Ezekiel, in chapters 16 and 23.

[87] Ex 38, 8.

[88] Cf. Lev 21.

such cults through the use of the word *znh* is well known from the Old Testament[89]. The word for adultery *nʾp* is used by the prophet Jeremiah in his polemics against non-Yahwistic or Yahwistic/syncretistic cults also in Jer 3, 9 and 5, 7. This prophetic view of adultery, *i.e.* adultery towards Yahweh who alone the people ought to worship and according to the rules stipulated by the prophets and the orthodox Yahwistic theologians, obviously has nothing at all to do with what some scholars have designated cultic prostitution, an alleged institution the vestiges of which cannot be found in the Bible.

2.2.1.4. The *nʿrh* as a *mrzḥ* Hostess

After this somewhat lengthy detour into the world of Ancient Near Eastern sacred prostitution, we shall return to the problem of the *nʿrh*, vital, in our opinion, to the understanding of the passage Am 2, 7b-8.

From the fact that the institution of cultic prostitution in the Old Testament must be assumed to be non-existent, and as Old Testament moral codes do not know of any objections to sexual intercourse, except the ones dealt with in the laws concerning adultery and blood relation, which could provoke such strong words of condemnation as implied in the use of the prophetic *ḥll*[90], it seems to follow, in contrast to what is normally assumed, that the sentence "a man and his father visit the maid" cannot refer to any sexual activity, but must be understood in some other way.

When the expression *hlk ʾl* is taken in a sexual sense, this has mostly been done as a consequence of the similarity between this expression and the expression *bwʾ ʾl*, which is used in the Bible with this meaning[91]. However, the expression *hlk ʾl*, occurring only in Gen 12, 1 and Jud 1, 10, in addition to Am 2, 7, is not used in this sense.

It follows further that if the sentence "a man and his father go to the maid, profaning my holy name" does not imply any sexual relationship, the whole sentence becomes meaningless unless one connects it with the following v.8:

> "In front of every altar they lie down, on garments taken as pledge, and in the house of their gods they drink the wine given as rates"[92].

If we want to find the solution to the problem of the *nʿrh*, v.8 is in fact our only viable approach. The main problem with regard to v.8 is connected with the setting of the scene: what kind of event is it that is described here? At first glance one would automatically think of a temple

---

[89] Cf. above n. 86.

[90] See above pp. 19-21.

[91] Gen 16, 2; 30, 3-4; 38, 8, Deut 22, 13, 2 Sam 16, 21-22.

[92] For details of this verse, see above notes 17-19.

as the setting where the event described took place. Undoubtedly, the scene has strong religious overtones ("in front of every altar", "in the house of their gods").

On the other hand, when considering the atmosphere of the situation depicted by the prophet, as well as the expressions "garments taken as pledge", and "wine given as rates", it does not quite follow that the scene described by the prophet takes place in a temple. After all, the terminology used by the prophet seems far more to imply an accusation towards the wealthy of Samaria for their economic exploitation of the poor (Am 2, 6-7a) than to refer to the complex taxation system of the temple.

In addition to this, the reference to altars does not constitute any problem. It is very likely that the palaces of the wealthy of Samaria had private altars[93]. If this is the case, we may easily understand what the prophet means when he refers to "the house of their gods".

When the description provided by the prophet in 2, 8 depicts an assembly of Samaritans in a private house or palace, it may seem that the solution to our problem is near at hand. In fact, we do not even have to go outside the book of Amos to find descriptions of feastal events like the one we have in Am 2, 8. Thus, we read in 3, 12:

> "Thus says Yahweh:
> As the shepherd rescues from the mouth of the lion two legs or a piece of an ear, so shall the Israelites be rescued, that are sitting in Samaria, in the corner of a couch and on Damascus divans[94]".

The prophet is here predicting the total annihilation of the inhabitants of Samaria. What is the most interesting in our connection is the reference to the luxurious seating arrangements. It is not unlikely that we have a reference here to the sumptous meals of the richer classes of the city. Admittedly, this text seems to lack any religious overtone. This goes for the whole of the context. It *may* be, however, that the reference in 3, 14 to the religious practice of the Israelites connected to the altars of Bethel bears on the passage 3, 12, as well.

The religious overtone, however, is not lacking in Am 4, 1 where we also have a description of some feastal event. In the same way as in Am 2, 8, wine plays an important factor in this context:

---

[93] On the problem of private altars very little has been written. That they did exist, however, is beyond doubt. One of the texts indicating this is Num 16 (cf. M. Löhr, *Das Räucheropfer im Alten Testament* (1927) 187. On Num 16, see in particular A. H. J. Gunneweg, *Leviten und Priester* (1965) 171-84). On the private altar from an archaeological point of view, see the references in *BRL* (1937) 20 and *BRL* ²(1977) 9.1 Cf. also J. B. Pritchard, "Tell Es-Saᶜidiyeh", *RB* 73 (1966) 574-76.

[94] On this verse, see below p. 182.

"Hear this word, you cows of Bashan in the mountains of Samaria, who oppress the poor (*dlym*), who crush the needy (*ʾbywnym*), and who say to their husbands: Bring, that we may drink!"[95]

The similarity between the scene described in Am 4, 1 and the one described in 2, 8 needs no further comment. The two passages may very well describe the same situation.

Even more illustrative and more important in our connection is the passage Am 6, 4-7:

"You that lie upon beds of ivory and sprawl upon your couches, eating young rams from the flock and fattened young cows from the cowshed, 5. you that sing songs accompanied by the lute, like David, and play on musical instruments, 6. you that drink wine out of bowls and anoint yourselves with the best of oils,...
7. Therefore they shall now head the procession of the captives, and the *mrzḥ*[96] of the sprawling shall come to an end".[97]

What we have before us here is the description of a meal. It is not, however, an ordinary meal. The word here left untranslated, *mrzḥ*, qualifies our description and tells us that we have to do with a sacred meal. As we see, this fits perfectly the descriptions of the prophet Amos in 2, 8 and 4, 1, too. As we have to do with the words of the same prophet, addressed to the same audience within a very limited period of time, there can be little doubt that the prophet in all three of these texts is referring to the same event: a sacred meal with a religious content which could not be accepted by the Yahwistic prophet.

The sacred meal played a very important role in the religiuos and social life of the Ancient Near East. Best known to us is the sacred meal of the so-called *mrzḥ* association. This association is known to us also in the Old Testament, namely from Am 6, 7 and Jer 16, 5. As I have described this association further below[98], I shall refrain from going into details here.

If, however, the passage Am 2, 8, as well as 4, 1 and 6, 7 must be regarded as giving descriptions of the assemblies of the *mrzḥ*, something which in my opinion seems very likely, the result will be that also the *nʿrh* of Am 2, 8 has to be connected to the *mrzḥ* in some way. From this, I would propose that the *nʿrh* mentioned in Am 2, 8 may have been some sort of a hostess attached to the *mrzḥ*.

---

[95] On this verse, see below pp. 37-44.
[96] As it is not easy to find an English word for the institution designated *mrzḥ*, I prefer to leave the word untranslated. For details on the *mrzḥ*, see below pp. 127-42.
[97] On this passage, see below pp. 127-28.
[98] Pp. 127-42.

This assumption would also explain the wrath of the prophet expressed in 2, 8 concerning the man and his father who go to the *nʿrh*; by doing so, they were in fact going to the *mrzḥ* in order to participate in the sacred meal. As this meal was heavily embedded in Canaanite religion and culture, it is only natural that it could not be accepted by the Yahwistic prophet.

Our thesis will also provide an explanation for the curious use of the expression "a man and his father". From our knowledge of the Ancient Near Eastern *mrzḥ* association we know that it was very much a family affair[99]. Each family[100] had its own *mrzḥ*; hence the expression "a man and his father".

A further distinct trait of the *mrzḥ* was that it was obviously something of the upper classes, of the wealthy in society. Consequently, we may well understand the criticism of the prophet when he speaks of oppression and exploitation, pledge and rates. What is more important in our connection though, is the fact that the *nʿrh* was not, as it is often assumed, someone of low rank, but rather someone belonging to the upper class. This, again, makes her connection with the *mrzḥ* association even more plausible[101].

---

99 See below, p. 131.

100 "Family" is here understood in a very wide sense of the word.

101 On the rank of the *nʿrh*, see above pp. 17-19.

CHAPTER THREE

THE PROPHET AS MISSIONARY. STUDIES IN AM 4, 1-13

3.1. *The Cows of Bashan*

The fourth chapter of the Book of Amos opens with the following address:

> "Hear this word, you cows of Bashan in the mountain of Samaria[1], who oppress the poor (*dlym*)[2], who crush the needy (*ʾbywnym*)[3], and who say to their husbands: Bring, that we may drink!"

Essential to a correct interpretation of the message contained in the fourth chapter of the Book of Amos is the expression "cows of Bashan (*prwt hbšn*)" in 4, 1. As I have discussed this expression on a previous occasion[4], I shall be content to summarize in broad outline the main conclusions reached at that time[5].

The majority of commentators who have written on it takes the expression "cows of Bashan" to be a reference to the women of Samaria.

In doing so, they take as their starting point the cattle of Bashan in Transjordan. The comparision by the prophet of the women of Samaria to the cattle of Bashan is, according to some scholars, brought about by the beauty and opulent charms of the Samaritan women, or, according to others, by the fact that the women addressed belong to the upper classes of society.

Accordingly W. R. Harper, in his commentary on Amos, writes about "the noble princesses who are now rebuked because of their sins"[6]. W. Nowack interprets the expression "als eine Bezeichnung der üppigen und gewalttätigen Weiber jener Grossen"[7]. E. Hammershaimb believes

---

[1] On Samaria in the Book of Amos and in the Bible, see below pp. 181-85.

[2] On this word, see below p. 81.

[3] On this word, see below p. 81.

[4] H. M. Barstad, "Die Basankühe in Am iv 1", *VT* 25 (1975) 286-97.

[5] Despite the many immaturities of this *Erstlingsarbeit* I am as convinced of the tenability of my theory today as I was at that time. What I did not know, however, was that A. Neher had already expressed a similar view with regard to the meaning of the formula *prwt hbšn* in 1950 (*Amos* pp. 82-85, 224, 273). Consequently, M. Bič was not the first one to connect the expression with Canaanite cults (*Das Buch Amos* (1969) 82ff.). The view taken by Neher was followed by R.Vuilleumer-Bessard (*La tradition cultuelle* (1960) 43) and later by J. D. W. Watts ("A Critical Analysis of Amos 4, 1ff", *Proc. SBL* (1972) 496, n. 4.). My own view was partly supported by A. J. Williams ("A Further Suggestion About Amos iv 1-3", *VT* 29 (1979) 206).

[6] W. R. Harper, *A Critical and Exegetical Commentary* (1905) 86.

[7] W. Nowack, *Die kleinen Propheten* (1922) 136.

that "the cows of Bashan" reflect the exuberant appearance of the Samaritan women[8]. Designations of the commentators like "edelste Rasse"[9] and "Rassevieh"[10] stresses the high social status of these so-called ladies. Also A. S. Kapelrud defines the Bashan cows as "the rich ladies of Samaria"[11]. S. Amsler, however, is content to state that "Amos interpelle les femmes de Samarie en les comparant au bétail de race de Basan, pâturages renommées de la Transjordanie"[12] and refrains from drawing the usual conclusion. One of the most recent commentators on Amos, J. L. Mays, expresses himself according to the old pattern when he states: "The Bashan-cows are the women of quality in Samaria, the pampered darlings of society in Israel's royalist culture"[13].

The commentators whom I have mentioned undoubtedly represent the ordinary scholarly view with regard to the meaning of the expression "cows of Bashan" in 4, 1. In what follows I am going to account for why I do not share this view. As it turns out, this is vital to the understanding of the total context in which Am 4, 1 stands.

The word "Bashan" appears several times in the Old Testament, in total some 58 times. It occurs 42 times in Num, Deut, Jos, Kings and Chr. Apart from one occurrence in Deut 33, 22, where the tribe of Dan is compared to a lion springing out from Bashan, Bashan is in these texts solely used in connection with the conquest, or in other historical/-geographical descriptions.

In the Psalter "Bashan" occurs in Pss 22, 13; 68, 16.23; 135, 11, and 136, 20. In the two last mentioned psalms the use of the word "Bashan" is of the same type as the one found in the historical books. The king of Bashan is here mentioned together with Sihon, king of the Amorites and some Canaanite princes.

In Pss 22 and 68, however, the matter is quite different. In both of these psalms there are obviously old mythological traditions underlying the use of "Bashan". In Ps 68, 16-17 the mountain Bashan is described in mythical terms which makes it possible to identify it with the *Götterberg*, Zaphon/Tabor/Hermon, etc.[14].

Also rather interesting is the occurrence of "Bashan" in Ps 22, 13[15]. In

---

[8] E. Hammershaimb, *Amos* (1967) 61-62.

[9] A. Weiser, *Das Buch der zwölf kleinen Propheten* (1956) 150.

[10] T. H. Robinson, *Die zwölf kleinen Propheten*^{3} (1964) 85.

[11] A. S. Kapelrud, *Central Ideas in Amos* (1961) 63.

[12] S. Amsler, *Amos* (1969) 72.

[13] J. L. Mays, *Amos* (1969) 72.

[14] Cf. the article "*har*" by S. Talmon, *TWAT* II (1977) 459-83, in particular paragraph V. The article is rich in bibliographical information.

[15] My previous assumption that the animal metaphor in this text corresponds to the use of animal metaphors *e.g.* in Pss 7, 3 and 10, 9 ("Die Basankühe in Am iv 1", *VT* 25 (1975) 289) is too superficial.

this context the expression *ʾbyry bšn* stands in *parallelismus membrorum* with *prym rbym*. Here, too, we should be aware of the fact that old mythological traditions underlie the use of these different expressions[16]. Compared to the Bashan tradition in Ps 68 mentioned above this turns out to be particularly interesting.

Finally, we meet with "Bashan" in ten different prophetic texts, namely Is 2, 13; 33, 9, Jer 22, 20; 50, 19, Ez 27, 6; 39, 18, Am 4, 1, Mi 7, 14, Nah 1, 4, and Zech 11, 2.

The use of "Bashan" in the prophetic tradition obviously differs from the use of this word in the other Old Testament texts, and it may seem legitimate to speak of a separate prophetic tradition in connection with the word.

In Jer 50, 19, Mi 7, 14, and Ez 39, 18 we find "Bashan" in a salvation oracle, addressed to the people. Playing on the national prestige of their fellow countrymen the prophets are drawing their attention to the past, towards the times when Carmel, Bashan, the hillsides of Ephraim, and Gilead (Jer 50, 19), Carmel, Bashan, and Gilead (Mi 7, 14), and Bashan (Ez 39, 18) were in their possession. The prophets are able to tell their people that these desirable regions, once taken away from them, shall once more come into their possession.

The last seven texts which have "Bashan" in them are all texts of doom. In the same way as with the salvation oracles mentioned above, the word "Bashan" seems to have been a common constituent of several judgement oracles, most of them addressed to foreign nations. Here, too, we must assume that the prophets are taking advantage of the national consciousness of the people.

Of the prophetic texts which have "Bashan" in them only Am 4, 1 and Jer 22, 20 are directed against the prophet's own people.

It is in connection with the background of the above mentioned texts that it has been maintained that the expression *prwt hbšn* in Am 4, 1 constitutes a comparison of the women of Samaria with the cattle of Transjordan, and that the simile reflects either the attractive looks or the high social status of these women.

The texts themselves, however, offer no factual evidence in support of such assumptions. Further, a comparison of women with cows, in a connection similar to the one we have here, is to my knowledge unknown. This goes both for the Old Testament as well as for the literature from the surrounding cultures[17].

---

[16] Cf. A. S. Kapelrud, "*ʾbyr*", *TWAT* I (1973) 45, III.1.

[17] Nor am I convinced by the explanation offered by S. Speier. Speier sees in the expression a *doppeldeutiger Ausdruck* where *bšn* is used as an equivalent to Arabic *baṯne*/*baṯane*, meaning "ein üppig gebautes Mädchen" ("Bemerkungen zu Amos", *VT* 3 (1953) 306-07). I find the explanation of Speier a little far-fetched.

Also the context of Am 4, 1 must be regarded as an objection to the common view on the expression "cows of Bashan". Our verse stands as the opening verse in a proclamation of doom. Leaving the doxologies of v.13 out of account[18], the words of doom take up the whole of Chapter 4.

We may divide the chapter the following way: Vv. 1-3, address and proclamation of judgement[19]. Vv. 4-5, a plea to sin, *i.e.* to participate in the cults at Bethel and Gilgal[20]. Vv. 6-11, enumeration of the different disasters which Yahweh has brought upon the people[21], and, finally, in v. 12, confirmation of the judgement.

In my opinion, there can be no doubt that the expression *prwt hbšn* in 4, 1 is a paraphrase for the whole of the Israelite people/inhabitants of Samaria. In what follows I intend to state the reasons for my assumption.

As one can see, both the preceding (3, 1ff.) and the succeeding (5, 1ff.) words of judgment are directed against the whole of the people of Samaria/Israel and not against any separate part of it. Also the rest of Chapter 4, containing the utterance of doom which is introduced through the address of 4, 1, concerns the whole of the people and not any particular group[22]. One may, in fact, feel tempted to ask why Amos should be content to address his words of doom to the upper class women of Samaria, when the following pronouncement regards the whole of Samaritan society.

One should further notice the formal agreement between the expressions *hyšbym bšmrwn bpʿt mṭh* in 3, 12 and *prwt hbšn ʾšr bhr šmrwn.* As one can see, the expression in 3, 12 stands as an apposition to *bny yśrʾl.*

Already these preliminary, rather superficial, contextual observations make it probable that the expression *prwt hbšn* may be regarded as including *all* inhabitants of the northern capital, rather than referring to some separate group among them.

If this is the case, in Chapters 3, 4 and 5 there are three different pronouncements of judgement, all containing several similar features. All three oracles of doom have as their introductory formula the expression *šmʿw hdbr hzh*, and all are addressed to the people of Samaria. The expression *prwt hbšn* of Am 4, 1, accordingly, must be understood as a metaphorical/poetical paraphrase. Such usages are well known from the

[18] On the question of the doxologies, see below pp. 79-80.

[19] On these verses, see further below pp. 43-44.

[20] See further on the passage below pp. 47-49 and 54-58.

[21] Cf. below pp. 58-75.

[22] Or at least not a group as particular as "the women of Samaria". The group to which the prophet is addressing himself is the rich upper class in their capacity as leaders, religious and political, of the people. Consequently, when addressing himself to this particular group, Amos is also addressing himself to the whole of the Samaritan people, or the whole of the northern realm, for that sake.

Old Testament, and one should not attempt to interpret them literally. Suffice to point to the expression *btwlt yśrʾl* in Am 5, 1. No one, I believe, would attempt to read this expression in a different way than as a determinative for the Israelite people.

As has already been suggested by some scholars[23] the solution to the problem of the expression "cows of Bashan" in the Book of Amos must be sought in the relationship of that expression to the Canaanite cult.

Already the determinative *bhr šmrwn* should attract some interest in this connection. Even if the expression "on the mountain of Samaria" in the present context serves the function of a rather general statement—an appositional remark meant to designate all the inhabitants of the city of Samaria—it may not be accidental that the prophet chooses to express himself in this way. Viewed against the background fact that the Canaanite Baʿal cult was most intimately connected with a holy mountain, it may well be that the expression *bhr šmrwn* implies more than has usually been thought[24]. However, one is not likely to come beyond a mere suspicion.

Also rather interesting is the expression *hʾmrt lʾdnyhm*. The word *ʾdn* is not the ordinary word for "husband" in the Old Testament[25]. Normally, "husband" is rendered by *bʿl*[26]. We may assume, therefore, that Amos wants to throw something into relief when he uses the word *ʾdn*.

ʾdn is frequently used in the Old Testament as a divine title for the god[27]. This was so also in Canaanite religion. In the Ras Shamra texts we read about El, the head of the Ugaritic pantheon, saying to another god (in all likelihood this other god is Baʿal): *ʾat. ʾadn. tpʿr*—"you shall be called *ʾadn*—lord"[28]. In fact, the title *ʾdn* was so intimately connected with the fertility god of ancient Syria/Palestine that in Hellenistic times the fertility god *par excellence* bears this title as his proper name[29].

There is also another possible explanation to the use of *ʾdn* in our verse. When Amos uses the word *ʾdn* instead of *bʿl*, he may be doing this in order to emphasize that the "cows of Bashan" are not "talking" to their real husband. The real husband of Israel is Yahweh[30].

---

[23] See n. 5 above.

[24] Cf. Jer 22, 20ff. For literature on the holy mountain, see n. 14 above.

[25] As far as I have been able to find out the word is used in this sense only in Gen 18, 12.

[26] Gen 20, 3, Ex 21, 3.22, Deut 22, 22; 24, 4, 2 Sam 11, 26, etc.

[27] O. Eissfeldt, "*ʾadn*", *TWAT* I (1973) 66.

[28] *CTA* 1, IV, 17.

[29] I am still inclined to think that the name of the god Adonis has a Semitic origin. It is perhaps unnecessary to mention that not everyone agrees on this difficult problem (see most recently S. Ribichini, "Per una riconsiderazione di Adonis", *RSF* 7 (1979) 164-65). On the god Adonis, see also further below pp. 149-50.

[30] Cf. Jer 3, 14. Here, too, the prophet is engaged in polemics against Canaanite cults.

The words uttered by the "cows of Bashan", *hbyʾh wnšth*, "Bring, that we may drink!", have always caused trouble to the commentators. Formerly, I was of the opinion that these words might perhaps be connected with the New Year Festival and the festival of the new wine which was thought to have been so prevalent within the Canaanite Baᶜal cult[31]. To-day, I am more in doubt about these matters. On the whole, the problem of the New Year Festival is very difficult and, at any rate, the drinking of wine alone provides very meagre evidence indeed for connecting the episode mentioned in Am 4, 1 with a New Year Festival.

If one really feels a need to penetrate behind the text of Am 4, 1 there seem to be other contexts which suit our purpose much better. Below I have given an account of the Ancient Near Eastern institution commonly known as the *mrzḥ*[32]. Above[33] I have mentioned the possibility of connecting Am 2, 7b-8 with this institution also. The question we should now ask ourselves is whether it might not also be possible to link Am 4, 1 to the *mrzḥ*. As far as I can see, there are good reasons for doing so.

Firstly, we should keep in mind that we are dealing with the words of one particular prophet, uttered to one and the same audience; namely the wealthy upper classes of Samaritan society. If the prophet is addressing the *mrzḥ* in 6, 4-6, about which there can be absolutely no doubt whatever[34], what would be more natural than to find traces of the same situation also elsewhere in his message, namely in 2, 7b-8 and 4, 1, and possibly also in 3, 12?

Secondly, our assumption that Am 4, 1 (as well as the other possible *mrzḥ* passages in Amos) may contain allusions to the *mrzḥ*, is not something which is plucked out of thin air. The great similarities both with regard to form and content of the passages in question can hardly be overlooked. With regard to Am 4, 1 we note the importance of the wine which seems to indicate a meal. We note further the religious overtone of the verse, indicated through the formula *prwt hbšn*, which may point towards a sacred meal. We also note the reference to the oppressing of the poor and needy, which points towards the upper classes of society. As I have indicated below[35] the *mrzḥ* was an institution reserved for the wealthy families of society.

As for the expression "cows of Bashan", the word *prh*, "cow", is far more interesting to us than the word "Bashan" when it comes to identifying the polemical overtone of the prophet in his use of the expression.

---

[31] H. M. Barstad, "Die Basankühe in Am iv 1", *VT* 25 (1975) 293.
[32] See pp. 127-42.
[33] See p. 33ff.
[34] The passage is treated in more detail below pp. 127-28, 138-42.
[35] See p. 139; also above p. 34.

There is no doubt in my mind that this term, in the way it is being used in Am 4, 1, should be connected with Canaanite cults[36].

Thus, in Hos 4, 16 we meet the word *prh* as a determinative for Israel following deities other than Yahweh. The adjective attached to *prh* in this context is *srrh*, usually rendered by "wild", "stubborn". From the context, in particular vv. 13-15 and no less, v. 14, "wanton", "licentious" may seem more appropriate. The word is used in this meaning in Prov 7, 11, where taking the *šyt zwnh* of v. 10 into consideration, it hardly could be translated in any other way.

The word *prh*, accordingly, may be considered as a prophetic invective, used as a determinative for the "apostate" people. This use of the word fits the context of Am 4, 1 perfectly[37].

Also Jer 2, 24 is of great interest in this connection. In this text, which is dominated by polemics against Canaanite cults (v. 20), the two nouns *prh* and *bkrh* (v. 23) occur as determinatives for the people who have left Yahweh and follow other deities. In v. 23 the Baᶜals in particular are mentioned. Unfortunately, the text is rather corrupt. However, there can be no doubt about the reading *prh*, no matter how the rest of the verse is interpreted. Jer 2, 24 consequently, is the third context where we find the word *prh* as a determinative for the people who worship deities other than Yahweh. Needless to say, this cannot be circumstantial.

Our interpretation of the expression *prwt hbšn* in Am 4, 1 is further supported by the verses following v. 1, especially vv. 4-5. In fact, the whole of Am 4, 1-12 is concerned with anti-Canaanite cult polemics. This is quite clearly shown *inter alia* in vv. 7-8: the main function of the Canaanite deity Baᶜal was to secure the rain and thereby provide fertility in field and meadow[38]. By throwing into relief the worship of the "cows of Bashan", *i.e.* the inhabitants of Samaria, the prophet can tell them that their worship is all wrong and can only lead to disaster. This they may see for themselves (Am 4, 6-11). All their cult has been good for nothing. Only Yahweh is the master of the rain, as well as of the other blessings of life.

---

[36] H. Gottlieb has made some very interesting remarks on Mi 4, 11-13 and the use of the word *ᶜglh*, "cow", as a designation for the Israelite people. He believes the designation to have roots in Canaanite cults. The suggestion of Gottlieb is undoubtedly of interest in our connection, and if it has not received the attention it deserves this can only be the result of its being written in Danish (H. Gottlieb, "Den tærskende kvie - Mi 4, 11-13", *DTT* 26 (1963) 167-71).

[37] I do not any more believe ("Die Basankühe in Am iv 1", *VT* 25 (1975) 295) that our text has anything to do with cultic prostitution. As I have attempted to demonstrate above (26-33), the evidence for the existence of any such institution in ancient Israel is virtually nil.

[38] Cf. in particular I Kings 18 (see below pp. 69-70). A text very similar to the one in Am 4, 7-8 is Jer 3, 3 (see below p. 70).

Comparing Am 4, 1ff to the preaching of the prophet Hosea, to mention only one example, we notice as an all-important feature of the message of the two prophets the effort to emphasize the mighty powers of Yahweh at the expense of the deity Baᶜal (Hos 2, 5.12). It is also within this context that we shall have to seek the explanation for the use by the prophet Amos of the expression *prwt hbšn* in his address to the Samaritans in Am 4, 1.

In his words against the "cows of Bashan" the prophet shows no mercy, hurling out his bitter view of their future:

> "Hear[39] this word, you cows of Bashan in the mountains of Samaria[40], who oppress the poor, who crush the needy, and who say to their husbands: Bring, that we may drink! 2. *ʾdny yhwh* has sworn by his holiness: Days will come upon them when they will take you away with hooks[41], and the rest of you with fishing hooks. 3. You shall go out through the breaches, one after another, and you will be taken into Harmon[42], says *yhwh*."

The nature of the religious worship of the "cows of Bashan" is further explained to us through the words of Amos in 4, 4-5, which must be regarded as the direct continuation of the words of doom in 4, 1-3.

3.1.1. A Digression. The Cow as a Fertility Symbol in the Ancient Near East. A Few Examples

If it were the case that the expression "cows of Bashan" in Am 4, 1 was a determinative for the inhabitants of Samaria worshipping deities other than Yahweh and partaking in the sacred meals of the *mrzḥ*, one would expect the particular use of *prh*, "cow", found in this verse to have its background in Canaanite mythological conceptions.

In fact, in the same way as the bull[43], the cow did play an important role as a fertility symbol of the Ancient Near East.

---

[39] Concerning the lack of consistency between the expression *prwt hbšn* and such forms as *šmᶜw, lʾdnyhm, ᶜlykm*, see H. M. Barstad, "Die Basankühe in Am iv 1", *VT* 25 (1975) 291, n. 14.

[40] On Samaria in the Book of Amos and in the Bible, see below pp. 181-85.

[41] The exact meaning of the words *snwt* and *syrwt dwgh* is at issue (cf. S. J. Schwantes, "Note on Amos 4, 2b", *ZAW* 79 (1967) 82-83, A. J. Williams, "A Further Suggestion About Amos iv 1-3", *VT* 29 (1979) 206-09). In relation to the cow metaphor, the picture of the cows being driven out with hooks in their noses suits the context well.

[42] Concerning the enigmatic Harmon cf. D. N. Freedman, F. I. Andersen, "Harmon in Am 4, 3", *BASOR* 198 (1970) 41.

[43] Cf. *i.a.* W. von Soden, "Stierdienst", *RGG*³ 6 (1962) 372-73, *WM* 1. Abt. B.1 (1965) Index, "Stier" p. 594, M. Weippert, "Gott und Stier", *ZDPV* 77 (1961) 93-117, J. M. Sasson, "The Worship of the Golden Calf", *Orient and Occident* (1973) 151-59, H. Motzki, "Ein Beitrag zum Problem des Stierkultes in der Religionsgeschichte Israels", *VT* 25 (1975) 470-85. Cf. also below pp. 50, 183, 188-89.

The relationship between fertility and cow seems to have been particularly outstanding in ancient Egypt. Among the many goddesses connected with or, wholly or in part represented by the figure of a cow, one may especially note Hathor and Isis, the two fertility goddesses *par excellence* of the Egyptian pantheon[44].

Of particular interest further is the goddess of birth, Meskhent (*mśḫn.t*), originally the personification of the birthplace[45]. The goddess wears on her head a badge identical with the hieroglyph for a cow's uterus[46].

Also in old Mesopotamian religion the cow seems to have played an important role in connection with the stimulation of fertility. Of particular interest is the mythological fragment about the moon-god and the cow Amat-Sîn. The myth relates how Sîn catches sight of a beautiful cow, grazing in the field. He feels drawn to her, and, in the disguise of a bull, he succeeds in leading her away from the flock and having intercourse with her. The cow conceives, and we read how she is about to give birth. Sîn sends for two goddesses to assist during the delivery, the one bringing water, the other oil. Finally a calf is born. The interesting thing about this myth, handed down in several versions, the "original" *Sitz im Leben* of which is lost to us, is that it does not exist as an isolated text, but always in connection with medical prescriptions concerning birth and delivery[47].

A variant of the same myth is also known from Asia Minor. In a Hittite myth, originally Hurrian, we read how the sun-god catches sight of a grazing cow and feels attracted to her. He descends from heaven in the shape of a youth and starts a conversation with the cow. Unfortunately the text is badly broken at this point, and it is impossible to get any meaning out of it. The text goes on with the story of the birth of a child in human shape by the cow. When the cow discovers that her offspring is in

---

[44] For a general survey, see H. Bonnet, *RÄRG* (1952) 402-05. On the goddesses in particular, see F. Daumas, "Hathor", *LÄ* II (1977) 1024-1033, J. Bergman, "Isis", *LÄ* III (1980) 186-203. A motif of particular interest was discussed by P. Matthiae, "Il motivo della vacca che allata", *RSO* 37 (1962) 1-31.

[45] H. Bonnet, *op. cit.* 458-59.

[46] Cf. F. L. Griffith, "Notes on Mythology", *PSBA* 21 (1899), and A. Gardiner, *Egyptian Grammar*² (1950) nr. 45, p. 466.

[47] *VAT* 8869 (*KAR* 196) was published by E. Ebeling, "Keilschrifttexte medizinischen Inhalts. IV.", *Archiv für Geschichte der Medizin* 14 (1923) 65-78. A duplicate, *K* 2413, was published by G. Meloni, "Testi assiri del British Museum", *RSO* 4 (1911-12) 559ff. See further F. M. Th. Böhl, "De maangod en de koe", *JEOL* 4 (1936) 202-04, F. Köcher, *Die babylonisch-assyrische Medizin*, B. III: 3 (1964) Nr. 248, W. G. Lambert, "A Middle Assyrian Tablet of Incantation", *Studies in Honor of B. Landsberger* (1965) 283-88, *id.*, "A Middle Assyrian Medical Text", *Iraq* 31 (1969) 28-39, J. van Dijk, "Une variante du thème "l'Esclave de la lune"", *Or* 41 (1972) 339-48. Cf. further R. Borger, *Handbuch der Keilschriftliteratur* B.1 (1967) 101.

human shape, she flies into a rage and threatens to eat it. The sun-god sees to it that the child is found by a poor fisherman from the town of Urma. The fisherman, being childless, takes the child and brings it home with him and presents it to his wife. Together they fool the neighbours into believing that the child was born to the fisherman by his wife. In this way they are able to keep the child[48].

The designation *Märchen*, given to this tale by some scholars[49] can hardly be said to be appropriate[50]. Viewed against the background of other Ancient Near Eastern texts, not least the very similar story from Mesopotamia about the moon-god and the cow, the Hittite story undoubtedly qualifies as a myth. Whether this myth has served particular purposes we do not know. However, it is easy to imagine that it served magical purposes as part of a ritual against childlessness. That the text in its present form has more the character of a *Märchen*, is quite another matter.

The most important attestations of the use of the cow motif in connection with the stimulation of fertility, with relevance to the Old Testament, are found in the Ras Shamra texts. In these texts the goddess Anath is often pictured in the shape of a cow, corresponding to the representation of Baᶜal as a bull[51].

The most interesting text from Ras Shamra in this respect is *CTA* 5, V, 17b-22. This text, representing the very climax in the Baᶜal cyclus[52], a last incident before the deity disappears, relates how Baᶜal meets with a young cow in the fields of *šḫlmmt* and has intercourse with her, with the result that she gives birth to a son. Unfortunately the text is broken immediately after this short intermezzo, and we get no further information as for the continuation of the story. It is, in fact, somewhat remarkable that scholars have failed to notice the conspicuous resemblance between this Ugaritic text and the Akkadian and Hittite myths mentioned above. It may further be worth mentioning that the Ugaritic word for "cow"

[48] *KUB* XXIV 7. Cf. also H. Ehelof, "Das Motiv der Kindesunterschiebung", *OLZ* 29 (1926) 766-69, H. G. Güterbock, *Kumarbi* (1946) 120-22. Whether *KUB* XXIV originally belongs together with "the story of Appu", *KUB* XXIV 8, as assumed by Güterbock, is more uncertain. I am not convinced that it is correct to put all the different fragments together into a "cyclus". For a transcription and translation of *KUB* XXIV 7, see J. Friedrich, "Churritische Märchen und Sagen", *ZA* 49 (1950) 224-33, commentary 247-53.

[49] J. Friedrich, *op. cit.* and more recently E. von Schuler in *WM* 1. Abt. B.1 (1965) 163.

[50] H. Ehelof, "Das Motiv der Kindesunterschiebung", *OLZ* 29 (1926) 766-69, already reacted against this classification in 1926.

[51] However, Baᶜal is never called a bull in the Ugaritic texts. This epithet is reserved for El (but see H. Gese, *Die Religionen Altsyriens* (1970) 129).

[52] J. C. de Moor, *The Seasonal Pattern* (1971) 183ff. and *passim*, A. Caquot, *Textes ougaritiques* (1974) 248-49, J. C. L. Gibson, *Canaanite Myths and Legends* (1978) 72.

used in this text is *prt*. This word corresponds to Hebrew *prh*, which occurs in Am 4, 1[53].

Further Ugaritic texts which have the cow motif are *CTA* 10, III, 20-22; 33-38; 13, 22.29; *CTA* 6, II, 28-30; *PRU* V, 124 *passim*.

It follows from the selection of examples of Ancient Near Eastern mythology presented above that the prophet has deliberately chosen the words which appear in Am 4, 1. It is certainly not due to coincidence when he addresses the Samaritan people worshipping deities other than Yahweh by the designation *prwt hbšn*.

3.2. *The Words of Amos against the Cults in Bethel and Gilgal* (Am 4, 4-5)

After the prophet Amos has attacked the inhabitants of Samaria for their oppression of the poor and needy and for their non-Yahwistic worship, he continues his religious polemics by attacking their participation in the cults at Bethel and Gilgal:

> "4. Go to Bethel and transgress (*wpšʿw*)! To Gilgal and multiply your transgressions (*hrbw lpšʿ*)! Bring in the morning your sacrifices (*zbḥykm*), every three days your tithes (*mʿśrtykm*). 5. Let the smoke of the leavened emerge as a thank-offering (*twdh*) and proclaim voluntary offerings (*ndbwt*), announce (them)."

Am 4, 4-5 is not the only passage in the Book of Amos which condemns the local cults at Bethel and Gilgal. Apparently these cults must have been very popular among the inhabitants of the northern realm. Thus, we read in Am 3, 14:

> "On the day that I punish Israel for its transgressions, I will punish the altars of Bethel, and the horns of the altar shall be cut off, and they shall fall to the earth[54]".

[53] Also Ugaritic *ʿglt*, appearing in the same text and corresponding to Biblical Hebrew *ʿglh*, is of great interest in this connection (see n. 36 above). Of other Ugaritic texts having the cow motif notice *CTA* 10, III, 20-20; 33-38; 13, 22.29, *CTA* 6, II, 28-30, *PRU* V 124 *passim*.

[54] The "horns of the altar" referred to in this text are known from archaeological excavations (cf. the picture published by A. Biran, "An Israelite Horned Altar at Dan", *BA* 37 (1974) 107, fig. 15. See also below p. 190). At Bethel no such altar has been found (see below pp. 51-52). Even if *qrn*, "horn", is commonly used in the Bible as a symbol for power (*e.g.* I Kings 22, 11, Mi 4, 13) and is well known from Ancient Near Eastern iconography (cf. E. D. van Buren, *Symbols of the Gods in Mesopotamian Art* (1945) 104-06) the meaning of the horns and the act described in Am 3, 14 are uncertain. It may be that the fall of the horns to the ground is a way to express the physical destruction of the altar. It may also be that the act described refers to a ritual of deconsecration or some other rite performed in connection with the altar (on the horned altar in the Bible, see further Ex 27, 2; 30, 2-3; 37, 25-26; 38, 2. In the sacrificial cult the blood of the slaughtered animal was smeared on the horns of the altar; Ex 29, 12; 30, 10, Lev 4, 7.18.25.30.34; 8, 15; 16, 18. Holding the horns of the altar gave right of asylum; I Kings 1, 50-51, 2, 28.)

Bethel and Gilgal is further mentioned in Am 5, 5-6:

> "Do not seek Bethel,
> do not go to Gilgal,
> or cross over to Beer-Sheba.
> For Gilgal shall go into exile
> and Bethel shall become nothing.
> 6. Seek Yahweh, and you shall live,
> or he will burn the House of Joseph like a fire,
> and it will devour, and there is no one to put out
> the flames for Bethel[55]."

The final passage in the Book of Amos which mentions Bethel is Am 7, 10ff. The famous episode related in this passage is of particular importance as it is the only passage in the Book of Amos which provides us with some biographical information. I quote vv. 10-13:

> "Amaziah, the priest of Bethel, reported to Jeroboam, king of Israel, saying: Amos is conspiring against you in the midst of Israel. The country cannot tolerate all his words. 11. For thus speaks Amos: Jeroboam shall die by the sword, and Israel shall go into exile away from its land. 12. And Amaziah said to Amos: O, seer, go, flee away to the land of Judah and eat (your) bread there, and there you prophesy (*tnb*ʾ). But in Bethel you are not to prophesy again, for this is the sanctuary of the king, a royal palace."

We learn from this passage that Bethel in the times of Amos was regarded as an important cult place, a royal sanctuary. This must imply that the cult performed at Bethel was the official cult of the royal dynasty. Consequently it will also have been the cult of the ruling classes of Israelite society. From the words of Amos we understand that the cult cannot have been Yahwistic, or that it may have been strongly syncretistic.

The information we get from the message of Amos concerning the actual contents of the cult performed at Bethel, however, is not overwhelming. The only passage which offers us some details of the cult is Am 4, 4-5, and what we can read here is not very informative.

The same goes for the cult place Gilgal. Of this place and its cult we are told even less.

A further problem concerning the cults at Bethel and Gilgal is that we know absolutely nothing about the relationship between the cult of the aristocrasy and the "popular" religion of the Israelite people.

As Bethel and Gilgal played such important roles in the religious history of the Israelite people, it may be worthwhile to take a further look at the biblical traditions concerning these two places. As we shall see, it is

---

[55] On this passage, see below p. 77ff.

not accidental that these places play such an important role in the religious life of the Israelites in the times of the prophet Amos.

3.2.1. Bethel in the Biblical Tradition

No biblical place name can show such a distinction throughout the early Israelite tradition as that of Bethel[56]. The name Bethel (according to the tradition its earlier name was Luz[57]) was already mentioned in connection with the patriarch Abraham. Abraham built an altar at Bethel and invoked the name of Yahweh[58]. More prominent is the place of Bethel in the Jacob story. Also Jacob built an altar at Bethel[59]. According to tradition it was also Jacob who gave Bethel its name[60].

In the conquest stories in the books of Joshua and Judges Bethel is frequently mentioned[61]. We also read that the prophetess and judge Deborah had her residence between Ramah and Bethel[62]. Bethel played an important role in the war between Israelites and Benjaminites[63]. It is in the same connection that we learn that Bethel was an important sanctuary of the Israelites in the times of the judges[64]. The great importance of Bethel is further attested by its being one of the towns where Samuel held office as a judge[65]. The "god of Bethel" is referred to in the consecration story of king Saul[66].

The most significant story in the Old Testament with regard to Bethel as a cult place is the story about the religious and political schism of King Jeroboam I, and his installation of the golden calves at Bethel and Dan[67].

A tradition of prophetic activity against Bethel and its cult is preserved in the peculiar story of the pronouncement of damnation against the altar of Bethel and its destruction in I Kings 13, 1-32.

---

56 On Bethel in the biblical tradition, see K. Galling, "Bethel und Gilgal", *ZDPV* 67 (1945) 26-43, C. A. Keller, "Über einige alttestamentliche Heiligtumslegenden I", *ZAW* 67 (1955) 162-68, W. J. Dumbrell, "The Role of Bethel in the Biblical Narratives", *AJBA* 2 (1974) 65-76, V. Maag, "Zum Hieros Logos von Beth-El", *Kultur, Kulturkontakt und Religion* (1980) 29-37.

57 Gen 28, 19; 35, 6, Jos 18, 13, Jud 1, 23.

58 Gen 12, 8. See also Gen 13, 3-4.

59 Gen 35, 1.7.14-15.

60 Gen 35, 7. See also Gen 31, 13.

61 Jos 7, 2; 8, 9.12.17; 12, 9; 16, 1-2; 18, 13.22, Jud 1, 22-26; 21, 19.

62 Jud 4, 5.

63 Jud 20, 18.26.31.

64 Jud 20, 26; 21, 2-4. Cf. J. Dus, "Bethel und Mispa in Jdc. 19-21 und Jdc. 10-12", *OrAnt* 3 (1964) 227-43. See also by the same author, "Ein richterzeitliches Stierheiligtum zu Bethel?", *ZAW* 77 (1965) 268-86.

65 1 Sam 7, 16 (with Mizpah and Gilgal).

66 1 Sam 10, 3 (on the deity Bethel, see below p. 167).

67 I Kings 12, 29-33. On this story, see also below pp. 188-89.

Bethel is also mentioned in the Elijah/Elisha stories. From these we learn that a brotherhood of prophets was staying at Bethel[68].

From the story of the temple reform of King Josiah (640/39-609/08) it is evident that non-Yahwistic or Yahwistic/syncretistic cults were dominant at Bethel. In the story we read how King Josiah broke down the altar and demolished the cult objects[69].

In view of the strong non-Yahwistic or Yahwistic/syncretistic contents of the cult at Bethel, it is indeed remarkable that we do not find Bethel more heavily attacked in the prophetic literature. It is commonly believed among scholars that the place name *byt ʾwn*, mentioned in Hos 4, 15; 5, 8 and 10, 15, is a disparaging reference to Bethel. This is often thought to be modelled on Am 5, 5b. However, a place name *byt ʾwn* is mentioned in the conquest stories in the books of Joshua and Samuel[70], and there is no reason why Hosea should not be preaching against *this* town. In one instance the tradition describes the town of *byt ʾwn* as being situated close to *byt ʾl*[71]. This makes the identification of the *byt ʾwn* of the conquest stories with the *byt ʾwn* of the Book of Hosea even more likely. Most probably it has been the reference in Hos 10, 5 to "the calf of Beth-Aven" which has made the scholars think of *byt ʾwn* as a substitute for *bytʾl*. However, most probably also Beth-Aven, being a self-contained even if less famous cult place than Bethel, also had its calf representation. The calf, or rather the bull, was the common way of picturing the male deity in ancient Syria, and in all likelihood bull figures were in use at all the different local cult places[72]. It may also be that Beth-Aven has been held to be a substitute for Bethel because Hosea in the same instance also refers to Gilgal. However, because Amos mentions Bethel and Gilgal together, there is no reason why Hosea should do so[73]. And as for the assumption by scholars that the exchange of Bethel with Beth-Aven in Hosea is modelled on Amos' use of *ʾwn* in 5, 5b, I believe that the words of Amos in 5, 5b are due more to a coincidence than to a conscious play on words[74]. Hosea does, however, mention Bethel twice in his preaching. Once he refers to the biblical tradition of Jacob who met God at Bethel[75], and once he men-

[68] II Kings 2, 2-3 (cf. also II Kings 2, 23-25).

[69] II Kings 23, 15-20 (cf. H. W. Wolff, "Das Ende des Heiligtums in Bethel", *Festschrift K. Galling* (1970) 287-98).

[70] Jos 7, 2; 18, 12, 1 Sam 13, 5; 14, 23.

[71] Jos 7, 2. There is no reason why a place Beth-Aven should not still have been in existence in the time of Amos and Hosea (against *e.g.* J. M. Grintz, "'ʿAi which is Beside Beth-Aven'," *Bib* 42 (1961) 215). Cf. also below p. 188.

[72] Cf. n. 43 above.

[73] In Hos 9, 15. Gilgal is mentioned alone, in Hos 12, 12 together with Gilead.

[74] Cf. Hos 12, 12.

[75] Hos 12, 5.

tions Bethel in an utterance of doom[76]. In the prophets after Amos and Hosea Bethel is hardly mentioned[77].

From the above it follows that Amos is the only prophet who systematically condemns the cult at Bethel in his preaching. In view of the great interest which this prophet shows in Bethel it is a pity that the archaelogical excavations carried out at Bethel have not revealed anything which could be of interest to us.

3.2.2. The Archaeology of Bethel

The site of ancient Bethel is commonly identified with modern *Bētīn*, north-east of Ramallah, north of Jerusalem. The site was excavated under W. F. Albright for the American Schools of Oriental Research and the Pittsburgh-Xenia Theological Seminary in 1934, and under J. L. Kelso for the American Schools of Oriental Research and Pittsburgh Theological Seminary in 1954, 1957, and 1960[78].

According to the archaeological evidence the story of the sanctuary at Bethel goes back to Chalcolithic times. This is demonstrated by a Chalcolithic water jar which has been dated to around 3500 B.C. The jar was found with sacrificial bones(?) still intact. In its early days the sanctuary consisted of an open air high place, where the top of the mountain served as an altar for the worshippers[79].

The further excavations, however, did not yield any significant results for the religious role played by Bethel in the religious history of Israel. In 1960 a building from Middle Bronze I was found immediately above the before-mentioned high place on bedrock. The building, thought to be a temple because of its situation on the high place, was dated to the 19th century B.C. One cannot fail to note that the evidence for the building being a temple is very meagre. It might just as well be the remains of a palace that the expedition of 1960 had discovered. No altar, nor any cult

---

[76] Hos 10, 5. The reference may be to the place or to the deity (on the deity Bethel, see below p. 167).

[77] Jer 48, 13 (may be a reference to the deity Bethel), Zech 7, 2.

[78] The excavation report was published by J. L. Kelso, *The Excavation of Bethel* (1968). The report is very "Albrightian" in spirit, and the present writer very often disagrees in the way it attempts to link the archaeological evidence to the biblical traditions (an illustrative exposure of the ways and methods of the Albright school of archaeology is found in the discussion between E. E. Campbell and J. Maxwell Miller, "W. F. Albright and Historical Reconstruction", *BA* 42 (1979) 37-47). On the archaeology of Bethel, see also M. Noth, "Bethel und Ai", *PJ* 31 (1935) 7-29, M. Wüst, "Bethel", *BRL*² (1977) 44-45. Further literature in E. K. Vogel, "Bibliography", *HUCA* 42 (1971) 17.

[79] J. L. Kelso, *The Excavation of Bethel* (1960) 45. 20-21. The claim that sacrificial blood was found on the open air altar has been challenged by D. L. Newlands, "Sacrificial Blood at Bethel?", *PEQ* 104 (1972) 155.

objects in the building were found[80]. The same applies for another building, also found in 1960, and also thought to be a temple, dated to Middle Bronze II[81]. Here, too, the evidence relating to the building is not of the kind that indicates with any degree of certainty whether it was a temple or a palace.

More important in our connection is the fact that none of the expeditions could find traces of the cult centre of Jeroboam I[82], nor anything which might shed any light on the cult at Bethel during the reign of Jeroboam II, the time of the prophet Amos.

To sum up: the total result of the archaeological work carried out at Bethel contributes nothing towards a better understanding of the religious life at Bethel which formed such an important factor of the religious life of ancient Israel.

3.2.3. Gilgal in the Biblical Tradition

At first sight the biblical traditions concerning Gilgal may seem more complicated than those concerning Bethel. If one takes a look at the new dictionary of Köhler/Baumgartner, one soon finds that the article "*glgl* II" informs us of several different Gilgals[83]. However, this most probably makes the matter more complicated than necessary. I hardly think that the biblical evidence allows for any such differentiation. As has also been maintained by several scholars, the most prolific starting point is to assume that the biblical references to *glgl* intend the one and the same geographical location near Jericho[84].

In the biblical tradition the name of Gilgal already appears in connection with the story of Moses. We read in Deut 11, 29-30 that Moses gives the name of Gerizim and Ebal as the names of the mountains on which the Israelites are to set a blessing and a curse, respectively, on entering the land of Canaan. The mountains are described as being situated opposite Gilgal[85].

In the conquest stories in the Book of Joshua Gilgal plays an important role[86]. In Jos 4, 19-24 we read how Gilgal is reached, and of the twelve stones which were set up there[87]. It is in the same connection that we first

---

80 J. L. Kelso, *op. cit.* 22-23.

81 *Ibid.* 26-27.

82 *Ibid.* 50-51.

83 *HAL*³, Lief. 1 (1967) 183.

84 Thus also K. Galling, "Bethel und Gilgal", *ZDPV* 67 (1945) 21, H.-J. Kraus, "Gilgal", *VT* 1 (1951) 182, F. Langlamet, *Gilgal et les récits de la traversée du Jourdain* (1969). 13. All these works provide excellent surveys of Gilgal in the biblical tradition.

85 Cf. O. Eissfeldt, "Gilgal oder Sichem", *Kleine Schriften*, B.5 (1973) 165-73.

86 Cf. F. Langlamet, *Gilgal et les récits de la traversée du Jourdain* (1969).

87 According to one theory also the stones provide the etymological explanation of the

learn of Gilgal as a cult place: the Israelites were circumcised at Gilgal[88], and they celebrated Passover there[89]. As the headquarter of Joshua, Gilgal plays an important role in the conquest of Canaan[90].

In the Book of Judges Gilgal is once mentioned together with Bethel[91], and once it is referred to as a cult place[92].

In the consecration story of Saul in 1 Sam 10 Gilgal is mentioned as the place where Saul and Samuel offered holocausts and communion offerings after the consecration (v. 8).

In 1 Sam 7, 16 Gilgal is mentioned together with Bethel and Mizpah as one of the centres where Samuel was judging Israel.

Gilgal is further mentioned as the place where Saul is proclaimed the first king of Israel[93]. It also served as his camp in the war against the Philistines[94]. In 1 Sam 15, 21 we learn that Gilgal was the cult place of Saul. In 1 Sam 15, 33 we read that "Samuel butchered Agag before Yahweh in Gilgal".

Gilgal is also mentioned in the story of David but, naturally enough, it does not play any major part in this story[94b].

Together with Bethel, Gilgal is mentioned in the Elijah/Elisha stories[95]. From these stories we learn that (as it was also the case with Bethel) a brotherhood of prophets had their residence at Gilgal[96].

From the above it follows that Gilgal, even if somewhat overshadowed by Bethel in fame, played an important role in the religious and profane history of Israel from the earliest times.

However, when we turn to the prophetic literature, we find that all references to Gilgal, with the exception of Mi 6, 5, appear in the two prophets Amos and Hosea. We find further that all the prophetic references to Gilgal, again with the exception of Mi 6, 5, are of a religio-polemical character. This is something which must be regarded as extremely important in view of the role prophesy played in the religious history of ancient Israel[97].

---

name Gilgal (G. Dalman, "Der Gilgal der Bibel und die Steinkreise Palästinas", *PJ* 15 (1919) 5-26). However, one should always keep in mind that etymological speculations of this kind are uncertain.

88 Jos 5, 2-9.

89 Jos 5, 10-12.

90 Jos 9, 6; 10, 6-7.9.15.43; 14, 6.

91 Jud 2, 1.

92 Jud 3, 19.

93 1 Sam 11, 14-15. According to a different tradition (1 Sam 10, 17-27) Saul was first elected king at Mizpah.

94 1 Sam 13, 4.7-8.12.15; 15, 12.

94b 2 Sam 19, 16.41.

95 II Kings 2, 1.

96 II Kings 4, 38.

97 See above p. 9ff. and below p. 82ff. and *passim*.

Unfortunately, the information we get from the biblical texts with regard to the contents of the cult performed at Gilgal is not very impressive. The polemical passages Am 5, 5[98] and Hos 4, 15 and 9, 15 refer to Gilgal as a place of wickedness which should be avoided by the Israelites. Am 4, 4[99] and Hos 12, 12[100] are the only passages which allow us a glimpse behind the scene, a not very informative glimpse.

3.2.4. The Archaeology of Gilgal

Gilgal is even more disappointing from an archaeological point of view. In fact, the location of the site remains a puzzle. This does not mean that there has been any lack of suggestions. Over the years biblical Gilgal has been identified with a number of different sites. Of the more recent attempts to identify the site I may mention Khirbet el-Mefjir[101], Tell el-Maṭlab[102], and Suwwānet eth-Thanīya[103]. As long as the question remains unsolved, we shall have to settle with the fact that we have no archaeological evidence of which we can make use.

3.2.5. The Transgressions of the Israelites at Bethel and Gilgal

As already mentioned the information offered by Am 4, 4-5 on the rites performed at the two cult places Bethel and Gilgal is very scarce:

> "4. Go to Bethel and transgress (*wpšʿw*)! To Gilgal and multiply your transgressions (*hrbw lpšʿ*)! Bring in the morning your sacrifices (*zbḥykm*), every three days your tithes (*mʿśrtykm*). 5. Let the smoke of the leavened bread emerge as a thank-offering (*twdh*) and proclaim voluntary offerings (*ndbwt*), announce (them)."

The sacrificial terms which we meet with in this text are all well known. It should be stressed, however, that our knowledge of the sacrificial system of ancient Israel and its development remains basically hypothetical[104].

zbḥ is the common word in the Old Testament for a blood sacrifice including a sacred meal[105]. Not infrequently, as in the present context, the

---

98 See below pp. 77-79.

99 See below pp. 54-58.

100 Cf. D. Grimm, "Erwägungen zur Hos 12, 12", *ZAW* 85 (1973) 339-47.

101 J. Muilenburg, "The Site of Ancient Gilgal", *BASOR* 140 (1955) 11-27.

102 O. Bächli, "Zur Lage des alten Gilgal", *ZDPV* 83 (1967) 64-71.

103 B. M. Bennett Jr, "The Search for Israelite Gilgal", *PEQ* 104 (1972) 111-22.

104 Among the basic works on the ancient Israelite sacrificial cult are R. Dussaud, *Les origines cananéennes du sacrifice israélite* (1921), R. de Vaux, *Les sacrifices de l'Ancien Testament* (1964), R. Rendtorff, *Studien zur Geschichte des Opfers* (1967), M. Haran, *Temple and Temple-Service* (1978).

105 The general article by J. Bergman, H. Ringgren, B. Lang, "*zbḥ*", *TWAT* II (1977) 509-31 provides a rich bibliography.

term is used of such rites within non-Yahwistic or Yahwistic/syncretistic cults[106]. Of particular interest in our connection is the assumption by Greenfield that the *zbḥ* was somehow connected with the *mrzḥ*-meal[107]. However, even if this may seem probable, it nevertheless remains hypothetical[108]. That the *zbḥ* was offered to the deity in the morning must be seen as a result of the general idea that the morning was an especially favourable time of the day[109].

The tithes (*mʿśrtykm*) are mentioned also together with the *zbḥym*. The tithes, which played such an important role in the religious life of ancient Israel[110], come under the same attack from the prophet as the sacrifices.

Finally, Amos mentions the sacrificial terms *twdh* and *ndbh* as forming a part of the rites performed at Bethel and Gilgal. As is the case with the other sacrifical terms occurring in the Old Testament the exact meaning and function of the *twdh* and the *ndbh* is not perfectly clear.

twdh is usually rendered by "thank-offering". The term is partly used independently[111], and partly in combination with other sacrificial terms[112]. *ḥmṣ*, a designation for food which is leavened[113], was not allowed to be used as a burnt-offering according to the sacred laws[114]. The only valid explanation to this prohibition must be that it was used in this way in non-Yahwistic or Yahwistic/syncretistic rites. In other sacrifices the use of leavened bread was allowed[115].

The second sacrifical term of Am 4, 5, *ndbh*, is usually translated by "voluntary offering". From the texts it follows that the *ndbh* may be of various kinds. Thus, according to Ez 46, 12 it may be a *ʿwlh* or a *šlmym*[116]. Thus, the two terms *twdh* and *ndbh* are not so much designa-

---

[106] The participation in such rites by worshippers of Yahweh was forbidden by the sacred laws (Ex 22, 19; 34, 15, Lev 17, 7. Cf. also Ex 32, 6, Hos 4, 14; 5, 6ff.).

[107] J. C. Greenfield, "Un rite religieux araméen et ses parallèles", *RB* 80 (1973) 48f.

[108] On the *mrzḥ* in general, see below pp. 128-38. On the *mrzḥ* in the Book of Amos, see above pp. 33-36, 42-44, and below pp. 127-28, 138-42. As for the cult criticism of Amos in 4, 4-5 in general, one should not fail to interpret this passage in the light of other cult-critical passages in the Book of Amos (see below pp. 111-18).

[109] Cf. J. Ziegler, "Die Hilfe Gottes 'am Morgen'". *Alttestamentliche Studien* (1950) 281-88.

[110] For bibliography and references, see *HAL*³, Lief. II (1974) 583-84, H.-F. Weiss, "Zehnte", *BHH* III (1966) 2208-09. Cf. also M. Weinfeld, *Deuteronomy and the Deuteronomic School* (1972) 213-15.

[111] Lev 7, 12, Jer 17, 26; 33, 11, 2 Chr 29, 31.

[112] *zbḥ htwdh*, Lev 7, 12; 22, 29, 2 Chr 33, 16, *zbḥ twdt šlmym*, Lev 7, 13.15.

[113] D. Kellermann, "*ḥmṣ*", *TWAT* II (1977) 1061-68.

[114] Lev 2, 11; 6, 10 (cf. Ex 23, 18; 34, 25). To eat leavened bread was also forbidden at times of feasts (Ex 12, 15; 13, 3-7, Deut 16, 3).

[115] Lev 7, 13; 23, 17.

[116] Cf. further Ezra 3, 5, 2 Chr 31, 14, Deut 16, 10, together with *ndr*: Lev 7, 16; 22, 18.21.23; 23, 38, Nu 29, 39, Deut 12, 6.17. Am 4, 5 is the only passage in the Bible which has *ndbh* together with *twdh*.

tions for particular sacrifices as they are determinatives for the circumstances under which the sacrifices took place.

Of particular significance when it comes to understanding the meaning of Amos' words against Bethel and Gilgal is the word *pšʿ*, occurring in v. 4 (*wpšʿw, hrbw lpšʿ*). The translation of the Hebrew word *pšʿ*, however, is not an easy task. When taking a look at the rendering of *NEB* of the noun *pšʿ* in its different contexts, we find that the range of words applied is considerable: "crime", "rebellion", "sin", "offence", "transgression", "wrong", "misdeed", "fault", "disobedience", "law-breaking", "treachery", "presuming", "misconduct", "falsehood", "disloyal acts", "iniquity", "impiety"[117]. On consulting the most current English translations of Am 4, 4, we find that *pšʿ* is rendered by "transgress" (*RSV*), "rebel" (*NEB*), and "sin" (*The Jerusalem Bible*).

When dealing with the words of Biblical Hebrew one should always take great care not to let one's knowledge of the Hebrew words become influenced by extra-textual evidence. Even if this may seem self-evident to anyone engaged in the difficult task of translating from one language to another, I believe this pitfall to be particularly imminent in the case of the biblical languages. Thus, a word rendered by English "sin", or its equivalents may undoubtedly, no matter what is its Hebrew origin, easily lead to one's opinion concerning the meaning of the word in question being coloured by the long traditions of Western Christian hamartiology. The Christian scholar, in particular, should always keep in mind that the theology of sin of the Christian religion, owing so much to Greek thought, is extraneous to the Old Testament[118].

The background for our view on *pšʿ* in Am 4, 4, consequently, must partly be the context of v. 4, and partly the use of *pšʿ* in similar contexts elsewhere in the prophetic literature.

The context of *pšʿ* in Am 4, 4 is quite clear: the verb is here used to describe the participation of the Israelites in the rites performed at Bethel and Gilgal. From the general attitude of the prophet in the present context, as well as from the description of the cultplaces Bethel and Gilgal elsewhere in the Book of Amos[119], it follows that the cults performed at these ancient places were non-Yahwistic or strongly Yahwistic/syncretistic. Our passage, consequently, gives expression to the very same cult criticism which we find in Am 5, 21-24[120], and should be interpreted against the background of this cult criticism.

[117] G. Te Stroete, "Sünde im Alten Testament", *Übersetzung und Deutung* (1977) 169-70.

[118] On *pšʿ* in general, see the survey by R. Knierim, "*pšʿ*", *THAT* II (1976) 488-95. See further R. Knierim, *Die Hauptbegriffe für Sünde im Alten Testament* (1965).

[119] See above pp. 47-51, below pp. 77-79.

[120] See below pp. 111-18.

The same prophetic use of *pš*ʿ that we have in Am 4, 4—namely as a technical term for the participation of the Israelites in non-Yahwistic or Yahwistic/syncretistic rites—is frequently found in other prophets, as well[121].

Quite commonly the phenomenon described by Amos in 4, 4-5 has been termed "apostasy" by the scholars who have commented upon this and related texts. The question we shall have to ask ourselves, however, is: can the description "apostasy" so frequently used by the scholarly world, really be said to be adequate for the situation depicted in Am 4, 4-5? Quite obviously, the use of the term "apostasy" can only be said to be legitimate if it really was the case that the inhabitants of the northern realm at the time of the prophet Amos were "orthodox Yahwists" who left their "original" Yahwistic faith and started to worship deities other than Yahweh.

Admittedly, this is the impression we do get when reading the Deuteronomic history. But can we really trust the Deuteronomic "history" in these matters? I should be inclined to think not.

Also the prophetical writings lead sometimes to the impression that they are describing an apostate people who have left their original faith and taken to the worshipping of non-Yahwistic deities. The prophets themselves held pretty clear views on what Yahwism was and how Yahweh should be worshipped. However, from the Bible itself[122], from archaeology[123], and from extra-biblical texts[124] we get the straightforward

[121] Is 1, 2; 43, 27; 46, 8; 48, 8; 59, 13; 66, 24, Jer 2, 8.29; 3, 13; 33, 8, Ez 2, 3; 18, 31; 20, 38, Hos 14, 10, Zeph 3, 11.

[122] No student of the Old Testament is unaware of the many remnants of syncretistic practises which are found scattered all over the biblical texts. A scholar who has been particularly interested in this aspect of the biblical texts is the Swede G. W. Ahlström. See in particular his *Aspects of Syncretism in Israelite Religion* (1963) and most recently "Heaven on Earth - At Hazor and Arad", *Religious Syncretism in Antiquity* (1975) 67-83. Of the vast literature relevant to this field one may note C. J. Labuschagne, *The Incomparability of Yahweh in the Old Testament* (1966), F. J. Helfmeyer, *Die Nachfolge Gottes im Alten Testament* (1968), H. D. Preuss, *Verspottung fremder Religionen im Alten Testament* (1971), J. P. Floss, *Jahwe dienen - Göttern dienen* (1975), M. Rose, *Der Ausschliesslichkeitsanspruch Jahwes* (1975). Cf. also n. 5, Chapter 1, above.

[123] In addition to the literature referred to in the works mentioned above n. 122, see the surveys by P. Welten, "Götterbild, männliches", *BRL*² (1977) 99-111, "Götterbild, weibliches", *ibid.* 111-119, "Göttergruppe", *ibid.* 119-22.

[124] The most interesting texts in this respect are obviously the Elephantine papyri. With regard to the date and origin of these extraordinary documents cf. E. G. Kraeling, *The Brooklyn Museum Aramaic Papyri* (1953) 42ff., P. Grelot, *Documents araméens d'Égypte* (1972) 37f. A further text worth mentioning is an inscription which was re-read by A. Lemaire in 1977 and which, according to his reading, contains the expression "the Ashera of Yahweh" (A. Lemaire, "Les inscriptions de Khirbet el-Qom et l'Ashéra de YHWH", *RB* 84 (1977) 595-608, in particular 603ff). According to Lemaire (p. 607) the reference is to a cult object and not to a goddess Ashera. The reference *may*, however, just as well be to a goddess Ashera. The matter is impossible to decide upon (cf. below p. 166).

message that only a very small percentage of the inhabitants of Israel adhered to the religion of the prophets of Yahweh. The religious system of orthodox Yahwism is in fact a post-prophetic creation, and rather than a time of apostasy and reform, the period of the prophet Amos should be viewed as a time of missionary activity.

This missionary activity of the prophet Amos is brilliantly demonstrated in the continuation of his words against the cultic activities at Bethel and Gilgal. In Am 4, 6-13 the purpose of the message of the prophet is to make the Israelites realize that their non-Yahwistic cults are unable to help them in their search for prosperity and life.

3.3. *The Prophet as Missionary. Am* 4, 6-13

3.3.1. The Text

6. "And I gave you cleanness[125] of teeth in all your towns, lack of bread in all your places. Yet you did not turn to me, says Yahweh.
7. And I also kept back from you the rain three months before the harvest. And I let it rain upon one town and upon another I did not let it rain. One field was rained upon, and a field upon which it did not rain dried up.
8. Two, three towns staggered to another town to drink water, but they could not get enough. Yet you did not turn to me, says Yahweh.
9. I struck you with scorching and mildew, and destroyed[126] your gardens and your vineyards, your fig-trees and your olive-trees the locust devoured. Yet you did not turn to me, says Yahweh.
10. I sent you a plague like the plagues of Egypt. I killed your young men with the sword at the same time as your horses were captured. I let the stench of your camp go up into your nostrils. Yet you did not turn to me, says Yahweh.
11. I overthrow you as God overthrew Sodom and Gomorrah, and you were like a brand snatched from the fire. Yet you did not turn to me, says Yahweh.
12. Therefore, I shall do thus to you, O Israel. And because I will do this to you, prepare to meet your god, O Israel.
13. For lo; He is the creator of mountains and the creator of wind, and reveals to man his mind. He who makes the morning darkness and walks on the heights of the earth. *yhwh ʾlhy ṣbʾwt* is his name."

---

[125] The major text witnesses LXX, Peshitta, Targum Jon. and the Vulgate have here "bluntness", "dullness" instead of "cleanness". The Hebrew *Vorlage* for this translation would probably have been *qhywn* and not the *nqywn* of MT.

[126] MT has *hrbwt.*

It is indeed a mighty piece of prophetic craftmanship we witness in this famous text. There can be little doubt that these powerful words made an impression on their audience.

When reading through the whole of Chapter 4 of the Book of Amos, we see that we may well regard the whole chapter as a coherent speech unit. We may divide this unit the following way: the people of Samaria are addressed (v. 1), the judgement is pronounced (vv. 2-3), the mistaken cultic activities of the Samaritans at Bethel and Gilgal are exposed (vv. 4-5), previous disasters among the Israelites due to their participation in non-Yahwistic or Yahwistic/syncretistic cults are ennumerated (vv. 6-11), the announcement/threat stating that as a result of the Israelites' not having changed their cultic activities, such disasters as the ones just mentioned by the prophet are still going to befall them is pronounced (v. 12), the doxology follows (v. 13).[127]

As the whole of Chapter 4 forms a consistent speech unit,[128] it follows that no part of the text should be allowed to be treated in isolation, but that each unit of the text must be viewed in light of the whole of the prophet's preaching in Chapter 4 (as well, of course, as in relation to the whole message of the prophet contained in the Book of Amos).

3.3.2. Am 4, 6-11(12) in the History of Research, and how it should be interpreted

The interpretation of Am 4, 6-12 is totally dependent upon how one chooses to interpret the prophetic movement in ancient Israel in general, as well as upon one's understanding of the prophetic message of Amos in particular.

With regard to the question of how the prophetic movement in ancient Israel is to be understood in general we have recently been witnessing a

---

[127] On the doxologies in the Book of Amos cf. below pp. 79-80.

[128] Against *e.g.* T. H. Robinson, *Die zwölf kleinen Propheten*[3] (1964) 87, who represent the not uncommon view that Am 4, 6-13 consists of several originally separate pieces which have been put together at a late stage in the handing down of the tradition. However, W. Rudolph ("Amos 4, 6-13", *Wort, Gebot, Glaube* (1970) 27-38) has argued convincingly that the passage Am 4, 6-13 should be regarded as a unity. But he does not believe that 4, 6-13 necessarily has any connection with the preceding vv. 4-5 (*ibid.* 28). In this I disagree with Rudolph. I believe that the whole of Chapter 4 should be regarded as a unity. H. W. Wolff (*Dodekapropheton* 2 (1969) 250-33) regards most of the passage 4, 6-13 as not the work of Amos. However, as far as I am able to judge, his reasons for doing so are vague and superficial and cannot be accepted. It is also noteworthy that the same scholar elsewhere ("Das Thema "Umkehr" in der alttestamentlichen Prophetie", *Gesammelte Studien* (1964) 139) refers to Am 4, 6-12 as evidence in support of his view that this prophet is preaching doom only with no prospect of salvation.

On the strophic structure of our passage cf. J. L. Crenshaw, "A Liturgy of Wasted Opportunity", *Semitics* 1 (1970) 27-37.

most interesting discussion among scholars on whether the prophets were to be regarded exclusively as preachers of doom, or whether there were also brighter tones, viz. a call for repentance and conversion, to be found in their preaching[129]. For my own part, I would without hesitation subscribe to the latter view[130]. And I would go even further than that. With regard to the prophet Amos I believe that the call for conversion constitutes the main aspect of his message and that the words of doom should be regarded as threats rather than pronouncements of doom and disaster. Of course we must read the words of doom as they stand in the text. But at the same time we should not forget to ask what was the *function* of these severe judgement oracles. Does the prophet simply want to inform the people that such and such is certainly going to happen, or is there a particular *intention* behind his words? Again I would subscribe to the latter view. In my opinion the words of judgement in the mouth of the prophet Amos serve missionary purposes. The prophet wants to urge his fellow countrymen to turn to Yahweh and worship him as their god. The other gods are unable to help them. It is not a coincidence that other deities do play a major role in the message of Amos[131], quite in contrast to what scholars have normally assumed[132]. As the all-powerful deity it is also Yahweh who is responsible for the misery of the people if they do not follow him as their god.

With Fohrer I believe that one might (purely for practical reasons) outline schematically the development of Old Testament religion—a development about which we are only allowed to speak very hypothetically—through five major impulses: "Mosaic" Yahweh religion, royalty, prophecy, "Deuteronomic" theology, and eschatology[133]. I also believe with Fohrer that the prophetic movement is the most important of these. I do, however, disagree with Fohrer with regard to the reason for the major importance of the prophetic movement. Thus, I do not agree with Fohrer's assertion that prophecy marks the transition from early/primitive religion to "Hochreligion", or the transition from local religion to world-religion[134]. Not only do the terms used by Fohrer in this connection lack support in the Old Testament texts themselves, but it is also hard to see that they stand up to modern anthropological and religio-theoretical research.

---

[129] See the illustrative survey by K. A. Tångberg, "Var Israels 'klassiske' profeter botspredikanter?" *TTK* 50 (1979) 93-105.

[130] Cf. also below pp. 78-79.

[131] See below pp. 118-26 and pp. 143-203.

[132] When consulting the literature on this subject one will soon find that such views as those quoted above 4-5 do represent scholarly *consensus*.

[133] G. Fohrer, *Geschichte der israelitischen Religion* (1969).

[134] *Op. cit.* 294-96.

The importance of the prophetic movement lies primarily in its role as mediator and link between what Fohrer has termed "die mosaische Jahvereligion", representing the early version of what was later to become the all-dominating religion in Israel, and the later Deuteronomic shape of this early form of Yahwism. The prophet must here be regarded as the forerunners of the Deuteronomists[135].

The problem of how the passage Am 4, 6-13 should be understood relates very much to the question of the relationship of the prophets to tradition, a question which has been much discussed in Old Testament scholarship recently. One of the most successful accomplishments of recent research has been to associate the preaching of the prophets with the Old Testament idea of the covenant. When the prophets accuse the Israelites of leaving Yahweh and of violating his commandments, they are in fact accusing the people of breaking the covenant with Yahweh.

Not all scholars, however, who have been engaged in this debate seem to hold quite identical views with regard to the contents of the Old Testament covenant concept. Roughly, we may nevertheless outline the idea of the Old Testament covenant in recent scholarship as a mutual agreement between Yahweh and the Israelite people, expressed through institutions like the cult, the amphictyony, etc., and with roots in the ancient history of Israel (the conquest story, the Sinai event, etc.). According to the common trend in Old Testament scholarship the basic message of the prophets was to tell the Israelites that they had not kept their covenant obligations towards Yahweh, their divine partner, and that they were now going to receive their deserved punishment[136].

By those scholars who seek to interpret the prophet Amos within a covenant context the pericope Am 4, 6-11(12.13.) has been regarded as particularly relevant. The covenant context of the prophet Amos has perhaps most consistently been advocated by Reventlow. According to this scholar, Am 1, 3 - 2, 6; 4, 6-11 and 9, 13-15 all represent different rituals performed by the prophet Amos. All the rituals are to be understood against the background of the covenant[137]. The theories of

---

[135] I do find it remarkable that so little research has been put into the highly important field of the relationship of the prophetic movement to the Deuteronomists. For references to some of the work which has been done, see F. Crüsemann, "Kritik an Amos im Deuteronomistischen Geschichtswerk", *ProblBiblTheol* (1971) 57. Cf. also W. Dietrich, *Prophetie und Geschichte* (1972).

[136] See *inter alia* R. E. Clements, *Prophecy and Covenant* (1965) 27-44. Cf., however, also by the same author, *Prophecy and Tradition* (1975) 22-23, modifying the tendency in the work first mentioned.

[137] H. Reventlow, *Das Amt des Propheten bei Amos* (1962) 75: "Das Amt des Amos... ist gebunden an die Institution der Bundesfestverkündigung, in denen dieser Jahwewille seine öffentliche Proklamation erfährt". A further conclusion reached by Reventlow with regard to Am 4, 6-11 is that the passage is modelled on the covenant curses of Lev 26 (*ibid.* 75-90).

Reventlow were in particular taken up and developed further by Brueggemann, who has termed the passage Am 4, 4-13 "a liturgy of covenant renewal"[138].

Basically the line taken by those who want to understand the prophets against the background of "Israelite covenant worship" is wrong. The prophets are much more to be regarded as the pioneers and the founders of the religion of ancient Israel than as a group of fervent reformists who took up earlier traditions of Israelite religion and attempted to reform the religious activity of the Israelites in accordance with these traditions[139]. Also, most of the argumentation put forward by those who seek to understand the prophetic movement against the background of Israelite covenant traditions is not valid.

Thus, the relationship of the prophets to the institution of the covenant was furthered by the attempts, in particular, of Mendenhall to explain Exodus 20 as an early covenant of Israel with Yahweh. Mendenhall based his theories on the comparison of the text of Ex 20 with Hittite treaty forms from the middle of the second millennium[140]. His thesis was to become a great success, and several scholars subscribe to his views[141].

However, more recent research has complicated considerably the possibility of finding any relationship between covenant and prophecy. McCarthy has argued convincingly that the Sinai event cannot be said to represent a treaty at all, but is rather to be classified as a theophany. Further, he has demonstrated, equally convincingly, that oriental treaty formulas came into usage in Israel only at a very late stage. McCarthy has thus taken the credibility out of the theories of such scholars as Mendenhall and Beyerlin[142].

It should further be noted that the thesis of the amphictyony which played such an important role in the theories of Mendenhall cannot be upheld any more[143].

---

[138] W. Brueggemann, "Amos iv 4-13 and Israel's Covenant Worship", *VT* 15 (1965) 1-15.

[139] In this respect I wholly subscribe to the views of Fohrer put forward in his article "Remarks on Modern Interpretation of the Prophets", *JBL* 80 (1961) 309-19. The article of Fohrer is a sound warning in these times. Unfortunately, it seems that very few scholars have followed the views expressed by Fohrer both in this article and elsewhere.

[140] See in particular G. E. Mendenhall, "Ancient Oriental and Biblical Law", *BA* 17 (1954) 26-46, and, "Covenant Forms in Israelite Tradition", *ibid.* 50-76.

[141] In particular one should note the *Habilitationsschrift* of W. Beyerlin, *Herkunft und Geschichte der ältesten Sinaitraditionen* (1961), which has been of great influence in the German scholarly world.

[142] D. J. McCarthy, *Treaty and Covenant* (1963), in particular 173ff. Criticisms of Mendenhall and Beyerlin are also found in his *Old Testament Covenant* (1973) *passim.* In the second edition of *Treaty and Covenant* (1978) the thesis of McCarthy that the Sinai narrative shows no resemblance to the treaty genre has been repeated with added evidence (277-98 *passim*).

[143] See below p. 102.

In more recent times theories concerning the influence of covenant ideas in the preaching of the prophets have come under attack for reasons of even greater consequence.

More and more it has dawned upon the Old Testament scholarly world that the traditional covenant theology, which is found in its most developed form in the Deuteronomic writings, is a late theological creation[144]. The most important contributions towards this recent change in the view of the the Old Testament covenant have been the works of Perlitt[145] and Kutsch[146]. After their publications[147] it is very unlikely that the traditional view concerning the relationship between the prophets and the covenant has any chance of surviving[148].

This fact has wide implications for other aspects of scholars' views of ancient Israelite prophecy as well. Quite a few current scholarly views of the role and function of Israelite prophecy are ultimately based on the assumed great influence of covenant theology on the prophets. Of these the most important ones are likely to be attitudes to the curses, on the so-called *ryb*-pattern, and on the use of the verb *šwb*. Am 4, 6-11(12.13) has been used as an argument for all these indications of covenant influence in the prophets.

Thus, it has been assumed that the use of curses in prophetic maledictions is directly dependent upon the use of curses in Ancient Near Eastern vassal treaties. Viewed against the background of the theories of Mendenhall and others mentioned above, this assumption is again regarded as a further proof that spiritually the prophets belong within the framework of the covenant. Such are the conclusions reached *inter alia* by Fensham[149], and by Hillers[150]. The latter, however, is not uncritical about his own conclusions. Even though he states towards the end of his treatise that the parallels between Ancient Near Eastern treaty curses and Old Testament passages are "principally due to the fact that throughout her early history up to the exile, Israel shared with her neighbours a com-

---

[144] Cf. also the modifications of Clements mentioned above n. 136.

[145] L. Perlitt, *Bundestheologie im Alten Testament* (1969).

[146] E. Kutsch, *Verheissung und Gesetz* (1973).

[147] A summary of the conclusions reached by Perlitt and Kutsch is found in R. Martin-Achard, "Trois ouvrages sur l'alliance dans l'Ancient Testament", *RThPh* 110 (1978) 299ff.

[148] As two of the most outstanding works representing the traditional view on the relationship of the prophets to the covenant, one may note W. Brueggemann *Tradition for Crisis* (1968), and J. Bright, *Covenant and promise* (1976).

[149] F. C. Fensham, "Malediction and Benediction in Ancient Near Eastern Vassal-treaties and the Old Testament", *ZAW* 74 (1962) 1-9, "Common Trends in Curses of the Near Eastern Treaties and *kudurru*-Inscriptions compared with Maledictions of Amos and Isaiah", *ZAW* 75 (1963) 155-75.

[150] D. R. Hillers, *Treaty-Curses and the Old Testament Prophets* (1964), *Covenant: The History of a Biblical Idea* (1969) 120-42.

mon legal form, the treaty, and that this form was adopted as a basic element in Israel's religion'', and that ''the prophets often used the traditional threats associated with the covenant when pronouncing doom on the people''[151], he is none the less fully aware of the possibility that both the treaty-curses and the Old Testament parallels simply reflect idioms in popular speech[152], and that this possibility represents a threat to his own conclusions.

In fact, there can be no doubt that the apparent parallels between the threats in the vassal treaties and speech forms in the Old Testament simply reflect that we have to do with a widely spread phenomenon within closely related cultures. The phenomena curse and blessing, malediction and benediction, play an all important role in the culture of the Ancient Near East, in treaties, in Akkadian *kudurru*-inscriptions, on tombs and sarcophagi, in the cult, in popular speech, *and* in Israelite prophecy[153]. When we consider how widespread the phenomenon in fact was, it is only natural that also the prophets of Israel make use of such forms in their speech. The strange thing would indeed have been if they had not done so. That we have to do with striking similarities in forms no one could deny. The important thing, however, is that we have no generic similarity; the prophets have their own form.

Similar objections to the ones brought against the relationship between the maledictions of the prophet and the curses of Ancient Near Eastern treaties may be brought against yet another literary *genre* which has played an important role in the attempt to link prophecy to the idea of the covenant; namely the so-called *ryb*-pattern.

The thesis of the *ryb*-pattern (as far as I know, the idea was first developed by Huffmon[154]) attempts to demonstrate that the prophetic ''lawsuit'' in fact is a covenant law-suit which reflects the covenant form. Here again, however, we should rather assume that we have to do with another widespread speech form in the Ancient Near East. The prophetic ''law-

---

[151] *Treaty-Curses and the Old Testament Prophets* 88.

[152] *Ibid.* 87.

[153] In addition to the book of Hillers mentioned above, see J. Pedersen, *Der Eid bei den Semiten* (1914), S. Mowinckel, *Psalmenstudien* V (1923), A. Parrot, *Malédictions et Violations de Tombes* (1939), J. Scharbert, *Solidarität in Segen und Fluch* (1958), J. Hempel, ''Die israelitischen Anschauungen von Segen und Fluch'', *Apoxysmata* (1961) 30-113, S. Gevirtz, ''West-Semitic Curses and the Problem of the Origins of Hebrew Law'', *VT* 11 (1961) 137-58, H. C. Brichto, *The Problem of ''Curse'' in the Hebrew Bible* (1963). Cf. also below p. 144.

[154] H. B. Huffmon, ''The Covenant Lawsuit in the Prophets'', *JBL* 78 (1959) 285-95. The thesis of Huffmon, which to-day is widely recognized among scholars, was further developed by G. E. Wright, ''The Lawsuit of God'', *Israel's Prophetic Heritage* (1962) 26-67, and particularly by J. Harvey, ''Le 'rîb-Pattern', *Bib* 43 (1962) 172-96.

suit'' provides us with no proof that the prophets were influenced by any covenant theology in their preaching.

Obviously, there are striking similarities between the message of the prophets and the Deuteronomic covenant theology[155]. This is something which we may easily explain as a result of the fact that in several respects the prophets were the forerunners of the Deuteronomists[156]. We must take great care not to interpret the prophets too uncritically in the light of the Deuteronomic writings. This, however, is what we do when we put things the other way around and state that the prophets are influenced by the covenant.

These considerations regarding the relationship of the prophets to the post-prophetic Deuteronomic theology of the covenant have implications for the meaning and the function of the word *šwb*, frequently occurring in the prophetic literature[157]. In the prophet Amos the word *šwb* occurs in 4, 6.8.9.10.11; 9, 14 (hiphil 1, 3.6.8.9.11.13; 2, 1.4.6). This word *šwb* has played an important part in the discussion of the relationship of the prophets to the covenant. In Amos Chapter 4 *šwb* has normally been translated by ''return''. This translation, of course, implied the return to Yahweh, the divine partner in the covenant, the obligations of which have been violated by the Israelites.

It is with interest that we note how scholars have specified more closely the semantic contents of *šwb* in this connection. H. W. Wolff, for instance, in a paper originally published in 1951, states with regard to *šwb* in Am 4: ''*šwb* betont ja hier nicht die Abkehr vom falschen Kult, sondern die Hinkehr zu Jahwe... im Sinne der *Rückkehr in das ursprüngliche Jahweverhältnis*''[158]. This assumption of Wolff concerning the semantic contents of the verb *šwb* has been supported by Holladay in his work on the word: ''The verb *šûbh*, in the qal, means: having moved in a particular direction, to move thereupon in the opposite direction, the implication being (unless there is evidence to the contrary) that one will arrive again at the initial point of departure''[159]. In his book Holladay

---

[155] See the work referred to above n. 136. For this reason it is also easily understood why so many scholars object to the view that the covenant is all post-prophetic (see *e.g.* J. Barr, ''Some Semantic Notes on the Covenant'', *BeitrAltTheol* (1977) 37-38). Obviously the whole problem rests on how we choose to understand the word ''covenant''. In order not to create complete chaos it may seem wise to reserve the term for the theological system found in Deuteronomic writings. This, of course, does *not* mean that similar thoughts are not found elsewhere in the Old Testament too, *e.g.* in the prophetic writings.

[156] Cf. above p. 61.

[157] For a detailed survey, see W. L. Holladay, *The Root šûbh in the Old Testament* (1958) 178-85.

[158] H. W. Wolff, ''Das Thema ''Umkehr'' in der alttestamentlichen Prophetie'', *Gesammelte Studien zum Alten Testament* (1964) 135.138.

[159] W. L. Holladay, *The Root šûbh* (1958) 53.

also operates with a particular convenantal usage of *šwb*. In Amos this use of *šwb*, according to Holladay, appears in Chapter 4, where it should be translated by "return to".

The translation of *šwb* by "return to" in Am 4 is followed unanimously to-day. This, I suspect, is largely the result of the fact that this translation fits so well into the general thesis that the prophet is accusing the Samaritans of breaking the covenant with Yahweh. It is, in fact, almost as if the above quoted definitions by Wolff and Holladay were made with the covenant in mind. However, when we know the historical/literary background of the Biblical covenant theology, it is obvious that the matter becomes more complicated.

It should further be noted that the definitions of *šwb* provided by Wolff and Holladay are too schematical and too simple. The earlier work by Dietrich on the word *šwb*, despite the fact that it is not of the same quality as the work by Holladay, is more varied in this respect[160]. There can be no doubt that the word *šwb* in the Old Testament may be translated also with other expressions than the "return to" of Wolff and Holladay[161].

Thus, with regard to *šwb* in Am 4, a context where the prophet attempts to convince his fellow countrymen that they should leave off worshipping the deities at Bethel and Gilgal and turn to Yahweh as their god, it seems to me that the translation "turn to" fits the text much better than the "return to" of Wolff and Holladay. If one, consequently, wants to stick to classificational slogans, one should here speak of "a missionary" rather than of a "covenantal" usage of the word *šwb*. That in Am 4 there is an appeal to conversion rather than an appeal to take up the covenant obligations again is supported also by other passages in Amos[162].

The assertion that the prophets are not influenced by any covenant theology in their preaching should, however, be modified somewhat. The problem is complicated by the fact that even if the prophets obviously do not speak of a covenant in the meaning of the word found in the late Deuteronomic writing, we nevertheless find that the prophets frequently

---

[160] E. K. Dietrich, *Die Umkehr (Bekehrung und Busse) im Alten Testament und im Judentum* (1936) 46ff.

[161] In this matter, of course, it must be regarded as utterly amateurish to resort to the dictionaries. The only valid judge must be the texts themselves. When this is said, however, I must say that I find W. Gesenius, *Hebräisches und aramäisches Handwörterbuch* (1915) gives the most reliable translations of the word *šwb* in the Old Testament. It is unfortunate that H.-J. Fabry, *Die Wurzel ŠÛB in der Qumran-Literatur* (1975) does not take more of the Old Testament material into consideration (see, however, p. 17, n. 28). The most recent survey of *šwb* in the Old Testament, J. A. Soggin, "*šūb*", *THAT* II (1976) 884-91, is content to follow Holladay uncritically. We have here a field which really calls for a fresh investigation.

[162] See below pp. 78-79.

refer to the traditions of ancient Israel. Thus, we find in the prophets references to election theology, the universalism of Yahwism, etc.[163]. There is nothing remarkable in this. Quite obviously the Deuteronomists did not *invent* the traditions underlying their theological interpretation of Israelite history. Once more, we are here witnessing how the prophets appear as the forerunners of the Deuteronomic movement. Quite another matter, of course, is the fact that the Deuteronomic view of the religious history of Israel, *and* the prophetic view of the same utilizing the stereotyped phrases of the Yahwistic tradition, must *never* be seen as a description of Israelite religious conditions as they really were. If *that* had been the case there would have been no need for the prophetic movement.

In Am 4, 6-11(12.13) we are witnessing the embitterment of the Yahwistic prophet Amos because his religion has not been accepted among the Samaritans in northern Israel. The people are unwilling to turn to the god who, in the eyes of Amos, is the only one that can help them. The long enumeration of disasters in our passage should not so much be seen as punishment for "sins" as it should be regarded as the proofs of a missionary that the present cultic activities of his audience cannot help to provide them with the necessities of life. They should rather turn to Yahweh. He is their god. He is able to help them.

Obviously, there is a punishment aspect attached to the enumeration of the disasters in Am 4 as well. But whereas this aspect of punishment in the Deuteronomic writings has become a major aspect, this is not so in Amos. It is the missionary aspect which is the most important in this chapter. The stress on doom and disaster appears only as a necessary supplement to the same.

3.3.3. The Disasters of Am 4, 6-11

In Am 4, 6-11 several calamities which have befallen the inhabitants of Samaria are mentioned: famine (v. 6)[164], lack of rain (vv. 7-8)[165], crop diseases and grasshoppers (v. 9)[166], war and pestilence (v. 10)[167], and disaster (v. 11)[168].

---

[163] *E.g.* Am 9, 7. On the matter in general cf. *i.a.* G. Fohrer, *Geschichte der israelitischen Religion* (1969) 287.

[164] *nqywn šnym*, literally "cleanness of teeth" (cf. n. 125 above).

[165] *gšm* is here the designation for the March-April rains (cf. P. Reymond, *L'eau, sa vie, et sa signification dans l'Ancien Testament* (1958) 19ff, 24.

[166] *gzm*, "grasshopper"? The meaning of the word is uncertain. The word occurs only here and in Joel 1, 4; 2, 25. For *šdpwn* and *yrqwn* cf. G. Dalman, *AuS* I, 2 (1928) 326-27.

[167] *dbr*, a designation for pestilence, cf. *HAL*³, Lief. I (1967) 203.

[168] The reference to Sodom and Gomorrah seems to have been a traditional constituent in words of doom (cf. Deut 29, 22, Jes 13, 19, Jer 49, 18; 50, 40). For a translation of Am 4, 6-13 see p. 58 above.

It is obvious that we have here before us disasters of ultimate importance to any society and particularly to an agricultural society. Each of the disasters mentioned in the text represents in its own way a threat of death and non-existence. From the history of religion we know that it has been a major task of religious cultic activity everywhere in the world to avoid disasters of the kind here mentioned. Old Testament religion is no exception in this. In fact, Old Testament religion is markedly *diesseitig* in its orientation. With regard to the question of rain it is also a fact that for climatical reasons ancient Israel was even more dependent than her neighbours upon a successful rainy season[169].

It is easy to imagine that in a society like Israel in the times of the prophet Amos, a time of many different gods and many different cults, the question could arise which deity was the most reliable and the most powerful. In times of crisis when the godhead seemed to pay no attention to their prayers, despairing worshippers might start to ask themselves whether the god they were worshipping really was able to help them in their distress. Or they might feel more attracted to the cult of a different deity than the one they usually worshipped for other reasons: social prestige, change in cultural environment, etc. These are all facts well known to us from the Old Testament. In fact, what we know to be the Yahwistic religion of Israel was born out of such a struggle between two competing cults, a struggle commonly (even if somewhat superficially) referred to as the struggle between "Yahwism" and "Baᶜalism"[170].

In this religious fight between two competing cults the question of fertility and prosperity stands at the very centre. To the Yahwistic prophets Yahweh is the only god who is really able to provide the people with the necessary goods of life. All the other deities are helpless and useless, idols carved in wood or stone.

According to the preaching of Amos in Am 4, 6-11 the worship of deities other than Yahweh has resulted in a series of disasters in Israel, and from v. 12 we learn that Israel has not seen the last of these disasters.

Quite naturally one tends to regard the disasters in Am 4, 6-11 as a punishment from Yahweh following the evil ways of the people. However, the exaggerated emphasis of scholars on the punishment aspect of the pericope has unfortunately overshadowed the fact that this aspect is only secondary. The real message of the prophet is to underline that it is Yahweh, and not the other deities, who provides life and prosperity. This fact is supported by the words of Amos in 5, 4-6 too, which also concern the cults at Bethel and Gilgal:

---

169 See G. Dalman, *AuS* I, 1-2 (1928) *passim*.

170 Cf. n. 122 above.

"For thus says Yahweh to the House of Israel:
Seek me and you shall live.
Do not seek Bethel,
do not go to Gilgal,
or cross over to Beer-Sheba.
For Gilgal shall go into exile,
and Bethel shall become nothing.
Seek Yahweh and you shall live,
or he will burn the House of Joseph like a fire,
and it will devour and there is no one to put out the
flames for Bethel"[171].

From the above it follows further that it is wrong to describe the struggle between the two competing cults as a struggle between Yahwism on the one hand and the Canaanite fertility cults on the other. Amos is trying to convince his fellow countrymen that it is Yahwism that is *the* fertility cult. From his point of view the other cults are unable to provide fertility and it would be wrong even to call them fertility-cults.

Rather than to attempt to interpret the message of the prophet Amos against the background of apostasy and punishment, the *Leitmotif* of the Deuteronomic theologians, one should, in the first instance, resort to the prophets preceding him.

Particularly illustrative in this connection is the story of the prophet Elijah in I Kings 18[172]. Despite the fact that the story bears witness to Deuteronomic encroachments, there can be little doubt that basically it is very old.

In the story we read about a severe famine in Samaria in the days of king Ahab (v. 2). The prophet Elijah has word from Yahweh that he should go and see the king. Yahweh will then provide the rain (v. 1). We have here all the main features of ancient Israelite religion: the deity as the provider of the rain, the prophet as the intercessory link[173], and the king as the religious head of the people[174].

---

[171] Cf. below pp. 77-79.

[172] On this very important text cf. A. Alt, "Das Gottesurteil auf dem Karmel", *Kleine Schriften* B.2 (1953) 135-49, R. de Vaux, "Les prophètes de Baal sur le mont Carmel", *Bible et Orient* (1967) 485-97, K. Galling, "Der Gott Karmel und die Ächtung der fremden Götter", *Geschichte und Altes Testament* (1953) 105-25, H. H. Rowley, "Elijah on Mount Carmel", *Men of God* (1963) 37-65, H. Seebass, "Elia und Ahab auf dem Karmel", *ZThK* 70 (1973) 121-36, F. C. Fensham, "A Few Observations on the Polarisation Between Jahweh and Baal", *ZAW* 92 (1980) 227-36, M. J. Mulder, *De naam van de afwezige god op de Karmel* (1979). I am grateful to Professor Mulder for sending me a copy of his inauguration lecture.

[173] Cf. below pp. 71-72, 73-74, 85-88, 105-08.

[174] The literature on this subject is enormous. Cf. J. A. Soggin, "*mælæk*", *THAT* I (1971) 908-20 *passim*.

When Ahab sees the prophet Elijah, he asks him whether the prophet is responsible for the disaster which has befallen his people. The answer of Elijah bears the mark of the Deuteronomist:

> "And he said: I have not brought Israel into calamity, but you have, and your family, because they have left the commandments of Yahweh and followed after the Baᶜals."

The rest of the chapter tells us the story of the tug of war between the prophets of Baᶜal and Elijah in order to decide whose god is the real god, *i.e.* which of the two deities is able to provide the necessary rain and bring the disastrous famine to an end.

The story told in I Kings 18, despite for the fact that it bears witness to having undergone marked changes during the process of its being handed down, provides us with many important insights into the religion of ancient Israel and into the struggle between the two religious main streams: Yahwish and Baᶜalism. No less interesting with regard to the words of Amos in 4, 6-11 is the stereotyped uttering of the people in v. 39, after Elijah has provided the life-bringing rain on behalf of his god Yahweh and the prophets of Baᶜal have failed their mission:

> "And all the people saw (this), and they fell on their faces and they said: Yahweh is god, Yahweh is god."[175]

In the prophet Jeremiah we are met with similar thoughts. In this prophet, however, the relationship of the Israelite people to Yahweh is described much more in accordance with a developed apostasy theology. In this respect the similarities between Jeremiah and the Deuteronomists are striking. The stereotyped phraseology of a theological kind which we find in Jeremiah represents a further development of what is found in the earlier prophets.

Jeremiah, too, interprets the past and tells of the worship of deities other than Yahweh and its consequence for the fertility of the land. In Jer 3, 3a he states:

> "And the showers were withheld and there was no spring-rain."

And in a similar context, in Jer 5, 24, we read:

> "And they do not say in their hearts: Let us fear Yahweh our god, who gives autumn-rain and spring-rain in its season and keeps for us the weeks fixed for the autumn."

[175] Cf. also H. M. Barstad, "*HBL* als Bezeichnung der fremden Götter im Alten Testament", *StTh* 32 (1978) 62. The exclamation *yhwh hwᵓ hᵓlhym* must have formed a part of some cultic ritual. The expression is semantically related to the formula *ḥy yhwh*, etc., which is treated in more detail below pp. 146-55.

Of great interest is further Jer 14. The chapter contains several features which may throw light upon Am 4, 6-12. The description in Jer 14, 1-6 of the drought and the lament reminds us of the description in Am 4:

> "The word of Yahweh which came to Jeremiah[176] concerning the drought. 2. Judah mourns[177] and her gates languish. They fall to the ground in lament, and the mourning cry goes up from Jerusalem. 3. Their mighty send their servants for water, they come to the cisterns. They do not find water. They return with empty vessels. They are ashamed and dismayed and cover their heads because of the ground which is dismayed. Because there is no rain on the land the farmworkers are ashamed, they cover their heads[178]. 5. Even the hind in the field abandons her new-born because there is no grass. 6. And the wild-asses stand on bare heights, they gasp for air like jackals, their eyes fail because there is no herbage."

Also the text following these verses contains some very interesting features. Immediately after the description of the lament and the drought a kind of confession of sins follows in v. 7a. It may seem, consequently, that this is some sort of liturgy with the prophet acting as an intercessant to the people[179]. Among other things, the liturgy comprises a prayer to Yahweh that he must not forget them, but help them in their great distress (vv. 8-9). However, Yahweh accuses the worshippers of sins that cannot be forgiven. He instructs Jeremiah that he is not to help this wicked people (vv. 11-12). The prophets who prophesy welfare and good days are not sent by Yahweh, who will see to it that the people are destroyed by sword and famine, the very same things which according to the other prophets are not going to befall them (vv. 13-18). It is not accidental, of course, that the prophetic words of doom and disasters present a future to the people filled with those very disastrous events which they sought to avoid through their cultic activities. This, I suspect, is an aspect of the prophetic words of doom which seems to have been left almost unnoticed by those who interpret the prophets as messengers of doom and disaster only, and fail to see the missionary aspects of their message.

In Jer 14, 20 there follows another confession of sin, and a further prayer for relief in distress (v. 21). Finally, in v. 22 there follows a rather interesting glorification in hymnic style:

> "Are there any among the Hubals[180] of the nations that can bring rain? Or can the heavens bring showers? Are not you the one, Yahweh, our god? We set our hope on you because you ar the one who makes all these things."

---

[176] MT is in a mess here. Cf. the current commentaries.

[177] For this mourning rite cf. Joel 1, 9.

[178] Cf. 2 Sam 15, 30, Est 6, 12.

[179] Cf. above p. 69 and below pp. 72, 73-74, 85-88, 105-08.

[180] On "the Hubals", see my article "*HBL* als Bezeichnung der fremden Götter", *StTh* 32 (1978) 57-65.

The liturgy of confession together with the pronouncements of doom continues in Chapter 15. The remnants of a liturgy preserved to us in Jer 14-15 are extremely important inasmuch as they provide us with a glimpse behind the scenes of ancient Israelite religion.

It is only natural to assume that this liturgy was accompanied by particular rites by means of which it was believed that one could provide the rain. And in fact, we do find remnants of such water rites in the Old Testament. Thus, we have a description of a water rite in the story of the prophet Elijah in I Kings 18 (vv. 30-35). Further reference to this rite is found in 1 Sam 7, 6, in the story of Samuel at Mizpah. It is with great interest that we note the context in which the description of the water rite in 1 Sam 7, 6 appears. Again it seems that we have all the details of the ritual found in Jer 14-15: polemics against the worshipping of deities other than Yahweh (1 Sam 7, 4), confession of sins (v. 6), and finally Samuel acting as an intercessor between Yahweh and the people.

Even further references to the water rite in the Old Testament are found in 2 Sam 23, 16 and possibly in Lam 2, 19[181].

It may seem strange that the water rite is not described in detail in the Old Testament. This could be explained, of course, as a result of the fact that the rite is Canaanite in origin and for this reason avoided in Yahwistic orthodox circles. This explanation, however, is not likely. In fact, we do not find any detailed catalogue with instructions for any aspects of the cult in the Old Testament. It is only a part of the whole which has survived and reached us. It is also worth noticing that we have no prohibition against the water rite either. Still another thing which points to the great importance of the water rite within the Yahwistic religion too is the fact that the rite plays an important role in Mishnaic and Talmudic literature. It is hardly likely that this would have been the case if the rite had been regarded by the orthodox Yahwists as a non-Yahwistic rite[182].

The lament in Joel 1-2[183] has also most probably a drought as its background (1, 11-12). This is seen quite clearly from the exhortation to praise following the granting of the prayer in 1, 19ff. We read in 2, 23:

> "Sons of Zion, be glad,
> rejoice in Yahweh, your god.
> For he gives you the early rain (*mwrh*) for righteousness and pours down rain (*gšm*) for you, early rain (*mwrh*) and late rain (*mlqwš*), as before[184]".

[181] On the water-rite cf. M. Delcor, "Rites pour l'obtention de la pluie", *RHR* 178 (1970) 117-32. Cf. also n. 182 below.

[182] On the water-rite in late Jewish tradition cf. D. Feuchtwang, "Das Wasseropfer und die damit verbundenen Zeremonien", *MGWJ* 54 (1910) 535-52, 55 (1911) 43-63.

[183] Cf. below pp. 83-84 and 95.

[184] MT has here unexpectedly *brʾšwn*. All the commentators, however, read *krʾšwn* with the Septuagint, the Vulgate and Peshitta.

And in Zech 14, 17 we read that those who do not participate in the eschatological worship of Yahweh in Jerusalem will have no rain. Even if this may seem to be a foreign element in the present context, there can be no doubt that the motif originates from a cultic context and thus supports the remarks above concerning the relationship between the rain that brings fertility and the worship of Yahweh[185] (cf. also Ez 34, 26).

In the writings of the Deuteronomists and in the Priestly Code the relationship between Yahweh and the life-giving rain has developed into a whole theological programme. We have here a late development of thought forms found in the early prophets. A prophet like Jeremiah though, has more in common with the Deuteronomists than with Amos in this matter.

The *locus classicus* of the late Israelite tradition is undoubtedly the passage Deut 11, 13-17:

> "And if you will really obey the commandments which I enjoin on you today, to love Yahweh your god and to serve him with all your heart and all your soul, (14) I will give the rain (*mṭr*) for your land in its season, early rain (*ywrh*) and late rain (*mlqwš*), and you shall gather in your grain, your wine, your oil. (15) And I will give grass in your fields for your cattle and you shall eat and be full. (16) Take care your heart is not deceived, and you yield and serve other gods and worship them, (17) and the wrath of Yahweh will burn against you and he will shut up the heavens and there will be no rain (*mṭr*) and the land will not give its produce, and you will quickly die from the land that Yahweh gives you."[186]

A further text of great interest is I Kings 8. In the prayer of Solomon the lack of rain appears as one of the disasters mentioned (vv. 33-34.37). Obviously, we have in this rather complicated text the remnant of an ancient ritual. We note in this context that all the disasters are regarded as punishments from Yahweh as a result of the people having sinned against him. After the confession of sin there follows the granting of the prayer and restoration of the previous favourable conditions.

Even if the problem of the life-bringing rain plays such an important role in Old Testament religion, it does not, however, constitute the only concern of the worshippers. As is the case also in Am 4, 6-11, we find that the mention of one disaster alone is extremely rare. Most commonly we find that lack of rain, famine, war, etc. appear in lists. The most frequent of these is the occurrence of the triple threat of "sword, famine, pestilence" (*ḥrb*, *rᶜb*, *dbr*). This formula is found several times in the prophet Jeremiah. In Jer 14, 12 Jeremiah is told by Yahweh not to act as

[185] Cf. B. Otzen, *Studien über Deuterosacharja* (1964) 211.

[186] Cf. also Deut 28, 12, 23-24 where curse or blessing is dependent upon whether the commandments of Yahweh are being obeyed or not. Cf. also 2 Sam 1, 21.

an intercessor for the people[187]. As a result of their transgressions all Yahweh will give them is "sword, famine, and pestilence". A similar story is found in Jer 21, 1-9[188]. In Jer 24, 1-9 the same triade occurs in a pronouncement of doom and in Jer 27, 8.13 the prophet uses the formula as a threat against those who are not willing to serve the king of Babylon. Further, Jeremiah applies the formula "sword, famine and pestilence" against the people who had disobeyed the words of Yahweh in Jer 29, 17-18 and 32, 24. In Jer 32, 36 the formula appears in relation with the worship of deities other than Yahweh, and in 44, 13 in connection with both disobedience and the worship of other deities. In Jer 34, 17 we find the formula used when the people break their promise to Yahweh and are unwilling to release the slaves in accordance with their agreement[189]. Finally, in Jer 42, 17.22 the interceding prophet tells the people that if they choose to go to Egypt and stay there, they will be punished with "sword, famine and pestilence".

In the prophet Ezekiel we find the triade *ḥrb*, *rᶜb*, *dbr*, in Ez 6, 11-12; 7, 15 and 12, 16 in relation to the people worshipping deities other than Yahweh.

Rather peculiar is the occurrence of the triade in the story in 2 Sam 24 of the census of David. We read in this story, which undoubtedly has an old prototype, how the king as a punishment for his transgression has to make a choice between "sword, famine, and pestilence."[190]

A variant of the triade just mentioned occurs in the important passage Jer 28, 8[191]. Here the formula "war (*mlḥmh*), disaster (*rᶜh*[192]), and pestilence (*dbr*)" is used.

Further triades are "pestilence (*dbr*), blood (*dm*), and sword (*ḥrb*)", appearing in Ez 28, 23 in a pronouncement against Sidon, and "sword (*ḥrb*), wild beasts (*ḥyh*), and pestilence (*dbr*)" in Ez 33, 27 in an utterance against the prophet's own people.

More comprehensive lists are "pestilence (*dbr*), famine (*rᶜb*), sword (*ḥrb*), scattering to every wind (*lkl-rwḥ ᵓzrh*)", occurring in a pronouncement of doom against Jerusalem in Ez 5, 12. The same utterance goes on in 5, 17 with "famine (*rᶜb*), wild beasts (*ḥyh rᶜh*), pestilence (*dbr*), blood (*dm*), and sword (*ḥrb*)". And in Ez 14, 13-23, also in a pronouncement against Jerusalem, famine (*rᶜb*), wild beasts (*ḥyh rᶜh*), sword (*ḥrb*), and pestilence (*dbr*)" is mentioned.

---

[187] On this text, see above pp. 71-72. Cf. also below p. 83.
[188] Cf. also below pp. 105-106.
[189] Cf. above Chapter 2, n. 35.
[190] The story corresponds to the story in 1 Chr 21, 10-14.
[191] For the context cf. below pp. 105-106.
[192] Several MSS have *rᶜb* for *rᶜh*. The common English translations (*RSV*, *NEB*, *Jerusalem Bible*) have "famine", not "pestilence" here.

In addition to such lists given above there are far more comprehensive catalogues of disasters which will befall the people in case they do not obey the laws of Yahweh and follow Yahweh as their god. Famous examples are the catalogues of Lev 26 and Deut 28. Rather than simple curses these catalogues represent whole theological programmes. These catalogues, too, however, have as their background the simple curse[193].

---

[193] Cf. above n. 153.

CHAPTER FOUR

RELIGIOUS POLEMICS IN AMOS 5

4.1. *The Composition and Contents of Chapter 5*

As in the message of the prophet contained in Am 4 the words of the present chapter seem, more or less, to constitute an ideological unity consisting of pronouncements of judgement and of accusations concerning the ethical and religious behaviour of the Israelites[1].

With regard to vv. 18-27 containing, among other things, the famous words about the "Day of Yahweh" (vv. 18-20) and the cryptic statement in v. 26 containing the words *skwt* and *kywn*, it is difficult to decide upon the original relationship of this text to the obvious unit vv. 1-17. It is equally difficult to decide whether or not in vv. 18-27 we are dealing with a series of disconnected Amos words which have been linked together by a compilator.

All these problems, however, are very considerably reduced by the fact that all these different verses belong within the same *ideological* context: they are all words by one prophet, directed towards the one and the same audience. Whether they were originally uttered on one particular or on several different occasions is of less importance. It should also be stressed in this connection that the means available for discerning the strata of a certain composition, late interpolations in a text, etc. is altogether rather illusory[2].

Vv. 1-17 may be divided the following way: v. 1. Introduction to the words of judgement through the formula *šmʿw ʾt-hdbr hzh*, "Hear this word!" The same formula is used in 3, 1[3] and 4, 1.

---

[1] For the translation of the text, see below pp. 77 (vv. 2-3), 77-78 (vv. 4-6), 81 (v. 11), 82 (vv. 16-17), 108-09 (vv. 18-20), 111 (vv. 21-24), 119 (v. 25), 119ff. (v. 26).

[2] The statement is not meant categorically, of course. When we consider the size of the Book of Amos, however, it must be regarded as quite obvious that we do not have at our disposal sufficient textual material to make such statements with regard to authenticity as may frequently be found in some of the most used commentaries. This does not imply that we are totally incapacitated when it comes to making critical observations on the text (cf. B. Vawter, "Prophecy and the Redactional Question", *No Famine in the Land* (1975) 127-39, where one will find at least one good example with regard to the Book of Amos).

[3] The attempt by W. H. Schmidt, "Die deuteronomistische Redaktion des Amosbuches", *ZAW* 77 (1965) 172-73, to take Am 3, 1 as a result of the Deuteronomic redaction of the Book of Amos was criticized by T. R. Hobbs, "Amos 3, 1b and 2, 10", *ZAW* 81 (1969) 384-87. Hobbs, too, however, regards 3, 1b as secondary. I cannot accept any of the reasons put forward for why Am 3, 1 is secondary as legitimate.

Amos defines his utterance as a *qynh*, a "dirge". The *qynh* being the lament for the dead, Amos uses a form taken from quite another sphere of life in his pronouncement of doom. V. 2 brings the lament itself:

> "She has fallen and will rise no more,
> the virgin Israel,
> prostrate on her land, with no one to raise her up."[4]

V. 3 gives another pronouncement of doom:

> "For thus speaks *ʾdny yhwh*: The city from which a thousand went out, shall have a hundred left, and the one from which a hundred went out, shall have ten left, for Israel."

The utterance of doom of v. 3 belongs together with v. 2 in a unity. Obviously, the figures appearing in this verse should not be taken literally. They are simply a means of describing the total annihilation of the Israelite people. Nor should the reference to the hundred and the ten that are left be regarded as references to an idea of "a remnant" as some scholars do[5]. As is the case with the description of the shepherd who rescues a pair of legs or a bit of an ear from the lion's mouth (3, 12) and of the man that carries the bones out of the ruined house (6, 10), the purpose of the description of the prophet in 5, 3 is to describe the total annihilation of the Israelites.

The verb *yṣʾ* used in v. 3 is a technical term for "going to war"[6].

The concept that *yhwh* punishes his people by means of war is also found in Am 2, 14-16; 4, 10; 7, 11. The phenomenon is commonly found in the prophetic writings[7].

V. 4 introduces a new and quite different section vv. 4-6:

> "For thus says *yhwh* to the House of Israel:
> Seek me and you shall live.
> Do not seek[8] Bethel,

---

[4] The use of the *qynh* metre in the preaching of doom is found in other prophets as well. Besides Am 5, 1 and 8, 10, cf. Jer 7, 29; 9, 9; 9, 19, Ez 2, 10; 19, 1; 26, 17; 27, 2.32; 28, 12; 32, 2. For a combination of the lament over the dead and the song of derision, see Is 14. For the *qynh* in general, see W. Zimmerli, *Ezechiel* (1969) 420-21.

[5] Cf. L. Markert, *Struktur und Bezeichnung des Scheltworts* (1977) 134, n. 73.

[6] *E.g.* Gen. 14, 18, Num 1, 3.20ff, Deut 20, 1; 23, 10, 1 Sam 8, 20; 18, 30, 2 Sam 11, 17; 18, 2-4.6.

[7] G. von Rad, *Der heilige Krieg* (1969) 62ff. Cf. above pp. 58 and 74-75, and below pp. 93ff.

[8] Pointing to the fact that the verb *drš* is never used in connection with a place name, O. Eissfeldt has suggested that the reference in Am 5, 5 is to the deity Bethel, rather than to the place name ("Der Gott Bethel", *ARW* 28 (1930) 16-17. On the deity Bethel, see also below p. 167). In view of 4, 4, however, as well as of the context in general, this is not likely. If *drš* were not used in connection with a place, it would be more reasonable to assume that here we have a pun on the "Seek me" of the preceding line. For a detailed treatment of the verb *drš*, see G. Gerleman, E. Ruprecht, "*drš*", *THAT* I (1975) 460-67, S. Wagner, "*drš*", *TWAT* II (1977) 313-29.

do not go to Gilgal,
or cross over to Beer-Sheba[9].
For Gilgal shall go into exile,
and Bethel shall become nothing,
Seek *yhwh* and you shall live,
or he will 'burn[10]' the House of Joseph[11] like a fire,
and it will devour, and there is no one to put out the
flames for Bethel."

Several scholars have maintained that there can be no original connection between vv. 1-3 and 4ff., or that the two pericopes are apparently contradictory[12]. This view is absolutely wrong and is the result of an incorrect interpretation of the message of the prophets in general, including Amos, which regards the prophets exclusively as preachers of doom and disaster. However attractive the view that Amos and his fellow prophets preach nothing but coming catastrophe and have no room for brighter prospects in their preaching may be[13], it does not correspond to the message contained in the preaching of the prophets.

What the message of the prophet really contains, however, has rightly been stressed by other scholars who see the prophetic message basically as a warning and an appeal to the contemporaries of the prophets to turn away from their moral and social misconduct and their worship of gods other than Yahweh and to turn to him as their sole deity[14]. Thus, the

[9] There is no reason to assume that the name of Beer-Sheba is secondary (thus *e.g.* H. W. Wolff, *Dodekapropheton* 2 (1969) 269 and 281). The main argument for this seems to have been that the name of Beer-Sheba is not repeated with a pronouncement of judgement as is the case with both Gilgal and Bethel in the same verse. We cannot, however, expect that the words of the prophet will always correspond with our ideas of verbal consequence. One could also argue, of course, that the condemnation of Beer-Sheba has disappeared during the handing down of the tradition. Even if Amos is the only prophet to mention Beer-Sheba, the condemnation of this cult place does play an important role in his religious polemics (see below pp. 188-201. On Bethel and Gilgal cf. above pp. 47-58.)

[10] The meaning of *ṣlḥ* in this context is uncertain. See M. Sæbø, "*ṣlḥ*", *THAT* II (1976) 552.

[11] On "Joseph", see L. Markert, *Struktur und Bezeichnung des Scheltworts* (1977) 139, n. 104.

[12] In quite recent times, however, when scholars have approached the text from a more literary angle, this view has not been the prevailing one (cf. the literature mentioned in n. 18).

[13] As representatives of this view on Amos we may mention R. Smend, "Das Nein des Amos", *EvTh* 23 (1963) 404-23, H. W. Wolff, *Dodekapropheton* 2 (1969) 124-25 and *passim*, *id.*, "Die eigentliche Botschaft der klassischen Propheten", *BeitrAltTheol* (1977) 547-57, H. H. Schmid, "Amos", *WuD* N.F. 10 (1969) 97, W. H. Schmidt, "Die prophetische 'Grundgewissheit'", *EvTh* 31 (1971) 630-50, *id.*, "Suchet den Herrn, so werdet ihr leben", *Studia G. Widengren... Oblata* (1972) 127-40, *id.*, *Zukunftsgewissheit und Gegenwartskritik* (1973) *passim.* Cf. also Chapter 3, n. 129 above. One consequence of this view must be that the *drš* of Am 5, 4-6 is to be understood ironically (cf. T. M. Raitt, "The Prophetic Summons to Repentance", *ZAW* 83 (1971) 35, n. 16).

[14] *E.g.* S. Amsler, "Amos, prophète de la onzième heure", *ThZ* 21 (1965) 318-28, J. M. Berridge, "Zur Intention der Botschaft des Amos", *ThZ* 32 (1976) 321-40, O. Keel, "Rechttun oder Annahme des drohenden Gerichts?" *BZ* NF 21 (1977) 200-18.

words of judgement of the prophet Amos are not meant as a final prediction of a catastrophe that is bound to come irrespective of how the Israelites behave. They should rather be classified as warnings and admonitions. As we find both social/moral and religious accusations together quite often in the Book of Amos, there should be no difficulties connected to the view that vv. 1-3 and 4-6 belong together as a unity. As the admonitions in vv. 4-6 concern the religious worship of the Israelites at the cultic centres Bethel, Gilgal, and Beer-Sheba[15], the words of doom in vv. 1-3 here are caused consequently by the religious behaviour of the Israelites.

There is a strong missionary aspect attached to the message of Amos in this text: worship the god that is really able to help you, or you will all be doomed! This particular aspect of the prophetic activity of Amos is more easily understood when viewed against the background of the pericope 4, 6-11, which gives expression to the very same idea[16]. It is equally important to place this motif within the greater context of the whole of the prophetic movement, which is something that commentators have not always done[17].

The admonition that the people shall seek Yahweh is repeated in v. 6. Here the admonition is followed by another kind of threat: if the Israelites do not take Yahweh as their god rather than other deities, Yahweh himself will destroy them.

With v. 7 a new theme is introduced in the unit: preaching of social justice combined with new words of doom.

With regard to composition the passage vv. 7-17 belongs among the more difficult ones and has generated not a few different solutions to the various problems[18]. Whereas some of the problems connected to this passage are minor[19], other undoubtedly belong to the most difficult within the Book of Amos.

Thus, the impression of a confused composition in vv. 7-17 is largely caused by the introduction of the two hymnic verses 8-9 that seem to

---

[15] Cf. n. 9 above.

[16] See above p. 58ff.

[17] Cf. the introduction above.

[18] In addition to the current commentaries, see in particular F. Hesse, "Amos 5, 4-6f", *ZAW* 68 (1956) 1-17, K. W. Neubauer, "Erwägungen zu Amos 5, 4-15", *ZAW* 78 (1966) 292-316, with emphasis on the final literary composition J. de Waard, "The Chiastic Structure of Amos v 1-17", *VT* 27 (1977) 170-77. That Am 5, 1-17 constitutes a chiasm has also been observed by C. Coulot, "Propositions pour une structuration du livre d'Amos", *RScRel* 51 (1977) 179-80. Cf. further L. Markert, *Struktur und Bezeichnung* (1977) 125-53.

[19] Thus I cannot see that the introduction of the plural participle *hhpkym* in v. 7, as against the singular of v. 6, represents any major problem (see *e.g.* J. D. W. Watts, "Note on the Text of Amos v 7", *VT* 4 (1954) 215-16) Irregularities of this kind are well known in Biblical Hebrew.

break up the unity of the text. The problem of these hymnic passages which must be viewed in connection with the occurrences of the hymnic passages in Am 4, 13 and 9, 5-6, is basically whether the verses stem from the mouth of Amos, or whether they belong to a later, redactional stage. If the latter is the case, there arises the problem of the dating of the hymns as well as what part they play in the final composition. There is also a problem connected to the composition of the "hymns" themselves: are we dealing with fragments of more comprehensive hymnic compositions or should the small units be regarded as isolated independent hymnic outbursts? With regard to vv. 8-9 there is also a particular problem connected to the inner relationship between the two verses[20].

When reading through the composition of Am 5, 1-17 as it is contained in MT, one does undoubtedly get the impression that vv. 8-9 represent a late addition to the text. I believe, however, that one cannot be too certain in this matter[21]. Thus, I doubt very much whether biblical scholarship with the help of means they have at their disposal to-day can actually decide with any degree of certainty whether passages like the one in question do go back to Amos or not. If for a moment, we think of the prophet as a preacher talking to his fellow countrymen, using all sorts of rhetorical techniques, it is not difficult to imagine that Amos used precisely the kind of incoherent composition, including the hymnic outbursts, which we find in Am 5, 1-17. After all, the prophets were not systematic logicians, but emotional religious preachers. Thus, when looking for the hand of a later editor or interpolator, one should rather search for attempts to make the preaching of the prophet more intelligible than for distortions in the composition.

I am not, however, going to discuss in detail the compositional problems of vv. 7-17[22]. What is most important is that this pericope differs from the preceding vv. 1-6 in one major respect: whereas vv. 1-6 concerns the religious behaviour of the Israelites, vv. 7-17 is concerned with their moral and social behaviour.

Vv. 7 and 10 give us the prophet's description of the people. They "turn justice (*mšpṭ*) to wormwood[23]", they "throw righteousness (*ṣdqh*)

[20] A comprehensive survey of the debate is found in W. Berg, *Die sogenannte Hymnenfragmente im Amosbuch* (1974).

[21] Even if most commentators explain the hymnic passages as late additions to the text, there have also been attempts to see them as the words of Amos himself (*e.g.* G. J. Botterweck, "Zur Authenzität des Buches Amos", *BZ* NF 2 (1958) 182-86).

[22] I am content to refer to the literature mentioned above n. 18.

[23] *lᶜnh*. Some scholars have pointed to the expression *hpk lmᶜlh*, "to turn upside down", which occurs in Jud 7, 13, and have changed *llᶜnh* in this verse to *lmᶜlh*. The emendation has support in the Septuagint. In view of Am 6, 12b, however, where a similar expression occurs, *lᶜnh* stands parallel to *rʾš*, "poison" (see H. W. Wolff, *Dodekapropheton* 2 (1969) 269).

to the ground[24]" (v. 7), they "hate him who judges in the gate", and "abhor the one that speaks honestly (*tmym*)" (v. 10).

In v. 11 there follows a judgement of doom, introduced by the particle *lkn*, followed by further accusations:

> "Therefore[25], because you "trample[26]" on the poor[27] and take grain tribute from him,
> you have built houses of hewn stone, but you shall not live in them,
> you have planted pleasant vineyards, but you shall not drink their wine[28]".

In v. 12 there follow further accusations regarding the transgressions of the Israelites: they "show hostility toward the righteous (*ṣdyq*)[29]", they "take bribes", and they "turn away the needy (*ʾbywnym*)[30] in the gate".

The request to keep silent in v. 13 is very difficult to understand. It could be that we here have to do with a late addition to the message of Amos. On the other hand, it must be regarded as methodologically unsound to presuppose a late addition whenever one fails to see the meaning of a passage within a context. It may well be that the text *is* meaningful, but that the modern interpreter does not see the meaning. I leave the problem of v. 13 open.

Vv. 14-15, an admonition to seek good (*ṭwb*) and not evil (*rʿ*) in order that one may live, and to hate evil (*rʿ*) and love good (*ṭwb*), and establish justice (*mšpṭ*) in the gate in order that Yahweh may be gracious to the remnant of Joseph, forms an exact parallel to the admonitions regarding the religious behaviour of the Israelites in vv. 4-6[31]. As is the case with the admonitions concerning religious behaviour in vv. 4-6, also vv. 14-15 aim at making the people observe the demands imposed upon them. These demands are, according to the prophet, the demands of Yahweh, and they cannot be separated from the worship of Yahweh. If the Israelites do not observe the laws of Yahweh, they are doomed. This is particularly well illustrated by the last pronouncement of judgement in the pericope 5, 1-17, vv. 16-17:

---

[24] Cf. Am 6, 12b. Cf. also Hos 10, 4.

[25] The introduction of the pronouncement of doom by the particle *lkn* is commonly found in the Book of Amos: 3, 11; 5, 16; 6, 7; 7, 17. On the particle in general, see W. E. March, "*Lākēn*: Its Functions and Meaning", *Rhetorical Criticism* (1974) 256-84.

[26] The meaning of the word *bwšskm* is uncertain (cf. H. W. Wolff, *Dodekapropheton* 2 (1969) 270).

[27] Amos focuses on the bad treatment of the poor in 2, 7; 4, 1; 8, 6 also. The word has been treated in detail by H.-J. Fabry, "*dal*", *TWAT* II (1977) 221-44.

[28] Cf. Is 17, 10-11.

[29] Cf. Am 2, 6. On this word, see K. Koch, "*ṣdq*", *THAT* II (1976) 507-30.

[30] The same word is mentioned in the enumeration of the social misdeeds of the Israelites in Am 2, 6; 4, 1; 8, 4.6. For this word, see the detailed treatment by G. J. Botterweck, "*ʾbywn*", *TWAT* I (1973) 28-43.

[31] See above pp. 77-78.

"Therefore[32], thus says Yahweh, *ʾlhy ṣbʾwt ʾdny*:
In all the squares there shall be lamentation[33],
and in all the streets they shall say: Woe! Woe![34].
And they shall call the farm-worker[35] to mourning,
and those skilled in mourning to lamentation[36].
In all the vineyards there shall be lamentation,
for I am going to pass through the midst of you,
says Yahweh."

4.2. *Lamentation and Fertility. A Few Remarks*

These last words of judgement in the pericope 5, 1-17 are very important and may be looked upon as a summing up of a main aspect of the prophetic message of Amos. Whereas the two earlier pronouncements of doom in the pericope, vv. 2-3 and 11, refer to the worship of deities other than Yahweh and to the social and moral transgressions of the people respectively, the words of judgement contained in vv. 16-17 refer to both vv. 2-3 and 11 and may, consequently, be regarded as a pronouncement of doom occurring as a result of both the religious and the social/moral behaviour of the Israelites. Again we have an example that the ethical preaching of the prophet Amos cannot be separated from his religious polemics.

Of particular interest in this connection are the contents of the pronouncement of doom contained in vv. 16-17. Great importance must be attached to the fact that the prophet is picturing the future catastrophe so closely connected to the farm-worker and the vineyard. The theme of the prophet's message is the very same as in 4, 6-11[37]. The fundamentals of life, prosperity and fertility, are here being concentrated in the one motif: the fertility of the vineyard. In ancient Palestine the deities were regarded as the securers of necessary fertility. According to Amos, however, Yahweh was the only one that was able to provide this fertility. If the Israelites did not follow him, they were doomed. In fact, Yahweh himself would cause the destruction. Thus, the punishment has two different

[32] Cf. n. 23 above.

[33] *mspd* is the lamentation over the dead. Cf. Gen 50, 10, Esther 4, 3. The prophets often use this *Gattung* in their messages of doom. Cf. Jer 6, 26; 48, 38, Ez 27, 31, Mi 1, 8.11, Zech 12, 10-11. Cf. also Is 22, 12, Joel 2, 12. Cf. also Ps 30, 12. The classic work on the lamentation for the dead is H. Jahnow, *Das hebräische Leichenlied* (1923).

[34] The word *hw*, most probably a variant of *hwy*, occurs only here (on *hwy*, see below n. 169).

[35] On *ʾkr*, see H. Gese, "Kleine Beiträge zum Verständnis des Amosbuches", *VT* 12 (1962) 432-36. The re-reading of the Masoretic text proposed by Gese for v. 17a (p. 434) is fascinating, but not necessary.

[36] MT is corrupt here; *ʾl* should stand before *mspd*.

[37] See above p. 58ff.

aspects attached to it: on the one hand Yahweh was the only god that *could* help the people, on the other, he himself would punish the people if they did not worship him and follow his divine commandments[38].

It is not difficult to see why Amos in his pronouncement of doom in 5, 16-17 has chosen to concentrate on the farmworker and his occupation. Of all the things which constituted a constant threat to life and prosperity, the lack of rain followed by crop failure was undoubtedly felt as the most imminent calamity which could befall the population of an agricultural society[39]. Again accordingly, we see that it is wrong to maintain that Amos (and the other prophets) were fighting against the fertility gods of their time. The most correct way to express what it signifies is to say that the concern of the prophet was to fight for the idea that there is only *one* fertility god, and that his name is Yahweh.

It is interesting to note that the theme of the lamenting farm-worker is known from the preaching of other prophets as well, indicating the importance of the lament in this connection. Thus we read in Jer 14, 4:

> "Because the ground is dried out[40], since there is no rain on the land, the hopes of the farm-workers are wrecked (*bšw ʾkrym*), and they cover their heads"[41].

And in Joel 1, 11:

> "Despair, you farm-workers (*ʾkrym*), lament, you vine-dressers
> (*krmym*), for the wheat, and for the barley,
> for the harvest of the field has been ruined"[42].

Here, too, the punishment of Yahweh must be seen as a consequence of both the moral and the religious behaviour of the Israelites: the lack of fertility follows both the worship of gods other than Yahweh and the disobedience of his divine laws.

It is with special interest that we note the mention of the mourning of the farm-workers (and the vine-dressers) in connection with crop failure. If we take a closer look at the texts in question, in particular Joel 1, 4-14, it seems as if the prophets refer to the lament of the farm-workers in connection with drought and crop failure in an established ritual. This also follows from the further context of Jer 14, 4.The pronouncement in Am 5, 16-17 consequently must be regarded as a reference to the public

---

[38] On the punishment aspect cf. also further below p. 84f.

[39] Probably the best insight in this is provided by the standard work by G. Dalman, *AuS*, in particular I, 1-2 (1928).

[40] The meaning of Hebrew *ḥth* in this context is uncertain. My translation is only a suggestion based on the context (for further suggestions, see W. Rudolph, *Jeremia* (1968) 98).

[41] For the greater context of this, Yahweh as the provider of the rain, cf. above p. 58ff.

[42] Cf. also the following verses.

lament[43] which will follow the disaster caused by the unwillingness of the Israelites to turn to Yahweh as their god and obey his commandments.

The public lament has several interesting features attached to it. Thus, A. S. Kapelrud has stressed a connection between the mourning rites in the Book of Joel and the lament over the disappearing fertility god in Ugaritic religion[44]. Even if this remains hypothetical, and even if one should not too hastily draw comparisons between the Old Testament and the Ugaritic texts, this possible aspect of the lament of the farm-workers in Joel deserves to be taken into consideration[45].

The main aspect, however, of the lament of the farm-worker in connection with the failing crop should be sought in the phenomenon of the general public lament, the occasional public fast ordered by the leaders when war, defeat, drought, grasshoppers, famine, etc. had occurred or was threatening[46].

The main function of the deity was to provide for the welfare of his people, and to see to it that none of these disastrous events occurred. The people, on their side, had to fulfil *their* obligations: the worship of their god in the cult and obedience to his divine laws. If they did not do this, they had no guarantee that the deity would keep his part of the agreement. An eventual occurrence of war, defeat, pestilence, drought, etc. might then be interpreted as the punishment of the god following the transgressions of the people. Either they had not been worshipping him properly, or they had disobeyed his rules for moral and social behaviour.

When the prophets (and following them the Deuteronomists) interpret the distress of the people, present or past, as the punishment of Yahweh

[43] Cf. on the public lament in addition to the present section also below pp. 103-08.

[44] A. S. Kapelrud, *Joel Studies* (1948) 30-31 and *passim*.

[45] One should keep in mind, however, that we have no evidence in the Old Testament which shows that there ever was a lament over the vanished fertility god in Israel. Even if the assumption that a "dying and rising" deity existed in the Ancient Near East has to be modified considerably (cf. below pp. 148-51), there can be no doubt that mourning rites in connection with the vanished deity have played a certain role in the fertility provoking cults. Thus, we *may* assume that similar rites were known in ancient Israel (Ez 8, 14!). Still, this all remains very, very hypothetical.

[46] Even if there are not many psalms of this literary genre to be found in the Book of Psalms (Pss 44, 60, 74, 79, 80, 83, and 89 all represent the public lament. These psalms, however, are mostly centering around the theme of the injustice committed by others on Israel), there are quite a few references to it scattered all over the Old Testament. In addition to the examples quoted above, particular mention should be made of the prayer of Solomon at the inauguration of the temple, I Kings 8, 22-53 (see in particular vv. 33-40). The most typical example of a public lament to be found in the Bible is the Book of Lamentations. Further on the public lament, see H. Gunkel, J. Begrich, *Einleitung in die Psalmen* (1933) 117-39, S. Mowinckel, *Offersang og Sangoffer* (1951) 192-226, C. Westermann, *Lob und Klage in den Psalmen*[5] (1977) 39-48, H. W. Wolff, "Der Aufruf zur Volksklage", *Gesammelte Studien*[2] (1973) 392-401.

because they have broken the agreement, i.e. they are worshipping deities other than Yahweh, and they are not following his commandments concerning moral and social behaviour, they are thus building on commonly accepted religious thought.

However, this interpretation of why disasters occur in society could also be used for missionary purposes.

A major task of the prophet was to intercede for the people in times when disasters of the kind just mentioned had occurred or were threatening[47]. It is also within this context that we have to understand the phenomenon of the "oracles against the foreign nations" which have played such an important part in ancient Israelite prophecy[48]. For purely missionary purposes the prophets were now able to use their techniques against their own compatriots too: if the people do not follow Yahweh, this and that will certainly happen to them; if they do not obey his moral commandments, such and such will occur. Thus, the oracles are not actually meant as the prediction of a coming catastrophe, but must be seen first and foremost as threats serving the ends of the prophets of Yahweh in the religious struggle between the two main religious forces "Yahwism" and "Baᶜalism". Hypothetically, we must assume that other prophets were doing the same for *their* gods. In the end, however, it was the prophets of Yahweh that won the victory. The other prophets are lost to posterity, or they appear in rather biased passages as "false prophets", etc.[49]

One of the "origins" of the so-called "classical prophecy of doom" in ancient Israel is accordingly to be found in the encounter between what we may superficially term "Yahwism" and "Baᶜalism"[50]. From this it follows that the great importance of the prophetic movement in the formation of what was later to become the classical Israelite religion can hardly be exaggerated.

A further aspect of the public lament which is also relevant to our thesis, is the aspect of penance. This particular aspect of the lament,

---

[47] It is quite remarkable that so little attention has been paid to the important intercessory role of the prophets. See, however, A. B. Rhodes, "Israel's Prophets as Intercessors", *Scripture in History and Theology* (1977) 107-130. Cf. also L. Ramlot, "Prophétisme", *DBS* 8 (1967-72) 1162-66.

[48] On the oracles against the foreign nations, see below pp. 97, 101, 103-108. Cf. also above Chapter 2, n. 2.

[49] In recent years research on the so-called "false prophets", "Baᶜal prophets", etc. has made some progress (cf. J. Crenshaw, "Prophecy, False", *IDBS* (1976) 701-02). It must be regretted that the great importance of the study of "non-canonical" prophets for the whole of the prophetic movement has not always been appreciated by scholars.

[50] It goes without saying that a designation like "Baᶜalism" is not very precise. Nor can it adequately cover the complete picture of the different religious cults in Israel at the time of the classic prophets (cf. above Chapter 3, notes 122-124).

expressed through fast and other rites[51], is probably as old as the lament itself. Actually, the phenomenon of penance is not easy to explain. We may assume, however, that its main purpose has been to make the god well-disposed towards his worshippers and change their present situation; change the war to their advantage, provide the necessary rain in a period of drought, etc.

An illustrative example is found in Jud 20. After we have been informed in v. 25 that eighteen thousand Israelites have been killed in the war against the Benjaminites, we learn from vv. 26-28:

> ''And all the Israelites and the whole people went up, and they came to Bethel, and they wept (*wybkw*) and they sat there in the presence of Yahweh. And they fasted (*wyṣwmw*) on that day until evening and offered burnt offerings (*wyᶜlw ᶜlwt*) and communion offerings (*wšlmym*) in the presence of Yahweh. And the Israelites consulted Yahweh (*wyšʾlw...byhwh*) (the ark of the covenant of God was there in those days, and *pynhs bn-ʾlᶜzr bn-ʾhrn* served before it in those days), and they said: Should we yet again go to war with our brothers[52] the Benjaminites, or should we stop? And Yahweh said: Go! For tomorrow I will give them into your hand.''

Equally interesting is the tradition preserved in 1 Sam 7. Despite the text clearly showing the hand of the Deuteronomist, it illustrates in a fine way the function of the public lament in ancient Israel. We read in vv. 3-6:

> ''And Samuel said to the whole of the House of Israel: If you turn to[53] Yahweh with all your heart and put away the foreign gods among you, and the Astartes, and direct your heart to Yahweh and serve him alone, he will deliver you from the hands of the Philistines. And the Israelites put away the Baᶜals and the Astartes and served Yahweh alone. And Samuel said: Gather all of Israel at Mizpah, and I will plead with Yahweh for you. And they

---

[51] The most characteristic rite of the public lament was the fast (*ṣwm*). We read of the fast as a constituent of the lament in Jud 20, 26, 1 Sam 7, 6, 2 Chr 20, 3, Ezr 8, 21-23, Neh 9, 1, Esther 4, 3; 9, 31, Is 58, 5, Jer 14, 12, Joel 1, 14; 2, 12.15, Jonah 3, 5. Cf. further H. Brongers, ''Fasting in Israel in Biblical and Post-Biblical Times'', *OTS* 20 (1977) 1-21. Other important rites in connection with the lament were the different sacrifices. In Jud 20, 26 we read about ''burnt offerings (*ᶜlwt*)'', and ''communion offerings (*šlmym*)'', and in Jud 21, 4 we read how the people built an altar in connection with the lament and performed the same sacrificial rites (*ᶜlwt* and *šlmym*). 1 Sam 7, 9-10 mentions the ''whole burnt offering'' (*ᶜwlh klyl*) in connection with the lament. *klyl* is somewhat problematic. The term could also be a designation for a particular kind of propitiatory sacrifice as we know it from Phenician and Punic practise (cf. *HAL*³ Lief. II (1974) 457). In Jer 14, 12 Yahweh tells the prophet that the public lament with fasting, burnt offering (*ᶜlh*), and cereal offering (*mnḥh*) will do them no good (cf. above pp. 71-72). The similarity between the context in Jeremiah 14 and Chapters 4-5 of Amos is conspicuous. A particular interesting rite in connection with the lament is the water rite (cf. above p. 72). Lament and water rite occur together in 1 Sam 7, 6 and Lam 2, 19 (?).

[52] MT has *ʾhy*.

[53] On the verb *šwb*, see above pp. 65-66.

gathered at Mizpah, and they drew water and poured it out in the presence of Yahweh. They fasted that day, and they said there: We have sinned against Yahweh. And Samuel judged the Israelites at Mizpah."[54]

This interesting text contains several of the ingredients of the public lament. Besides the war situation, there is also, apparently quite unmotivated, mention of a water ritual, whose purpose it was to provide rain in a period of drought[55]. We have here either an indication that the water ritual was a fixed constituent of the public lament in times of crisis, or that the Deuteronomic redactor has mixed two different traditions regarding the cult place Mizpah together; one telling of a ritual in connection with the war against the Philistines, the other of a public lament in connection with a drought. The confession of sin is also interesting and bears witness to the penance character of the lament[56].

One of the best illustrations I have found with regard to the situation described by Amos in 5, 16-17 and similar descriptions in the other prophets is a late Syriac psalm handed down among the works of Ephraem Syrus[57]. The following example stands out from the rather rigid theological severeness of Syrian Christianity and provides us with a brilliant illustration of the persistence of popular religion in an agricultural society. The translation is that of Brockelmann[58]:

"Lasst uns Trauer anlegen, damit der Himmel
  sich bedecke zum Regen.
Wir wollen dumpfes Geschrei erschallen lassen
  damit der Donner in den Wolken ertöne.
Die Stimmen des Gebetes sollen fliegen,
  damit Blitze zum Regen gesandt werden.
Die Erde möge mit Tränen genetzt werden
  damit sie auch vom Regen benetzt werde.
Wir wollen die Schleusen der Augen zum Weinen öffnen,
  damit auch die Wolken geöffnet werden.
Die Stimme unseres Bittens wird zwingen
  den Höchsten, unsere Stimme zu erhören.
Weil unsere Stimme nicht bei ihm gehört ward,
  hörte auch seine Stimme auf bei uns zu tönen,
  und der Donner seiner Wolken schwieg.
Weil die Tränen unseres Weinens versiegten,
  versiegten seine Stimme von unseren Äckern.
Denn er dürstet sehr nach unserem Worte,
  so wie das Feld nach seinen Güssen.

---

[54] For further examples, see the references mentioned above n. 46.
[55] Cf. above p. 72.
[56] On the confession of sins cf. above pp. 71-72.
[57] *Sancti Ephraem Syri hymni et sermones*. Ed. T. J. Lamy, T. III (1889) col. 97.
[58] C. Brockelmann, "Ein syrischer Regenzauber", *ARW* 9 (1906) 518-20.

Er wünscht nicht dass wir fallen,
da er durch Tränen die Schuldscheine löscht.
Wir wollen den Leib im Gebet schwitzen lassen,
damit die Wolke Regen ergiesse.
Wir wollen ein wenig dürsten,
damit die Saat vom Regen gesättigt werde.
Wir wollen ein wenig fasten,
damit die Sättigung durch die Wolke gross werde"[59].

It would be illegitimate, of course, to maintain that the situation described in this Syriac psalm applies automatically for Am 5, 16-17 and the related Old Testament passages also. The core of the situations described, however, are identical. Consequently, the psalm quoted illustrates very well the situation in which the farm-workers of ancient Israel found themselves in times of drought.

From the Syriac lament we learn that much of the purpose of the ritual is to be found in what nowadays has been termed homeopathic or imitative magic, *i.e.* rituals based on the assumption that things which resemble each other can influence each other[60]. This, I believe, provides us with a plausible explanation of some of the rites connected to the lament in the Old Testament also (the water rite, the mourning, etc.).

In Am 5, 16-17, however, we see how the prophet has turned the old ideas upside down. He gives a description of the lament as his audience would recognize it from times of drought and crop failure. But he offers them no consolation. To Amos, the situation of the public lament represents yet another way of expressing the judgement of Yahweh. Rather than providing the rain, Yahweh will cause disaster: "For I am going to pass through the midst of you, says Yahweh."

The situation of Am 5, 16-17 is not unlike the one described in 1 Sam 7[61]. But this time there is not going to be any "Go! For tomorrow I will give them into your hand", which was the answer one would normally expect from the priest or the prophet as intercessor[62].

A similar situation following a public lament is described in Jer 14, 11-12. Yahweh informs the prophet Jeremiah that he is not going to intercede for the people:

"And Yahweh said to me: Do not pray for the well-being of this people. For when they fast, I will not listen to their cry, and when they offer burnt offering and cereal offering, I will not accept them. For I will make an end to them with the sword, with famine and with pestilence."[63]

[59] It is with a certain interest that we compare this ancient hymn to the popular prayers and rituals for provoking rain in twentieth century Palestine (see G. Dalman, AuS I: 1 (1928) 133-54.

[60] The difficult problem of magic has been much disputed in recent years (cf. J. Waardenburg, *Approaches to the study of Religion.* Vol. 1 (1973) index under "Magic" pp. 702-03, However, I cannot go into this here.

[61] Cf. above pp. 86-87. [62] Cf. above n. 47. [63] Cf. above p. 71-72.

4.3. *The "Day of Yahweh" in Amos* 5, 18-20

4.3.1. Preliminary Remarks

One of the most intriguing passages in the prophetic message of Amos is the reference in 5, 18-20[64] to the "Day of Yahweh". This is also the passage in the Book of Amos which has most emphatically left its mark on the history of research. However, when dealing with a text as puzzling as Am 5, 18-20, it is important that the scholar does not let himself become side tracked by the history of research. Undoubtedly, this is something which may easily happen when an exegetical problem has a history of research as long and as complicated as is the case with the problem of the "Day of Yahweh" in the Old Testament. On the other hand, the history of research has played such an important part in the discussions of the problem, and seems to be so intermingled with it, that we simply cannot allow ourselves to avoid it.

4.3.2. The "Day of Yahweh" in Recent Scholarship. A Short Outline

The growing interest in the Biblical Hebrew expression *ywm yhwh* after the turn of the century was primarily due to its relevance for the discussion on Old Testament eschatology. A natural starting point for a short survey of the history of research of the "Day of Yahweh" is consequently the German scholar Hugo Gressmann.

Like so many scholars after him[65], Gressmann connected *ywm yhwh* with the wars of Yahweh and *inter alia* pointed to Arabic *yaum* as a designation for the wars of the Arabs in Arabic literature as a parallel[66]. He himself rejects this explanation as being too narrow however[67], and takes the problem up on a broader basis[68]. His conclusions were that the concept of *ywm yhwh* constitutes the very essence of Old Testament eschatology, an eschatology originating from a common Near Eastern conception of an imminent cosmic catastrophe, and ultimately stemming from Babylonian mythology[69].

With Sigmund Mowinckel's *Psalmenstudien* II[70] a new era was

---

[64] The text is translated below pp. 108-109.

[65] See below n. 85.

[66] H. Gressmann, *Der Ursprung der israelitisch-jüdischen Eschatologie* (1905) 143: "Der Tag Jahwes = Der Schlachttag, die Schlacht Jahwes".

[67] *Ibid.*

[68] *Ibid.* 143-58.

[69] *Ibid.* 160 and *passim.*

[70] The ideas of Mowinckel regarding *ywm yhwh* are found scattered in various of his works. In addition to *Psalmenstudien* II (1922) *passim*, see in particular "Jahves dag", *NTT* 59 (1958) 1-56, 209-29.

inaugurated in research on the "Day of Yahweh". Although obviously inspired by him, Mowinckel opposes Gressmann in several respects. While Gressmann and others on the whole interpret *ywm yhwh* as an eschatological concept, Mowinckel connects this view with his own theories on the Enthronement Psalms and the origin of eschatology. In accordance with his thesis that eschatology is originally to be regarded as a projection of cultic events—as they were performed at the New Year Festival—into the future, Mowinckel maintains that the source for the eschatological term *ywm yhwh* must be sought in the cult and that, in fact, it originally signifies the day of the cultic enthronement of Yahweh[71].

In this development from cult into eschatology, Mowinckel finds Am 5, 18-20 to be of vital importance. This prophet's use of the term *ywm yhwh* constitutes the very turning point in the development of Old Testament eschatology: all the prophets following Amos proclaim the "Day of Yahweh" as a day of disaster for Israel. Thus, the foundation is laid for a gradual detachment of the "Day" from the original, cultic context into a new, eschatological one, a development which may have roots in a prophetic tradition but which becomes explicit for the first time in the preaching of Amos[72].

Here it becomes obvious how far Mowinckel has distanced himself from Gressmann who held eschatology to be pre-prophetic. According to the latter, eschatology must even "aus der prähistorischen Epoche stammen"[73]. In opposition to Gressmann, Mowinckel claims moreover that eschatology is a genuine Israelite phenomenon. He is here in accordance with E. Sellin[74] offering, however, a different solution to the problem of the origin of eschatology than Sellin's reference to *das Sinaiereignis*. Sellin,

---

[71] Mowinckel was not the first one, however, to see *ywm yhwh* as a cultic event. Thus, G. Hoffmann called attention to the possibility of *ywm yhwh* in Amos being a festal day as early as 1883 ("Versuche zu Amos", *ZAW* 3 (1883) 112). That P. Volz (*Das Neujahrsfest Jahwes* (1921)) made observations similar to those of Mowinckel regarding the relationship between the New Year Festival and the development of Israelite eschatology, is also well known. Volz, too, pointed to the cultic element in the "Day of Yahweh" (*op. cit.* 15). Less known is A. J. Wensinck, "The Semitic New Year and the Origin of Eschatology", *AcOr* 1 (1923) 158-99. Both with regard to the origin of eschatology and the origin of the "Day of Yahweh" Wensinck maintains theories similar to those of Mowinckel.Even though Volz was not explicitly mentioned in his work, Wensinck seems nevertheless to have been influenced by him (see especially pp. 188-99). As for the definition of the term "eschatology" it is important to be aware of the fact that the view held by Mowinckel in the early twenties underwent considerable development as time went by. For a most readable article on this, see J. H. Grønbæk, "Zur Frage der Eschatologie in der Verkündigung der Gerichtspropheten", *SEÅ* 24 (1959) 5-21.

[72] *Psalmenstudien* II (1922) 248, 272, and especially 318-19. See also "Jahves dag", *NTT* 59 (1958) 17-21.

[73] H. Gressmann, *Der Ursprung der israelitisch-jüdischen Eschatologie* (1905) 147.

[74] E. Sellin, *Der alttestamentliche Prophetismus* (1912) 172-83.

accordingly, is more in accord with Gressmann about the nature of the "Day of Yahweh"[75].

When Mowinckel's interpretation of the idea of *ywm yhwh* immediately seemed to turn out a success, this was due not least to the positive response his theories concerning the Enthronement festival were met with, and the fact that he was able to link these theories to his view of the "Day of Yahweh".

A scholar like G. Hölscher already subscribed to Mowinckel's view in 1925[76], and over the years quite a few scholars have fallen in with Mowinckel and his "cultic" view of the "Day of Yahweh". Among them we find names like A. S. Kapelrud[77], J. D. W. Watts[78], J. Morgenstern[79], R. Largement and H. Lemaitre[80], R. E. Clements[81], J. Lindblom[82], K.-D. Schunck[83] and J. Gray[84].

But naturally the views of Mowinckel regarding the "Day of Yahweh" were not allowed to pass unchallenged. Notably the last decades have seen quite a variety of alternative solutions to the problem of *ywm yhwh*.

One of those who opposed Mowinckel, and who did so with the greatest success if one may judge from the response his thesis has been met with, was the German scholar Gerhard von Rad.

Taking his starting point in a *form- und traditionsgeschichtliche* method, von Rad sought to ascertain whether the concept and the expression *ywm yhwh* might form part of any particular Gattung. After having examined the idea in its various contexts, he was in the position to demonstrate that the "Day of Yahweh" had its roots far back in Israelite tradition and that

---

[75] E. Sellin, *op. cit.* 113 and *Das Zwölfprophetenbuch* (1922) 192-93. The fact that Sellin in the latter work maintains that the punishment of Yahweh will happen on a "Festtag", however, modifies his earlier view somewhat.

[76] G. Hölscher, *Die Ursprünge der jüdischen Eschatologie* (1925) 9. The view put forward by Hölscher in this work, however, differs from the one maintained by him in his long article "Sigmund Mowinckel som gammeltestamentlig forsker", *NTT* 24 (1923) 133.

[77] A. S. Kapelrud, *Joel Studies* (1948) 55 and *passim*, *Central Ideas in Amos* (1961) 71ff. *The Message of the Prophet Zephaniah* (1975) 84, 61-64, 80-87.

[78] J. D. Watts, *Vision and Prophecy in Amos* (1958) 68-76, cf. also *ibid.* 81-84.

[79] See *inter alia* J. Morgenstern, "Amos Studies", *HUCA* 11 (1936) 124, 12-13 (1937-38) 19. 48ff, 15 (1940) 304.

[80] R. Largement, H. Lemaitre, "Le jour de Yahweh", *Sacra Pagina* (1959) 259-66.

[81] R. E. Clements, *Prophecy and Covenant* (1965) 107-10.

[82] See *inter alia* J. Lindblom, "Gibt es eine Eschatologie bei den alttestamentlichen Propheten?" *StTh* 6 (1952) 84, *Prophecy in Ancient Israel* (1962) 316ff and *passim.*

[83] K.-D. Schunck, "Der 'Tag Jahwes' in der Verkündigung der Propheten", *Kairos* 11 (1969) 14-21. However, Schunck does not always seem to have shared this view. Thus, in his article "Strukturlinien in der Entwicklung der Vorstellung vom 'Tag Jahwes'". *VT* 14 (1964) 329-30 he adheres to the view of Gerhard von Rad (see below n. 85) on the origin of the expression *ywm yhwh.*

[84] J. Gray, "The Day of Yahweh", *SEÅ* 39 (1974) 5-37.

it originated from the institution of "Holy warfare"[85]. Accordingly, *ywm yhwh* must be considered to be an act of war, referring to the day when Yahweh rises against his enemies in battle and conquers them.

Von Rad, too, exposed himself to criticism. The most massive, and indubitably also the most reponsible attack on von Rad's position has come from the Jewish scholar M. Weiss[86]. Nevertheless, there can be no doubt that the theories of von Rad concerning the "Day of Yahweh" come closest to an *opinio communis* on the origin of the idea of *ywm yhwh* in recent years[87].

Mention should also be made of the American scholar, F. M. Cross who, in an original and most inspiring paper, has attempted to combine the theories of Mowinckel and von Rad and maintains that *ywm yhwh* must be interpreted both as "the day of victory in holy warfare" and as "the day of Yahweh's festival"[88].

In addition to these classic solutions of Mowinckel and von Rad, there are also other theories on the origin and the meaning of the idea of the "Day of Yahweh". I will only mention a few names and the theories connected to them.

In 1948, L. Černy, opposing Mowinckel and the so-called "Myth and Ritual" school but following Gressmann, sought to demonstrate that the idea of *ywm yhwh* constituted the very essence of Old Testament eschatology, an eschatology with roots far back in ancient Israelite tradi-

---

[85] In his study *Der heilige Krieg im alten Israel*, originally published in Zürich in 1951, von Rad does not seem to be aware of any connection between the institution of "Holy War" and the idea of *ywm yhwh* at all, or at least he does not mention any such connection. Yet he does quote a passage from a book by Julius Wellhausen taken from a context in which Wellhausen points to a possible connection between the two (p. 14). Later, von Rad was to come to advocate his view of the relationship between the institution of "Holy War" and *ywm yhwh* on several occasions. See in particular "The Origin of the Concept of the Day of Yahweh", *JSS* 4 (1959) 97-108 and *Theologie des Alten Testaments* II (1961) 133-37.

Von Rad was far from being the first scholar to point to a connection between "Holy War" and *ywm yhwh*. Already before the turn of the century Julius Wellhausen had called attention to the relationship between the two phenomena (*Israelitische und jüdische Geschichte* (1897) 27). Later, several scholars pointed out this connection long before von Rad took up the view. See *inter alia* J. P. M. Smith, "The Day of Yahweh", *AJT* 5 (1901) 512, H. Gressmann, *Der Ursprung der israelitisch-jüdische Eschatologie* (1905) 143, S. R. Driver, *The Books of Joel and Amos* (1907) 185, W. W. Cannon, "The Day of the Lord in Joel", *CQR* 103 (1926-27) 50-51.

[86] M. Weiss, "The Origin of the 'Day of the Lord' - Reconsidered", *HUCA* 37 (1966) 29-60. According to this scholar "day" is a theophanic description.

[87] See *inter alia* G. Eggebrecht, *Die früheste Bedeutung und der Ursprung der Konzeption vom "Tage Jahwes"* (1966), J. R. Wilch, *Time and Event* (1969) 95, H. W. Wolff, *Dodekapropheton* 2 (1969) 299-300, E. Haag, "Der Tag Jahwes", *BiLe* 13 (1972) 517-25.

[88] F. M. Cross, "The Divine Warrior", *Biblical Motifs* (1966) 11-30. The views of Cross were later taken up by R. W. Klein, "The Day of the Lord", *CTM* 39 (1968) 517-25.

tion[89]. According to this view, Černy interprets *ywm yhwh* in Am 5, 18-20 strictly eschatologically. He does not, however, have many followers.

More recently, F. J. Hélewa has called attention to the connection between *ywm yhwh* and the idea of the covenant[90]. Similar views were expressed also by F. C. Fensham[91] and most recently by C. van Leeuwen[92].

A scholar like A. J. Everson, again, refutes an eschatological interpretation of the concept, which he believes to have come into existence only in late, post-exilic time, and instead emphasizes the historical contents of *ywm yhwh*[93].

4.3.3. *ywm yhwh* in the Message of the Prophets

A cursory glance through the prophetical books of the Old Testament gives the impression that the formula *ywm yhwh* is a set phrase which gives expression to one particular idea in the prophetic message. Consequently, it must be considered unwise to attempt to look for an explanation to the "day of Yahweh" in Amos 5, 18-20 without having first considered the function and meaning of the expression in the other prophets. As we see, there is in fact sufficient evidence for an attempt to explain the occurrence of *ywm yhwh* in Amos based on the background of the general prophetic conception of the idea.

It must likewise be regarded as unwise to focus attention too much on the problems connected to the origin of the concept of the "Day of Yahweh". This, of course, does not imply that knowledge of the background of the concept *ywm yhwh* cannot contribute towards an understanding of how the idea is being used in its present context[94], only that the danger is near at hand (as is obvious in much of the secondary

---

[89] L. Černy, *The Day of Yahweh* (1948) *passim.*

[90] F. J. Hélewa, "L'origine du concept prophétique du "Jour de Yahvé"", *ECarm* 15 (1964) 3-36.

[91] F. C. Fensham, "A possible origin of the concept of the day of the Lord", *Biblical Essays* (1966) 90-97. I am indebted to Professor Fensham for sending me his article.

[92] C. van Leeuwen, "The Prophecy of the *YÔM YHWH* in Amos 5, 18-20", *OTS* 19 (1974) 113-34.

[93] A. J. Everson, "The days of Yahweh", *JBL* 93 (1974) 329-37, *The Day of Yahweh as Historical Event* (1969), "Day of the Lord", *IDBS* (1976) 209-10.

Referance should further be made to J. G. Trapiello, "La noción del "Dia de Yahve" en el Antiguo Testamento", *CuBi* 26 (1969) 331-36, maintaining that the concept *ywm yhwh* has an Israelite origin, and that it expresses the expectation of the historical manifestation of Yahweh for the benefit of his people, and to C. Carniti, "L'espressione "il giorno di JHWH", *BeO* 12 (1970) 11-25, asserting that the concept of the "Day of Yahweh" is without any tradition in the religious history of the Israelite people, but came into being with the preaching of the prophet Amos.

[94] An interest in background information, in fact, plays a major part throughout the whole of the present investigation of the Book of Amos.

literature on the phenomenon) that research into the background may obscure a simple reading of the idea in the prophetic context, the very context which was the reason for investigating into the background of the idea in the first place.

When we want to inquire into the meaning behind the prophetic expression *ywm yhwh*, it is important not to confine oneself rigidly into considering only the passages that contain the expression *ywm yhwh expressis verbis.* These passages are Is 13, 6.9, Ez 13, 5, Joel 1, 15; 2, 1.11; 3, 4; 4, 4, Am 5, 18 (bis).20, Ob 15, Zeph 1, 7.14(bis), Mal 3, 23. Together with these occurrences *expressis verbis* we should also group the indefinite *ywm lyhwh*, occurring in Is 2, 12, Ez 30, 3 (LXX and Peshitta omit *l*), and Zech 14, 1. However, in addition to these, we find several passages which obviously reflect the same idea, using a different formula. Some of them are found in the same texts which have *ywm yhwh expressis verbis*, and some are found elsewhere. The main point, however, is that the similarities between the two groups of texts are so striking that there can be little doubt that these other phrases give expression to the same idea as does *ywm yhwh.* Among these formulas related to the expression *ywm yhwh*, we note in particular *ywm ʿbrt yhwh*, "the day of the wrath of Yahweh", in Zeph 1, 18[95], *ywm ḥrwn ʾpw*, "the day of his burning anger", in Is 13, 13[96], *ywm ʾp-yhwh*, "the day of Yahweh's anger", in Zeph 2, 2-3[97], *ywm nqm*, "day of vengeance", in Is 34, 8; 61, 2; 63, 4[98].

But the idea of the "Day of Yahweh" is reflected also in quite a few other passages in the prophetic literature where the word *ywm* does not appear at all. Thus, rather than to look for the linguistic label "*ywm*" one should rather look for the actual *content* of the passages. A typical example of this is Jer 4, 27-29 which has all the ingredients of the *ywm yhwh* passages, but which lacks *ywm ipsissimum verbum.* Thus, we have in this passage the context of judgement, description of war, and of cosmic darkness[99].

For practical reasons, however, in what follows I shall concentrate on the so-called "classical" *ywm yhwh* passages[100].

---

[95] Cf. *ywm ʿbrh* in Zeph 1, 15. Cf. also Prov 11, 4.

[96] Cf. Lam 1, 12: ... *ʾšr hwgh yhwh bywm ḥrwn ʾpw.*

[97] Cf. *bywm ʾp-yhwh* in Lam 2, 22, *ywm ʾpw* in Lam 2, 11, *ywm ʾpk* in Lam 2, 21.

[98] Cf. also *ywm nqmh* in Jer 46, 10. For further references see E. Jenni, *THAT* 1² (1975) 724.

[99] Cf. V. Eppstein, "The Day of Yahweh in Jer 4, 23-28" *JBL* 87 (1968) 93-97.

[100] Further, on *ywm* see E. Jenni in *THAT* 1² (1975) 707-26, in particular 723ff. Cf. also M. Sæbø, "yôm", *TWAT* III, Lief. 4-5 (1980) 559-61, 566-86. Of other expressions of interest in this connection particular mention should be made of the frequently occurring *bywm hhwʾ.* The discussion whether this formula should be considered as an "eschatological" technical term, seems to have resulted in the opinion of P. A. Munch (*The Expression bajjôm hāhūʾ* (1936)) that the expression in question is not an eschatological

All the passages referred to above relating to the "Day of Yahweh" have an emphasis on the negative character of the "day" as an event of doom and disaster in common. This utterly negative character of the "Day of Yahweh" is elaborated further in the oracles in which the *ywm yhwh* passages occur.

The most characteristic element in the descriptions of the "Day of Yahweh" is undoubtedly the element of war. Thus, we read in Is 13, 4-6:

> "Listen! A rumbling in the mountains as of a great nation. Listen! The noise of kingdoms, of nations gathering together. *yhwh ṣbʾwt* is mustering a host for battle.
> They come from a distant country, from the end of the heavens, *yhwh* and the instruments of his wrath, to destroy the whole earth. Wail, for *ywm yhwh* is near (*qrwb*), it comes like destruction from *šdy*[101]."

And in Joel 2, 2b-9 there is a description of the army invading on the terrible "Day of Yahweh" (mentioned *expressis verbis* in vv. 1 and 11):

> "Like dawn spread over the mountains, a great and powerful nation, such as has never been seen before, nor will ever be again in the ages to come. Before them fire devours, and behind them a flame burns. Like the garden of Eden is the land before them, and behind them a wasted desert. Nothing escapes them. Like the appearance of horses is their appearance, and like horses they run. It is like the rattle of chariots leaping on the tops of the mountains, like the sound of the flame of the fire devouring the stubble, like a powerful nation ready for battle. Before them nations tremble, all faces grow pale. Like warriors they run, like soldiers they mount the wall. They march each on his way, and they do not turn[102] from their paths. They do not jostle each other, each marches in his path. They 'burst through the weapons'[103], they do not break off. They rush upon the city, they leap on to the wall, they climb into the houses, they enter the windows like a thief..."

And in Zech 14, 1-3:

> "See! A day is coming for Yahweh when the spoils taken from you will be divided among you. And I will gather up all the nations against Jerusalem to battle, the city will be captured, the houses plundered and the women ravished. Half of the city shall go into captivity, but the rest of the people shall not be cut off from the city. And Yahweh will go forth[104] and fight against those nations like the day he fought on the day of battle"[105].

---

term, but always appears as a temporal adverb, becoming the *opinio communis* (see *e.g.* J. Jeremias, *Theophanie* (1965) 97, n. 1, H.-M. Lutz, *Jahwe, Jerusalem und die Völker* (1968) 130, n. 2). I find the discussion somewhat artificial. At the same time as the term *bywm hhwʾ* obviously is a temporal adverb, it must be equally obvious that when the term occurs as a determinative in connection with the expression *ywm yhwh* it is as eschatological as the expression *ywm yhwh* itself.

[101] Further descriptions of war follow in the text. See in particular vv. 15ff.

[102] Reading *yʿwtwn* instead of MT *yʿbṭwn*, "they take a pledge". The reading has support in the Peshitta, the Septuagint and in the Vulgate.

[103] The translation is that of RSV. The Hebrew of MT is not easily understood.

[104] For *yṣʾ* as a technical term for "going to war" cf. above p. 77.

[105] Cf. B. Otzen, *Studien über Deuterosacharja* (1964) *passim*.

In addition to these more detailed descriptions of war in the prophetic *ywm yhwh* passages, we find further references to war in several other passages. Of these one may note: the reference to the battle on the day of Yahweh in Ez 13, 5. Joel 1, 15 uses the same phrase as in the war text of Is 13 quoted above (v. 16): "*ywm yhwh* is near, it comes like destruction from *šdy*". Zeph 1, 16 describes the day as "a day of trumpet and battle cry against the fortified cities and against lofty corner towers", and in Ez 30 the word "sword" (*ḥrb*) occurs frequently (vv. 4, 5, 6, 11, 17, 21, 22, 24, 25), unambiguously pointing towards the war-like character of the "Day of Yahweh".

Consequently when reading through the prophetic *ywm yhwh* passages, one is given the impression that the most conspicuous feature of the texts which relate to the "Day of Yahweh" is the description of war.

However, the description of war is not the only medium available to the prophets in their portrayal of the "Day of Yahweh". Another conspicuous trait of the descriptions is the depiction of darkness and cosmic changes[106]. Of the relevant passages we note in particular: Is 13, 10: "the stars of heaven and their constellations will not let their light shine, the sun will be dark (*ḥšk*) when it rises, and the moon not shed its light", Ez 30, 18: "the day shall be dark (*ḥšk*)", Joel 2, 2: "a day of darkness (*ḥšk*) and gloom (*ʾplh*), a day of cloud (*ʿnn*) and darkness (*ʿrpl*), and in v. 10: "the earth quakes, the heavens tremble, the sun and moon darken (*qdrw*) and the stars stop shining", Joel 3, 3-4: "And I will give portents (*mwptym*) in the heavens and on the earth, blood and fire and columns of smoke (*tymrwt ʿšn*). The sun will be turned into darkness (*ḥšk*) and the moon into blood, before the great and terrible day of Yahweh comes", Joel 4, 15: "Sun and moon darken and the stars stop shining (= Joel 2, 10b), Zeph 1, 15b: "a day of cloud and darkness (= Joel 2, 2)".

Of other characteristics of the terrible "Day of Yahweh" we may note: drought (Ez 30, 12, Joel 1, 20, cf. Is 34, 9), doom for other deities (Ez 30, 13, Zeph 1, 4), lack of food (Joel 1, 10ff.).

The *ywm yhwh* passages in the prophetic text leave no doubt as to the meaning of the idea of the "Day of Yahweh" in the message of the prophets: the formula *ywm yhwh* and related expressions refer to the *ywm*, *i.e.* the time[107] when Yahweh destroys his enemies in war. The "Day of

---

[106] Cf. below n. 175.

[107] It is commonly accepted that *ywm*, usually rendered by "day", also has the meaning "time". Cf. E. Jenni, *THAT* I² (1975) 711ff. This does not imply, of course, that one should change the translation of *ywm yhwh* from the "Day of Yahweh" to the "Time of Yahweh".

Yahweh'' is mostly described as an event in the future, but there is also evidence that the description may refer to past events[108].

Vital to the understanding of the idea of the ''Day of Yahweh'' in the prophets is the awareness of the fact that the overwhelming majority of the ''Day of Yahweh'' passages occur in oracles against foreign nations. When I use the strong term ''overwhelming'' in this connection, it is mainly due to the several passages in the prophetic texts which obviously reflect the idea of the ''Day of Yahweh'' without mentioning *ywm yhwh expressis verbis*[109]. However, also quite a few of the classic *ywm yhwh* passages occur in oracles against foreign nations: Is 13, 6.9 (against Babylon), Ez 30, 3 (against Egypt), Is 34, 8 (against Edom), Is 63, 4 (against Edom).

Further, several of the passages which have *ywm yhwh* connect the oracles against the foreign nations with oracles of prosperity for Zion. This ''Jerusalem-theology'' in connection with the idea of the ''Day of Yahweh''—doom for the nations, prosperity for Jerusalem—is particularly conspicuous in the contexts of Joel 4, 14, Ob 15, Zech 14, Zeph 1, Is 2, 12[110].

Jerusalem is not the concern of the prophet Amos[111]. However, we must assume that the scheme ''doom for the foreign nation—prosperity for one's own nation'' formed a part of the prophet's pronouncement against the foreign nation in the North as well as in the South. Consequently it is against this background that we should attempt to understand the words of Am 5, 18-20, where we are given to understand that the people were actually ''longing for'' the ''Day of Yahweh''.

The problem of the prophetic use of the formula *ywm yhwh* cannot be isolated from the problem of the prophetic oracles against the foreign nations, of which they form an inherent part. However, before we turn our attention to the problem of the use of oracles against foreign nations in the prophets, it may be useful to take a look at the scholarly discussion regarding the origin of the idea of the ''Day of Yahweh''.

4.3.3.1. The Origin of the Idea of the ''Day of Yahweh'' in the Prophets. A Few Remarks.

The problem of the origin of the concept of the ''Day of Yahweh'' may not seem to concern this investigation. However, as the discussion of

---

[108] Cf. A. J. Everson, ''Day of the Lord'', *IDBS* (1976) 209, who rightly points to texts like Is 22, 1-14, Jer 46, 2-12, Lam 1, 2; 1, 12, Ez 13, 1-9 as evidence of this.

[109] Cf. above p. 94.

[110] On the relationship between the Zion theology and the ''Day of Yahweh'', see in particular H.-M. Lutz, *Jahwe, Jerusalem und die Völker* (1968) 130-46 and *passim*, G. W. Ahlström, *Joel and the Temple Cult of Jerusalem* (1971)62-97 and *passim*.

[111] Cf., however, above Chapter 2, n. 12.

origin has played a dominating, in my view far too dominating, role in scholarly discussion, it is only natural that a few words should be said on the matter. I do not intend going into many details of the discussion[112], but will focus attention on the two theories which have found support among the majority of scholars, namely the cultic origin alleged by Mowinckel and the theory of von Rad concerning the origin of the idea in the institution of holy war.

A basic argument by those who maintain that *ywm yhwh* is a cultic event, or at least originates from a cultic event, is that several passages in the Old Testament itself seem to indicate that *ywm* is used as a designation for a cultic feast.

Undoubtedly, there *are* instances in the Old Testament where *ywm* is used as a designation for some festal event.

In Hos 2, in a long rebukc against the Israelites for their participation in non-Yahwistic worship, we read in v. 15 that the people will be called to account for their *ymy hbᶜlym*, their Baᶜal festivals. Among the offensive contents of these festivals are mentioned offerings.

In Hos 9, 5, in a context where the prophet portrays the tragic future of Israel, he asks: "What will you do on the day of the festival (*mwᶜd*), on the day of the feast of Yahweh (*ywm ḥg-yhwh*)?" Probably the reference is to the feast of ingathering, the Sukkoth feast, which was among the most significant of the ancient Israelite festivals[113].

Also the phrase "on the day of our king" in Hos 7, 5 is most probably a reference to some Yahweh festival, despite the attempt made by most scholars to see the expression as a reference to the political king[114].

Further passages in the Old Testament which have *ywm* as a designation for a festal event are Hos 12, 10 and Esther 9, 22.

Even if the evidence cannot be said to be overwhelming, it is sufficient to show convincingly that the Biblical Hebrew word *ywm* in the Old Testament does occur, among other things, as a designation for a cultic festal event.

---

[112] Cf. the literature referred to in the survey above notes 66-100.

[113] Cf. J. L. Mays, *Amos* (1969) 127.

[114] Of all the scholars who have commented upon this interesting text only S. Mowinckel (*Psalmenstudien* II (1922) 43, cf. also 190, 202, 213), H. S. Nyberg (*Studien zum Hoseabuche* (1935) 44), G. Östborn (*Yahweh and Baal* (1956) 34 and 42), and R. Vuilleumier-Bessard (*La tradition cultuelle* (1960) 44) take Hos 7, 5 as referring to a cultic event. Mowinckel, however, is the only one that reads the passage as a reference to a Yahwistic cult. In this I believe that he is right. The use of the word *ywm* as a designation for certain cultic feasts has interesting parallels in Akkadian (cf. B. Landsberger, *Der kultische Kalender der Babylonier und Assyrer* (1917) 12, R. Largement, H. Lemaitre, "Le jour de Yahweh dans le contexte oriental", *Sacra Pagina* (1959) 259-66). I will mention the most interesting of these parallels in more detail below.

In Mowinckel's discussion concerning the origin of the "Day of Yahweh" Assyrian/Babylonian religious texts played an important role. In fact, the Old Testament usage of *ywm* as a designation for a cultic feast does have interesting parallels in Akkadian religious texts. I shall be content to mention the most important ones.

A most interesting text is found in the series *Ludlul bēl nēmeqi*[115]. In tablet II, 16, the worshipper in his despair compares himself to the unhappy person who has not participated in the cult: *ib-ṭi-lu u4-mu ili i-še-ṭú eš-še-ši*, "who has done nothing on holy days, and despised sabbath". Yet, we read further on (1.25): "The day for reverencing the god (*u4-m pa-la-aḫ ilī^meš^*) was a joy to my heart". Although we cannot say for sure, it is possible that we here have a reference to the New Year Festival[116].

Another interesting text was published by F. Thureau-Dangin in 1922[117] and printed with a transliteration and translation the same year[118]. The text, which is an omen text copied by a priest in Uruk in the time of the Seleucids, concerns the ritual of the Akitu-festival. Obv. 20 to rev. 15 of the text contains 23 predictions concerning the *ūm il āli*, the "Day of the city god", and the possibility that it will rain, thunder, hail, storm, etc. on that day[119].

Still another Akkadian text, *K* 2801, obv. 40, has the expression *ūm ili* as a designation for certain cultic feasts[120].

Even more interesting in our connection are the texts which mention the name of a particular deity in relation to the "day". One such text is *K* 2302, which tells of the days of various gods[121].

In *CT* 29, 49, 1.28 we read: [*i-na Nipp*]*ur ina u4-mi ^il^Enlil*.., "in Nippur on the day of Enlil..."[122]. The reference is obviously to some cultic feast or celebration.

In a text published by V. Scheil[123] the "Day of Adar" is mentioned, and here, too, the reference must be to some cultic feast[124].

---

115 The quotations from this series are taken from W. G. Lambert, *Babylonian Wisdom Literature* (1960) 38-39. For earlier literature see *ibid.* 27-28.

116 See 1.26.

117 F. Thureau-Dangin, *Tablettes d'Uruk* (1922) nr. 9 (pl. XX). Cf. R. Borger, *Festschrift Böhl* (1973) 44f.

118 F. Thureau-Dangin, "Les fêtes d'Akitu", *RA* 19 (1922) 141-48.

119 Cf. E. Weidner, "Der Tag des Stadtgottes", *AfO* 14 (1941-44) 340-42.

120 First published by B. Meissner, "Die Bauinschriften Asarhaddons", *BASS* 3 (1898), obv. 40, p. 232, pl. 291. For a more up to date edition, see R. Borger, *Die Inschriften Asarhaddons* (1956) 81.

121 Published by C. Virolleaud, "Nouveaux fragments inédits", *Babyloniaca* 1 (1907) 201-03. A part of the text (lines 13-26, and not the part which interests us in this connection) is translated by Virolleaud, "Textes pour servire à l'histoire de la religion assyro-babylonienne", *RSEHA* 12 (1904) 270-71.

122 Cf. the edition of the duplicate Rm 155 in *ZDMG* 68 (1914).

123 V. Scheil, *Textes élamites-sémitiques* (1908) nr. 14, obv. 5.

124 *Op. cit.* nr. 70 and nr. 73.

The same goes for the texts *VAT* 4075 and *VAT* 4094 where the obligatory deliveries for the *ūm* ^{d}*Ellil* and *ūm* ^{d}*Bēl* are mentioned respectively[125].

Thus, for the background of the above-mentioned texts there can be no doubt that the assumption that *ywm* may be used as a designation for a cultic festal event in the Hebrew Bible is widely supported by Akkadian texts.

But how does this relate to the "Day of Yahweh" as a day of judgement and destruction which is how we meet the phenomenon in the message of the prophets?

According to the defenders of a cultic view of the "Day of Yahweh" a development has taken place from "day" being a designation for a cultic feast to it being a futuristic/eschatological idea where Yahweh destroys his enemies in battle[126].

However, a closer scrutiny of the texts and their contents reveals that there is no textual evidence in support of any such theory. This goes for both the Old Testament and the Akkadian texts[127]. "Day" as a designation for certain cultic feasts and "day" as a designation for the time when Yahweh destroys his enemies have generically nothing to do with each other. Both linguistic phenomena are easily understood within their own contexts and rather than to talk of a development from the one to the

[125] *VAS*, H. 5 (1908) Nr. 23 and Nr. 67.

[126] The classic study, of course, being S. Mowinckel, *Psalmenstudien* II (1922).

[127] Building so many of his theories on Akkadian parallels, Mowinckel postulated a similar development as having taken place within Assyrian-Babylonian religion with regard to the "day". He is able to point to a clear parallel in Akkadian in the expression "måtte din forferdelige dag nå dem" ("Jahves dag", *NTT* 59 (1958) 19), which he found in G. Hölscher, *Die Ursprünge der jüdischen Eschatologie* (1925) 13. Hölscher, however, does not say anything about where he took his text from. Even if the text undoubtedly belongs to the series *Maqlû*, the arrangement of the text is not quite like that of Tallqvist (K. Tallqvist, *Die assyrische Beschwörungsseries Maqlû* (1894) I, 117 and II, 121). The reading of Hölscher referred to by Mowinckel, "dein furchtbarer Tag möge sie erreichen", however, is the same as we find in Tallqvist. This text quoted by Mowinckel and Hölscher is the only text I have found which could be said to be comparable to the Biblical Hebrew usage of *ywm yhwh* where the destruction of enemies plays a main role. All the other occurrences of Akkadian *ūmu* in combination with some negative idea are not comparable (for references, see the article "*ūmu(m)*", *AHW* Lief. 15 (1979) 1419. The Assyrian-Babylonian hemerologies which have played a certain role in the discussion are not relevant (for references to literature on the hemerologies, see W. von Soden, *TWAT* III, Lief. 4/5 (1980) 562)). However, the one text referred to by Mowinckel and Hölscher does not carry any weight as evidence. Thus, the reading of "day" in this text has been rejected by Assyriologists. Already by the new edition of *Maqlû* in 1937. G. Meier had changed the reading of Tallqvist to "dein wütendes Wetter" (*Die assyrische Beschwörungssammlung Maqlû* (1937) 11 and 18). Even if other readings have been suggested (*CAD* 4 (1958) 433: *UD-ka ez-zu likšussunuti* - "may your fierce ūmu-demon catch them"), Meier's 1937 reading seems to have been commonly accepted (cf. Å. W. Sjöberg, E. Bergmann, *The Collection of the Sumerian Temple Hymns* (1969) 100, M.-J. Seux, *Hymnes et prières* (1976) 379). This takes the last of any credibility out of Mowinckel's Akkadian parallel.

other, one should realize that, based on what textual evidence we do have, the two linguistic usages of "day" have existed side by side. When we take into consideration the wide semantic range of the Semitic word for "day", there is nothing remarkable in this[128].

Another main argument for relating the "Day of Yahweh" to the cult has been the occurrence of *ywm zbḥ yhwh* in Zeph 1, 8[129]. But this text must be viewed along with other texts in the Old Testament which have *zbḥ* as a figure of speech for Yahweh's punishment. Thus, there is nothing cultic in the description of slaughter depicted in Is 34, 1-8. In this oracle against Edom *zbḥ* occurs in v. 6. The description of Yahweh's slaughter here reminds one of the description of the goddess Anath in the Ugaritic texts[130], and *may* be a reflection of the same mythological theme. The same goes for Ez 39, 17-20 (*zbḥ* in v. 17). The same theme is found also in the oracle against Egypt in Jer 46, where we have a description of the "Day of Yahweh" (*zbḥ* in the portrayal of the slaughter in v. 10). Rather than to translate *zbḥ* by "sacrifice" in these passages, the translation "slaughter" seems more appropriate.

The main aspect of these texts, however, is the aspect of war, and the fact that they appear in oracles against foreign nations. It may further be worth mentioning that we find exactly the same theme expressed in an Assyrian oracle against foreign nations[131].

The decisive reason for the great attraction of a cultic interpretation of the "Day of Yahweh" though, was Mowinckel's theory concerning the cultic origin of eschatology. No doubt connecting of the "Day of Yahweh" to the theories of Mowinckel of the enthronement festival of Yahweh at the great New Year festival must have had a fascinating effect on the scholarly world in the years following its publication[132]. The fact that Mowinckel himself was later to change his view on the nature of Israelite eschatology, does not seem to affect this[133]. When scholars take a cultic view of *ywm yhwh* they are more or less following the thesis developed by Mowinckel.

However, despite the power of attraction that Mowinckel's theory might have, it rests on insecure ground. Not only does it represent the

---

[128] See the survey of E. Jenni in *THAT* I[2] (1975) 707-26 and of W. von Soden, J. Bergman, M. Sæbø in *TWAT* III, Lief. 4-5 (1980) 559-86.

[129] *E.g.* S. Mowinckel, "Jahves dag", *NTT* 59 (1958) 7, J. Gray, "The Day of Yahweh", *SEÅ* 39 (1974) 29.

[130] In particular *CTA* 3, II, 4-41. Cf. most recently J. Gray, "The Blood Bath of the Goddess Anat in the Ras Shamra Texts", *Festschrift Schaeffer* (1979) 315-24.

[131] Cf. M. Weippert, ""Heiliger Krieg" in Israel und in Assyrien", *ZAW* 84 (1972) 481-82.

[132] For Mowinckel's theories concerning the Enthronement Festival, the origin of eschatology, and the "Day of Yahweh", see above all *Psalmenstudien* II (1922) 211-314.

[133] See above n. 71.

major problem of whether the ancient Israelites in fact did celebrate a New Year Festival the way we know the Assyrians and Babylonians did[134] but, regardless of the point of view which is taken in this matter, it remains a fact that the theory of the enthronement festival and the rites connected to it according to Mowinckel must be regarded as highly hypothetical and without any base in the texts of the Old Testament. Admittedly, the theories of that scholarly giant Sigmund Mowinckel *are* attractive. In this matter, however, the texts themselves must be the sole judges.

This brings us to the other major theory concerning the origin of the "Day of Yahweh", viz. that of Gerhard von Rad, who sees the origin of *ywm yhwh* in the "holy war" traditions of pre-monarchical Israel[135].

Taking as our starting point the texts themselves, it may seem that the theory of von Rad provides us with a reasonable explanation for the origin of the "Day of Yahweh" in the prophets. As we have seen[136], the descriptions of *ywm yhwh* in the prophetic literature are primarily descriptions of war-like events. And the war-motif does play an all-important role in the early traditions of Israel[137], having led to the terminology "holy war"[138].

With "holy war", however, von Rad did not mean *any* "holy war". To him "holy war" in the Old Testament constituted a particular Israelite institution without parallels in the surrounding cultures, and closely connected to the alleged institution of the "amphictyony"[139].

Recent research, however, has not only made it clear that the classical amphictyony-theory as developed by Noth[140] cannot any longer be upheld[141], but also that the views of von Rad concerning the institution of "holy war" must be revised completely. Thus, M. Weippert has

---

[134] See D. J. A. Clines, "New Year", *IDBS* (1976) 627f.

[135] G. von Rad, "The Origin of the Concept of the Day of Yahweh", *JSS* 4 (1959) 97-108, *Theologie des Alten Testaments* II (1961) 133-37.

[136] See above pp. 95-96 and *passim.*

[137] In addition to the classic study of G. von Rad, *Der heilige Krieg* (1951), the most recent monographs on the subject are R. Smend, *Jahwekrieg und Stämmebund* (1963) and F. Stolz, *Jahwes und Israels Kriege* (1972). For an extensive bibliography, see M. Weippert, "Heiliger Krieg in Israel und in Assyrien", *ZAW* 84 (1972) 463, n. 13.

[138] The designation "Holy War", of course, should be taken as a rather wide term applying to all warfare which involves religion.

[139] G. von Rad, *Der Heilige Krieg* (1951).

[140] M. Noth, *Das System der Zwölf Stämme Israels* (1930).

[141] Of the authors who have criticized the amphictyony thesis I may mention N. P. Lemche, *Israel i dommertiden* (1972). The book by Lemche is also worth noticing for its evaluation of the Greek evidence (cf. by the same author, "The Greek "Amphictyony" – Could it be a Prototype for the Israelite Society in the Period of the Judges?" *JSOT* 4 (1977) 48-59), A. D. H. Mayes, *Israel in the Period of the Judges* (1974), C. H. J. de Geus, *The Tribes of Israel* (1976).

demonstrated quite convincingly that holy war ideology is a common Ancient Near Eastern phenomenon (also in the whole of the ancient world, for that matter)[142]. In ancient warfare the gods would always play an important part, and for this reason it is impossible to make any distinction between "profane" and "holy" war in the ancient world. One important consequence of this with regard to the Old Testament is that the ideology of "holy war" did not cease to exist in Israel with the introduction of the monarchy, as von Rad had assumed. The importance of the article by Weippert can hardly be exaggerated when we know for a fact that the views of von Rad have gone down in the history of research as the official view of the scholarly world on "holy war" in ancient Israel.

The fact that the views of von Rad concerning the institution of "holy war" in ancient Israel cannot any longer be upheld does not, however, affect the connection between the "Day of Yahweh" and "holy war" terminology which we find in the texts. Our problem is how this relationship is to be understood. As we shall see, a possible solution to this problem may be found in the institution which produced the texts in which we find the idea of *ywm yhwh* represented, namely the institution of ancient Israelite prophecy itself.

4.3.3.2. The "*Sitz im Leben*" of the "Day of Yahweh" in the Prophets

As demonstrated above[143], the most conspicuous trait about the *ywm yhwh* passages is that they occur in oracles against foreign nations. Consequently, the next step is to assume that the relationship of the prophets to the "Day of Yahweh" must be sought in the oracles against the foreign nations.

When glancing through the secondary literature on ancient Israelite prophecy, one is indeed surprised to find that so little attention has been paid to the matter of the oracles against foreign nation[144]. Despite the fact

---

[142] M. Weippert, ""'Heiliger Krieg" in Israel und Assyrien", *ZAW* 84 (1972) 460-93. Cf. also N. Gottwald, "War, Holy", *IDBS* (1976) 942-44. Also the book by F. Stolz (above n. 137) is in agreement with many of the criticisms put forward by Weippert with regard to the theories of von Rad (and Smend, above n. 137) concerning the institution of "Holy War".

[143] See above p. 97.

[144] Thus, the now classic work by C. Westermann, *Grundformen prophetischer Rede* (1960) deals only very briefly with the matter. In fact, we may even read in this otherwise excellent book that the view of Gunkel (see H. Schmidt, *Die grossen Propheten* (1915) IL) that the oracles against the foreign nations is the basic prophetic speech form has been a hindrance to prophetic research (*op. cit.* 18). The present writer, however, is more inclined to agree with Gunkel in this matter than with Westermann (of the literature on the oracles against the foreign nations that we do have, see above Chapter 2, n. 2 and below n. 147).

that these oracles occupy large parts of the message of the prophets[145] the commentators of the prophetic books have mainly been interested in the prophets as proclaimers of doom and destruction to their own people. But obviously the oracles against the nations as uttered by the classic prophets of ancient Israel must have had a *function* or they would hardly have occupied such a dominant place in their message.

Among the scholars engaged in the study of the oracles against the nations in the books of the prophets interest has mainly centred around the question of origin. Most commonly the origin of the oracles against the nations is found in the "holy war" traditions of pre-monarchical Israel[146]. In the pre-monarchical situation the role of prophets in connection with the "holy war" is indisputable[147]. In addition to the Old Testament evidence we also now know quite a few extra-biblical sources which may throw interesting light upon this connection between prophecy and "holy war" in the Ancient Near East[148].

What, now, of the relationship of the earlier prophets to the later, so-called classic ones? Traditionally, ever since the days of Gustav Hölscher[149] the Old Testament scholarly world has drawn a sharp line between the early and the late prophets of Israel[150]. However, there can be no doubt that this differentiation of scholars between early and classic prophecy cannot be upheld, at least not to the degree that it has been

[145] *E.g.* Am 1, 1-2, 3, Is 13-23, Jer 46-51, Ez 25-31. In fact, *all* the prophetic books in the Old Testament, with the exception of the Book of Hosea, contain oracles against the foreign nations.

[146] A classic study is that of R. Bach, *Die Aufforderungen zur Flucht und zum Kampf im alttestamentlichen Prophetenspruch* (1962). The major weakness of this otherwise excellent study is that the author is too dependent upon the theories of von Rad concerning the institution of "Holy War". This has prevented him from drawing several interesting conclusions from his material.

[147] Cf. J. S. Ackermann, "Prophecy and Warfare in Early Israel", *BASOR* 220 (1975) 5-13, J. H. Hayes, "The Usage of Oracles against Foreign Nations", *JBL* 87 (1968) 81ff.

[148] A survey of the most important extra-biblical evidence relating to biblical prophecy is found in H. B. Huffmon, "Prophecy in the Ancient Near East", *IDBS* (1976) 697-700. The most important texts outside the Bible itself are those found at ancient Mari (see in addition to the literature mentioned by Huffmon in particular, A. Malamat, "Prophetic Revelations in New Documents from Mari and the Bible" *Volume du Congrès*: *Genève* 1965 (1966) 207-27, E. Ellermeier, *Prophetie in Mari und Israel* (1968), W. L. Moran, "New Evidence from Mari on the History of Prophecy", *Bib* 50 (1969) 15-56, J. S. Holladay, "Assyrian Statecraft and the Prophets of Israel", *HThR* 63 (1970) 29-51, J. F. Ross, "Prophecy in Hamath, Israel, and Mari", *HThR* 63 (1970) 1-28). One of the most recent commentators on the relationship between Mari and Israelite prophecy, E. Noort, has rightly warned against making too much out of the comparisons (*Untersuchungen zum Gottesbescheid in Mari* (1977), 92 and *passim.*

[149] G. Hölscher, *Die Propheten* (1914).

[150] C. Westermann, "Propheten", *BHH* 3 (1966) 1496-1512 presents us with a pretty accurate description of how the scholarly world in general sees the relationship between early and late prophecy.

done[151]. There are, in fact, more similarities than differences between the two, the main difference being that of the earlier prophets we have records of their doings, but few words, whereas in the case of the later prophets the matter is the reverse; we do have their words, but the records about them are restricted to what scattered information we find in their own words[152].

On the background of the researches of Stolz and Weippert on holy warfare in ancient Israel, and on the background of the relationship between the "Day of Yahweh" and the oracles against the nations and "holy war", as well as on the background of the continuity between early and late prophecy, we shall have to assume that the oracles against the nations in the prophetic books, including the words about the "Day of Yahweh", reflect the fact that the classic prophets of ancient Israel also were exercising the ancient task of intermediating between Yahweh and the people in times of war.

True enough, the pronouncement of doom against the prophets' own fellow countrymen occupy a large part of their message. As we have seen in the case of Amos, this phenomenon served missionary purposes[153]. This main task of the prophets, however, does not necessarily exclude or contradict their other task as intercessors in times of war and crisis[154]. The assumption that the prophets of the 8th and the 7th centuries, in addition to preaching doom and social justice to their fellow countrymen also performed prophetic tasks of the kind mentioned above, in fact provides us with the only acceptable solution to the problem of the oracles against the foreign nations which otherwise must be regarded as totally extraneous elements in the prophetic books[155].

This assumption has support in the Old Testament texts also. The word of Jeremiah in his encounter with Hananiah in Jer 28, 8 presents us with the prophet's own definition of prophecy (irrespective of the context of this particular episode):

---

[151] Among scholars who have warned against making a too sharp distinction between the earlier and the later prophets of ancient Israel we find names like J. Lindblom, *Prophecy in Ancient Israel* (1962), A. Malamat, "Prophetic Revelations" *Volume du Congrès: Genève 1965* (1966) 208, n. 2, J. A. Soggin, *Introduction to the Old Testament* (1976) 216ff. Concerning the background of the present prevailing interest in prophecy and tradition, it may seem strange that the sharp distinction between "primitive" and "classic" prophetism is still widespread.

[152] Cf. K. Baltzer, *Die Biographie der Propheten* (1975) 107ff.

[153] See above p. 58ff. It should not be overlooked in this connection that we find the very same phenomenon in earlier prophecy also (see *e.g.* the story of Elijah in I Kings 21, 17-26, or the story of Micaiah in I Kings 22, 13-23).

[154] Cf. *inter alia* above p. 85.

[155] Cf. also above pp. 11-14, 85, 97, 101.

> "The prophets that were before you and before me from ancient times prophesied against many countries and against great kingdoms war, disaster, and pestilence."

Equally illustrative is a passage like Jer 21, 2. We read how Jerusalem is besieged, and how the king sends an official and a priest to Jeremiah:

> "Ask (*drš-nʾ*) Yahweh for us, because Nebuchadrezzar, king of Babylon, is making war with us. Perhaps Yahweh will do with us according to his wonderful deeds and make him withdraw from us."

The main point of the story, as has been demonstrated by scholars[156], is that Yahweh does not help against the enemy, but that he sides with him against the inhabitants of Jerusalem. The information offered to us in this story, however, also shows us something else which is of importance, namely that the task of the prophets in the days of Jeremiah in times of war was the very same as it was with the early Israelite prophets: to intercede with Yahweh on behalf of his people[157]. If this had not been the case, it is highly unlikely that the king would have addressed himself to Jeremiah in the first instance. That the prophet, when asked, does not give the expected answer is quite another matter[158].

Consequently rather than stress that the oracles against the nations and the "Day of Yahweh" have their *origin* in the "holy war" traditions of Israel, one should accept as a fact that they also in their *present* context constitute a part of what has been termed "holy war". "Holy war" never ceased to exist in Israel until after Israel ceased to exist as a nation. It was not until the Israelites ceased to make war at all that these and other traditions which we find in the prophetic writings could become "eschatological" and thus released from their original *Sitz im Leben*[159].

What, then, was the *Sitz im Leben* of the prophetic oracles against the foreign nations, the context within which we also find the words of the prophets concerning the "Day of Yahweh", the terrible day when Yahweh is going to destroy his enemies in battle?

The most likely place to search for the *Sitz im Leben* of this prophetic activity is the public lament[160]. This was the occasion when people and priests congregated in times of crisis to ask Yahweh for help. In ancient

---

[156] Cf. J. A. Soggin, "Der prophetische Gedanke über den Heiligen Krieg", *VT* 10 (1960) 79-83, H. Weippert "Jahwekrieg und Bundesfluch in Jer 21, 1-7", *ZAW* 82 (1970) 396-409.

[157] Cf. n. 47 above. Cf. also Jer 7, 16, Mi 3, 5.

[158] Cf. above p. 85ff.

[159] One of the conclusions to be drawn from this is that eschatology is basically a late phenomenon in the religious history of Israel. On the complicated discussion of Old Testament "eschatology" we have a fine introduction in *Eschatologie im Alten Testament.* Hg. v. H. D. Preuss (1978).

[160] Cf. above n. 46. Cf. also above pp. 82-88.

Israel the worst disaster alongside the lack of rain for the fields was without doubt war. In those times of crisis it was the task of the prophet to interpret the words of Yahweh to the people and to encourage them in their distress[161]. A classic example is the story in Jud 20, 26-28[162]. Equally illustrative is the story told in Jer 21, 2[163]. A further text worth noting in this connection is Ps 74, 9. In this public lament the priest complains to Yahweh:

> "Our signs (*ʾwttynw*) we do not see. There is no longer any prophet (*nbyʾ*), and there is no one among us that knows for how long"[164].

Obviously this text must not be taken as evidence for the non-existence of prophecy in Israel at the time the lament was composed. What we have here is more likely a figure of speech which underlines the distress of the situation. In all likelihood the prophet was introduced on the scene after this complaint of the priest. Of particular interest is further the fact that the term *ʾwttynw* most probably refers to "holy war"[165].

The most convincing evidence in favour of the assumption that the oracles against the nations and the "Day of Yahweh" in the prophets have the public lament as their *Sitz im Leben*, however, follows from the fact that at least three of the passages in which references to the "Day of Yahweh" occur are found within the context of the public lament. These three texts are Is 13, 6, Ez 30, 3 and, above all, Joel 1, 14-15.

Consequently the question whether or not the "Day of Yahweh" is cultic ought to be viewed in another light. The term cultic used in connection with *ywm yhwh* was always identified with Mowinckel's view concerning the "day". However, von Rad too claimed that *ywm yhwh* was cultic in as much as the institution of "holy war" was embedded in different accompanying rites. And if the idea of the "Day of Yahweh" is to be connected with the ancient Israelite public lament, it must also be regarded as cultic, *i.e.* related to the institution of Yahweh worship and accompanied by certain rites.

The main problems in relation to the assumption that the "Day of Yahweh" is located within the oracles against foreign nations and belongs within the institution of the public lament are centred in the public lament itself. In fact, we are rather ignorant when it comes to the details regarding this cultic institution. That the public lament was performed in times of crisis we do know[166]. But was it performed in times of

[161] Cf. above p. 85ff.
[162] See above p. 86.
[163] See above p. 106.
[164] Cf. Lam 2, 9, Ez 7, 26.
[165] H.-J. Kraus, *Psalmen* B. 1 (1966) 517.
[166] See above p. 84.

crisis only? Could it not also be possible that the public lament formed part of the rituals performed at the regular cultic feasts in ancient Israel, as a kind of prophylactic ritual, so to speak? If this is the case, the theories of Mowinckel concerning the "Day of Yahweh" will also have to be taken into consideration. This is so irrespective of one's view of Mowinckel's theories concerning the enthronement festival or the New Year Festival[167].

Unfortunately, our knowledge is these matters is very restricted, and we shall have to await future research into the important cultic institution of the public lament before anything more definite can be said about the problem.

4.3.4. Amos 5, 18-20

With this background information we can now turn to the words of Amos concerning the "Day of Yahweh". Immediately after he has described to the Israelites how they are to participate in the public lament when Yahweh has taken fertility away from them (vv. 16-17)[168], Amos says concerning the "Day of Yahweh" in 5, 18-20:

> "Woe[169] to those who long for (*hmtʾwym*) the day of Yahweh! What will the day of Yahweh be to you? It is darkness (*ḥšk*) and not light (*ʾwr*). It is as when a man runs from a lion, and a bear meets him, or he comes home and leans his hand on the wall, and a snake bites him.

[167] *Psalmenstudien* II (1922) 211-314.

[168] For the text, see above pp. 81-82.

[169] The woe-form was probably taken over by the prophets from quite another sphere of life. The debate about the original "*Sitz im Leben*" of this form, however, clearly shows that scholars have been unable to agree. Thus, S. Mowinckel maintained that the origin of the woe oracle was the curse (*Psalmenstudien* V (1923) 2, 119ff). In this he was followed *inter alia* by C. Westermann (*Grundformen prophetischer Rede* (1960)136-42). E. Gerstenberger, on the other side, attempted to demonstrate that the woe oracle, as well as the bliss oracle, stemmed from the wise men's reflections about the conditions of the world ("The Woe-Oracles of the Prophets", *JBL* 81 (1962) 249-63). Among his followers we find H. W. Wolff, (*Amos' geistige Heimat* (1964) 12-23, *Dodekapropheton* 2 (1969) 298). Whereas Gerstenberger pointed to the different functions of the woe oracle in the wisdom traditions, Wolff is of the opinion that it ultimately goes back to the lament over the dead. That the woe oracle has its origin in the lament for the dead is, as far as I am able to judge, the most likely solution to the problem. Obviously there is no need to limit its function to the wisdom traditions of the clans. Among the scholars who have assumed that the woe oracle has its origin in the lament over the dead, we find R. J. Clifford, "The Use of HÔY in the Prophets", *CBQ* 28 (1966) 458-64 and W. Janzen, *Mourning Cry and Woe-Oracle* (1972). Whereas the majority of scholars assumes that the two interjections *ʾwy* and *hwy* are used identically, G. Wanke has attempted to demonstrate that a distinction should be made between the two ("*ʾwy* and *hwy*", *ZAW* 78 (1966) 215-18). According to Wanke, *ʾwy* is to be understood as a cry of dread, lamentation and peril, whereas *hwy* stems from the lamentation for the dead. I do not believe that this distinction is necessary. For a survey of the occurrences of *hwy* in the Bible, see H.-J. Zobel, "*hwy*", *TWAT* II (1977) 382-88.

> Is not the day of Yahweh darkness (*ḥšk*) and not light (*ʾwr*), and gloom (*ʾpl*) with no brightness (*ngh*) in it?"

The woe utterance contained in Am 5, 18-20 is a pronouncement of doom to those who "long for" the "Day of Yahweh". Again we see how the prophet has directed his words *against* the Israelites, rather than against their "enemies", *i.e.* the group or groups whom they themselves expected to be struck by that terrible "Day of Yahweh". The wrath of Yahweh was not expected to turn against those who worshipped him in the cult. This is also the reasons why the people had "longed for" *ywm yhwh*.

A reflection of the same usage of *hitpaʿel* of *ʾwh*, "to long for", "to wish", is found in a most interesting text in Jer 17. I quote vv. 14-18:

> "Heal me, Yahweh, and I shall be healed. Save me, and I shall be saved. For you are my praise. Look! They say to me: Where is the word of Yahweh? Let it come! But I did not fail to follow you as a shepherd, I did not long for (*htʾwyty*) a day of disaster (*ʾnwš*). You know that what came forth from my lips was in front of you. Do not be a terror to me, you are my refuge on the day of disaster (*rʿh*). Let my persecutors be put to shame, but let not me be put to shame, let them be terrified, but let not me be terrified. Bring upon them a day of disaster (*rʿh*) and destroy them with double destruction."

The similarities between this text in Jeremiah and the one of Am 5, 18-20 are not difficult to see. Even if there is no direct mention of *ywm yhwh* in the Jeremiah text, the very same idea of the destruction of one's opponents is expressed through the formulas *ywm ʾnwš* and *ywm rʿh*[170]. The language of Jeremiah in this prayer represents exactly the kind of language which we find in the laments in the Book of Psalms[171]. The prophet is here using the stereotype language of the cult when expressing his own personal needs. From our two examples, Jer 17, 14-18 and Am 5, 18-20, may we perhaps guess that the wish or longing for the day of disaster for one's enemies was a fixed formula in the lament? Such an assumption, however, must be regarded as highly hypothetical when considering how meagre our evidence is.

In 5, 18-20, however, Amos makes it quite clear to his audience, as Jeremiah did during the siege of Nebuchadrezzar[172], that the wrath of Yahweh may very well turn against the Israelites rather than being a help and support to them. He does this by stating the negative aspect of the "Day of Yahweh" as we know it from the descriptions in the Old Testa-

[170] That *ywm rʿh* may have the same function as *ywm yhwh* is seen *inter alia* in Jer 51, 2. In this oracle against Babylon *ywm rʿh* is described as an event of war.

[171] W. Rudolph, *Jeremia* (1968) 117-19.

[172] See above p. 106.

ment of *ywm yhwh*[173]: the "day" is darkness and not light. The pronouncement that the "Day of Yahweh" is "darkness, and not light" is the only information we get regarding this event in the message of Amos, and if it had not been for the fact that we have further descriptions of *ywm yhwh* in the words of other prophets, we should not have known very much about the phenomenon at all. It may well be that the portrayal of darkness and cosmic disturbances in connection with the "Day of Yahweh" is related to the description of Yahweh's theophany that we know from the Old Testament, ultimately stemming from ancient Canaanite lore[174], but most probably belonging within the common Ancient Near Eastern vocabulary to express chaos, disorder, and lack of prosperity[175].

In the present context the negative description of *ywm yhwh* is further stressed through thc use of the simile of a man who flees from a lion, but meets a bear, or who believes himself to have arrived home safely, and is bitten by a snake. These comparisons, probably taken from the wisdom traditions[176], underline what the prophet has already said about those who "long for" the "Day of Yahweh". Those who believe that they are safe on this day will find that the day is a disaster to them.

If the assumption that the idea of the "Day of Yahweh" belongs within the ritual of the public lament is correct, this opens the possibility of a connection between .vv. 16-17, which depicts a public lament, and the pronouncement on *ywm yhwh* in vv. 18-20. In fact, both vv. 16-17 and vv. 18-20 are more easily understood when we read them in the light of each other. With the "Woe" of 5, 18 Amos turns the "Woe! Woe!" of the people in vv. 16-17 back on themselves. Not only will there be drought and disaster in the land, but what is even worse is that all their lamenting is only going to add to their disaster.

---

[173] See above pp. 93-97.

[174] Cf. Hab 3, 11. I disagree with those who take this passage to be late (*e.g.* J. Jeremias, *Theophanie* (1965) 98). Even if it may be late in the present context, we have to do with an ancient theme.

[175] With regard to the Old Testament the classic study is S. Aalen, *Licht und Finsternis* (1951). Of more recent literature, admittedly of uneven quality, I mention: J. Hempel, "Die Lichtsymbolik im Alten Testament", *StGen* 13 (1960) 352-68, *id.*, "Licht, Heil und Heilung im biblischen Denken", *Antaios* 2 (1961) 375-88, R. Von Ungern-Sternberg, "Die Bezeichnungen "Licht" und "Finsternis" im Alten Testament', *DtPfrBL* 65 (1965) 642-46, A. P. B. Breytenbach, "The Connection between the Concepts of Darkness and Drought as well as Light and Vegetation", *De fructu oris sui* (1971) 1-5. Cf. also S. Aalen, "*ʾwr*", *TWAT* I (1973) 160-82. See further W. von Soden, "Licht und Finsternis in der sumerischen und assyrisch-babylonischen Religion", *StGen* 13 (1960) 647-53, H. Ringgren, "Light and Darkness in Ancient Egyptian Religion", *Liber Amicorum* (1969) 140-50, C. J. Bleeker, "Some Remarks on the Religious Significance of Light", *JANES* 5 (1973) 23-34.

[176] H. W. Wolff, *Amos' geistige Heimat* (1964) 11.

4.4. *Amos and the Sacrificial Cult.* 5, 21-24

After the prophet has uttered his words about how the "Day of Yahweh" is going to turn out a disaster for the Israelites, he continues his criticism of their religious activities by attacking their sacrificial cult. We read in 5, 21-24:

> "I hate, I despise your feasts (*ḥgykm*)[177]. I will not smell your sacred assemblies (*ʿṣrtykm*)[178]. Even if you offer me burnt offerings (*tʿlw-ly ʿlwt*[179])...[180]. I am not pleased with your cereal offerings (*mnḥtykm*)[181], nor do I take any delight in the communion offering (*šlm*)[182] of fattened beasts. Take away from me the noise of your songs (*šryk*)[183], I will not listen to the tunes of your stringed instruments (*nblyk*)[184]. Let justice (*mšpṭ*) roll like water and righteousness (*ṣdqh*) like an ever-flowing stream."

It is a well known theme in the prophetic preaching that we meet with here. Besides Am 4, 4-5, one has only to think of passages like Is 1, 10-17, Jer 6, 20; 7, 21-23; 14, 12, Hos 6, 6, Mi 6, 6-8 to see that we have a pattern.

Formerly, these and similar statements in the prophetic books were regarded as indications that the prophets denounced all cultic activity on the whole. The originator and foremost exponent of this strongly negative attitude to the cult was Julius Wellhausen, whose understanding of "der ethische Monotheismus der Propheten" was quite incompatible with any positive evaluation of the cult[185]. In the years following the publication of Wellhausen's book the majority of scholars were to accept his views concerning the relationship between cult and prophetism[186].

---

[177] Cf. the survey with a comprehensive bibliography by G. J. Botterweck, B. Kedar-Kopfstein, "*ḥag*", *TWAT* II (1977) 730-44.

[178] Cf. Is 1, 13, Joel 1, 14. The term is used of the seventh day of the Mazzoth-festival (Deut 16, 8) and of the eighth day of the Feast of Booths (Lev 23, 36, Num 29, 35, Neh 8, 18, 2 Chr 7, 9). In II Kings 10, 20 it is used of a Baʿal festival. Cf. E. Kutsch, "Die Wurzel *ʿṣr* im Hebräischen", *VT* 2 (1952) 57-69, in particular 69.

[179] On this sacrifice cf. R. de Vaux, *Les sacrifices de l'Ancien Testament* (1964) 28-48, R. Rendtorff, *Studien zur Geschichte des Opfers im Alten Testament* (1967) 74-118.

[180] MT is corrupt. For a survey of the different suggestions regarding the attempt to restore the text, see H. W. Wolff, *Dodekapropheton* II (1969) 303-04.

[181] On this sacrifice cf. R. Rendtorff, *Studien zur Geschichte des Opfers im Alten Testament* (1967) 119-33.

[182] Cf. on this sacrifice R. de Vaux, *Les sacrifices de l'Ancien Testament* (1964) 28-48. The sacrificial term occurs in the singular only here in Amos.Cf., however, W. Eisenbeis, *Die Wurzel šlm im Alten Testment* (1969) 72-73.

[183] Cf. R. Ficker, "*šīr*", *THAT* II (1976) 895-98.

[184] This instrument, probably a kind of a harp, is often mentioned in the Old Testament in cultic contexts (cf. 1 Sam 10, 5, 2 Sam 6, 5, Pss 57, 9; 81, 3; 92, 4; 108, 3; 150, 3; Neh 12, 27, etc.).

[185] J. Wellhausen, *Israelitische und jüdische Geschichte*[3] (1897) 110-13.

[186] See *e.g.* E. Sellin, *Das Zwölfprophetenbuch* (1922) 53 and *passim*, A. Weiser, *Die Prophetie des Amos* (1929) 318-19.

Here, too, the man to go against the crowd was Sigmund Mowinckel. In his epoch-making studies in the Book of Psalms, Mowinckel attempted to demonstrate that the cult constituted the very centre of religious life in ancient Israel[187]. After Mowinckel the pendulum was to swing in the opposite direction, especially in Scandinavia where the strong appreciation of the cult was to become a main characteristic of any approach to the Old Testament.

The basic content of this new view on the cult critical passages in the prophets is that when the prophets denounce the cultic feasts and the offerings of the people they are not denouncing the cult *an sich*, but only the perverted and syncretistic usages of the cult, stemming from the Canaanite Baᶜal cult, or that they are also criticizing an empty cult where the worshippers participate automatically at the same time as they ignore the ethical and social commandments of Yahwch. This is more or less, where the problem now stands, even if not everyone can agree that the final solution to this intricate problem has been reached[188].

If we take a closer look at the passages in which the prophets speak critically of the cult and let these texts speak for themselves, one is in fact tempted to say Wellhausen was right. Indeed some of these polemical passages against the cult seem at first glance to indicate that the prophets wanted to reject the cultic celebrations entirely.

On the other hand, one should not assume beforehand that all the anti-cult polemical utterances of the prophets are of the same kind and state the same idea. A passage like Mal 1, 10 gives us an indication of this. In this late verse, stemming from the Persian period, we have the approximate words of the classic prophets regarding the cult. The meaning of the apparently anti-cult criticism of this author, however, is rather a lofty appraisal of the cultic services, and has nothing to do with the ideas concerning the cult which we find in the period of classic prophecy. What is being criticized in Mal 1, 10 is the use of faulty sacrificial animals, not the cult itself. The cult is being condemned only because the regulations concerning the quality of the sacrificial animals were neglected by the

[187] For a summing up of the views of Mowinckel on the role of the cult in the religion of ancient Israel, see his book *Religion og kultus* (1950).

[188] Of the vast literature on the subject cf. P. Volz, "Die radikale Ablehnung der Kultreligion durch die alttestamentlichen Propheten", *ZSTh* 14 (1937) 63-85, A. S. Kapelrud, "Cult and Prophetic Words", *StTh* 4 (1950) 5-12, H. H. Rowley, "Ritual and the Hebrew Prophets", *JSS* 1 (1956) 338-60, R. Hentsche, *Die Stellung der vorexilischen Schriftpropheten zum Kultus* (1957), E. Würthwein, "Kultpolemik oder Kultbescheid", *Tradition und Situation* (1963) 115-37, M. J. Buss, "The meaning of "Cult" and the Interpretation of the Old Testament", *JBR* 32 (1964) 317-25, H.-J. Hermisson, *Sprache und Ritus im altisraelitischen Kult* (1965), M. Sekine, "Das Problem der Kultpolemik bei den Propheten", *EvTh* 28 (1968) 605-09, H. Schüngel-Straumann, *Gottesbild und Kultkritik vorexilischer Propheten* (1972).

priests (cf. Lev 22, 22-25). Clearly, this is not the same kind of criticism which we find in the prophets.

The fact that such different attitudes can be hidden behind seemingly quite similar words concerning the sacrificial cult makes it necessary to take a closer look at the meaning and context of the different anti-cult passages in the prophetic literature. For the sake of simplicity I shall quote only the most important texts.

In the prophet Hosea, the contemporary of Amos, we read in 6, 4-6:

> "What shall I do with you, Ephraim? What shall I do with you, Judah? Your loyalty (*ḥsd*) is like a morning cloud, like the dew that goes away quickly. Therefore, I have kept (them down) through the prophets, slaughtered them by the words of my mouth...[189]. For I desire loyalty (*ḥsd*) and not sacrifice (*zbḥ*), knowledge of god rather than burnt offerings (*ᶜlwt*)."

Immediately after this passage of complaints regarding the loyalty of the Israelites there follows the declaration of the prophet that the people have violated the covenant (*bryt*). This brings the statement of the prophet in close connection with Deuteronomic thought, the phraseology of this last declaration being clearly Deuteronomic[190].

We note with interest that the words of Hosea against the sacrificial cult are far less strict than those of Amos quoted above. Hosea simply states that there are certain qualities which Yahweh wants from the Israelites other than the cultic ones (cf. 4, 1). It is more appropriate to say that this prophet makes the value of the cult relative than to claim that he rejects it. Concerning the background to the preaching of the prophet Hosea in general, as well as the background to the statement in 6, 4-6 that the loyalty of the Israelites is "like a morning cloud" and "like the dew that goes away quickly", the most obvious assumption is that the cult-critical words of this prophet in 6, 4-6 concern the non-Yahwistic or Yahwistic/syncretistic cultic rites in which the Israelites participated. This said, it may seem strange that Hosea does not use stronger words against the cult.

We further read in Mi 6, 6-8:

> "With what shall I come before Yahweh, bow down before God on high? Should I come before him with burnt offering (*ᶜwlwt*), with one year old calves? Will he be pleased with thousands of rams, or ten thousand rivers of oil? Should I give my first-born for my transgression, the fruit of my body for the sin of my soul?—He has told you, man, what is good, and what Yahweh requires from you: to do justice (*mšpṭ*) and to love loyalty (*ḥsd*) and to walk humbly with your god."

---

[189] MT has here further: *wmšpṭyk ᵓwr yṣᵓ*, which does not seem to be meaningful in the context.

[190] M. Weinfeld, *Deuteronomy and the Deuteronomic School* (1972) 367 and 340 nr. 5.

These words of Micah do not seem to stand in any particular context or to be addressed to any particular audience. They are rather to be regarded as a general theological statement of the prophet[191]. For this reason we do not get any clue from the context for the meaning of the passage. As it stands, however, the passage in Micah seems to imply more or less the same as the passage from Hosea quoted above does: Yahweh does not require sacrificial offerings. This does not mean that he *rejects* them; they are, however, unnecessary.

Also this passage in Micah is ideologically closely related to the thought of Deuteronomy. Particularly striking are the resemblances between what is said in Mi 6, 8 and Deut 10, 12 (cf. also 6, 5).

A more comprehensive argument against the cultic sacrifices is found in Is 1, 11-17:

> "What are all your sacrifices (*zbḥykm*) to me, says Yahweh. I am sated with burnt offerings (*ᶜlwt*) of rams and the fat of calves. I am not pleased with the blood of bulls or lambs or goats. When you come to see[192] my face, who demands this from you: the trampling down of my courts? Do not continue to bring worthless cereal offerings (*mnḥt-šwʾ*). This is a disgusting incense to me. New Moon and Sabbath, assemblies! I cannot endure wickedness and feast (together). My soul hates your New Moons and your festivals. They are a burden to me. I am tired of bearing (them). When you stretch out your hands, I will hide my eyes from you. Even when you multiply your prayers, I will not listen. Your hands are full of blood. Wash and make yourselves clean. Take away the evil of your doings from before my eyes. Cease to do evil. Learn to do good. Seek justice (*mspṭ*), assist the oppressed[193], help the fatherless to his right, plead for the widow."

This text of Isaiah is comprehensive enough to provide us with a full explanation of the attitude of the prophet towards the sacrificial cult. As compared to the words of Hosea in 6, 4-6 or the words of Micah in 6, 6-8 these words of Isaiah seem to be more negative. In this way they are more similar to the words of Amos in 5, 21-24. In fact, it may seem as if Amos and Isaiah do reject sacrifices on the whole. After Mowinckel's research, however, this is unlikely to be the case.

The passage Is 1, 11-17 also informs us why the prophet denounces the cult: the participants in the sacrificial rites follow the rules laid down for the cultic celebrations, but they do not follow the rules laid down by Yahweh for moral and social behaviour. Able to bring the offerings, they are at the same time unable to do justice towards the weaker ones among

---

[191] Cf. J. L. Mays, *Micah* (1976) 138.

[192] Reading *lirʾôṯ* with one Syriac ms.

[193] The passive reading is not the one of MT, but is has support from several of the versions.

their fellow citizens. But the cult is worthless when its participants have blood on their hands.

The conclusion we have to draw from Is 1, 11-17 does not imply that the prophet is altogether critical of the cult. There is no reason why he should not accept the cultic celebrations of the people if at the same time they fulfill the ethical demands of Yahweh.

We have noted above the striking similarities between the critical passages in Hosea and Micah to certain ideas and phrases in Deuteronomy. Also Is 1, 11-17 shares common elements with Deuteronomy. Thus, the regulations concerning the rights of the fatherless and the widow[194] play an important role in Deuteronomy[195]. It is further worth mentioning that the word *ṭrḥ*, "burden" in Is 1, 14 occurs elsewhere in the Old Testament only in Deut 1, 12.

Another interesting feature of Is 1, 11-17 is the close similarity between v. 15 and Jer 14, 12[196], and between v. 16 and Am 5, 14-15[197].

The last prophet to be taken into account with regard to the relationship of the prophets to the cultic sacrifices is Jeremiah. In Jer 6, 20 we read:

> "What is frankincense brought from Sheba or fragrant cane from a distant country? Your burnt offerings (*ᶜlwtykm*) are not acceptable, and your communion offerings (*zbḥykm*) do not please me."

This statement by Jeremiah gives expression to the general disapproval of Yahweh concerning the sacrifices of the people. The passage appears apparently isolated in a pronouncement of doom and gives us no indication as to what causes the disapproval of Yahweh with regard to these sacrifices. If we are allowed to view the passage in the light of what we find in the following chapter of the Book of Jeremiah, however, we are much better off. In Jer 7, 21-24 we read:

> "Thus says Yahweh *ṣbʾwt*, the god of Israel: Add your burnt offerings (*ᶜlwtykm*) to your communion offerings (*zbḥykm*) and eat flesh![198] For I did not speak to your fathers, and I did not command them on the day that I brought them out of the land of Egypt regarding burnt offering (*ᶜlh*) or communion offering (*zbḥ*). For this is what I commanded them: Listen to my voice and I will be your god and you shall be my people, and you shall walk in all the way that I command you, that you may prosper."

---

[194] For a general survey, see F. C. Fensham, "Widow, Orphan and the Poor", *JNES* 21 (1962) 129-39.

[195] Cf. Deut 10, 18; 14, 29; 16, 11.14; 24, 17.19.20.21; 26, 12.13; 27, 19. Cf. also Jer 7, 6; 22, 3.

[196] Cf. below p. 116.

[197] Cf. above p. 81.

[198] We note with interest that we here have an ironic invitation by the prophet and consequently a parallel to what we find in Am 4, 4-5 (cf. above p. 54).

Whereas the reason for the prophetic denunciation of the sacrificial cult in Is 1, 11-17 seems to be the lack of moral and social values of the cult participants, the context of Jer 7, 21-24 seems to indicate that the reason for the prophet's dissatisfaction with the cult is the cult itself. According to Jer 7, 17-18 and 30ff (there can be no doubt that these verses belong within the same ideological unity as vv. 21-24) Jeremiah's dissatisfaction with the cult is caused by its "pagan" or syncretistic usages. Of all the anti-cult polemical texts which we have quoted so far this text of Jeremiah is, in addition to Am 5, 21-24[199], the only one which connects the negative view of the cult directly to the non-Yahwistic or Yahwistic/syncretistic contents of the cult.

A further, interesting feature of the passage Jer 7, 21-24 is the remarkable reference to the traditions of Israel and the statement that Yahweh did not give any regulations concerning sacrifices when he brought the Israelites out of Egypt[200]. The conclusion we have to draw from this passage in Jeremiah is that the cultic sacrifices seem to be without any religious value.

If the critical anti-cult passages in the prophets quoted above show striking similarities with Deuteronomic ideology and phraseology, this is even more so the case with the passage Jer 7, 21-24. Particularly striking are the phrases "you shall be my people"[201], and "that you may prosper"[202]. Also in the continuation of the passage 7, 21-24, where the prophet describes the "apostasy" of the fathers and states that the present generation is still worse than the generation of the fathers, we find Deuteronomic phraseology[203].

One last cult polemical passage in the prophets which should also be mentioned in this connection is Jer 14, 11-12:

> "And Yahweh said to me: Do not pray for the well-being of this people. For when they fast, I will not listen to their cry, and when they offer burnt offering (*yᶜlw ᶜlh*) and cereal offering (*mnḥh*), I will not accept them. For I will make an end to them with the sword, with famine, and with pestilence."

Some details of the relationship between this passage in Jeremiah and Amos Chapter 5 have been mentioned above[204]. When taking a closer

---

199 In view of Am 5, 25-26 there cannot be the least doubt that Am 5, 21-24 concern the worship by the Israelites of deities other than Yahweh.

200 Cf. Am 5, 25 (see below pp. 118-19).

201 Cf. Deut 4, 20; 7, 6; 14, 2; 26, 18; 27, 9. Cf. also Jer 11, 4; 13, 11; 24, 7; 30, 22.25; 31, 32; 32, 38.

202 Cf. Deut 4, 40; 5, 16.26; 6, 3.18; 12, 25.28; 22, 7. Cf. also Jer 42, 6.

203 Cf. H. Ringgren, "ʾb", *TWAT* I (1973) 14-15. As this theme is quite frequent in the Old Testament, however (cf. Ringgren, *op. cit.* 16 and *passim*, E. Jenni, "ʾb", *THAT*² (1975) 13), it may be more correct to regard Jeremiah as the originator of this aspect of "father-theology".

204 Above pp. 70-72.

look at the context of Jer 14, 11-12, one sees that there are several features of the text that are found in Am 4-5 also. In agreement with the description of the lack of rain in Am 4[205], there is a description of lack of rain in Jer 14, 1ff too. Further on this is interpreted as the punishment of Yahweh following the transgressions of the people. Other kinds of punishment—war, famine—are, as is the case in Am 4, also described. One conclusion of Jer 14 (v. 22) is that it is Yahweh who provides the rain. Consequently also this chapter fulminates against syncretistic practices.

The attempt to draw any conclusions from these critical anti-cult passages in the prophets is not easy. In the texts there is no systematic treatise of the prophets' view of the sacrificial cult. What occasional statements we do have, do not allow us to draw any final conclusions with regard to the relationship of the prophets to the cult. Thus, we do know that the prophet Isaiah in Is 1, 11-17 denounces the cult because at the same time the participants in the cultic rites do not obey the commandments of Yahweh on moral and social behaviour. We also know that the prophet Jeremiah in 7, 21-24 denounces the cult because it is syncretistic. But does this automatically imply that if the worshippers referred to in Is 1, 11-17 had behaved in a morally and socially unreproachable manner, or if the cult referred to in Jer 7, 21-24 had not been syncretistic, these prophets would have approved of the sacrificial cult?

Obviously, this is how we would pose the question. However, it is equally obvious that the question cannot be put that way. The prophets reacted to what they *saw* in society, they reacted to particular occasions, under various circumstances. It is hardly *fair* to ask them for a reflective view on the nature of the cult. Their message is a simple message: follow Yahweh as your only god and obey his divine commandments for moral and social behaviour.

Again we should try to remember that the generally accepted thesis which attempts to see the prophets as participants in an ongoing war between traditional Israelite faith and Canaanite religion is not correct. There was no such thing as traditional Israelite religion before the time of the Exile in the way the Deuteronomists would have us believe. Yahweh was only one of several gods that were worshipped in ancient Israel. The Yahwistic prophets in the times of classic prophecy fought, as the Yahwistic prophets before them had done, for the recognition of Yahweh as the sole god of Israel. Through this fight they laid the foundation for what was later to *become* what we have come to know as classic Israelite religion. It is in the light of this that we shall also have to view the anti-cult passages in the prophetic books.

---

205 Cf. above p. 58ff.

We have noted above the many similarities to Deuteronomic phraseology in the words of the prophets against the sacrificial cult. This fact adds further evidence to the assumption that the prophets must be regarded as the forerunners of Deuteronomy and the Deuteronomists.

However, we should note further that the similarities between the anti-cult polemical passages of the prophets and Deuteronomy are not restricted to the phraseology. Thus, one of the conclusions which we *have* to draw from these passages of the prophets, if we pay attention to the texts, is that the sacrificial cult is *unnecessary*. Even if the prophets do not in fact forbid the cultic sacrifices (which would indeed have been impossible), they make the value of the cultic sacrifices *relative*.

In this they are closely followed by Deuteronomy. Whereas the sacrificial cult according to the Priestly Code is something which should be practised for its own sake, in order to please the deity, Deuteronomy holds that the godhead has no need of sacrifice. Basically, Deuteronomy holds the view that the offerings should be consumed by the offerer in the sanctuary and shared by the needy, the poor, the alien, the orphan, the widow, and the Levite. Through the sacrifice the offerer expresses his gratitude towards the deity. Besides the already mentioned humanitarian aspect of providing food for the needy, this aspect of expressing gratitude is, according to Deuteronomy, the only purpose of the sacrificial cult[206].

Much more than what has been outlined above can hardly be said on the problem of the critical anti-cult passage Am 5, 21-24. Altogether, we are here on insecure ground. What we do know, however, are the reasons for the harsh polemic of the prophet Amos against the cult. When Amos attacks the sacrificial cult in 5, 21-24 he is doing so for the very same reason that caused his attack on the cult in 4, 4-5[207]: the non-Yahwistic contents of the cult in which the Israelites participated. This fact follows irrevocably from the words allowing immediately after the denunciation of the cultic sacrifices in 5, 21-24, the words in 5, 25-26 which explicitly mention the names of non-Yahwistic deities.

4.5. *Amos* 5, 25-26

Of the two verses 5, 25 and 5, 26, v. 25 does not cause us any major problems. Taking the *h* of *hzbḥym* as a *hē interrogative*, as is done almost unanimously by the commentators[208], we may translate the verse the following way:

---

[206] Further on this, see M.Weinfeld, *Deuteronomy and the Deuteronomic School* (1972) 210ff.
[207] See above pp. 54-58.
[208] Cf., however, R. Dobbie, "Amos 5, 25", *TGUOS* 17 (1959) 62-64.

> "Did you bring me sacrifices and cereal offering the forty years in the desert, House of Israel?"

The built-in answer to this rhetorical question is, of course: "No! You did not." This verse has to be regarded as a direct continuation of the denunciation of the cultic sacrifices in vv. 21-24. The reference to the desert period[209] in connection with the denouncement of cultic sacrifices is also found in the passage Jer 7, 21-24 critical of the cult[210].

If v. 25 leaves us with no problems to speak of, the same cannot be said of v. 26. Without hesitation I would characterize Am 5, 26 as the most difficult passage in the whole Book of Amos. This is the more regrettable as the passage is the only one in the prophet's message, beside 8, 14[211], which gives us the names of different deities that were worshipped by the Israelites in the time of Amos.

If we take a look at the current English translations of v. 26, we find that they do not differ very much from each other:

> "No! But now you shall take up the shrine of your idol king and the pedestals of your images, which you have made for yourselves" (*NEB*).

> "You will carry away Sakkuth, your king, and Kaiwan, your star god, the images that you have made for yourselves" (*NAB*).

> "So now you must shoulder your king Sakkut, and Kaiwan your star-god, idols you have manufactured" (*Moffatt*).

> "You shall take up Sakkuth your king, and Kaiwan your star-god, your images, which you have made for yourselves (*RSV*).

> "Now you must shoulder Sakkuth your king and Kaiwan your god, those idols you have made for yourselves (*Jerusalem Bible*).

We notice that all the current English translations, with the exception of *NEB*, take the two Hebrew words *skwt* and *kywn* which occur in Am 5, 26 to be the names of two deities, Sakkuth and Kaiwan. The identification of the two deities Sakkuth and Kaiwan in this verse is widely supported by those scholars who have commented on this difficult passage[212].

---

[209] Cf. S. Talmon, "The "Desert Motif" in the Bible", *Biblical Motifs* (1966) 31-63, which is also rich in bibliographical information.

[210] Cf. above pp. 115-16.

[211] On Am 8, 14 see below pp. 143-201.

[212] See *inter alia* C. C. Torrey, "On the Text of Amos 5, 26", *JBL* 13 (1894) 61-62, A. van Hoonacker, *Les douze petits prophètes* (1908) 252, E. Burrows, "Cuneiform and Old Testament", *JThS* 28 (1927) 184-85, E. A. Speiser, "Note on Amos 5, 26", *BASOR* 108 (1947) 5-6, E. Würthwein, "Amos 5, 21-27", *ThLZ* 72 (1947) 151, S. Erlandsson, "Amos 5, 25-27", *SEÅ* 33 (1968) 82, H. W. Wolff, *Dodekapropheton* 2 (1969) 304, 310, W. Rudolph, *Joel - Amos - Obadja - Jona* (1971) 206, "Schwierige Amosstellen", *Wort und Geschichte* (1973) 160. Not all these scholars, however, believe that the words contained in v. 26 (or v. 25) go back to Amos (thus *e.g.* Wolff and Würthwein regard these words as later additions to the text).

However, despite the fact that the scholarly world seems more or less to have agreed upon the identification of the two Assyrian/Babylonian deities Sakkuth and Kaiwan, we can hardly accept this identification as unproblematic. Thus, the reading given by modern interpreters of Am 5, 26 differs widely from the way the ancient versions read the text.

In the ancient versions there is no reference to a deity Sakkuth at all. Most of them read the *skwt* of MT as *sukkat*, taking the word as Hebrew *skh*, meaning "cover", "hut". This accounts for the reading *mšknʾ* of the Peshitta, *tēn skēnēn* of the Septuagint and Symmachus, *tous syskiasmous* of Aquila, and *tabernaculum* of the Vulgate. Targum Jonathan, on the other hand, simply reproduces *sykwt* which may, of course, be a reference to the deity Sakkuth, but in all likelihood the Targums have not understood MT and are content to reproduce the text. The reading *horasin* of Theodotion should also be mentioned.

The "tabernacle" or "shrine" of the versions seems to give good sense in relation to the *wnśʾtm* of MT which indicates the carrying around of some sacred object in procession[213]. The usage corresponds to the ones known to us from Assyrian-Babylonian religion, described by the verb *našû*(*m*) II[214]. On the other hand, this usage may apply to the carrying around of the statue of the deity Sakkuth as well.

When it comes to a closer determination of what the Israelites were carrying around, the *mlkkm* of MT, the versions cannot agree at all.

The Peshitta, accordingly, takes the *mlkkm* of MT as a reference to the deity Milcom. So does Aquila. The Septuagint, on the other hand, reads the name of the deity referred to as Moloch. The Vulgate does the same . The only two text witnesses which follow MT are Theodotion and Symmachus, who both read *tou basileōs hymōn*. The *ptkrykwn* of the Targums seems quite unexpected.

When we come to the name of the second deity referred to in the MT, we find that the versions seem to be more in agreement with each other. The Peshitta gives the *kywn* of MT as *kʾwn*, the Targums have *kywn*, in accordance with MT. Aquila and Symmachus read *chioun*, the Septuagint has, somewhat unexpectedly, *Raifan*[215].

Altogether, we do not get any help from the versions when it comes to an attempt to solve the difficult problems of how to understand the two Hebrew words *skwt* and *kywn* in Am 5, 26. We do, however, learn one important thing from the versions in this matter: the Hebrew text of Am 5, 26 was already corrupt and unintelligible in their time. For this reason

213 Cf. Ex 25, 14, 1 Sam 2, 28, Is 45, 20; 49, 22; 52, 11; 66, 12, Jer 10, 5.
214 Cf. *AHW* II (1972) 764, 3b.
215 The most likely explanation of this is an early reading of *R* for *K* of the Greek translators. Cf. Acta 7, 43 (cf. E. Haenchen, *Die Apostelgeschichte* (1969) 235, n. 3).

there is little use in trying to reconstruct the text on the basis of the versions. In fact, none of them seem to have had any clues for the meaning of this difficult text[216].

The problem of Am 5, 26, however, does not consist of the interpretation of the two terms *skwt* and *kywn* alone. There is also a problem connected to the *wnś'tm* in this verse. Does this verb refer to a past or a future event, or maybe even to a present one? Here, too, the opinions of the scholars have differed widely.

Thus, we note that all the English translations of v. 26 quoted above take *wnś'tm* as a reference to the future. This, of course, is something which fits the context perfectly. As an introduction to the pronouncement of doom in v. 27, we may well understand that the prophet tells his audience that they are to bring their deities with them into exile. As the result of having worshipped deities that are unable to help them, the enemy will conquer the country and the people will go into exile. When leaving their country they will take in procession with them the deities that were unable to help them avoid disaster when carried around in solemn cultic procession. The irony of this prophetic picture is superb.

When consulting the ancient versions, we find that they have unanimously taken the *wnś'tm* as a reference to the past, to the forty years in the desert referred to in v. 25. This, however, is the most unlikely interpretation of the verse. It simply does not make sense[217].

Finally, there is the possibility of taking the verb as referring to the present situation: "But now you carry..." This interpretation was suggested *inter alia* by Gevirtz[218]. I find this interpretation hard to accept.

The problem of how to understand the *wnś'tm* of MT will have to be decided from the background of the contextual evidence. The present tense suggestion is difficult to accept. However, there can be no doubt that the event referred to is one which took place in the time of Amos, and not an event preceding him. This leaves us, in fact, with the possibility of retaining the past tense of the versions, translating "But you carried...", and understanding this as a reference to what had been going on in the Samaritan cult in Amos' own time. Whether this is the correct way to understand the passage, or whether it should be read as a reference to a future event as described above, is hard, if not impossible, to decide[219].

---

[216] For this reason I believe that an attempt to restore the meaning of Am 5, 26 on the basis of the ancient versions is unlikely to succeed. For an attempt to restore the verse on the basis of the Septuagint, see C. D. Isbell, "Another Look at Amos 5, 26", *JBL* 97 (1978) 97-99.

[217] This interpretation was earlier much favoured (cf. *e.g.* N. Schmidt, "On the Text and Interpretation of Amos 5, 25-27", *JBL* 13 (1894) 11.

[218] S. Gevirtz, "A New Look at an Old Crux", *JBL* 87 (1968) 276.

[219] For a survey of the different possibilities cf. S. Erlandsson, "Amos 5, 25-27", *SEÅ* 33 (1968) 77-80.

What we may agree upon, however, is that the text of Am 5, 26 refers to some non-Yahwistic cult in Samaria in the time of the prophet Amos.

However, this does not bring us any closer to the *content* of the verse. We still do not know what the prophet was saying about the foreign deities worshipped, or even who they are. This statement may seem somewhat exaggerated, but this is nevertheless where we stand. It remains a fact that MT is corrupt and offers an awkward syntax. The text as it stands may hardly be translated in any other way than the following:

> "And you carried *skwt*, your king and *kywn*, your images, a star which you have made for yourselves."

When consulting the secondary literature, one will find that there has been no lack of attempts to restore this text and make it meaningful. However, modern translators have been as unable to solve the textual problems of Am 5, 26 as the ancients[220]. As far as I can see, the student of Am 5, 26 has three options. He may choose among the many available suggestions the one that he thinks is the most likely. Or, if he cannot appreciate any of the dishes offered on the menu, he can propose a new recipe himself[221]. Or, finally, he can accept for a fact that it lies beyond his capacity to solve this particular problem. I have settled for the third option. As far as I am able to judge, quite a few of the suggested solutions to the textual problem of Am 5, 26 are acceptable. Which one is the more acceptable , however, I find impossible to decide. We shall simply have to accept that we are unable to solve all the *cruces* of the Hebrew Bible with the means at present available to us.

With regard to the two Hebrew words *skwt* and *kywn*, I have shown above that the majority of the modern English translations[222], as well as the majority of scholars[223], have taken these words to be the names of the Assyrian-Babylonian deities Sakkuth and Kaiwan. Even if this reading is an old one[224], it must have arisen in the wake of the so-called Pan-Babylonian movement[225]. As we have seen, it has prevailed up till today,

---

[220] There is no need to present the different solutions in any detail here. I am content to refer to the literature mentioned in the text.

[221] One of the most ingenious recent attempts to solve the *crux* of Am 5, 26 is the one by S. Gevirtz, "A New Look at an Old Crux", *JBL* 87 (1968) 267-76. Gevirtz may very well be right in his new suggestion, of course, but who can say?

[222] See above p. 119.

[223] Above n. 212.

[224] It is with interest that we note how the Bible of Luther changed the translation of Am 5, 26 from following the words of the Vulgate to identifying the two words *skwt* and *kywn* as the two deities "Siccuth" and "Chiun" (*Martin Luthers Deutsche Bibel 1522-1546.* 11.B. 2.H (1960) 240 and 4.B. *Bibelrevisionen* (1923) 237.

[225] See *inter alia* E. Schrader, "Assyrisch-Biblisches", *ThStKr* 47 (1874) 332 and *passim.*

and may now be regarded as the *opinio communis* of the scholarly world[226].

As far as I can see, the success of the identification of the two deities Sakkuth and Kaiwan was particularly furthered by the fact that two deities by that name were mentioned together in an Akkadian religious text. The text in question is the one known by the name of Šurpu, a collection of Akkadian incantations and prayers. Tablet II of this series contains invocations to different deities with a request to forgive and relieve those sick who are suffering as a result of their moral or cultic offences. In the long enumeration of different deities we find in 1.180 the mention of the two deities *dSAG.KUD* and *dSAG.UŠ*[227]. Of these two ideograms *SAG.UŠ* is the best known, being the ideogram for Akkadian *kajamānu*, which, among other things, is a name for the planet Saturn[228]. Consequently, it has been assumed that *kywn* in Am 5, 26 is the name of the Assyrian-Babylonian deity Saturn. Obviously, this assumption may seem to have some support in the text. Even if the word *kwkb*, "star", represents the major syntactical problem of our verse, it is attested by all the ancient versions. This makes it unlikely that the word is a late addition to the text.

On the other hand, however, the comparison to *kajamānu* in Akkadian is not uncomplicated. Thus, the importance of the planet god Saturn in Assyrian-Babylonian religion is not as great as perhaps one would like to think. By far the majority of the "*kajamānu*" texts are of an astronomical character. The majority of these, again, are non-religious. In fact, in the Assyrian-Babylonian religion Saturn is the only planet which was *not* related to one of the major deities[229].

In addition to this, *kajamānu*, as an appellative meaning "steadfast", was used for other deities as well[230]. This brings us to ask the question whether it could not be possible that it is *this* usage which is also reflected in *kywn* in Am 5, 26?[231]. Altogether our actual knowledge of Assyrian-Babylonian history of religion is not very impressive and it would conse-

---

[226] Thus, the translation of Am 5, 26 of NEB (above p. 119), which takes the versions more into account, stands rather isolated today.

[227] E. Reiner, *Šurpu* (1958) 18.

[228] For references, see *CAD* 8 (1971) 36-38, *AHW* 1 (1965) 420-21.

[229] W. von Soden, "Licht und Finsternis in der sumerischen und babylonisch-assyrischen Religion", *StGen* 13 (1960) 651. Professor von Soden has kindly informed me that he believes that the reason for this is that this planet was the last one to be discovered by the astronomers.

[230] For Shamash see *inter alia* S. Langdon, *Babylonian Penitential Psalms* (1927) 52 (also in A. Schollmayer, *Sumerisch-babylonische Hymnen und Gebete* (1912) 55), for Sin see *inter alia* S. Langdon, "A fragment of a series of Ritualistic Prayers", *RA* 12 (1915) 191.

[231] The etymological implications of the name of the deity *kywn* already played an important role for the translators of the Lutheran Bible (cf. above n. 224.). See further above n. 230 and M.-J. Seux, *Épithètes royales* (1967) 131ff.

quently be wise not to give the Akkadian evidence too much weight in this matter[232].

More important than the Akkadian evidence is the fact that Akkadian *kajamānu* as a designation for the planet Saturn was also taken over by other languages of the Ancient Near East, Syriac, Persian, Arabic. This adds considerably to the possibility that *kywn* in Am 5, 26 is also the Hebrew name for the planet Saturn.

Among the extra-biblical texts the Syriac ones are the most important to us. One should keep in mind, however, that these texts are all from late Christian times, and for this reason they do not carry much weight except as additional evidence[233]. One of the more important Syriac texts is the one by Ephraem Syrus which shows that Saturn was identified with Kaiwan in Edessa[234].

If the reference to *kywn* in Am 5, 26 is a reference to the deity Saturn, this becomes particularly interesting in the light of the great importance of Saturn in late West-Semitic religion. Besides the late Syriac evidence mentioned above, we have very little reliable evidence for a Saturn cult in ancient Syria/Palestine. In the colonies in Africa, however, Saturn played an all-important role for centuries. The cult of Baal-Ḥammōn is one example of this[235], Baal-Qarnaim another[236]. In fact, the Saturn cult in Africa was the dominating religion of the area for quite a while, especially after it merged with the Latin Saturnus[237]. However, despite the merging with a Latin deity the main features of the African Saturn were basically Semitic. For this reason we may speak of "the African Baᶜal"[238].

With regard to the word *mlkkm* preceding *kywn* in MT, we noticed above that this word was taken either to be a reference to the deity Milcom, or to the deity Moloch, or as an appellative "your king" of a deity Sakkuth. Seeing that MT is corrupt and hardly can be reconstucted, we shall have to admit that all three suggestions are accep-

---

232 On the problems in connection with the writing of a systematic treatment of Assyrian-Babylonian religion cf. J. Nougayrol, "Einführende Bemerkungen zur babylonischen Religion", *Theologie und Religionswissenschaft* (1973) 28-46 *passim*.

233 References to the Syriac texts are found in C. Brockelmann, *Lexicon Syriacum* (1928) 322.

234 *Ephraemi Syri opera omnia*, ed. P. Benedictus (1740) 2, 458C.

235 *WM* 1 Abt. B.1 (1965) 271-72.

236 *Ibid.* 272-73.

237 An excellent survey of the evidence of Saturn worship in the classical world is given by J. A. Hild, "Saturnus", *Saglio* 4 (1911) 1083-90. Cf. also *PRE* 2.R. 2.B (1923) 218-23.

238 The standard work on Saturn worship in Africa is M. Leglay, *Saturne Africain. Histoire* (1966) and *Saturne Africain. Monuments.* I-II (1961-66).

table[239]. Which one of the suggestions is to be preferred is to some degree dependent upon how one chooses to understand the *skwt* of MT.

The fact that a deity Sakkuth is mentioned together with the deity *ka-jamānu* in one Akkadian text[240] does not tell us much. Obviously the two deities have nothing in common, and when they are mentioned together in one text, this must be regarded as purely coincidential. None of the Akkadian texts which refer to a deity Sakkuth gives any reason to believe that the two deities have anything in common. Nevertheless, a deity Sakkuth *may* have been worshipped in Samaria in the time of Amos[241]. We are not likely to come anywhere closer than this to the problem of the deity Sakkuth.

In connection with the assumption of the Septuagint (and the Vulgate) that the reference is to the deity Moloch[242] there is one little detail which could still be worth mentioning. If Amos really mentions Moloch and Saturn together, this is particularly interesting seen against the background that both of these deities, Moloch in Israel and Saturn in Africa, were associated with child sacrifices[243].

From the above it follows that there is not really much we can say about the cults referred to in Am 5, 26. As we have seen, the evidence

---

239 For references to the deity Sakkuth, see A. Deimel, *Pantheon Babylonicum* (1914) 231, K. Tallquist, *Akkadische Götterepitheta* (1938) 440. Prayers to Sakkuth were published by S. Langdon, *Babylonian Liturgies* (1913) 124-30. It *may* be that we have a reflection of this deity in the name *skwt bnwt* mentioned in II Kings 17, 30. If this is the case, the reading of the versions (above p. 120) appears to be more uncertain (see, however, also K. Koch, *Amos* B.2 (1976) 41). Also Moloch is a well known deity from the Old Testament. After Eissfeldt had attempted to demonstrate that the passages in which scholars had found references to a deity *MLK* were in fact references to a particular kind of sacrifice (*Molk als Opferbegriff im Punischen und Hebräischen* (1935)), the deity Moloch disappeared from the scholarly world for a while. Today, however, Eissfeldt has hardly any followers, and the existence of a deity Moloch is almost unanimously accepted by the scholars (cf. *e.g.* M. J. Mulder, *Kanaänitische goden in het Oude Testament* (1965) 63-64, D. Plataroti, "Zum Gebrauch des Wortes *MLK* im Alten Testament", *VT* 28 (1978) 286-300, M. Weinfeld, "Burning Babies in Ancient Israel", *UF* 10 (1978) 411-13, J. Ebach, U. Rüterswörden, "ADRMLK, "Moloch" und BA^{c}AL ADR", *Festschrift Schaeffer* (1979) 216-26). This, however, does not imply that we know very much about the deity Moloch, except for the fact that he was probably associated with child sacrifices (this has been disputed *inter alia* by M. Weinfeld, *op. cit.*). The problems in connection with the deity Moloch are caused largely by the fact that *mlk* is a quite ordinary appellative for the deity in the Ancient Near East and forms a part of many deities' names (*e.g.* Milchom, Melqart, Malik, Malakbēl (who, incidentally, was identified with Saturn in Palmyra (*WM* 1.Abt. B.1 (1965) 452-53)). Cf. further J. A. Soggin, "mǽlæk", *THAT* I (1971) 908-20, *CAD* 10, 1 (1977) 164, *DISO* (1965) 152-53. On Milcom, the god of the Ammonites, cf. I Kings 11, 5.7.33, 2 Sam 12, 30, II Kings 23, 13, Jer 49, 1.3, Zeph 1, 5 (references to literature on this deity is found in *HAL*[3] Lief. II (1974) 561.

240 Cf. above p. 123.

241 Cf. II Kings 17, 30. Cf., however, also below pp. 159-63.

242 Cf. above n. 239.

243 Further on this cf. A. R. W. Green, *The Role of Human Sacrifice* (1975) *passim.*

does not allow us to draw any conclusions. The only conclusion we may draw from this extremely difficult text is that the verse contains polemics against non-Yahwistic deities, and that these deities were of a planetary character[244]. As for the identification of the different deities in this text, the identification of the deity Saturn/Kaiwan may seem relatively secure. As for the other deity(ies) referred to in this text, the evidence is too meagre to allow for any conclusions.

---

[244] This is not surprising when one considers all the references in the Old Testament to planet worship (cf. in particular *ṣbʾ hšmym* in Deut 4, 19; 17, 3, II Kings 17, 16; 21, 3.5, 24, 4f, Jer 8, 2; 19, 13, Zeph 1, 5. Cf. C. A. Keller, *Nahoum, Habacuc, Sophonie* (1971) 189).

CHAPTER FIVE

AM 6, 4-6. THE *MRZḤ* INSTITUTION

5.1. *Structure and Contents of Am* 6, 1-14. *The Text of Am* 6, 4-7

The sixth chapter of the Book of Amos also appears to form a coherent unity, the composition being rather similar to that of the preceding chapters. However, instead of the stereotyped introduction formulas *kô ʾāmar yhwh* (1, 3.6.9.11.13; 2, 1.4.6) and *šimʿû haddāḇār hazzæ* (3, 1; 4, 1; 5, 1), this new pronouncement of doom opens with the woe oracle 6, 1-2. Then there follows the reason for the pronouncement in vv. 3-6, and the pronouncement itself in vv. 7-11. In vv. 12-13 there follow further descriptions of the people's outrages, followed by a final word of judgement in v. 14.

We note once more the twofold accusation of the prophet against the Israelites, one religious (vv. 4-6 and 13) and one moral (vv. 3 and 12). As always with the prophet Amos these two kinds of accusation are intimately bound together and cannot be separated from each other.

The passage which contains the religious polemics, vv. 4-7, may be translated as follows:

V.4. "You that lie upon beds of ivory and sprawl upon your couches, eating young rams from the flock and fattened young cows from the cowshed,

V.5. you that sing songs[1] accompanied by the lute, like David[2], and play on[3] musical instruments[4],

V.6. you that drink wine out of bowls[5] and anoint yourselves with the best of oils[6].

---

[1] For the translation, see J. A. Montgomery, "Notes from the Samaritan", *JBL* 25 (1906) 51.

[2] Several commentators erase *kĕdāwîd* from the text. I do not know if this is correct.

[3] This translation is suggested by Arabic *ḥasaba ʿalā* (Cf. *Bibliotheca Geographorum Arabicorum.* Ed. de Goeje, pars 7 (1892) 123, lines 13ff).

[4] Cf. M. Buttenwieser, "*bkly ʿz lywh*", *JBL* 45 (1926) 156-58.

[5] *mzrq* is a cultic term, meaning "bowl", "basin". *HAL*³ (see Lief. II (1974) 537 for all references) translates the word with "Sprengschale". From the etymology of the word this does seem to be the best translation. However, there is no reason to believe that the word was *always* used in the meaning "Sprengschale". All we may say is that according to the etymology of the word this was its original meaning. Thus, one should not read the words of Amos in 6, 6 as a reference to drinking wine in abundance as some commentators do. From Am 6, 6 it follows that *mzrq* can also be a designation for a drinking bowl. The main thing, however, is that the word is used only in cultic connections.

[6] Cf. P. Welten, "Salbe und Salbgefässe", *BRL*² (1977) 260-64. For an example of an anointment bowl used in the cult, see *ibid.* the article "Kultgeräte", 2c, Abb. 45, 7.

V.7. Therefore[7] they shall now head the procession of the captives, and the *mrzḥ* of the sprawling[8] shall come to an end."

When consulting the current commentaries on these verses, it will soon appear that not everyone associates the contents of vv. 4-6 with religious polemics. Quite a few scholars still adhere to the old view that the prophet here criticizes the opulent feasting of the upper classes of the northern realm, with eating and drinking to excess[9]. Even if this obviously may form a part of the objection of the prophet, however, it does not provide us with a satisfactory explanation for the words of doom uttered by the prophet Amos in this context. The explanation should rather be sought in the word *mrzḥ* — for the present left untranslated — of v. 7. The important implications of the word *mrzḥ* for a proper understanding of the words of the prophet in Am 6, 4-6 have more and more impressed the scholarly world[10]. However, as these implications are above all bound up in the existence of the *mrzḥ* "institution" in the cultures surrounding ancient Israel, it seems right to give a short survey of the general Ancient Near Eastern evidence relating to the *mrzḥ* before anything more is said about the context of Am 6, 4-6.

5.2. *The Ancient Near Eastern mrzḥ Evidence. A Survey*

A. The Old Testament

The only place in the Old Testament besides Am 6, 7 which has the word *mrzḥ* is Jer 16, 5. We read in 16, 1-6:

V.1. "The word of Yahweh came to me and said:

V.2. Do not take yourself a wife and do not have sons and daughters in this place.

---

[7] On *lkn*, see above Chapter 4, n. 25.

[8] Cf. v. 4.

[9] See *e.g.* A Neher, *Amos* (1950) 116-17, A. Weiser, *Das Buch der zwölf kleinen Propheten* (1956) 178-79, T. H. Robinson, *Die zwölf kleinen Propheten* (1964) 93-95, E. Hammershaimb, *Amos* (1967) 91-98, J. L. Mays, *Amos* (1969) 116-17, H. W. Wolff, *Dodekapropheton* 2 (1969) 320-22. It should be mentioned, however, that quite a few scholars have stressed that there is more to these verses than average opinion seems to recognize. In this group we find *inter alia* V. Maag, *Text, Wortschatz und Begriffswelt* (1951) 168, S. Amsler, *Amos* (1969) 219, M. Bič, *Das Buch Amos* (1969) 131-34. All the scholars mentioned are influenced by the important, but sadly neglected article by H. Gressmann, "Η ΚΟΙΝΩΝΙΑ ΤΩΝ ΔΑΙΜΟΝΙΩΝ," *ZNW* 20 (1921) 224-30.

[10] Thus we notice with interest that *HAL*[3] Lief. II (1974) 599 renders *mrzḥ* in Am 6, 7 by "Kultfeier mit Gelage". As recently as in 1979, however, one can still meet a translation like: "Aus ist es mit der Lustbarkeit der üppig daliegenden" (R. Meyer, "Gegensinn und Mehrdeutigkeit", *Festschrift Schaeffer* (1979) 603).

V.3. For thus says Yahweh of the sons and of the daughters who are born in this place, and of their mothers who bore them and of their fathers who begot them in this land:

V.4. They will die terrible deaths, they will not be lamented, they will not be buried. They will be dung on the surface of the ground, and they will perish by the sword and by famine, and their corpses will be food for the birds of the sky and for the beasts of the earth.

V.5. For thus speaks Yahweh: Do not enter a *byt mrzḥ* and do not go to lament, and do not bemoan them, for I have taken my peace away from this people, says Yahweh, the merciful and compassionate[11].

V.6. Both great and small will die in this land. They will not be buried and they will not be lamented and no one will cut himself for them nor shave his head for them."

The text goes on in v. 7 by describing further rites of mourning which will not take place. Then there follows the new prohibition in v. 8 against entering a banquet house (*byt-mšth*[12]). From v. 9, where there is mention of bride and bridegroom, it follows that the prohibition concerning the *byt-mšth* is not related to the prohibition concerning the *byt mrzḥ*, and we shall leave vv. 8-10 out of account.

The reasons given by Jeremiah for this pronouncement of doom is clearly seen from vv. 11, 13 and 18 which all mention specifically the worship of deities other than Yahweh.

We notice further the fact that entering the *mrzḥ* house is quite clearly objected to by the prophet. Following the words of the prophet in v. 4 one might have expected the prophet to continue: "And they will not enter a *mrzḥ* house, and they will not go to lament, and they will not bemoan them..." Instead of this we get the prohibition. In the light of vv. 11, 13 and 18 this can only mean that the reason for the pronouncement is to be found in the fact that the people *do* enter the *mrzḥ* house. This place, consequently, was not only a place where mourning in connection with the funeral took place but it was at least in the context from which the prophet Jeremiah speaks in the present passage, also connected with non-Yahwistic rites. Much more is not likely to be learned from this passage in Jeremiah[13].

---

[11] Literally "mercy and compassion".

[12] Cf. *HAL*[3] Lief. II (1974) 617.

[13] Several interpreters seem to believe that the words of Jeremiah in vv. 1-3 concern the prophet's personal life (cf. W. Rudolph, *Jeremia*[3] (1968) 109ff, J. Bright, *Jeremiah*[2] (1968) 107). This, however, is not correct. The way in which the prophet expresses himself is the form in which he presents his words of doom and has nothing to do with Jeremiah's private affairs.

B. An Ostracon from Elephantine

The Jewish garrison at Elephantine has given us many valuable insights into the religious life of the Israelites in an age of syncretism[14]. Also with regard to the *mrzḥ* institution the Elephantine colony can offer us some information. Thus, an ostracon, originally published by A. H. Sayce[15] and later studied by M. Lidzbarski[16], was translated as follows:

> "An Ḥaggai. — Ich sprach/mit Ašian wegen des Geldes/für die festliche Veranstaltung (*mrzḥ*ʾ). So erwiderte er/mir, nämlich dem Itô:/Ich will es nun geben/Ḥaggai oder/Jigdol. Sprich/mit ihm,/da wird er es geben/euch."

Evidently also the Jews of Elephantine have celebrated a *mrzḥ*. However, in view of the rather fragmentary character of our evidence, it is unfortunately not possible to get any further particulars about the *mrzḥ* at Elephantine. We notice that Lidzbarski has translated the word *mrzḥ*ʾ with "festliche Veranstaltung". We do not know, however, whether the reference in this ostracon really is to a feast. As we shall see below[17] we have also evidence which points towards the *mrzḥ* being some kind of an institution. The same may well apply for the *mrzḥ*ʾ at Elephantine, and if the reference is to some festal event, there is no evidence to tell anything about the contents of this feast. One should not fail to mention, however, the attempt made by B. Porten in his distinguished monograph on the military colony at Elephantine to form an idea of the character of the *mrzḥ* feast against the background of other Ancient Near Eastern *mrzḥ* evidence[18]. However fascinating his thoughts may appear, it should be kept in mind that the scanty material hardly allows for any such perspicuity.

Nevertheless the occurrence of the *mrzḥ* at Elephantine must be considered to be of great significance, not least when viewed against the background of the northern realm of Israel as a possible point of departure for the Jewish soldiers who in the 5th century inhabited the island of Elephantine at the southern border of Egypt.

C. The Marseilles Tariff

The word *mrzḥ* also occurs in a Punic inscription found in the old harbour of Marseilles, dating to the third century B.C.[19] Towards the end of

---

[14] Cf. above Chapter 3, n. 124 and below pp. 167-78.
[15] A. H. Sayce, "An Aramaic Ostracon from Elephantine", *PSBA* 31 (1909) 154-55.
[16] M. Lidzbarski, *Ephemeris* III (1915) 119-21 (= *RES* 1295).
[17] Cf. pp. 131-37.
[18] B. Porten, *Archives from Elephantine* (1968) 184.
[19] *CIS*, Pars prima, t. 1, 165. Cf. also *RAO* IV 343, M. Lidzbarski, *Handbuch* (1898)

this famous inscription, where specifications of the various sacrifices of the temple of Baal Saphon and stipulations of the charges which were to be paid to the priests are given, we may read:

16. "Every clan[20] and every family[21] and every *mrzḥ ʾlm* and
17. everyone that sacrifices [shall pay]/to these people a tribute at the sacrifice, according to what is stipulated in the written pi[ece]."[22]

In this text we see that the word *mrzḥ* is used at the level of "clan" and "family", and that it is associated with a certain deity. Obviously, this "gathering of the deities" here appears to be some kind of large "cultic" association. It is quite clearly not a designation for a festal event.

D. A Phoencian Inscription from Piraeus

An inscription discovered in 1887 and dating from the year 96 B.C.[23] relates the decision of the Sidonian colony of Piraeus to garland a certain *šmʿbʿl*, son of *mgn*, a principal of the temple and the buildings in the forecourt of the temple. The honour (being a typical Greek usage) is bestowed upon him, we learn, as a reward for his building the temple-court and performing all his duties. What particulary arouses our interest is the opening line of the inscription:

> "On the fourth day of the *mrzḥ* in the fourteenth year of the people of Sidon..."

The term *mrzḥ* is here obviously the designation for some feast or celebration. It *may* have been celebrated annually, and we understand that it lasted for at least four days. On the actual contents of the feast, however, we get no further information.

428, *idem*, *Altsemitische Texte*. H.1 (1907) nr. 63, G. A. Cooke, *Textbook* (1903) nr. 42, H. Gressmann, *Altorientalische Texte*² (1927) 448-49, F. Rosenthal, *ANET*² (1955) 502-03, J.-G. Février, "Remarques sur la grand tarif", *CByrs* 8 (1958-59) 35-43, M. G. Guzzo Amadasi, *Le iscrizioni feniche e puniche* (1967) 169-82, *KAI* 1 (1962) nr. 69, Tafel VI (for further literature, see the commentary in *KAI* II (1964) 83-87).

[20] For *mzrḥ* cf. Biblical Hebrew *ʾzrḥ*. Cf. also *DISO* (1965) 146. The interpretation suggested by A. van Branden, "Notes phéniciennes", *BMB* 13 (1956) 94-95 is evidently wrong.

[21] For *špḥ* cf. Biblical Hebrew *mspḥh*. Cf. also *DISO* (1965) 316.

[22] In these instructions to the participants of the sacrificial cult the ends of the lines are unfortunately missing. This does not, however, affect the word *mrzḥ*, the meaning of which we may infer from the parallel expressions in the text.

[23] The inscription was first published by E. Renan, *CRAI* (1889) 12-13. Cf. also *RAO* II 390 nr. 2, IV 344, V 210, M. Lidzbarski, *Handbuch* (1898) 425, *idem*, *Altsemitische Texte* H.1 (1907) nr. 52, G. A. Cooke, *Text-Book* (1903) nr. 33, *RES* 1215 (see for earlier literature), *Corpus Inscriptionum Atticarum*, Suppl. pars V 1335b, *KAI* 1 (1962) nr. 60 (for further literature, see the commentary in *KAI* II (1964) 73-74).

If we compare this inscription to the one found at Marseilles we may assume that the *mrzḥ* was also a designation for the feast of the *mrzḥ* association. The Piraeus inscription connects the *mrzḥ* to the temple of the Sidonians at Piraeus, and the person by the name of *šmʿbʿl* was probably an outstanding member of a *mrzḥ* association in Piraeus.

E. The Nabatean Evidence

In a Nabatean inscription, first published by G. Dalman[24], we read:

1. "Remembered be *ʿbydw br wqyh l*[25]
2. and his comrades, the *mrzḥ* of *ʿbdt*,
3. the god."

Admittedly, it is not easy to make any sense out of this rather fragmentary inscription. Thus, it is easily understood why scholars have disagreed over the interpretation of several of its words. As it is unlikely that much can be said about the historical background of the inscription[26], we are content to notice that also in this text *mrzḥ* seems to be a designation for some sort of cultic community[27]. It is further with interest that we note the relationship of this religious institution to the dead[28].

Recently, also another Nabatean inscription relating to the *mrzḥ* institution has been made known to the scholarly world. The inscription was published by A. Negev[29] and relates to

> "a dam (built) by... the sons of Saruta, the *mrzḥ* of Dushara, the god of Galia in the year 18 (= 98 A.C.)..."

It is interesting to note that the *mrzḥ* association, which had a clearly religious foundation was also engaged in such a practical enterprise as the building of a dam.

If J. Starcky is right in his correction of another Nabatean inscription published by Negev[30], it is possible that we have still another occurrence of *mrzḥ* in Nabatean[31]. This, however, remains rather uncertain.

---

[24] G. Dalman, *Neue Petra-Forschungen* (1912) nr. 73. Cf. also M. Lidzbarski, *Ephemeris* III (1915) 278 and *RES* 1432.

[25] For this reading cf. R. Savignac, "Notes de voyage", *RB* 10 (1913) 440.

[26] Cf., however, J. Starcky, *Pétra et la Nabatène* (1966) 972 and 1015.

[27] Cf. the comment of G. Beer on the root *ḥbr* in his review of Dalman, *Neue Petra-Forschungen* (1912) in *ZDMG* 67 (1913) 561-62.

[28] Cf. the text of Jeremiah quoted above pp. 128-29.

[29] A. Negev, "Nabatean Inscriptions", *IEJ* 13 (1963) 113-17.

[30] J. Starcky, *Pétra et la Nabatène* (1966) 919.

[31] Cf. J. Naveh, "Some Notes on Nabatean Inscriptions", *IEJ* 17 (1967) 187-89, B. Porten, *Archives from Elephantine* (1968) 182, n. 126. Cf. also O. Eissfeldt, "Neue Belege für Nabatäische Kultgenossenschaften", *MIOF* 15 (1969) 217-27.

F. The Palmyrean Evidence

The community which has contributed most towards increasing our knowledge of the Ancient Near Eastern *mrzḥ* institution is undoubtedly the Palmyrean. Even if the religion of ancient Palmyra can be said to be Semitic in its foundation[32], however, one should take care not to apply the Palmyrean *mrzḥ* evidence uncritically to the Old Testament. The culture of Palmyra was strongly syncretistic, and we cannot close our eyes to the possibility that the *mrzḥ* institution developed under some influence from, for example, the Greek *thíasos*[33]. Used with some caution though, I believe the Palmyrean evidence to be of considerable significance.

Undoubtedly the most interesting of the Palmyrean inscriptions was published by H. Ingholt in 1926[34]. The inscription, dating from A.D. 242/243, informs us of the merits of a *mrzḥ* leader in this year and offers us valuable information, especially on the duties of the different members of the *mrzḥ*. The particular occasion was the resignation of the *mrzḥ* leader Jarḥai Agrippa from this term of office[35]:

1. "[In the mo]nth of *tšry* (in) the year 555 (= A.D. 242/243)
2. under the leadership of the *mrzḥ* of *yrḥy ʾgrpʾ*, (son of)
3. *yrḥy*, / (son of) *ydy ʿbl*, (son of) *ʿgʾ*, (son of) *yʿt*, who
4. served the gods and was in charge of/the distribution[36]
5. the whole year and gave matured[37] wine / to the priests
   the whole year from his (own) house, and wine in leather-
6. sacks[38] / he did not bring from the West[39]. Remembered and
7. blessed (be) / *prṭnks* and *mlkwsʾ*, his sons, and *ʿgylw*, the

---

[32] J. G. Fevrier, *La religion des palmyréniens* (1931) 233-37.

[33] This problem cannot be taken up here. Cf. *inter alia* Du Mesnil du Buisson, *Les tessères et les monnaies* (1962) 465-74 and *passim*. For the *mrzḥ* association in Palmyra, see further two important books J. Février, *La religion des palmyréniens* (1931) 201-08 and J. T. Milik, *Recherches d'épigraphie proche-orientale* I (1972) *passim*.

[34] H. Ingholt, "Un nouveau Thiase à Palmyre", *Syr* 7 (1926) 128-41. Cf. also Milik, *op. cit.* 262. Cf. also *ibid.* 151, 153, 279-80.

[35] Cf. Milik, *op. cit.* 262.

[36] *qsmʾ* was connected with Hebrew *qsm* and translated by "divination" by Ingholt (cf. above n. 43). The word should rather, I believe, be connected with Arabic *qisma*, "distribution", "allotment", "apportionment" (cf. J. Pedersen, *Der Eid bei den Semiten* (1914) 12). This fits the context perfectly and underlines the meritoriousness of the *mrzḥ* leader. Probably the expression *lbt ksm[ʾ]* in the fragment published by Cantineau (*Syr* 17 (1936) 348-49) should be rendered by: "for the house of distribution", *i.e.* "storehouse". This offers an interesting parallel to the *bt dwdʾ*, the "kettle-house" of the present inscription 1.8.

[37] *ʾsq*, aphel of *slq*. Cf. *DISO* (1965) 193-94.

[38] Cf. Ingholt, "Un nouveau Thiase", *Syr* 7 (1926) 134. Cf. also *DISO* (1965) 79, *zq*.

[39] Cf. Du Mesnil du Buisson, *Les tessères et les monnaies* (1962) 487.

8. scribe, / and *zby*, son of *šʿdʾ*, who is in charge of the
9. kettle-house[40] / and *yrḥbwlʾ*, the cupbearer, and all the assistants."

Another inscription, an altar inscription, first published by M. E. Littmann[41] and dating from the year A.D. 34[42] relates of the altar that it was erected in honour of the gods Aglibol and Malakbel[43] by the members of the *mrzḥ*.

Still another inscription, first published by M. Sobernheim[44], then studied by Clermont-Ganneau[45], dating from A.D. 118, tells of the erection of a statue in honour of a man by his daughters *brbnwt mrzḥwth dy kmry bl*, *i.e.* "on the occasion of his leadership of the *mrzḥ* of the priests of Bel".

A fourth, bilingual inscription, dated to the year A.D. 203[46], opens with the following line: *brbnwt mrzḥwt slmʾ*... "when *slmʾ* was in charge of the *mrzḥ*..." The reading is somewhat uncertain, but is confirmed by the Greek text[47].

The remaining inscriptions from Palmyra relating to the *mrzḥ* are written in Greek. None of them can be said to be of vital importance for our understanding of the *mrzḥ* institution, but for the sake of completion I will mention them briefly.

An inscription published and in part reconstructed by J. Cantineau[48] relates to a certain Bolanos(?)... head (*symposíarchos*) of the *thíasos* of the priests of Bel...

An inscription published by W. H. Waddington[49], dated to the year A.D. 266, relates to the erection of a statue of a certain Septimius Worod, *symposíarchos* of the *thíasos* of the priests of Bel.

Most probably we have a reference to the *mrzḥ* also in another Greek fragment, *RES* 2158[50].

---

[40] "Kitchen"? Ingholt (above n. 34) translates the function of the man as "chef de cuisine".

[41] M. E. Littmann, "Deux inscriptions religieuses", *JA* (1901) 374-81. Cf. also *CIS* II 3980, *RES* 284, *RAO* IV 374-81, M. Lidzbarski, *Ephemeris* 1 (1902) 343-45, G. A. Cooke, *Text-Book* (1903) 302-03, J. T. Milik, *Recherches* I (1972) 119f.

[42] When J. Février, *La Religion* (1931) dates the inscription to the year A.D. 132, this must be due to his mixing the date of *RES* 284 with *RES* 285.

[43] On these deities, see J. Février, *La religion* (1931) *passim*, H. Gese, *Die Religionen Altsyriens* (1970) 227f, *WM* Abt. 1. B. 1 (1965).

[44] M. Sobernheim, *Palmyrenische Inschriften* (1905) nr. 7.

[45] *RAO* VII 11-12. Cf. also M. Lidzbarski, *Ephemeris* II (1908) 281-82, *RES* 2129.

[46] Also published for the first time by M. Sobernheim (n. 44 above) nr. 44. Cf. *RAO* VII 22-24, M. Lidzbarski, *Ephemeris* II (1908) 303-05, *RES* 2152.

[47] Cf. *RAO* VII 22.

[48] J. Cantineau, "Inscriptions Palmyréniennes", *RA* 27 (1930) 38ff.

[49] W. H. Waddington, *Inscriptions* (1870) nr. 2606a.

[50] First published by M. Sobernheim, *Palmyrenische Inschriften* (1905) nr. 44, Cf. also J. Février, *La religion* (1931) 203.

In addition to the inscriptions, several tesserae found at Palmyra furnish us with valuable information on the *mrzḥ* association, in particular R.nrs. 27, 30, 31, 32, 33, 34, 35, and 301[51]. The major value of the tesserae lies in their interesting illustrations.

On the front side of nr. 27 are depicted two priests, lying at full length on a sofa with a cup in their hands. They both stretch their right hands upward, one of them holding a little twig, the other a palm branch. Below the illustration we may read: *kmry dy* [*bl*] - "the priests of Bel". On the other side of the tessera there is another priest. He, too, lies on a sofa, above which there is a conventionalized vine. To the right there is a palm, below an inscription in two lines: *ḥyrn ʿtnwry* / *ṣ*(?)*lmy rb mrzḥʾ* -"*ḥyrn ʿtnwry* / *ṣlmy*, head of the *mrzḥ*. Similar tesserae are nrs. 30, 31, 32 (this one is dated to the year A.D. 444 = 132/33), 33, 34, and 35.

Thus, on the reverse of nr. 34 a priest is portrayed in an upright position, sacrificing incense on a fire-altar situated between him and a radiant, mailed god who leans upon a lance or a sceptre. On the obverse of nr. 301 an Apollo-Nebo is depicted in an upright position, naked and with bent legs. His right hand is placed upon his head, and with his left hand he is holding a lyre which lies upon a small column. From his left shoulder hangs a gown, and to the left stands a kindled fire-altar. On the reverse of the tessera there is an illegible inscription, in the first line of which, however, we are able to read *bny mrzḥʾ*, "the members of the *mrzḥ*".

The *mrzḥ* association is also mentioned in a tessera published by C. Dunant[52]. On the obverse of the tessera a goddess sitting on some sort of a camp stool is depicted. Dressed in a tunic, she holds a lance or a sceptre in her left hand, a crown in the other. On the reverse we can read the following inscription: "The *mrzḥ* of *bʿltk* and *tymʾ* (on the) 5th day (of the celebration?)"[53].

G. The Ugaritic *mrzḥ* Texts

The importance of the Ugaritic *mrzḥ* texts can hardly be exaggerated. Not only are they of a very great age, but they also bear witness to the existence of the institution in a milieu where influence from the Greek *thíasos* association was non-existent. If it had not been for the Ugaritic evidence, in fact, it is hardly likely that use could have been made of the evidence given above in an attempt to find out what was hiding behind the word *mrzḥ* occurring in Jer 16, 5 and Am 6, 7.

[51] The numbers refer to H. Ingholt, *Recueil des tessères* (1955).
[52] C. Dunant, "Nouvelles tessères," *Syr* 36 (1959) nr. 12.
[53] Cf. J. T. Milik, *Recherches* I (1972) 110-11, 119, 169.

The evidence on *mrzḥ* from ancient Ugaritic is not only written in two different languages, Akkadian and Ugaritic, but it is also totally different in character depending on the language used. Whereas the Akkadian texts describe the daily life of the inhabitants of Ugarit and deal with relations between human beings, all the Ugaritic texts (with two exceptions) are mythological texts and deal with the doings of gods. Obviously, this implies that we have to take precautions if we also want to apply the mythological material for comparative purposes.

In Akkadian the name of the *mrzḥ* institution is *marzaʾu.* As we have no further attestation of this word in Akkadian, we must assume it to be a loanword from Ugaritic[54].

The first Akkadian text to be published which contained a reference to the *mrzḥ* institution was *RS* 14.16[55]. In this text we read about the *lú.meš ma-ar-zi-ḫi*, the members of the *mrzḥ.* Unfortunately a lacuna makes it impossible to read what is said about these members of the *mrzḥ.* From the context, however, we may assume that they were people of consequence.

The next text which is of interest to us is *RS* 15.88, which deals with a royal confirmation of property[56]. We read that Niqmepa, son of Niqmadu and king of Ugarit, had built a *bît lú.meš mar-za-i*, a *marzaʾu* house, and given it to its members for ever. In a later text, *RS* 15.70[57], we learn that the son of this king has taken the house of the *marzeʿu* of Šatrana and given them the house of Ibramuzi instead. The text continues by laying down that in the future the house taken from the members of the *marzeʿu* will always belong to the son of the king, the heir apparent, whereas the new house given to the *marzeʿu* of Šatrana never will be taken from them, but forever belong to the members and their sons.

Also *RS* 18.01[58] provides us with some interesting information concerning the *mrzḥ* institution in ancient Ugarit. This international legal text relates the division of an area comprising the wine fields of the Hurrian Ištar, lying in the border district between Ugarit and Siyanni between the *mrzḥ* of Ari and the *mrzḥ* of Siyannu.

Of the texts written in Ugaritic, *RS* 19.103[59], a register of estates belonging to (?) several *mrzh* institutions, and a text which was illegally taken from Ras Shamra and sold to an American university[60], dealing

[54] Cf. W. von Soden, *AHW* II (1972) 617, *CAD* 10, 1 (1977) 321.
[55] C. Virolleaud, "Six textes de Ras Shamra", *Syr* 28 (1951) 173.
[56] *PRU* III (1955) pl. XX. Transliteration and translation 88.
[57] *PRU* III (1955) pl. XVII. Transliteration and translation 230.
[58] *PRU* IV (1956) pl. LXXVII. Transliteration and translation 230.
[59] *PRU* V (1965) 47. Cf. *UT* 2032.
[60] P. D. Miller, "The *Mrzḥ* Text", *CRST* (1971) 37-48. Cf. also M. Dahood, "Additional Remarks on the *Mrzḥ* Text", *ibid.* 51-54.

with some economic transaction of a *mrzḥ* institution, are the only texts similar to the Akkadian ones mentioned above. The rest of the Ugaritic texts which mention the *mrzḥ* are all mythological.

The most interesting of the mythological texts is *RS* 24.258, dealing with a banquet given by El, the head of the Ugaritic pantheon, to the other gods[61]. The essence of the feast seems to be eating and drinking to excess, resulting in the total collapse of El in his own excrement. I quote part of the text:

15b. El sits in his *mrzḥ*[62],
16. El drinks wine till satiety, must till inebriety.
17. El goes to his house, proceeds
18a. to his court[63].

The exact meaning of the word *mrzḥ* in this context is not easy to grasp. There can be no doubt, however, that the word has to do with the feasting and celebration mentioned in the lines preceding and following line 15b. It is likely that the solution to the riddle lies in line 15a which, for reasons of illegibility, I have left out of account. If the line could have been read, one might have been able to determine the exact meaning of the word *mrzḥ* on the basis of the parallelism likely to have existed between the two lines. From the continuation of our text (lines 17f), it is evident that the *mrzḥ* is not identical with the house of El. This fact is rather puzzling in view of the first lines of the text, of which lines 15b-18a form a part, where we read that El is making preparations for a banquet in his house. On the basis of what contextual evidence we do have, *mrzḥ* in this text is either a designation for a particular kind of banquet, or a name for the house in which this banquet took place[64].

---

[61] For the bibliography on this text, see H. M. Barstad, "Festmahl und Übersättigung", *AcOr* 39 (1978) notes 1 and 3. Cf. also K. J. Cathcart and W. G. E. Watson, "Weathering a Wake", *PIBA* 4 (1980) 50-52. I am grateful to Professor Cathcart for sending me an offprint of this article.

[62] J. C. de Moor, "Studies in the New Alphabetic Texts from Ras Shamra I", *UF* 1 (1969) 172, bases his translation of 1.15b: "Ilu remained seated among his *mrzḥ*-guests", on a reconstruction of the illegible 1.15a. I do not believe that this is possible. S. E. Loewenstamm has rightly remarked on 1.15a: "Der Text kann nich rekonstruiert werden ("Eine Lehrhafte ugaritische Trinkburleske", *UF* 1 (1969) 75).

[63] For *ḥtr*, see H. P. Rüger, "Zu RŠ 24.258", *UF* 1 (1969) 205.

[64] Obviously the mythological texts in which the *mrzḥ* appears belong to a different realm than the *mrzḥ* texts which relate to the daily life of ancient Ugarit and cannot be used uncritically to throw light upon the latter. In this respect, however, the text RS 24.258 is different from the other mythological *mrzḥ* texts written in Ugaritic. In its present form the story of El in his *mrzḥ* is followed by a series of medical prescriptions concerning over-eating and constipation. Elsewhere ("Festmahl und Übersättigung", *AcOr* 39 (1978) 23-30) I have attempted to demonstrate that the *whole* of RS 24.258 in its present form should be understood as a medical text. If the assumption is correct, the most likely place to look for the "*Sitz im Leben*" of RS 24.258 would be within the context of the sacred

It is most probable that *mrzḥ* is also mentioned in the famous poem of the goddess Anat, col. IV, line 4[65], where we read that the god *Ḵṯr*-and-*Ḫss* comes to deliver a message to El, while the latter sits in his *mrzḥ*. Unfortunately the text is rather broken and not easy to understand. If we translate *mrzḥ* in accordance with *RS* 24.258 mentioned above, however (cf. lines 9-10), at least a part of the text becomes meaningful[66].

The last text from ancient Ugarit to offer us information on the *mrzḥ* institution is the enigmatic *CTA* 21, one of the famous Rephaim texts[67]. Lines 1, 5 and 9 of this text contain the word *m(?)rzʿy*, probably referring to some person connected with the *mrzḥ* institution[68]. To make any further comments on this highly obscure text, however, would require a study of its own.

5.3. *The mrzḥ of Am 6, 4-6 against its Ancient Near Eastern Background*

I have presented the main bulk[69] of the evidence relating to the Ancient Near Eastern *mrzḥ* institution above. It is quite clear that the material, although apparently abundant, is far from sufficient for an exhaustive knowledge of the history and development of the institution. In addition to this even if we keep ourselves strictly within the borders of the Syrian/Palestinian religious world, chronological and geographical distances make it very unlikely that the institution was homogeneous. Not least important is the religious development which took place during the Hellenization of the Syrian religious world. For such and similar reasons it is obvious that we cannot equate the evidence relating to the

---

meals of the *mrzḥ* association. Thus, also the mythological text RS 24.258 may throw some interesting light upon the *mrzḥ* of the inhabitants of ancient Ugarit.

[65] *CTA* 1. The text was first published by C. Virolleaud, *La déesse ʿAnat* (1938). Cf. also U. Cassuto, *Ha Elah Anat* (1951) 91-100, G. R. Driver, *Canaanite Myths and Legends* (1956) 74-77, A. Caquot, *Textes ougaritiques* (1974) 293-314, J. C. L. Gibson, *Canaanite Myths* (1978) 39-40, 130-31.

[66] See above p. 137.

[67] The text was first published by C. Virolleaud, "Les Rephaïm", *Syr* 22 (1941) 1-30. Cf. further, G. R. Driver, *Canaanite Myths and Legends* (1956) 66-67, C. H. Gordon, *UT* 122, A. Caquot, *Textes ougaritiques* (1974) 479-80, J. C. L. Gibson, *Canaanite Myths and Legends* (1978) 135-36.

[68] Cf. also *UT* 19.2313.

[69] I have left out of consideration a few references to Semitic *thiasoi* in the Greek world (Delos, Thura, etc.). One may here compare the outline given by P. J. Morin, *The Cult of Dea Syria in the Greek World* (1960) *passim.* I have also left out of account the late Jewish evidence. All the references to the late Jewish evidence is found in J. Lewy, *Wörterbuch über die Talmudim and Midraschim* B. III (1924) 247 (cf. also M. Jastrow, *A Dictionary of the Targumim* Vol. 2 (1903) 840). For a survey of the late Jewish evidence, see O. Eissfeldt, "*marzeaḥ* und *marzĕḥāʾ*," *KlSchr* V (1973) 136-42. I have also left out the Arabic evidence (for a reference to the Arabic evidence, see O. Eissfeldt, *op. cit.* 136, n. 3). On the *mrzḥ* in general, see further B. D. Bryan, *Texts relating to the Marzeah* (1973).

Ancient Near Eastern *mrzḥ* institution and use it as a basis for a more comprehensive study.

Yet I believe that it is possible to draw a few general conclusions with regard to the religious and social phenomenon of the *mrzḥ* association. The main importance of the *mrzḥ* evidence is that it bears witness to the existence in the Ancient Near East of a social and religious association of the same kind as is also known from other cultures. Phenomenologically the *mrzḥ* institution is related to such institutions as for example, the Greek *thíasos* and the nordic *Gilde*[70], to mention only two examples. Being so richly attested, as well as widespread over several centuries, it is obious that the importance of the *mrzḥ* institution in society must have been considerable. Even if the character of the association was predominantly religious, it is beyond doubt that its social and economical influence was extensive, the members being people of consequence in society. Thus, both the Old Testament[71], the Nabatean[72], and the Ugaritic[73] evidence demonstrates beyond doubt that the *mrzḥ* members belonged to the upper classes of society. And from the rich evidence in Palmyra it may seem as if the institution entirely permeated Palmyrean society.

Apparently the main feature of the *mrzḥ* was the banquet. The sacred meal of the *mrzḥ* members is attested at Elephantine[74], at Piraeus[75], at Palmyra[76], at Ugarit[77] and in Am 6, 4-6[78]. That also the funerary banquet plays a certain role in the life of the *mrzḥ* institution is seen from Jer 15, 5[79] and from one Nabatean inscription[80]. Of the funerary character of the *mrzḥ*, however, our knowledge is rather limited[81].

---

[70] A most thorough survey of the Greek evidence is found in C. Lécrivain, "Thíasos", *Saglio* t. 5 (1912-19) 257-66. On the Nordic "gilde", see: H. Søgaard, S. Ljung, V. Niitemaa, G. A. Blom, "Gilde", *KLNM(N)* B. 5 (1960) 299-313.

[71] In addition to Am 6, 4-6 cf. also see above pp. 33-36.

[72] See above p. 132.

[73] See above p. 136.

[74] See above p. 130. However, we have no certain proof that *mrzḥ* in the Elephantine ostracon is a designation for a sacred meal.

[75] See above p. 131.

[76] See above p. 133ff.

[77] See above p. 137f.

[78] See above pp. 127-28. Cf. also above pp. 33-35.

[79] See above pp. 128-129.

[80] See above p. 132.

[81] Recently M. H. Pope has advocated the view that the Song of Songs should be interpreted against the background of the Ancient Near Eastern *mrzḥ* institution (*Song of Songs* (1977) 228-29 and *passim*). The most important feature of the *mrzḥ*, according to Pope, is the funeral feast. Pope, however, is building too much on late Christian evidence. Even if the funerary feast most probably formed a part of the life of the *mrzḥ* association, it is highly unlikely that it played the role attributed to it by Pope. At least there is no textual *evidence* for this. The connection between the Song of Songs and the *mrzḥ* remains uncertain (cf. J. Sasson, "On M. H. Pope's *Song of Songs*", *MAARAV* 1 (1978-79) 188-90).

That the sacred meal played an important role in the *mrzḥ* association is not surprising. The importance of the sacred meal in the history of religion in general[82] and throughout the ancient Semitic world in particular is well known[83].

The sacred meal seems to be most frequently attested in the ancient Syrian religion. In addition to the Old Testament evidence[84], we note how in the Ras Shamra texts the gods of the Ugaritic pantheon apparently take every opportunity to instigate a banquet with eating and drinking[85].

The sacred meal is further richly attested in several Syrian sanctuaries in Hellenistic times. Again Palmyra is our main witness. From the text published by Ingholt in 1926 quoted above[86] we find several references to wine and functionaries related to the storage and the serving of wine and food. With regard to the tesserae of Palmyra[87], E.Seyrig has convincingly demonstrated that their function was to be used as admittance cards to the sacred banquets of the *mrzḥ*[88]. The great importance of the banquet for the *mrzḥ* is attested by archaeology as well.

From Palmyra are known several rooms, commonly called "triclinia" from the three benches going around three of the four sides of the room, which were obviously used by the members of the *mrzḥ* for the celebration of their sacral banquets[89]. Similar rooms have been found all over the Syrian world, bearing witness to the great importance of these sacred meals. Thus, we know such triclinia from the Nabataean temples[90], from

---

[82] Cf. the survey with literature by A. Ström, "Abendmahl I", *TRE* B. 1 (1977) 43-47.

[83] Cf. *e.g.* R. Frankena, *Tākultu* (1953) for Assyrian-Babylonian religion, M. Delcor, "Repas cultuels esséniens", *Religion d'Israel* (1976) 320-44 for Qumran, J. Ryckmans, "Le repas rituel dans la religion Sud-arabe",*Symbolae Biblicae et Mesopotamicae F. T. M. de Liagre Böhl dedicatae* (1973) 237-34 for Arabia. Rich in relevant information is also C. H. Greenewalt, *Ritual Dinners in Early Sardis* (1978).

[84] Cf. *e.g.* 1 Sam 9, 12ff; 20, 5ff, Deut 12, 7; 27, 7. Ez 18, 12; 24, 11; 46, 19-24. Of particular importance in the Old Testament was the Passover meal. Cf. Ex 12, 1-11 and 12-51, Deut 16, 1-8, II Kings 23, 21-23, 2 Chr 35, 1-19.

[85] One only has to think of texts like *CTA* 4, III, 39-44; 4, IV, 31-39; 4, V, 106-109; 4, VI, 39-60; 3, I, 2-17; 22, 12-35, *RS* 24.252, *RS* 24.258. Of these text both *RS* 24.258 and *CTA* 22 concern the *mrzḥ*.

[86] See above pp. 133-34.

[87] See above p. 135.

[88] H. Seyrig, "Les tessères palmyréniennes", *Mémorial Lagrange* (1940) 51-58.

[89] H. Ingholt, "Five Dated Tombs from Palmyra", *Ber* 2 (1935) 63-68, 79-82, R. Amy, "Recherches dans la nécropole", *Syr* 17 (1936) 247-52, H. Ingholt, "Inscriptions and Sculptures", *Ber* 5 (1938) 138-39 (cf. also pl. L, I). J. Starcky, "Autour d'une dédicace", *Syr* 26 (1949) 59-62, R. du Mesnil du Buisson, *Les tessères et les monnaies* (1962) 475-93, especially 485-88, J. T. Milik, *Recherches d'épigraphie proche-oriental* I (1972) 141-217 *passim.*

[90] N. Glueck, *Deities and Dolphins* (1969) 162-91.

Dura-Europos[91], from Chirbet Semrīn[92], from Antioch-on-the-Orontes[93], as well as from several Syrian sanctuaries both in and beyond the Syrian-Phoenician borders[94]. Even if there is no direct evidence of the *mrzḥ* association in *all* these places, the rich attestations of religious banquet rooms make it possible to assume their existence.

It is against this picture of the Ancient Near Eastern sacred meal that we shall have to view the words of the prophet Amos in 6, 4-6. The objection of the prophet does not concern the opulent feasting to excess of the morally decadent upper classes in Israelite society[95]. The banquet described by the prophet in 6, 4-6 is the sacred meal of a Samaritan *mrzḥ* association, and the banquet is condemned for its connections with non-Yahwistic deities rather than for its immorality[96]. When viewed against this background, not only the text of 6, 4-6 becomes more meaningful in its context, but the existence of the *mrzḥ* meal in Samaria at the time of the prophet Amos may also throw interesting light upon several other passages in the Book of Amos, as well[97].

That the text of Am 6, 4-6 refers to a *mrzḥ* association of basically the same character as we find represented all over the ancient Syrian/Phoenician world must be considered beyond doubt. For this reason it is regrettable that O. Eissfeldt, one of the scholars who has paid much attention to the Ancient Near Eastern *mrzḥ* association[98], held the view that the word *mrzḥ* occurring in Jer 16, 5 and Am 6, 7 was derivated from a root *rzḥ* with the basic meaning "schreien", whereas the *mrzḥ* of the other West-Semitic languages is a derivation from a root *rzḥ* II with the basic meaning "sich vereinen"[99]. Eissfeldt, consequently, could accept no connection between the *mrzḥ* of the Bible and the *mrzḥ* of the Syrian religious world. Needless to say, such etymological speculations as those

---

[91] *The Excavations of Dura-Europos* [III] (1932) 5, M. Rostovtzeff, *Caravan Cities* (1932) 178-79, J. Starcky, "Autour d'une dédicace", *Syr* 26 (1949) 65.

[92] D. Schlumberger, "Neue Ausgrabungen", *AA* 50 (1935) 607-10, *idem*, *La Palmyrène du Nord-Ouest* (1951) 101-05.

[93] W. A. Campbell, "Archaeological Notes", *AJA* 42 (1938) 205-18.

[94] For further references cf. J. Starcky, "Autour d'une dédicace", *Syr* 26 (1949) 62-67 and D. Schlumberger, *La Palmyrène du Nord-Ouest* (1951) 101-05. The latter gives references to evidence of the sacred meal in non-Semitic religions, as well.

[95] Cf. above p. 128.

[96] From Am 5, 26 and 8, 14 there can be no doubt that the polemics against foreign deities play a major role in the preaching of Amos (on Am 5, 26, see above pp. 118-26, on 8, 14, see below).

[97] Cf. above pp. 33-36, 42-43, 55.

[98] In addition to the works by Eissfeldt mentioned in n. 31 and n. 69 above, and in n. 99 below, one may note "Kultvereine in Ugarit", *Ug* VI (1969).

[99] O. Eissfeldt, "Etymologische und archäologische Erklärung", *OrAnt* 5 (1966) 165-76.

of Eissfeldt concerning the word *mrzḥ* do not amount to much when confronted with the *contextual* evidence[100].

---

[100] As far as I have been able to find out, very few scholars have followed Eissfeldt in his ingenious, but artificial attempt to explain the occurrences of *mrzḥ* in the Old Testament as derivations from *rzḥ* I, and all the other occurrences of *mrzḥ* as derivations from *rzḥ* II.

CHAPTER SIX

THE DEITIES OF AM 8, 14

6.1. *The Structure and Contents of Chapter 8. The Text of 8, 14*

As is also the case with the other chapters in the Book of Amos, the message contained in Chapter 8 seems to constitute an ideological unity[1]. We may divide the chapter in the following way: vv. 1-2: The vision of the fruit-basket, the fourth vision in the Book of Amos[2]; v. 3: A word of judgement; vv. 4-6: The prophet's accusation against the outrages of the people. We notice the moral/social character of the charge. Vv. 7-13: Pronouncement of doom. This final utterance of doom is immediately followed by another accusation in v. 14, this time of a religious/cultic character. Being connected to the preceding passage through the participle *hnšbʿym*, the accusation in v. 14 also serves the function of giving the reason for the pronouncement of doom[3].

Consequently the structure of this chapter is very similar to what has been found earlier in Amos: corresponding to the denouncing of the moral behaviour of the prophet's contemporaries there is the condemnation of their religious practice. Again it is obvious that the common view which regards the prophet Amos as not concerned with polemics against non-Yahwistic or Yahwistic/syncretistic cults but as a moral castigator only, cannot be upheld[4].

The condemnation of the religious cults of the Israelites is obviously never so evident in the message of Amos as in 8, 14:

> ... *hnšbʿym bʾšmt šmrwn wʾmrw ḥy ʾlhyk dn wḥy drk bʾr-šbʿ wnplw wlʾ-yqwmw ʿwd.*
>
> "... those who swear by *ʾšmt šmrwn* and say: By the life of your god, Dan, and by the life of *drk bʾr -šbʿ*. And they shall fall and never raise again".[5]

---

[1] V. 8 should probably be treated on the same level as the so-called doxologies in the Book of Amos. On the authenticity of the doxologies, see above pp. 79-80.

[2] Cf. 7, 1-3. 4-6. 7-8; 9, 1-4. For 8, 1-2 see in addition to the current commentaries B. D.Rahtjen, "A Critical Note on Am 8, 1-2". *JBL* 83 (1964) 416-17, S. E. Loewenstamm, "A Remark on the Typlogy of the Prophetic Vision", *Tarb* 34 (1965) 319-22 (in Hebrew).

[3] It is possible that the use of the participle has here contributed towards weakening the impression that v. 14 gives a description of the behaviour which has led to the pronouncement of the words of judgement in vv. 7-13. The common structure of the Book of Amos, a description of the outrages of the people closely followed by the particle *lkn*, introducing the judgement, is stylistically more likely to emphasize the behaviour of the Israelites as the reason for doom (cf. 3, 11; 5, 16; 6, 7; 7, 17).

[4] Cf. the introduction above p. 4ff.

[5] There is no reason whatever to remove the statement *wnplw wlʾ-yqwmw ʿwd* from its

Am 5, 26 and 8, 14 are the only passages in the Book of Amos where the names of particular deities are distinctly mentioned. To the student interested in the religious polemics of the prophet Amos, this implies that these two passages deserve particular attention. Unfortunately, the text of Am 5, 26 is corrupt and does not encourage any major investigation[6]. In the case of Am 8, 14, however, this is not the case. For this reason I have decided to deal in detail with the exegesis of this one verse. Taking its importance into consideration, I find it natural that Am 8, 14 should occupy a central position in this study.

6.2. *Swearing by the Deity*

It is with particular interest that we note that Am 8, 14 not only contains the names of different deities worshipped in Samaria at the time of the prophet Amos, but that the verse also contains a reference to swearing by the name of the god.

The oath plays an important role both in the Old Testament and in the Ancient Near Eastern world. The comprehensive and complex oath institution in the Old Testament—being primarily of a juridicial character, but with profound social and religious implications—cannot be dealt with here[7]. I find the definition given by F. Horst particularly appropriate: "Der Eid soll im Alten Testament wie in der Umwelt Zusagen und Aussagen bekräftigen, ihnen Verlässlichkeit, Verbindlichkeit und Unverbrüchlichkeit geben. Er ist adfirmatio. So erscheint er als Versprechenseid, Prozesseid und Bekenntniseid. Der Mensch schwört Eide, aber Gott auch."[8]

What is of the greatest interest to us is obviously the oath in its religious context. From the Old Testament itself it follows quite clearly that swearing by the name of Yahweh was expected of the Israelites. So

---

present context and place it at the beginning of the verse as has been done by several of the German commentaries (cf. *inter alia* K. Marti, *Das Dodekapropheton* (1904) 219, W. Nowack, *Die kleinen Propheten* (1922) 163, E. Sellin, *Das Zwölfprophetenbuch* (1922) 215, V. Maag, *Text, Wortschatz und Begriffswelt* (1951) 56, T. H. Robinson, *Die zwölf kleinen Propheten* (1964) 102, W. Rudolph, *Joel, Amos, Obadja, Jona* (1971) 268. For some reason this change in the text of MT seems to be peculiar to the commentaries written in the German language. As far as I know, none of the English or French major commentaries has undertaken this transfer.

For the prophetical use of the formula *npl-qwm* cf. also Am 5, 2, Jes 24, 20, Jer 8, 4; 25, 27.

[6] On Am 5, 26, see above pp. 118-26.

[7] The classic work on the oath in the Ancient Near East is still J. Pedersen, *Der Eid bei den Semiten* (1914). Among more recent works one may note F. Horst, "Der Eid im Alten Testament", *EvTh* 17 (1957) 366-84, *idem*, "Eid. II. Im AT," *RGG*³ B.2 (1958) 349-50 (with literature), M. R. Lehmann, "Biblical Oaths", *ZAW* 81 (1969) 74-92. Cf. also above Chapter 3, n. 153.

[8] F. Horst, "Der Eid im Alten Testament", *EvTh* 17 (1957) 366.

important was the duty of swearing by the name of Yahweh that it was regarded on a level with the actual worship of the god. The following examples should illustrate this sufficiently:

> "You shall fear Yahweh your god, you shall serve him,
> and swear by his name (*wbšmw tšbᶜ*)." (Deut 6, 13.)

> "You shall fear Yahweh your god, you shall serve him,
> cling to him, and swear by his name (*wbšmw tšbᶜ*)." (Deut 10, 20.)

> "And the king shall rejoice in God, all who swear by him
> (*kl-hnšbᶜ bw*) shall boast." (Ps 63, 12a-b. MT).

In the same way as swearing by the name of Yahweh is closely connected to the worship of the god and is expected of the Israelites as a duty, swearing by gods other than Yahweh is synonymous with idolatry:

> "... that you do not mingle with these people who are still left among you. Do not mention the names of their gods, do not swear by them (*wlʾ tšbyᶜw*), do not serve them and do not worship them, but cling to Yahweh your god as you have done to this day." (Jos 23, 7-8).

> "I will raise my hand against Judah, and against all the inhabitants of Jerusalem, and I will cut off from this place what is left of *bᶜl*, the name of the idol-priests together with the priests, and those worshipping on the roofs the host of heaven, those who worship and swear to Yahweh (*hnšbᶜym lyhwh*) and yet swear by Milcom (*whnšbᶜym bmlkm*)". (Zeph 1, 4-5)[9].

All these passages show clearly the close connection between the worship of a god and swearing by him in the Old Testament. In the light of Am 8, 14, a passage like Jer 12, 16 turns out as particularly interesting:

> "And it shall happen if they really learn my people's ways, and to swear by my name (*lhšbᶜ bšmy*) 'By the life of Yahweh (*ḥy yhwh*)', as they taught my people to swear by Baᶜal (*lhšbᶜ bbᶜl*)."[10]

What makes the passage Jer 12, 16 so interesting is that here, as in Am 8, 14, we have an example of the prophet's denunciation of swearing by the oath formula *ḥy* + the name of a deity. From Jer 12, 16 we learn that the people have been swearing by the formula *ḥy bᶜl*. In Am 8, 14 other deities are mentioned in connection with the formula.

Swearing by the life of a god, a king, or even a high-ranking official in order to validate or strengthen the oath was a widespread phenomenon in the Ancient Near East. Well known from the Old Testament is the oath formula *ḥy yhwh*[11]. In accordance with the close connection between

---

[9] Cf. also Is 19, 18; 45, 23; 65, 16.

[10] The syntax of this verse in MT is awkward.

[11] See besides *TWAT* and *THAT sub voce* especially M. Greenberg, "The Hebrew Oath Particle *ḤAY/ḤĒ*", *JBL* 76 (1957) 34-39, H. J. Kraus, "Der lebendige Gott", *EvTh* 27 (1967) 169-200.

swearing by the deity and worshipping him, the reference of the prophet Amos to swearing by three different deities in Am 8, 14 informs us of the worship of these deities by the contemporaries of the prophet. Apparently the formula *ḥy* + the mention of the name of a deity is the only oath giving rise to prophetic concern in the Old Testament. The related phenomenon involving kings or others was never regarded as illicit[12].

6.2.1. The Oath Formula *ḥy*

The interpretation of the oath formula *ḥy* + the name of a deity constitutes a problem in itself. A particular problem connected with the interpretation of the formula is caused by the fact that *ḥy* in MT is vocalized in two different ways: before the name of *yhwh*, and other designations for the god of Israel, the particle is vocalized *ḥay*. Before the names of all other deities, as well as before human beings, however, it is vocalized *ḥê*. Obviously, this is not the place to go into details with regard to this problem. I am inclined, however, to agree with those who regard this difference in vocalization merely as "*eine rabbinische Finesse*"[13].

How, then, should this particular Semitic oath formula be translated? M. Greenberg has argued convincingly that *ḥy* in this oath formula should be taken as a noun in the construct state[14]. In this he is undoubtedly right, and it is regrettable that the rendering of the expression *ḥy yhwh* with "Yahweh is alive if..." is still widely maintained, instead of the correct "by the life of Yahweh"[15].

---

[12] The occurrences of *ḥy yhwh* in the Old Testament are all listed in *HAL*³ (1967) 295. For the occurrence of the formula in two Lachish ostraca, see *KAI* 193, 9 and 196, 12. For the formula *ḥy ʾny*, see *HAL*³ (1967) 295. Similar formulas found in the Old Testament are *ḥy ʾl* in Job 27, 2 and *ḥy hʾlhym* in 2 Sam 2, 27. Also the formula *ḥy-npšk* (1 Sam 1, 26; 17, 55; 20, 3; 25, 26, 2 Sam 14, 19, II Kings 2, 2.4.6; 4, 30), which is used in addressing both God, kings, priests, and prophets, is related to the formula *ḥy* + the mention of a name. The particle *ḥy* used of other figures than Yahweh in Old Testament oath formulas is not frequent, but the phenomenon occurs. In Gen 42, 15-16 Joseph in Egypt swears by the life of Pharaoh, the Pharaoh being regarded as a god (cf. n. 16 below), and in 2 Sam 15, 21 the formula *ḥy yhwh* occurs together with *ḥy ʾdny* used of the king. It is not likely that this double oath is a result of Egyptian influence as supposed by Kraus ("Der lebendige Gott", *EvTh* 27 (1967) 173-74). In addition to swearing by the god swearing by high-ranking members of society was quite common in the Ancient Near East. Thus, it must have been known in Israel also. Nor can swearing by the king in 2 Sam 15, 21 be used as an argument in the discussion on divine kingship in Israel.

[13] For the discussion, see M. Greenberg, "The Hebrew Oath Particle", *JBL* 76 (1957) 36, V. Maag, *Text, Wortschatz und Begriffswelt* (1951) 147-48. This explanation is the more probable as *ḥay* is used not only before *yhwh*, something which *might* have been explained phonologically (cf. Greenberg *loc. cit.*), but before *ʾl* and *ʾlhym* as well. This vocalization, of course, was no invention of the Masoretes, but reflects a manner of reading that came into existence due to reverence for the God of Israel.

[14] M. Greenberg, "The Hebrew Oath Particle", *JBL* 76 (1957) 36-39.

[15] M. Greenberg, *op. cit.* p. 37, n. 18, rightly opposes the reading of L. Köhler in Job 27, 2 (cf. also L. Köhler, *Lexicon* (1958) 292): "Es gilt Jahwes Leben wenn..." I agree

This strong connection between the act of swearing and the life of a god/king/person is by no means peculiar to the Old Testament only. The phenomenon is well attested all over the Ancient Near East, and was particularly frequent in Ancient Egypt[16] and in Assyria/Babylonia[17]. In fact, swearing by the life of someone was so common that in Akkadian the very word for oath, *nīšu(m)* II, actually means "oath by the life". Correspondingly, the expression *nīš* + king/deity means "to declare the life of" the king or deity concerned[18]. And in Egyptian the word for "life", *ʿnḫ*, is the word for "oath" as well[19]. Also the Arabs know of swearing by the life[20].

The question which we shall have to ask next is whether the use of *ḥy* + the name of the deity in Am 8, 14 can offer us any information beyond the mere fact that the prophet is here concerned with polemics against those who worship non-Yahwistic deities. In other words: does the particle *ḥy* reveal anything regarding the actual content of the cults or the character of the deities mentioned?

It may be of interest in this connection that in Ps 18, 47 (= 2 Sam 22, 47) we find the formula *ḥy yhwh* in a context which has nothing to do with swearing. Consequently, one ought to render *ḥy yhwh* in this text differently from the oath formula *ḥy yhwh*:

> "Yahweh is alive, blessed be my rock,
> exalted the god of my salvation."

Some scholars, and the Swedish historian of religion Geo Widengren in particular, are of the opinion that in Ps 18, 47 and texts similar in their views there are traces of the worship of a dying and rising deity. In addition to Ps 18, 47 Widengren bases his view on several Old Testament passages, among them Am 8, 14[21]. If Widengren and his followers are right, it goes without saying that this has considerable consequences for our view on the cults mentioned in Am 8, 14. But is it really possible that Widengren is right?

---

with Greenberg that this rendering in fact would be blasphemous. It has not been maintained in *HAL*³. Among more recent commentators on the oath formula C. A. Keller still rendered the phrase "lebendig ist Jahwe, wenn ich dies tue bzw. nicht tue" as recently as in 1976 ("*šbʿ* ni", *THAT* II (1976) 860).

[16] For a survey, see J. A. Wilson, "The Oath in Ancient Egypt", *JNES* 7 (1948) Table I, p. 151. Cf. also *RÄRG* (1952) 164 and P. Kaplony, "Eid", *LÄ* 1 (1975) 1189-90.

[17] A survey on the oath in Assyria/Babylonia is given by M. San Nicolò, "Eid", *RLA* B.2 (1938) 305-15.

[18] W. von Soden, *AHW* II (1972) 797-98.

[19] A. Erman und H. Grapow, *Aegyptisches Handwörterbuch* (1921) 26.

[20] See J. Pedersen, *Der Eid bei den Semiten* (1914) 17-18. Cf. also the modern Hebrew usage *bḥyy*, "I swear": "By my life!".

[21] G. Widengren, *Sakrales Königtum* (1955) 62-76. See also by the same author, "Konungens vistelse i dödsriket", *SEÅ* 10 (1945) 77.

With regard to Am 8, 14 there can be no doubt about the fact that this passage is easily explained against the background of the Old Testament usage of swearing by the deity worshipped in the cult[22]. With regard to the specific character of the deities mentioned in this text, nothing decisive can be said before we have taken a closer look at the different deities against their Ancient Near Eastern background. In the actual *text* of Am 8, 14, however, there is no support whatever to the assumption of Widengren that we have here a reference to the worship of dying and rising deities.

If we proceed to Ps 18, 47, the text with constitutes Widengren's main witness for his assumption concerning the dying and the rising deity, one would need a very vivid imagination indeed to see anything more in this text than a mere hymnal statement or outcry of triumph. Again there is nothing in the text which could support Widengren's assertion that the text gives evidence of the worship of Yahweh as a dying and rising deity. Consequently, one is not surprised to find that most of the commentators on this problem disagree with Widengren in his view of these texts[23].

Still, the problem is somewhat more complicated than it may seem to be from the way opponents to an interpretation of Yahweh as a rising and dying deity in the Old Testament have expressed it. If there really was widespread worship of a dying and rising deity in the Ancient Near East in the first millennium B.C., there is good reason to assume that this phenomenon was known in ancient Palestine as well. And if this particular cult could in some way be connected to the formula *ḥy* + the name of the dying and rising god, obviously this would call for a thorough investigation into the whole of the Old Testament in order to try to establish whether references to such a cult could be found. It would not be sufficient merely to claim that such traces are not likely to be found.

The problem, however, is the matter of the dying and rising deity itself. Whereas it was earlier commonly accepted that a cult of a dying and rising deity not only existed in the Ancient Near East but was also widely spread, this view has been called in question during the last decades. This is not the place to give any detailed survey of this important change within the history of religion in the Ancient Near East, so I shall be content to mention shortly the main contributions within the field.

A major breakthrough came in 1955 when von Soden published his important article "Gibt es ein Zeugnis dafür dass die Babylonier an die

[22] Cf. above p.144ff.

[23] Cf. *inter alia* H. Ringgren, *Israelitische Religion* (1963) 78, W. Schmidt, "Baals Tod und Auferstehung", *ZRGG* 15 (1963) 4, n. 23, H.-J. Kraus, "Der lebendige Gott", *EvTh* 27 (1967) 180-81.

Wiederaufstehung Marduks geglaubt haben?''[24] It is well known that the god Marduk played an important role in discussions about the Ancient Near Eastern belief in a dying and rising deity. As a result of the enormous influence of a book by H. Zimmern on the Babylonian New Year Festival published in 1918[25], the view was widely held, and still is by many scholars, that the Babylonian god Marduk was worshipped as a dying and rising deity. Zimmern built his thesis mainly on the Akkadian text *KAR* 143[26], the very text that von Soden in his 1955 article maintains has nothing to do with Marduk's dying and rising at all[27]. We may in the same connection, also mention the instructive article by Gurney on the god Tammuz[28].

The most important development within this field, however, is to be found in recent contributions concerning the Phoenician deity Adonis, regarded as the dying and rising deity *par excellence.* What Zimmern achieved for Marduk, Baudissin achieved for Adonis. Mainly as a result of the now classic work of that great scholar[29], generations of scholars have believed in the dying and rising of the Phoenician Adonis. Nor can the importance of J. G. Frazer's famous book on dying and rising deities be exaggerated[30]. It remains a fact that even if the social anthropologist Frazer is regarded as hopelessly amateurish in his methods by professional anthropologists, his views on a deity like Adonis have been, and are likely to be, I am afraid, extraordinary tenacious of life within scholarly groups where methodology is not taken too seriously[31].

---

[24] *ZA* 17 (1955) 130-66. See also by the same author, ''Ein neues Bruchstück des assyrischen Kommentars zur Marduk-Ordal'', *ZA* 18 (1957) 224-34.

[25] H. Zimmern, *Zum babylonischen Neujahrsfest* (1918).

[26] *KAR* 143 was published by E. Ebeling, *Keilschrifttexte aus Assur religiösen Inhalts*, B.1 (1915-19). The duplicate, *KAR* 219, was published in vol. 2, appearing after the book by Zimmern.

[27] Cf. also *WM* Abt. 1. B.1 (1965) 97.

[28] O. R. Gurney, ''Tammuz Reconsidered'', *JSS* 7 (1962) 147-60. See, however, T. Jacobsen, *Toward the Image of Tammuz* (1970) 73-101.

[29] W. W. Baudissin, *Adonis und Esmun* (1911). Here, too, the research of Zimmern is of vital importance inasmuch as Baudissin takes all his Babylonian material from Zimmern's book *Der babylonische Gott Tamūz* (1909).

[30] J. G. Frazer, *The Dying God* (1911). Cf. also by the same author, *Adonis, Attis, Osiris* (1914).

[31] This said, it should be mentioned that criticisms of Frazer's methods have occupied a significant place within methodological discussions in social anthropology throughout this century. On the whole I believe that the necessary criticism of this (and other) epoch-making intellectual giants of the past ought to reflect a more ''methodological'' understanding of the necessity of reading a man's achievement in the light of his social and intellectual environment than what has often been the case. Frazer's enormous influence contradicts the often condescending treatment he has been given by some of his modern critics. Very short, but responsible appraisals of Frazer are found *inter alia* in A. de Waal Malefijt, *Religion and Culture* (1970) 53-55, E. E. Evans-Pritchard, *Theories of Primitive Religion* (1975) 27-29.

As for the connection between Frazer and Baudissin, it is not possible to state to what

With regard to the interpretation of Adonis and related deities it is today possible to discount the theory of Adonis as a dying and rising god as a Frazerian concept strongly influenced by the wish to demonstrate that Christianity was not an innovation, but that all its essential features are to be found in earlier religions. It has been maintained, in fact, that this was the major intention of the whole *Golden Bough*, and I believe this is correct[32]. This "christianization" of Adonis and other deities of the Ancient Near East soon resulted in the common belief that these gods were worshipped as dying and rising deities, thus constituting an adequate counterpart to the later Christian belief in the death and resurrection of Christ.

Recently, important articles have been published by Colpe and Will[33], demonstrating that there is no evidence whatever in support of this widely held view[34].

The semantic untenability of classifying deities like Marduk, Tammuz, Adonis, Attis, Osiris, etc. as dying and rising deities obviously takes the last of the credibility out of Widengren's interpretation of Am 8, 14. It also takes the credibility out of the attempt to interpret the formula *ḥy aliyn bʿl*, occurring in *CTA* 6, III, 2.8.20, as a cultic cry in relation to the resurrection of Baʿal. In this myth, which relates the story of Baʿal's death and return to life in accordance with the absence and return of fertility[35], scholars have found yet another example of a dying and rising

extent Baudissin is dependent upon Frazer. Baudissin writes in the introduction to *Adonis und Esmun* (1911) VI-VII that he totally agrees with Frazer with regard to the meaning of the different myths, but not with regard to their origin. As for the relationship between the alleged worship of Adonis as a dying and rising deity and the Christian religion, he is undoubtedly far more reserved than Frazer (*ibid.* 522ff). Nevertheless, in the introduction to the 3rd edition of *Adonis, Attis, Osiris* in 1914 Frazer gives expression to his high regard of Baudissin's book. On the whole, however, it is evident that Baudissin did not approve of Frazer's methodological approach (cf. O. Eissfeldt, "Vom Lebenswerk eines Religionshistorikers", *ZDMG* 80 (1926) 109-11).

[32] E. E. Evans-Pritchard, "Religion and the Anthropologists", *Bl* 41 (1960) 110.

[33] C. Colpe, "Zur mythologischen Struktur der Adonis-, Attis- und Osiris-Überlieferungen, *lišān mitḫurti* (1966) 23-44, E. Will, "Le rituel des Adonies", *Syr* 52 (1975) 93-105. These scholars were not the first ones, however, to express doubt as to the resurrection of Adonis. Already in 1933, Roland de Vaux expressed himself very critical of the common view on the god Adonis. He was of the opinion though, that the resurrection of Adonis was celebrated at a very late stage in Egypt ("Sur quelques rapports entre Adonis et Osiris", *RB* 42 (1933) 31-56). The most recent commentator on Adonis is S. Ribichini, "Per una riconsiderazione di Adonis", *RSF* 7 (1979) 163-74.

[34] Obviously, the semantic untenability of classifying these gods as "dying" and "rising" does not affect the phenomenon that the deities in question disappear and return in relation to the change of the seasons, probably reflecting the disappearance and return of fertility. At the same time, however, it should be kept in mind that the theme of the disappearing deity is only one of several themes associated with Adonis and related deities.

[35] For an introduction, bibliography, and translation of this myth, see A. Caquot, *Textes ougaritiques* (1974) 225-71. The most recent edition of the text is found in J. C. L. Gibson, *Canaanite Myths and Legends* (1978) 68-81.

deity in the Ancient Near East. Against the background of the above, however, this interpretation can scarcely be maintained.

Any attempt to interpret the difficult Ugaritic myths today will have to take into account not only the Ugaritic myths, but the whole mythic world of the Ancient Near East in order to try to work out the structure and the meaning of these myths. As the theme of the disappearing god is fairly common in Ancient Near Eastern myths, the occurrence of this theme in the Ugaritic myths should be viewed also in the light of the other, related myths. Even if little systematic work has been carried out within this field[36], we know at least enough to be able to state that there is no evidence of any dying and rising deity to be found in these myths. The usefulness, and even possibility, of isolating one formula like *ḥy aliyn bʿl* and giving it a content of such wide-reaching consequences as has been done is dubious, to say the least.

The expression *ḥy aliyn bʿl* in *CTA* 6, III, 2.8.20 is probably best explained in the light of the expression *ḥy yhwh* in Ps 18, 47. As mentioned above[37] this expression should be defined as a triumphal/hymnic outcry. The occurrence of the phenomenon in Ps 18, 47 is best understood when viewed against the broader context of the concept of the "living god", represented by expressions like *ʾlhym ḥyym*, *ʾlhym ḥy*, and *ʾl ḥy*. Any attempt to distinguish between these three different Old Testament expressions is not prolific.

The problem with the notion of the "living god", however, is that it is not easily translated into English. Especially dangerous in a case like this is the tendency to what James Barr has called "hypostatization of linguistic phenomena"[38]. For this reason it may seem wise to make a little detour and take a closer look at the occurrences of the "living god" in their context.

(Deut 5, 26). Moses gives an account of the people's reaction after they have heard the deity speak out of the fire. The point of the story is the danger attached to witnessing the theophany, a well known religious phenomenon[39]:

---

[36] It is remarkable that so much work has gone into the philological elucidation of the Ancient Near Eastern mythological material, whereas comparatively little has been achieved with regard to the problems connected to the nature and meaning of the myths. A book of general interest—despite its rather meagre treatment of Canaanite myths—is G. S. Kirk, *Myth* (1970). Another book worth mentioning is P. Xella, *Problemi del mito nel Vicino Oriente* (1976). For an attempt to apply structural methods on Ugaritic mythological texts, see D. L. Petersen, M. Woodward, "Northwest Semitic Religion", *UF* 9 (1977) 233-48. An important article is R. A. Oden, "Theoretical Assumptions", *MAARAV* 2 (1979-80) 43-63. Cf. also n. 55 below.

[37] P. 148.

[38] J. Barr, "Hypostatization of Linguistic Phenomena", *JSS* 7 (1962) 85-94.

[39] Cf. H. M. Barstad, "Der rasende Zeus", *Tem* 12 (1976) 172-73.

"For who could possibly stay alive after having heard, like we have, the voice of ᵓ*lhym ḥyym* speaking out of the midst of the fire?"

(Jos 3, 10). Giving his instructions to the tribes before the cross over the river Jordan, an event happening in a miraculous way when the river stops running and the tribes cross over dryshod (vv. 14-17), Joshua states:

"By this you shall know that ᵓ*l ḥy* is among you and will certainly drive away from you the Canaanites, the Hittites, the Hivites, the Perizzites, the Girgashites, the Amorites and the Jebusites."

(1 Sam 17, 26). From the story of Goliath who has come to scorn Israel:

"And David said to the men that stood near him: What shall be done for the man who kills this Philistine and takes away the disgrace from Israel? For who is this uncircumcised Philistine that he should insult the armies of ᵓ*lhym ḥyym*?" (cf. also v. 36).

(II Kings 19, 4). From the story of Sennacherib's invasion of Judah in the year 701 B.C. All the towns of Judah, except Jerusalem, have fallen, and the king of Assyria sends his men to Jerusalem to inform king Hezekiah that he cannot trust Yahweh to save the city from the Assyrians. King Hezekiah sends a message to the prophet Isaiah, saying among other things:

"Perhaps Yahweh your God heard all the words of the cup-bearer whom his master, the king of Assyria, sent to insult ᵓ*lhym ḥy*, and will rebuke the words which Yahweh your God has heard..." (cf. also v. 16. II Kings 19, 4.16 = Is 37, 4.17).

(Jer 10, 10). After having given a description of non-Yahwistic deities, underlining their impotency, Jeremiah proclaims:

"But Yahweh is the true God, he is ᵓ*lhym ḥyym* and the everlasting king. At his wrath the earth quakes, the nations cannot endure his rage."

(Jer 23, 36). Towards the end of a tract against the false prophets, there comes this statement about the "burden"[40] of Yahweh:

"And the 'burden' of Yahweh you shall mention no more, for the 'burden' shall be a man's own word, and you twist the words of ᵓ*lhym ḥyym*, of Yahweh Sabaoth, our God."

(Hos 2, 1 MT). Hosea, in an oracle on the future (the context is difficult and it is uncertain where the verse belongs in the composition):

---

[40] Vv. 34-40. The rendering of Hebrew *ms*ᵓ by "burden" is uncertain. Even if the translation is correct, it is not easy to see what is meant with "burden" in this context. As this does not affect the formula ᵓ*lhym ḥyym*, however, I will not go into this problem.

> "And the number of the Israelites will be like the sand of the seashore which cannot be measured or counted. And in the place where they were told: "You are not my people," they will be called: 'Children of ʾ*l ḥy*'."

(Ps 42, 3). In this song of lament, the singer bewails the absence of God:

> "My soul thirsts for God, for ʾ*l ḥy*. When shall I come to see the face of God? V. 4. My tears are my food—day and night and all day long they say to me: Where is your God?"

(Ps 84, 3). In a hymn to the temple of Yahweh:

> "My soul longs for, yea, yearns for the courts of Yahweh,
> my heart and my flesh sing with joy to ʾ*l ḥy*."

When reading through these occurrences of statements concerning the "living god" it seems obvious that it is not possible in the light of the context to state that the expression means anything in particular. It is, for instance, quite possible to exchange the expression by the name of Yahweh. This operation does not alter the basic meaning of the statements occurring in the different verses where we find references to the "living god". In the texts which we have quoted, consequently, it seems that the function of the expressions ʾ*lhym ḥyym*, ʾ*lhym ḥy*, and ʾ*l ḥy* is solely to serve as titles for Yahweh.

Obviously there is some historical reason for these expressions having become designations for Yahweh. In their present context, however, speculations on the etymology of the expressions are of no importance, and may even lead to over-interpretation of the texts[41].

A further problem lies in the *relationship* between the formulas *ḥy yhwh* in Ps 18, 47 and *ḥy aliyn bʿl* in *CTA* 6, III, 2.8.20 and the statements concerning the "living god" presented above. The occurrences in Ps 18 and *CTA* 6 reflect an ancient usage and are not quite comparable to the statements where the "living god" appears as a Yahwistic title. It is likely, however, that these Yahwistic titles originate in the usage found in Ps 18, 47 and *CTA* 6, III, 2.8.20.

In 1964 Delekat attempted to demonstrate that the expression ʾ*l ḥy* should be connected with the word *ḥy* in 1 Sam 18, 18, meaning "Sippe". The original meaning of the expression accordingly, would have been something like "the god of the family"[42]. Delekat can hardly be right in this assumption. He did, however, stress one important aspect with regard to the meaning of the word *ḥy* in this connection, stating that

---

[41] Even a sober scholar like H. Ringgren is able to state with regard to the formula "the living god": "Die Deutung als "der aktiv Eingreifende" oder "der offensichtlich Anwesende" scheint sich also zu bestätigen" (*TWAT* II (1977) 892).

[42] L. Delekat, "Zum hebräischen Wörterbuch", *VT* 14 (1964) 27-28.

the word never means "living" in the sense of "active", but always "living" as opposed to "dead"[43].

This, of course, is a correct observation, which may relate to swearing by the life of a god as well. But what does it mean when one says that the god is not dead? The historical background for the Old Testament statements about the "living god" is probably best explained against the background of the *Götterpolemik*. To the followers of Yahweh the other deities are dead gods, unable to act, or to help the people who worship them. Only Yahweh is a living god. A reminiscence of this polemical side of statements about the living god is found in Jer 10, 10, quoted above[44]. It follows from this passage that a "living god" is a "true" god, a "real" god.

A further support of this is found in Ps 106, 28. In this passage the expression *zib̲ḥê met̲îm*, "sacrifices of the dead" occurs. These words have been interpreted quite commonly as a reference to a cult of the dead. Already Baudissin, however, maintained that the expression should rather be regarded as implying polemics against non-Yahwistic deities; the gods referred to are dead in the sense that they are not real gods[45]. Even if *mtym* is used in this way only in Ps 106, 28, the assumption has some support in the late Jewish tradition on the use of this word in Mishna ᵓAbot III, 3, ᶜAboda Zara II, 3, Jub 22, 17 and Sib 8, 384. A parallel to this particular use of *mtym* in Ps 106, 28 is found also in the use of the word *nblh*, "corpse" concerning the deities in Jer 16, 18. Also Lev 26, 30, referring to the idols as *pgry*, "corpses", bears witness to the same polemical tradition. It is within this context that we shall have to regard the expressions *ḥy yhwh* and *ḥy aliyn bᶜl* in Ps 18 and *CTA* 6 respectively. Admittedly, we do not have the polemical situation witnessed to in these texts. Yet, there seems to be no better way in which these two expressions may be explained.

Before we leave the formula *ḥy*, in the oath and without the oath, there is one more verse which should be mentioned. In Hos 4, 15 we may read:

> "Though you play the harlot, O Israel, do not let Judah become guilty. Do not go to Gilgal, do not go up to Beth-Aven, do not swear: *ḥy-yhwh.*"

I have mentioned above[46] the close relationship between the act of swearing by (the life of) the deity and the worship of the same deity. As a

---

[43] *Ibid.*

[44] P. 152.

[45] W. W. Baudissin, *Studien zur Semitischen Religionsgeschichte.* H.1 (1911) 102. Cf. also *TWAT* II (1977) 521-22. Together with several other words this expression represents a technical term for false gods (cf. the general survey by O. Eissfeldt, "Gott und Götzen im Alten Testament", *ThStKr* 103 (1931) 158-60).

[46] Pp. 145-146.

result of this swearing by Yahweh was in fact expected of the Israelites as a duty[47]. In the light of this the statement of Hosea in 4, 15 seems to stand out in striking contrast to normal religious practice. No wonder that Widengren also took this passage as evidence in support of his theory of Yahweh a a dying and rising deity[48]. As we have seen, however, this view can hardly be upheld[49]. The passage Hos 4, 15 is quite easily understood when viewed in the light of the other anti-cult passages in the prophets. The cult to which Hosea is referring in this verse must have been a strongly syncretistic one. As he would have denounced any cult which was not purely Yahwistic, he would also have denounced swearing by the name of Yahweh on the same terms[50]. The statement of the prophet in Hos 4, 15, consequently, is no more contradictory than the other anti-cult passages which we find in prophetic literature.

6.3. *The Deities of Am 8, 14*

6.3.1. Preliminary Remarks

In addition to the statement concerning swearing by the different deities, Am 8, 14 does not offer us any details of the cults denounced by Amos on this occasion. Of the three different deities referred to, one is anonymous located at, or at least, related to, the cult place Dan; the other two are named *ʾšmt* of Samaria and *drk* of Beersheba. When consulting current translations and commentaries on Am 8, 14, it is easy to find a great variety of opinions on how the names of these three deities should be interpreted. The task we have set ourselves, accordingly, is not an easy one. Even if we could identify the different deities mentioned in this verse, it would not bring us any further than simply knowing their names. As everyone knows, the name of an Ancient Near Eastern deity does not often yield any information about the cult of the deity. In fact, today the names of several thousand deities from all over the Ancient Near East are known[51]. Only a few of the many gods and goddesses were worshipped as major deities. Of these again only a very few were worshipped over a larger area and were popular over long periods. We even know next to nothing about the nature and the cult of many of the famous

---

[47] *Ibid.*

[48] Cf. also Is 48, 1, Jer 4, 2; 44, 26.

[49] See above pp. 148-51.

[50] Cf. above pp. 111-18.

[51] By far the most impressive number of gods is known from Assyrian/Babylonian religion. A. Deimel, *Pantheon Babylonicum* (1914) lists more than 3000 deities (cf. also K. Tallquist, *Akkadische Götterepitheta* (1938)). Even a relatively small society like ancient Ugarit knew the names of more than 250 deities (J. C. de Moor, "Ugarit", *IDBS* (1976) 930).

deities. As for the great number of minor deities, our knowledge is mainly restricted to their names.

An additional difficulty which we have to deal with when attempting to identify the name of a deity is caused by the fact that quite a few of the names may be second names, appellatives, etc. for one of the major deities. Obviously, an appellative may be used of different deities, as well[52].

A further difficulty consists in the relationship between proper names and appellatives: when is the name a "proper" personal name, and when is it only an appellative? Is is at all possible to distinguish between the two in practice? As we will see in the course of the present investigation this problem is a relevant one[53].

Our problems, however, do not stop here. Even if we are able to identify the name of a certain god or goddess in the Old Testament, and then find the same name in an extra-biblical text, we have virtually no guarantee that the two deities bearing identical names are identical in character, *i.e.* that the two different texts refer to the same deity. Even if there should really be a historical connection between the two deities, the local history of one of the deities may very well have provided this deity with quite distinctive features which it did not have when it was introduced into the new pantheon from another place. This problem, obviously, becomes quite apparent when it comes to certain appellatives which were later to become personal names. A typical example would be the name *bʿl*, the most wide-spread divine name in the ancient Syrian/Palestinian world. Even if we are well acquainted with the nature of this deity from the mythological texts of ancient Ugarit, this does not enable us to use this knowledge uncritically on all the Baʿals of the ancient Syrian world. A classic exponent of such illegitimate methodological behaviour is *e.g.* W. F. Albright, who states about the gods (?) (I suppose) of the Ras Shamra texts: "Since there is, in general, only a vague relationship between the divinities which figure most prominently in the mythological tablets found at Ugarit and the most popular deities worshipped in the city itself, we can scarcely be far wrong in supposing that the myths were more or less common to all the Canaanites and were in no way peculiar to Ugarit[54]". No one, I trust, would express himself as simply as that today. Several scholars have contributed towards creating a sounder methodological climate within this field since the days of Albright[55].

[52] Typical examples of such appellatives are *bʿl* and *mlk*.

[53] Cf. e.g. below pp. 165-66.

[54] W. F. Albright, *Archaeology and the Religion of Israel*² (1946) 71-72.

[55] Cf. *inter alia* A. Caquot, "Problèmes d'histoire religieuse", *La Siria nel tardo bronzo* (1969) 61-76. See also the methodological reflections in P. Xella, *Il mito di Šhr e Šlm* (1973) 24-32. Cf. also n. 36 above.

Already from these rather superficial methodological considerations it follows that the proposed attempt to solve the problems of the deities of Am 8, 14 is unlikely to yield many results. Yet I believe that the undertaking should be attempted.

6.3.2. The Goddess Ashima of Samaria

As indicated by the heading of the present section I believe that the name of the goddess worshipped in Samaria in the time of Amos and mentioned in Am 8, 14, is a goddess Ashima. Although this identification has already been suggested by quite a few scholars[56], several others have also argued against it. For this reason we shall first take a look at the main arguments which have been put forward against an identification with this goddess.

The main witness against an identification with the goddess Ashima is MT itself. The vocalization of MT, *hannišĕbāʿîm bĕʾašĕmaṯ šomrôn*, may be translated into English: "those who swear by the guilt of Samaria". Various scholars render the expression this way, believing that the word "guilt", "sin" refers to the Golden Calf at Bethel. Among these scholars we find Harper[57], Hoonacker[58], Hammershaimb[59], and to some extent Wolff[60].

Others translate *ʾšmt* also by "guilt", "sin", but do not specify any closer what the expression refers to. Here we find names like Kapelrud[61], Rudolph[62], Knierim[63].

Wellhausen, too, is of the opinion that the text refers to the Golden Calf at Bethel. He therefore makes a correction to MT and reads insted *ʾl byt-ʾl*[64]. Obviously, one cannot help thinking that a major alteration of the text like Wellhausen's seems far more forced than simply taking *ʾšmt* as a reference to the goddess Ashima, but then, of course, this was in the days of the proud "Ich lese". Several of the older German commentaries followed Wellhausen. We find names like Marti[65], Nowack[66], Sellin[67]

---

56 See below p. 158.
57 W. R. Harper, *A Critical and Exegetical Commentary* (1905) 184.
58 A. v. Hoonacker, *Les douze petits prophètes* (1908) 227.
59 E. Hammershaimb, *The Book of Amos* (1970) 128.
60 H. W. Wolff, *Dodekapropheton* 2 (1969) 371-72.
61 A. S. Kapelrud, *Central Ideas in Amos* (1961) 49.
62 W. Rudolph, *Joel, Amos, Obadja, Jona* (1971) 268.
63 R. Knierim, "ʾšm", *THAT* I (1971) 253.
64 J. Wellhausen, *Die kleinen Propheten*³ (1898) 93-94.
65 K. Marti, *Das Dodekapropheton* (1904) 219-20.
66 W. Nowack, *Die kleinen Propheten* (1922) 163.
67 E. Sellin, *Das Zwölfprophetenbuch* (1922) 215-16.

among them. Also Leahy seems to agree with Wellhausen[68]. Maag, too, makes a major change in the consonantal text and reads Ashera for Ashima[69].

By far the greatest number of commentators on this text, however, takes *ʾšmt* as a reference to a goddess Ashima. This is particularly evident in the case of scholars who have taken the Elephantine evidence into account[70]. It is sufficient to mention names like Neher[71], Watts[72], Kellermann[73]. Most probably Amsler belongs to this group as well, even if he does not mention Ashima by name, but is content to assume that we have to do with a corruption of an original proper name[74].

In a group by himself stands Robinson. Viewing the passage in the light of the Elephantine texts, this scholar assumes that the deity in question is not Ashima, but Asham-Bethel, a deity mentioned in these texts[75].

A further argument against the identification of the goddess in Am 8, 14 with Ashima is provided by the Old Testament tradition contained in II Kings 17, 29ff. This tradition has been used, *inter alia* by Mays in his commentary on Amos. In accordance with some of the commentaries mentioned above, Mays translates the expression: "They who swear by the guilt of Samaria". According to Mays, however, this is a late addition to the text introduced in order to connect the words of the prophet Amos to the later Ashima cult which, according to the tradition preserved in II Kings 17, 29ff, was introduced into Samaria after the fall of the city to the Assyrians in the year 722/21 B.C.[76]. Mays is not the first one, of course, to notice that the tradition in II Kings 17 actually denies the possibility that Ashima was worshipped in Samaria at the time of the prophet Amos[77]. Strangely enough, however, very few scholars have taken this into account when dealing with the problem of *ʾšmt* in Am 8, 14. As the passage II Kings 17, 30 seems to contradict our assumption that we have a reference to the deity Ashima in Am 8, 14, we shall have to take a closer look at this verse and its context.

---

[68] M. Leahy, "The Popular Idea of God in Amos", *IThQ* 22 (1955) 68-73.

[69] V. Maag, *Text, Wortschatz und Begriffswelt* (1951) 55-56. Maag is here following several of the older commentaries (cf. the references given by Harper in *A Critical and Exegetical Commentary* (1905) 184).

[70] On the Elephantine evidence, see below pp. 167-78.

[71] A. Neher, *Amos* (1950) 125.

[72] J. D. W. Watts, *Vision and Prophecy in Amos* (1958) 44.

[73] D. Kellermann, "ʾšm", *TWAT* 1 (1973) 472.

[74] S. Amsler, *Amos* (1965) 237.

[75] T. H. Robinson, *Die zwölf kleinen Propheten* (1964) 103-04.

[76] J. L. Mays, *Amos* (1969) 149.

[77] See E. König, "Die Gottheit Aschima", *ZAW* 34 (1914) 17, and most recently B. Porten, *Archives from Elephantine* (1968) 176.

6.3.2.1. The Ashima of II Kings 17, 30 and the Ashima of Am 8, 14

Even if we do find a reference to a goddess Ashima in II Kings 17, 30, it is, of course, possible to maintain that this fact has no bearing whatever on the problem of Ashima in Am 8, 14. Thus, Ashima *may* have been a rather common name for a goddess, and even if there is a tradition that an Ashima was imported into Samaria at a certain time, it may very well be that the Samaritans worshipped a goddess by that name even before this alleged event. That Ashima may have been a well-known name for a goddess may be indicated by the determinative *šmrwn.* If there was only one Ashima, would one then have expected the prophet to use this geographic determination?

Yet such objections may seem to be rather artificial. As we have at hand a tradition like the one found in the story in II Kings 17, 24-41, which quite clearly seems to deny the existence of any Ashima cult in Samaria at the time of the prophet Amos, it is obvious that we shall have to take this tradition into account when dealing with the problem of Ashima in Am 8, 14.

The story in II Kings 17, which relates the introduction of foreign nations into Samaria by the king of Assyria, is well known. Quite often the story is referred to as the story of the ''origin of the Samaritans''. In it we read how the king of Assyria takes people from Babylon, Cuthah, Avva, Hamath and Sepharvaim and settles them in the towns of Samaria. The story informs us that the new inhabitants of the Samaritan towns do not at first worship Yahweh, and that Yahweh for this reason sends lions among them, killing several of them. When this comes to the knowledge of the king of Assyria, he orders one of the priests who had been deported from Samaria to return to his home-country, settle down there, and teach the inhabitants to worship the god of the country, *i.e.* Yahweh. The priest goes, settles down in Bethel, and teaches the people to worship Yahweh.

We are further informed how each nation worships its own god. The men from Babylon make a statue of Succoth-benoth, the men from Cuthah make a Nergal, the men from Hamath make an Ashima, the men from Avva a Nibhaz and a Tartak, and the men from Sepharvaim burn their children in honour of Adrammelech and Anammelech. At the same time all these nations worship Yahweh in addition to their own gods (vv. 24-34a).

Vv. 34b-40 relate the covenant between Yahweh and his people and the obligation of the people to observe all the commandments of Yahweh, and the prohibition against the worship of gods other than Yahweh.

In v. 41 the contents of v. 33 that the foreign nations in Samaria worshipped Yahweh in addition to their own gods is repeated.

If we want to make use of the information provided by this story of the introduction of several foreign gods, including the goddess Ashima, into Samaria, we shall have to regard the account as an historical source. Our problem, then, is to what extent this document can be said to be a reliable historical source, whether it is unhistorical, but still contains some historical information, or whether it must be discarded as totally unreliable and consequently of no interest whatever to the problem of the goddess Ashima in Am 8, 14.

As our story forms a part of the so-called "Deuteronomic history", which is no history at all, but rather a theological re-writing of the traditions of ancient Israel, it is quite obvious that it is only with the utmost care that we can utilize the information which is here offered to us[78]. As it turns out, II Kings 17 seems to be even more complicated as regards historicity than most passages of the "Deuteronomic History".

Already a cursory glance at the passage 17, 24-41 gives us the impression that there are considerable problems connected to the historicity of this story. This applies not only to the legendary story of the attacking lions. Also the main feature of the story, the account of the king of Assyria worrying about the foreign nations not knowing how to worship Yahweh and ordering one of the Yahwistic priests to return to Samaria and settle down in Bethel in order to teach them to worship Yahweh, is more than unlikely[79].

And if most of the content of the story gives an unhistorical impression, both structure and composition add considerably to this impression. Here we see how the different sources are connected in a not too successful way. Most conspicuous is the obvious contradiction in vv. 33-34. In v. 33 we learn that the nations were worshipping Yahweh, presumably as a consequence of the instruction given them by the priest of Yahweh in Bethel. At the same time they continue to worship their own gods. In v. 34b, however, we read that they did not worship Yahweh at all. The

---

[78] The most comprehensive recent contributions on the linguistics and literary structure of II Kings 17 are the articles by G. Baena, "El vocabulario de II Reyes 17, 7-23. 35-39", *EstB* 32 (1973) 357-84, "Carácter literario de II Reyes 17, 7-23", *EstB* 33 (1974) 5-29, "Carácter literario de II Reyes 17, 13. 35-39", *EstB* 33 (1974) 157-79.

[79] Despite the attempt by S. M. Paul, "Sargon's Administrative Diction in II Kings 17, 27", *JBL* 88 (1969) 73, to account for the behaviour of the king of Assyria by referring to Sargon's general administrative policy and the fact that an Assyrian cylinder inscription found at Khorsabad describes how the king, in his attempt to Assyrianize all the different people in the new capital, saw to it that they were instructed in how to serve the king and the gods, we can hardly accept the possibility that Sargon would be so eager as to instruct the different nations in Samaria how to worship Yahweh, the national god of Israel.

reason for this contradiction is quite clearly that the passage, vv. 34b-40, originally did not concern the foreign nations in Samaria at all but contained accusations directed against the Israelites. Only by adding the repetition of what is stated in v. 33 in v. 41 has the author[80] managed to make a whole, even if a somewhat incoherent one, out of his different sources.

A preliminary conclusion to these rather superficial reflections concerning the passage II Kings 17, 24-41 must be that the main purpose of the composition it to provide an explanation for the origin of the strongly syncretistic rites in Samaria at the time of the author. This is suggested to us also by the explanatory notes in vv. 34 and 40. The whole passage, consequently, is quite unhistorical.

As several scholars have reached similar conclusions recently, it seems unnecessary to treat the passage more in detail. The markedly unhistorical character of the story in question was stressed particularly by H. H. Rowley in 1962[81], and has later been treated in detail by *inter alia* R. J. Coggins[82] and J. MacDonald[83]. The latter have been particularly interested in the linguistic evidence for separating the different sources. Of importance in our connection are the conclusions reached by MacDonald concerning vv. 29-33, the passage which contains the references to the different foreign deities, including the goddess Ashima. MacDonald writes of these verses: ''A polemical passage, probably very late in view of the many stylistic features that mark these verses as homogenous''[84].

From the above it follows that the account of the goddess Ashima being introduced into Samaria after the fall of Samaria to the king of Assyria is unhistorical and constitutes no evidence against the existence of an Ashima cult in Samaria in the time of the prophet Amos.

The question remains, however, whether this is the same as saying that the story of II Kings 17 is without *any* interest to the interpreter of Am 8, 14, or whether after all it may have some bearing on this text.

It is important in this connection to bear in mind the way literature was produced in Israel in ancient times. The authors of the biblical nar-

---

[80] Obviously, the word ''author'' is not very adequate used in connection with traditional literature. As long as it is not misunderstood, the term may still be retained.

[81] H. H. Rowley, ''The Samaritan Schism in Legend and History'', *Israel's Prophetic Heritage* (1962) 208-22. According to Rowley the whole of II Kings 17, 24-41 is unhistorical and post-exilic.

[82] R. J. Coggins, ''The Old Testament and Samaritan Origins'', *ASTI* 6 (1968) 35-48.

[83] J. MacDonald, ''The Structure of II Kings 17'', *TGUOS* 23 (1969-70) 29-41.

[84] J. MacDonald, *op. cit.* 39. Viewed against the evidence of Rowley, Coggins, and MacDonald, we can hardly accept the attempt to historize the story in II Kings 17, 24-41 by Paul (see n. 79 above), nor indeed the somewhat apologetic article by E. A. Parker, ''A Note on the Chronology of II Kings 17, 1'', *AUSS* 6 (1968) 129-33.

ratives would hardly qualify for the title "author" in the modern sense of the word. Like in the rest of the Ancient Near East, in Israel it was not regarded as *comme il faut* to use one's phantasy or imagination in the production of literature, poetry or prose. The task of the author was rather to attempt to make use of whatever material was available to him. He found his material within the mass of different traditions handed down from generation to generation, the sum of it constituting the cultural heritage of the Israelite people, a part of which is known to us today as "the Old Testament".

As for the ways in which these traditions were handed down through the generations, we are still basically ignorant. Yet, many valuable insights have been gained within this field during the last decades[85]. It would be wrong to call the Old Testament traditions historical in a modern sense of the word. Detached from their late redactional context, it turns out that a great number of the traditions are very old. As many of them reflect historical conditions they may also contain much valuable information if utilized with caution. Thus, it is very unlikely that the Old Testament traditions were invented by the redactors of the stories; they should always be regarded as taken over, and handed down.

In the case of the story of the goddess Ashima in II Kings 17 to discard this story as totally unhistorical does not imply that there is no reliable information to be gleaned from this story. Obviously, we cannot accept the "historical" information that the goddess Ashima was introduced into Samaria after the fall of the country to Sargon. With regard to the connection between the goddess Ashima and the two geographical names Samaria and Hamath, however, the case is different. From the tradition utilized by the redactor/author of the story contained in II Kings 17 we may assume with certainty that the goddess Ashima was connected to the two places Samaria and Hamath.

The name Hamath is most probably the Syrian city-state of the Middle Orontes, frequently referred to in the Old Testament[86]. As this state was conquered by Sargon in the year 720 B.C. and Assyrians settled there[87],

---

[85] Cf. the survey given by G. W. Coats, "Tradition Criticism, OT", *IDBS* (1976) 912-14. Cf. also R. B. Coote, "Tradition, Oral, OT", *ibid.* 914-16.

[86] For the relationship between Hamath and the Old Testament, E. G. Kraeling, *Aram and Israel* (1918) *passim* is still valuable. On the history of the Aramean city-states in general, see A. Alt, "Die syrische Staatenwelt vor dem Einbruch der Assyrer", *ZDGM* 88 (1934) 233-58. On Hamath in general, see the survey by J. D. Hawkins, "Hamath", *RLA* 4 (1972-75) 67-70, and most recently A. de Maigret, *La citadella aramaica di Hama* (1979). On the literary evidence from Hamath, see in particular *KAI* nrs. 203-213, J. C. L. Gibson, *Textbook* II (1975) 6-18, B. Hrozný, "L'inscription "hittite"-hiéroglyphique d'Apamée", *Syr* 20 (1939) 134-35, J. Læssöe, "A Prayer to Ea, Shamash, and Marduk from Hama", *Iraq* 18 (1956) 60-67. Cf. also J. D. Hawkins, *op. cit.* 68-70.

[87] See J. D. Hawkins, *op. cit.* 69.

it is also likely that the very late account of Hamathite settlers in the towns of Samaria sent there by Sargon (as well as the settlement of the other nations referred to in the same account) contains reliable traditions. This has some support also in Assyrian evidence from the period[88].

Unfortunately our knowledge of the history of Hamath is not sufficient to provide us with many details about the religious history of the place[89]. Even if we do know something about the religion of ancient Hamath[90], so far nothing has been found which could throw any light upon the goddess Ashima mentioned in II Kings 17, 30.

More important in this connection is the linking of the tradition in II Kings 17, 30 of the goddess Ashima to Samaria. Even if the story in II Kings 17 opposes *de facto* the possibility of an Ashima cult in Samaria as early as the eighth century B.C., we have seen that this tradition is late and unhistorical. In linking the name of the deity Ashima to the name of Samaria, however, the tradition itself in fact *supports* the assumption that the deity referred to by Amos in 8, 14 is the goddess Ashima. The fact that the reference of the prophet in 8, 14 may be to the name of the city rather than to the name of the area is not important in this connection. When in 8, 14 the prophet Amos adds the geographical determination *šmrwn* to the name of the goddess, this is probably a result of the name of the goddess being known from the surrounding cultures, *e.g.* Hamath as well.

Consequently rather than as evidence against mention of a deity Ashima in Am 8, 14, the story of II Kings 17 should be regarded as evidence supporting such a reading of the text.

There are, however, other objections against the identification of *ʾšmt šmrwn* with "Ashima of Samaria" which should be mentioned. One obvious objection is the claim that one ought to read the text as it stands. Even if the tradition makes it probable that there was an Ashima cult in Samaria in the time of the prophet Amos, this does not necessarily imply that this deity must be mentioned in Am 8, 14. Following MT as it stands, *ʾšmt šmrwn* would have to be rendered (as it also has been done[91]) by the "sin", "guilt" of Samaria. According to the context, the reference would still be to some deity. We should not, however, be able to identify the deity behind this expression. For this our evidence would be too scarce. The attempt, consequently, to see the "sin", "guilt" of Samaria as a reference to the calf at Bethel can only be regarded as unfounded guesswork[92].

---

88 Cf. above n. 79.
89 See n. 86 above.
90 See the references to the epigraphic remains of Hamath mentioned in n. 86 above.
91 See above p. 157. 92 Cf. above notes 57-60.

On the whole, I do not believe that it is possible to retain the reading of MT here. The word *ʾšmh*, being the feminine derivation of the root *ʾšm*, is a very late word and was probably not in use as early as in the time of the prophet Amos. All occurrences of this word are found in such late works as P (Lev 4, 3; 5, 24.26; 22, 16) and the Chronicler (Ezr 9, 6.7.13.15; 10, 10.19, 1 Chr 21, 3, 2 Chr 24, 18; 28, 13; 33, 23). In addition to these occurrences there is the very late Ps 69, 6[93].

One could assume, however, that *ʾšmt* was introduced into the text at a late stage, as a substitute for the name of the original deity. In that case it would be possible to retain the reading of MT and translate *ʾšmt* with "sin" or "guilt". The phenomenon would correspond in a way to the phenomenon of replacing the name of Baʿal with *bšt*, or different deities with *šqwṣ/šqṣ*, which we find in the Old Testament[94]. If this be the case, obviously we have no means of finding out what was the original name of the deity of Samaria mentioned in Am 8, 14.

Altogether I do not believe that *ʾšmt* was introduced into the text at a late stage. If this really had been the case, it is not likely that this particular word would have been chosen to replace the name of the original deity, especially when we know that a goddess with a very similar name was worshipped in Samaria. As a deity bearing a name consisting of the root *ʾšm* must have been rather well known all over the Ancient Near East[95], it is not likely that the later Jewish tradition would have been ignorant of the existence of a deity Ashima.

For this reason the simplest solution to the riddle of *ʾšmt šmrwn* in Am 8, 14 is to take the expression as a reference to "Ashima of Samaria", worshipped in the Northern realm in the time of the prophet Amos. When this cult was introduced into Samaria we do not know. The only thing we may say for certain is that the cult was still popular in late, post-exilic times when the account in II Kings 17 went through its final redactional stage.

If we compare the two different references to the goddess Ashima occurring in the Old Testament, II Kings 17, 30 and Am 8, 14, we soon find that the name of the goddess is spelled in two different ways. In II Kings 17, 30 the name of the goddess is written *ʾšymʾ*, in Am 8, 14 (in the construct state) *ʾšmt*. The fact that the final consonant of the name in II Kings 17, 30 is an *ʾaleph* and not a *hê* is most easily explained as a consequence of the late date of the passage[96]. In late texts the Aramaic

---

[93] Cf. D. Kellermann, "*ʾšm*", *TWAT* I (1973) 472.

[94] *bšt* for Baʿal occurs in Jer 3, 24; 11, 13, Hos 9, 10, *šqṣ* for Milcom in I Kings 11, 5, for Kemosh in I Kings 11, 7.

[95] See below p. 167ff.

[96] Cf. above p. 161.

orthography ʾ*aleph* for *hê* is not uncommon[97]. Noth's assertion that we cannot tell for certain the gender of the name in II Kings 17 is strange[97a].

Further there is the matter of the long *î* in the spelling of the name in II Kings 17, 30. Thus, some scholars have maintained that there can be no connection between the goddess mentioned in II Kings 17, 30 and the ʾ*šm*-element of the divine names in the Elephantine papyri[98], for the reason that the name of Ashima in II Kings 17 contains an original long *î*[99]. It is, however, not possible to lay any great weight on the quantity of the vowel in this connection. Even if *matres lectionis* are widely used to denote naturally long vowels, there is no real consistency in their usage[100]. Consequently there are no objections for regarding the spelling of II Kings 17, 30 as a variant of the word in the Elephantine texts and in Am 8, 14.

One should also, when dealing with MT, keep in mind the very late character of the text. Even if we assume the tradition in itself to be reliable, this fact allows for a certain freedom when dealing with problems like the one in question. Quite often students of the Old Testament tend to forget that the language of Biblical Hebrew is quite different from the Hebrew of, for example, the time of the prophet Amos.

If the reference in Am 8, 14, in accordance with our assumption, is to the goddess Ashima, there is also a problem attached to the grammatical construction *b*ʾ*šmt šmrwn* itself. If ʾ*šmt* really represents a personal name, we have here an example of a proper name in the construct state, something which is regarded as grammatically impossible.

There is more than one explanation to this phenomenon. Firstly, we must reckon here with the possibility that we have to do with a deliberate minor change in the consonantal text by the Massoretes in accordance with their reading "sin", "guilt". This assumption, however, is not absolutely necessary. The impossibility of ʾ*šmt* in Am 8, 14 being a personal name as a consequence of its appearing in the construct state is an objection to the identification with the deity Ashima which was already raised by König in 1914[101]. I am not wholly convinced, however, that the name of a deity cannot appear in a construct connection. How should one, for

---

[97] See *e.g.* W. Gesenius, *Gesenius' Hebrew Grammar* (1963) § 224 h. (To those who prefer to take the name as an Aramaism, see for the fluctuation between terminal *hê* and terminal ʾ*aleph* H. H. Rowley, *The Aramaic of the Old Testament* (1929) 39-50.)

[97a] M. Noth, *Die israelitischen Personennamen* (1928) 124.

[98] On the Elephantine evidence, see below pp. 167-78.

[99] M. Noth, *Die israelitischen Personennamen* (1928) 124, M. H. Silvermann, "Aramean Name-types", *JAOS* 89 (1969) 703, n. 71.

[100] S. Moscati, *An Introduction to the Comparative Grammar* (1969) 50, J. Blau, *A Grammar of Biblical Hebrew* (1976) 8. The same applies for Biblical Aramaic (F. Rosenthal, *A Grammar of Biblical Aramaic* (1961) 11).

[101] E. König, "Die Gottheit Aschima", *ZAW* 34 (1914) 17.

example, explain the name *yhwh* in the expression *yhwh ṣbʾwt* if not by regarding *yhwh* as *nomens regens* in a construct connection?[102] And what about the Ugaritic goddess *a̱trt ym*?[103]. And an expression like the Ugaritic *a̱trt ṣrm*, "Aṯirat of the Tyrians"[104], is not unlike *ʾšmt šmrwn* of Am 8, 14. Even if one should not make comparisons too automatically between Ugaritic and Hebrew, the similarity is indeed conspicuous.

In addition to this König also accepted that the appearance of a proper name in the construct state was possible in cases where the proper name was not a real proper name, but originally an appellative that had come into use as a proper name[105]. In the case of the goddess Ashima we must reckon with the possibility that we have to do with some sort of an appellative of a deity that was later turned into a proper name[106].

The problem of relationships between proper names, appellatives, and appellatives being used as proper names is indeed a most difficult one. To my knowledge the problem has not been treated in detail. From the Old Testament texts it is often quite impossible to make any distinction between real proper names and appellatives used as proper names.

Besides the matter of the spelling of the name there is also another difference between the mention of Ashima in II Kings 17, 30 and Am 8, 14 which it is worth noticing. In II Kings 17, 30 we note that the text states that the men from Hamath *made* an Ashima (*ʿśw ʾt-ʾšymʾ*). The same verb is used also in connection with the deities of the other nations. The phrase seems to indicate that a statue was made of the deity. We have here a clear parallell to some of the texts which relate to the goddess[107] Ashera[108].

Beyond the information that a statue was made of the goddess Ashima according to II Kings 17, 30, a possible connection between the goddess and the city state Hamath, also according to II Kings 17, 30, and that her cult was denounced by the prophet Amos in the middle of the eighth century B.C. in Samaria, the information offered us on this deity by the Old Testament is virtually nil. If we want to know anything more about the goddess Ashima, we shall have to turn to extra-biblical evidence. As we shall see, a goddess by the name of Ashima must have been rather widely worshipped in the Ancient Near East. For obvious reasons, the Elephan-

---

[102] On this expression, see *HAL*³ Lief. 2 (1974) 378, 5a.

[103] References to the texts are found in R. E. Whitaker, *A Concordance* (1972) 43.

[104] *CTA* 14, IV, 198 and 201.

[105] E. König, *Historisch-comparative Syntax* (1897) § 280 g. Cf. also § 285 h.

[106] On the etymology of Ashima, see below p. 167ff.

[107] I cannot accept the assumption made by some scholars that *ʾšrh* in the Old Testament is never a designation for a deity, but is always used of a cult symbol (thus *e.g.* E. Lipiński, "The Goddess Aṯirat", *OLoP* 3 (1972) 116).

[108] On Ashera, see the survey by J.C. de Moor, "*ʾšrh*", *TWAT* 1 (1973) 473-81.

tine papyri are the most important extra-biblical documents available in this connection.

6.3.2.2. The Goddess Ashima and the Elephantine Papyri

It was only after the publication of the Elephantine papyri that the discussion about the biblical Ashima really started.

In the famous temple tax list that was found in 1906/07 and published for the first time in 1911[109] there occur the names of the three different deities *yhw*, *ʾšmbytʾl* and *ʿntbytʾl*[110]. Ever since this text was published scholars have been attempting to solve the riddle of these divine names[111]. So far, however, no general agreement has been reached.

As the name *ʾšmbytʾl* is the only one of the three divine names in the Elephantine temple tax list which may throw any light upon the goddess Ashima in the Old Testament, we shall leave the two other divine names out of account. Ironically, these are at the same time the two unproblematic ones of the three. Whereas both *yhw* and the two elements *ʿnt* and *bytʾl* are well known to us from the Ancient Near Eastern history of religion[112], there are many difficulties attached to the *ʾšm* element of the compound name *ʾšmbytʾl*. For this reason it may seem wise first to give a survey of the most important contributions towards the solution of this *crux*. At the same time, the survey will provide examples of the different etymologies that have been suggested for this name.

One of the first scholars to comment upon the name *ʾšmbytʾl* in the Elephantine temple tax list was Ungnad[113], who identified the *ʾšm* element with the Babylonian pest-god Išum[114]. Grimme[115] explained *ʾšm* as a form of *šm*, "name", with a prosthetic *ʾaleph*. He was the first scholar to offer this explanation which was later to be the one most widely accepted. Grimme maintains further that there is a connection between *ʾšm* in the

---

109 E. Sachau, *Aramäische Papyrus und Ostraka* (1911) Tf. 17-19.

110 A. Cowley, *Aramaic Papyri* (1923) Nr. 22, 123-25.

111 As far as I know, no one ever followed J. N. Epstein in his attempt to explain these names as personal names ("Jahu, AŠMbēthel und ANTbēthēl", *ZAW* 32 (1912) 139-45).

112 For the god *yhwh/yhw* see *HAL*³ (1974) 377-78, *THAT* I (1975) 701-07, *TWAT* III, Lief. 4-5 (1980) 533-54. For the god *bytʾl* see R. Kittel, "Der Gott Betʾel", *JBL* 44 (1925) 123-53, O. Eissfeldt, "Der Gott Bethel", *ARW* 28 (1930) 1-30, H. Seyrig, "Altar Dedicated to Zeus Betylos", *The Excavations at Dura-Europos* (1933) 68-71, J. P. Hyatt, "The Deity Bethel and the Old Testament", *JAOS* 59 (1939) 81-98, J. T. Milik, "Les papyrus araméens d'Hermoupolis", *Bib* 48 (1967) 565-77. For the goddess Anat, see U. Cassuto, *Hā-ʾĒla ʿĂnāth* (1951), *WM* Abt. 1. B.1 (1965) 35-41, A. S. Kapelrud, *The Violent Goddess* (1969), H. Gese, *Die Religionen Altsyriens* (1970) 156-60, A. Caquot, *Textes ougaritiques* (1974) 85-92, F. O. Hvidberg-Hansen, *La déesse TNT* I (1979) 81-105.

113 A. Ungnad, *Aramäische Papyrus aus Elephantine* (1911) 41.

114 On this god cf. *WM* Abt. 1. B.1 (1965) 90-91.

115 H. Grimme, "Die Jahotriade von Elephantine", *OLZ* 15 (1912) 11-17.

Elephantine text and the goddess Ashima in II Kings 17, 30 and probably also in Am 8, 14. According to Grimme, the late Hellenistic evidence for the existence of a deity Simia(os) is also related to the ʾšm element in Elephantine[116]. Meyer[117], too, believes that there is a connection between ʾšm and Ashima in II Kings 17, 30 and Am 8, 14. König, on the other hand[118], follows Ungnad and believes that ʾšm is etymologically related to the Babylonian deity Išum. He assumes a relation with the Ashima of II Kings 17, but not with Am 8, 14, where he changes MT and reads Ashera for Ashima[119]. His main argument for not identifying Ashima in Am 8, 14 is the account of her late introduction into Samaria in II Kings 17[120]. Lemonnyer, again, identifies ʾšm etymologically as "name"[121]. He is able to accept a possible connection with Ashima in II Kings 17, but finds the connection with Am 8, 14 doubtful[122]. Also Lidzbarski[123] thought ʾšm to be the Semitic "name" with a prosthetic *ʾaleph*. He identified the same root in both II Kings 17, 30 and Am 8, 14 in the goddess Ashima. He further thought the same root to be present in the name of the god Eshmun also, as well as in the late Hellenistic attestations of the deity Simia(os). Because of the difference in sibilants, however, he was later to change his view with regard to the late Hellenistic evidence[124]. Cowley[125] is tempted to follow Ungnad and König in the identification with the Babylonian Išum, but thinks it more likely that the deity in question is the same as the one mentioned in II Kings 17, 30 and Am 8, 14. Albright[126] follows Grimme and believes ʾšm to be the Semitic "name". To Albright, however, the element ʾšm does not represent a proper deity's name, but is rather to be regarded as a divine attribute that has been hypostasized (as is the case with the elements *ḥrm* and *ʿnt*, also found in the Elephantine papyri). Albright has later been followed in this view by Silvermann[127], and most recently by Teixidor[128]. The god

[116] Cf. below pp. 178-80.

[117] E. Meyer, *Der Papyrusfund von Elephantine*[2] (1912) 58. Concerning the relationship between Elephantine ʾšm and Am 8, 14, Meyer gives the credit for connecting the two to Gressmann, whereas Grimme (cf. n. 115 above) points to Hüsing as the originator of the idea.

[118] E. König, "Die Gottheit Aschima", *ZAW* 34 (1914) 17f., 23ff., 27ff.

[119] I believe the last one to suggest this solution was V. Maag (cf. n. 69 above).

[120] On the historical value of the account of II Kings 17 cf. above 158ff.

[121] A. Lemonnyer, "Achima", *RSPhTh* 8 (1914) 294.

[122] *Ibid.* 295-96.

[123] M. Lidzbarski, *Ephemeris* B.3 (1915) 247.

[124] *Ibid.* 260-61.

[125] A. Cowley, *Aramaic Papyri* (1923) XIX.

[126] W. F. Albright, "The Evolution of the West-Semitic Divinity", *AJSL* 41 (1924-25) 93, *Archaeology and the Religion of Israel*[3] (1953) 174.

[127] See below n. 145.

[128] J. Teixidor, *The Pagan God* (1977) 31. Teixidor, too, takes the element ʾšm etymologically to be the Semitic "name".

Eshmun, according to Albright, has no connection to the ʾšm element, but should rather be identified with the god Šulman[129]. Noth, again, opposes all the suggested etymologies for ʾšm save one[130]. According to this scholar there is no connection whatever between this element and the Semitic "name", nor between ʾšm and the goddess Ashima mentioned in II Kings 17, 30, and possibly in Am 8, 14. Nor is there any connection to the Babylonian deity Išum. In fact, we do not know the etymology of ʾšm in the Elephantine texts at all. There *may*, however—still according to Noth—be a possible connection between ʾšm and the god Eshmun, as well as to a few theophorous Old Testament personal names where the element is found. With Aimé-Giron[131] a totally new attempt to solve the etymological riddle of ʾšm was introduced on the scene. Supported by his own philological/etymological speculations Aimé-Giron was able to reconstruct an original form **ʾasîm* or **wasîm*, "sign", "token". According to Aimé-Giron, this "sign" of the deity was originally a deified part of the temple. As a main witness in his argumentation he introduces, moreover, the term *semeion* from Lucian's *De Syria Dea*[132]. He further believes the ʾšm of Elephantine to be the male equivalent to the goddess Ashima and thus connected to the Ashima of II Kings 17, 30 and Am 8, 14. Vincent, too[133], believes that ʾšm is the male parallel to the goddess Ashima mentioned in II Kings 17, 30 and Am 8, 14. He further believes that ʾšm is connected to the deity Eshmun, also identical with the god Šulman. In this last respect Vincent adheres to the view advocated by Albright[134]. Also the late, Hellenistic evidence relating to the deity Simia(os) is, according to Vincent, connected with the Elephantine ʾšm element. Kraeling[135], again like several before him, connects ʾšm with the Semitic "name", and translates *ʾšmbytʾl* with "the name of Bethel". He thinks the name is a designation for the spouse of the deity Bethel. As a parallel phenomenon he refers to the expression *ʿštrt šm bʿl*, "Astarte, the name of Baʿal", in the inscription of the Phoenician king Eshmunazzar, dated to ca. 300 B.C.[136]. Also Porten[137] believes that there is a connec-

[129] W. F. Albright, "The Syro-Mesopotamian God Šulman-Ešmûn", *AfO* 7 (1931-32) 164-69.

[130] M. Noth, *Die israelitischen Personennamen* (1928) 122-26.

[131] M. Aimé-Giron, *Textes araméens d'Égypte* (1931) 113-17. Cf. also "Additions et corrections" p. [IV].

[132] On the late Hellenistic evidence relating to the goddess Ashima, see below pp. 178-80.

[133] A. Vincent, *La religion des Judéo-araméens* (1937) 545f., 654-80.

[134] Cf. above n. 129.

[135] E. G. Kraeling, *The Brooklyn Museum Aramaic Papyri* (1953) 90.

[136] This was already done by Lemonnyer, "Achima", *RSPhTh* 8 (1914) 295, n. 1. Cf. also W. F. Albright, "The Evolution of the West-Semitic Divinity", *AJSL* 41 (1924-25) 93, n. 2 (the reference given by Albright, however, is incorrect).

[137] B. Porten, *Archives from Elephantine* (1968) 172.

tion between ʾšm in the Elephantine papyri and the goddess Ashima in II Kings 17, 30. He opposes an identification with the deity of Am 8, 14, however, and assumes that the name of the deity originally referred to in this passage was deliberately changed into the word for "guilt", in the same way as the names of deities like Kemosh and Milcom were changed into *šqṣ*, "abomination"[138]. According to Porten there is also a possible link between ʾ*šm* and the late Hellenistic Simia(os), but this remains uncertain[139]. Milik[140], again, follows the tradition of explaining ʾ*šmbytʾl* as the "name of Bethel". The deity "Name" is also, according to Milik, found in II Kings 17, 30 and Am 8, 14, and in the Hellenistic god/goddess Simios/Simia. Not all the late Hellenistic references which seem to contain this divine element, however, are of the same kind. One should differentiate between three roots, each representing a different deity[141]. With Astour[142] a completely new attempt to solve the etymology of ʾ*šm* is introduced again. This scholar connects Elephantine ʾ*šm*, Ashima in II Kings 17, 30 and Am 8, 14, as well as the Phoenician Eshmun to the Ugaritic name *Iṯm*, occurring once in the divine double name *Šgr w Iṯm*[143]. According to Astour, Ugaritic *iṯm* corresponds to Hebrew ʾ*šm*, "guilt"[144]. The name, consequently, should be explained as a result of "guilt-offering" being personified and deified. After Astour, Silvermann has commented on the Elephantine ʾ*šm* on various occasions[145]. Silvermann follows Albright[146] and opposes the common view that the element ʾ*šm* is the name of an independent deity. The same goes for an element like *ḥrm*. These roots appear nowhere as names of gods, but solely as parts of composite names. Silvermann does not, however, take up Albright's view with regard to deified, divine attributes; the elements should rather be seen as hypostazations of cultic terms connected to the temple. With regard to ʾ*šm* he holds a similar view to Astour[147], who relates the word to

---

[138] *Ibid.* 176 (cf. above n. 94).

[139] *Ibid.* 172, n. 101.

[140] J. T. Milik, "Les papyrus araméens d'Hermoupolis", *Bib* 48 (1967) 567-68.

[141] J. T. Milik, *Recherches d'épigraphie proche-orientale* I (1972) 408: "Il convient de distinguer très rigoureusement entre *simyâ*, *semyâ*, "étendard, signum", *šamayâ*, "le Ciel" et eventuellement *šim*, *šem* et *šimâ*", (le) Nom"; les discussions récentes sur le dieu Étendard souffrent beaucoup de cette confusion" (cf. also the following pages). I do believe, however, that Milik is too optimistic when he claims the possibility of undertaking such a distinction (cf. below 283).

[142] M. C. Astour, "Some New Divine Names from Ugarit", *JAOS* 86 (1966) 281-82.

[143] RS 24.643, 1.9 (first published in *UG* V).

[144] Cf., however, D. Kellermann, "ʾ*āšām* in Ugarit?", *ZAW* 76 (1964) 319-22.

[145] M. H. Silvermann, "Aramean Name-Types in the Elephantine Documents", *JAOS* 89 (1969) 702-09, "Onomastic Notes to 'Aramaica Dubiosa'", *JNES* 28 (1969) 193-94. Cf. also his unpublished dissertation *Jewish Personal Names in the Elephantine Documents* (1967).

[146] Cf. above n. 126.

[147] Cf. above n. 142.

Biblical Hebrew *ʾšm* and believes that it is some kind of sacrifice. *ḥrm* he explains in accordance with Biblical Hebrew *ḥrm* as a "property sacred to God"[148]. As these terms are not designations for real gods it goes without saying that there can be no connection between them and the goddess Ashima of the Old Testament. As additional evidence in support of this view, Silvermann further points to the original long *î* in the name of the goddess in II Kings 17, 30[149] and to the fact that the *ʾšm* element in Elephantine is masculine, whereas the Old Testament Ashima is a goddess[150].

Against the background of this survey of the different views on the nature of the element *ʾšm* in the temple tax list from Elephantine, we shall take a closer look at the divine name *ʾšmbytʾl* in order to see to which extent this deity can be said to be of any relevance to the goddess Ashima mentioned in II Kings 17, 30 and Am 8, 14.

Consisting of the two different names *ʾšm* and *bytʾl*, the Elephantine Ashim-bethel may seem to provide us with yet another example of the so-called "double-deities" of the Ancient Near East. The phenomenon is well known, even if it cannot be said to be frequent[151]. Far too little is known about these deities to say anything certain about their specific nature[152]. In some instances we have a combination of the names of two male deities, in others a combination of one male and one female. There are, however, also instances when we do not know for certain whether one of the elements of the name is male or female[153].

With regard to the divine names consisting of two male elements we have examples where this phenomenon undoubtedly represents the fusing of two different deities[154]. This, however, does not entitle us to

---

[148] Compare also the views held by N. Aimé-Giron, *Textes araméens d'Égypte* (1931) 111-13 and "Additions et corrections", p. [IV]. Cf. also E. Bresciani, "Nuovi documenti aramaici dall'Egitto", *ASAE* 55 (1958) 279.

[149] On this argument, see above p. 165.

[150] Thus also A. van Hoonacker, *Une communauté judéo-araméenne* (1915) 79, M. Noth, *Die israelitischen Personennamen* (1928) 124, n. 3.

[151] On the Phoenician and Punic double-deities, see *KAI* II (1973) 88-89.

[152] The remarks of Röllig (n. 151 above) on the problems related to the Phoenician and Punic double-deities apply for the other Ancient Near Eastern double-deities as well.

[153] An illustrative example of this is provided by the Moabite deity *ʿštr kmš* mentioned in the Mesha inscription from the 9th century B.C. (*KAI* nr. 181, 1.17). References to the discussion whether this deity is male or female is found in *KAI* II (1973) 176-77. See further the references in J. C. L. Gibson, *Textbook* I (1973) 81. According to Gibson, the deity in question is male. So also Röllig. Even if it may seem reasonable to assume that these scholars are right, the problem can hardly be solved on the basis of the form *ʿštr* alone. The assertion that the Moabite deity in question is the first known example of a double deity (*KAI* II (1973) 176 and 89) is hardly correct. Already Ugaritic deities such as *kṯr.w ḫss* (R. E. Whitaker, *A. Concordance* (1972) 368-69) and *šgr w iṯm* (cf. above p. 170) must be regarded as examples of double-deities.

[154] A typical example of this would be the god Eshmun-Melqart. When we first meet

claim that all double-gods whose name consists of two male elements are the result of such an amalgamation of two different deities.

With regard to the double-deities whose names consist of one female and one male name the problem is more intricate. In some instances we undoubtedly have examples of androgynous deities[155].

In the case of the divine names *ʾšmbytʾl* and *ʿntbytʾl* in the Elephantine temple tax list, I think the problem is even more complicated. If these names are to be regarded as examples of double-deities we get one deity male + male and one deity female + male. That the element *ʾšm* in the first mentioned name is male, is, as far as I am able to judge, beyond doubt. Normally one would not find the problem of double-deities in a text remarkable. In this case I think that it is. Firstly, it is somewhat strange to find two double-deities mentioned in the same instance. Even if the phenomenon is not uncommon, it is not frequent. Secondly, the fact that the last part of both names is the deity Bethel is more than remarkable. If the two deities mentioned in this text really were double-deities we would have one male deity + Bethel and one female deity + Bethel. Even if the name *ʿnt-bytʾl could* be taken as "Anath of Bethel", *i.e.* "Anath, the consort of Bethel", there is no plausible explanation for *ʾšmbytʾl*. I also find the "Anath of Bethel" hard to accept.

In fact, I doubt very much that the two divine names Ashim-bethel and Anath-bethel are examples of double-deities. The last element of these two divine names, *bytʾl*, should rather be taken as referring to Bethel in the northern realm of Israel. As both the deity Ashim and the deity Anath were well known in the Ancient Near East[156], it was only natural that the Jews of Elephantine, when they emigrated from their home-country and brought the local cults with them, would call their deities "Ashim of Bethel" and "Anath of Bethel". Does not this phenomenon in fact form a close parallel to the phenomenon we have in Am 8, 14 where Amos denounces the cult of *ʾšmt šmrwn*? So we have an Ashim of Bethel and an Ashima of Samaria.

---

with the name of the god Eshmun, in the 7th-century treaty of king Asarhaddon of Assyria, the name of the god, *dIa-su-mu-nu*, is mentioned together with the name of the god Melqart, *Mi-il-qar-tu* (R. Borger, *Die Inschriften Asarhaddons* (1956) 109. Later, the names of the two deities have fused together into the name of a single god Eshmun-Melqart (*CIS* I 16, 6.23.24.28).

[155] Cf. H. Gese, *Die Religionen Altsyriens* (1970) 137.

[156] On *ʾšm/h/t*, see above and below *passim.* On Anath, see n. 112 above. From the Bible we know that Anath was known also in Israel. The name of the goddess has survived in geographical names (cf. Kapelrud, *The Violent Goddess* (1969) 12). Even if there is no mention of the cult of the goddess in the biblical texts, we may not conclude that her cult was unknown in northern Israel in the first millennium B.C. In fact, the Elephantine evidence points to the contrary.

It is with interest that we note that the deity Ashim-bethel is attested also elsewhere (So is Anath-bethel, for that matter[157]). In a Greek inscription from Kafr Nābo, dated to the year A.D. 224, a deity Symbetylos is mentioned[158]. This deity has been connected to the Old Testament Ashima on various occasions, and after the discovery of the Elephantine papyri, naturally to Ashim-bethel. Obviously Symbetylos reflects the same name as found in the Elephantine temple tax list. Even if some scholars have disputed any connection between these two deities[159], the similarity between the two names is too striking to be coincidental. With regard to the nature of the deity Symbetylos the information available to us is too scarce to be of any real value. All we can say is that the deity in question probably must be male.

Our interest in the Elephantine *ʾšmbytʾl* in connection with the Samaritan Ashima, is undoubtedly increased by the connection of the Elephantine Ashim to Israelite Bethel. Unfortunately the god Ashim is not mentioned again in the texts until late Hellenistic times[160].

This, however, does not give any cause to raise doubts about the existence of this deity. The existence of a deity Ashim among the Arameans is proved through the many theophorous Aramean personal names from Elephantine and elsewhere containing the name of this deity.

The most frequent of these names is *ʾšmrm*, "Ashim[161] is exalted[162]",

---

157 R. Borger, "Anath-Bethel", *VT* 7 (1957) 102-04. Borger's short article is very important as it clearly demonstrates that Albright was wrong when claiming that the Elephantine composite divine names were "theological speculations" and not names of deities (p. 104).

158 *IGLS* II (1939) nr. 376 1. I.

159 Among those opposing any connection between the Greek/Syriac Symbetylos and the Elephantine Ashim-bethel are E. König, "Die Gottheit Aschima", *ZAW* 34 (1914) 29-30, M. Noth, *Die israelitischen Personennamen* (1928) 124, n. 5, M. H. Silvermann, "Aramean Name-Types", *JAOS* 89 (1969) 703. Among those who believe that there is a connection between the two are H. Grimme, "Die Jahotriade", *OLZ* 15 (1912) 14-15 (Grimme was, as far as I know, the first one to make this suggestion), N. Aimé-Giron, *Textes araméens* (1931) 115, J. P. Hyatt, "The Deity Bethel" *JAOS* 59 (1939) 86, J. T. Milik, "Les papyrus araméens", *Bib* 48 (1967) 568-69, B. Porten, *Archives from Elephantine* (1968) 172-73, *idem*, "The Religion of the Jews of Elephantine", *JNES* 28 (1969) 119.

160 Cf. below pp. 178-80.

161 I have chosen to vocalize with a initial *a* in accordance with the Masoretic vocalization of the name of the goddess Ashima. On *šm* with a prostethic *ʾaleph* as the most probable etymology for the name of the deity, see below p. 175ff. At any rate the vocalization of Elephantine *ʾšm* is bound to be a matter of guessing (cf. the vocalization *ʾušm* by Gibson, *Textbook* II (1975) 43).

162 Theophorous names with the element *rym/rwm*, "to be high above", "to be exalted", are frequent in the Semitic languages (cf. in particular, M. Noth, *Die israelitischen Personennamen* (1928) 145-46 and *passim*, H. B. Huffmon, *Amorite Personal Names* (1965) 261-62, F. Gröndahl, *Die Personennamen* (1967) 182-83, F. L. Benz, *Personal Names* (1972) 408-09.

occurring in the names *ʾšmrm br nbwnd*[163], *ʾšmrm br ʾšmšzb*[164] and *ʾšwhrm br ʾšmrm br ʾšmšzb*[165]. The last two names contain also the Ashim name *ʾšmšzb*, meaning "Ashim rescued"[166]. *ʾšmrm* is further attested in one of the inscriptions on an Aramaic sarcophagus from South Saqqarah where we read the name *bytʾlzbd br ʾšmrm*[167]. We note with interest that the publisher of these texts holds the Arameans in question as originating in Syria[168]. The last occurrence of the name *ʾšmrm* is on one of the wooden tablets of the so-called Michaelidis Collection[169]. In the same text there also occurs another Ashim name, *ʾšmmdbḥ*[170]. This last name has caused some bewilderment as it seems to consist of the names of two different deities. The phenomenon, however, is not unknown[171]. The main problem with the texts of the Michaelidis Collection lies elsewhere. According to several scholars these texts are modern forgeries[172]. If this really is the case, it goes without saying that they are of no interest to us.

Further Ashim names are *ʾšmkdry br ʾpʿ*[173] and *ʾšmzbd br šwyn*[174].

It is further with interest that we note that a god Ashim was known among the Phoenicians also. Thus, on a Phoenician seal, probably from the 8th Century B.C., there occurs the name *btʾšm*, "the daughter of Ashim"[175]. Even if this female name is known only from this text, it parallels other theophorous names constructed in the same way. Best known is probably *btbʿl*, "the daughter of Baʿal"[176]. A much later example of a Phoenician Ashim name is *šmʾdn bn ḥʾr hkty* on a funeral stela from Kition, dated to the 3rd Century[177]. As we see, the name *šmʾdn*, "Ashim

---

163 A. Cowley, *Aramaic Papyri* (1923) nr. 53, 9.

164 E. G. Kraeling, *The Brooklyn Museum Aramaic Papyri* (1953) nr. 8, 11.

165 *Ibid.* nr. 11, 12.

166 Cf. *DISO* (1965) 296.

167 N.Aimé-Giron, *Textes araméens d'Égypte* (1931) nr. 110.

168 *Ibid.* 106.

169 E. Bresciani, "Nuovi documenti aramaici", *ASAE* 55 (1958) 277, *recto* 9.

170 *Ibid. recto* 5.

171 For references, see J. K. Stark, *Personal Names in Palmyrene Inscriptions* (1971) 78 under *bʿšmn.*

172 J. Naveh, "Aramaica Dubiosa", *JNES* 27 (1968) 317-25. See also B. Porten, *Archives from Elephantine* (1968) 168, n. 69, M. H. Silvermann, "Onomastic Notes", *JNES* 28 (1969) 192-96.

173 A. Cowley, *Aramaic Papyri* (1923) nr. 53, 6. This name is interesting for its obvious Babylonian origin and may best be compared to Babylonian names like *Marduk-ku-dur-ri-ŠEŠ* and *dÉ-a-ku-dúr-ri-ib-ni* (see *CAD* 8 (1971) under *kudurri* C a) 3). Cf. also B. Porten, *Archives* (1968) 332.

174 E. G. Kraeling, *The Brooklyn Museum Aramaic Papyri* (1953) nr. 8, 12, meaning "Ashim gave".

175 N. Avigad, "An unpublished Phoenician Seal", *Hommages à A. Dupont-Sommer* (1971) 3-4.

176 F. L. Benz, *Personal Names* (1972) 102.

177 O. Masson, "Recherches sur les phéniciens dans le monde hellénistique", *BCH* 93 (1969) 699. Cf. also J. Teixidor, "Bulletin d'épigraphie sémitique 1970", *Syr* 47 (1970) 371, nr. 72.

is Lord'', is here written without the prosthetic *ʾaleph.* This is rather interesting when compared to the name *btʾšm* mentioned above. It seems that the name of the deity in Phoenician is written both with and without the prosthetic vowel. A variant of *šmʾdn* is *šmʾdny*, "Ashim is his/my Lord"[178].

The examples mentioned above should adequately demonstrate that a deity Ashim existed in the Ancient Near East, worshipped over a large area. As we shall see, a deity by that name was known also in late Hellenistic times[179]. For further *ʾšm/šm* names, one may consult the current name-lists[180].

Against the background of the above, it should further be clear that the theories of Albright and Silvermann that the element *ʾšm* does not represent a real deity, but only "theophorous elements", or theological speculations, are unfounded[181]. The personal names which I have mentioned above would hardly have been constructed the way they have been unless a deity existed by the name of Ashim.

A problem in connection with the deity Ashim is the etymology of the name. Most commonly scholars explain the word *ʾšm* as being identical with the common Semitic "name"[182]. If this is correct, we *may* here have an interesting parallel in the late Jewish practice of referring to the god Yahweh as *hšm.*

Basically, however, I do not believe that it is possible to give any final answer to the problem of the etymology of Ashim. When I believe that the word for "name" may provide the most probable explanation to the problem of the etymology of Ashim, this is only because this *seems* to represent the most likely solution to the problem. Thus, the *ʾaleph* of *šm* is easily explained as an *ʾaleph prostheticum*[183]. There is further evidence in West Semitic texts that *šm* is used as an appellative of a deity. As we know, the step from appellative to proper name is not far in the Ancient Near Eastern history of religion. This could also provide an explanation

---

[178] B. Delavault, A. Lemaire, "Une stèle 'molk' de Palestine", *RB* 83 (1976) 577-78. For theophorous names constructed in this way, see F. L. Benz, *Personal Names* (1972) 260-61.

[179] Cf. below pp. 178-80.

[180] Cf. n. 162 above. Cf. also most recently, I. J. Gelb, *Computer-Aided Analysis of Amorite* (1980) 189ff.

[181] Cf. above p. 168.

[182] Thus, all the scholars mentioned in n. 162 above, with the exception of M. Noth, favour this etymology. Cf. also the remarks by R. Zadok, "Geographical and Onomastic Notes", *JANES* 8 (1976) 118-20.

[183] On this phenomenon, see H. H. Rowley, *The Aramaic of the Old Testament* (1929) 17, n. 1, R. Degen, *Altaramäische Grammatik* (1969) § 22, J. A. Fitzmyer, *The Aramaic Inscriptions* (1967) 77 and 88, J. Friedrich, W. Röllig, *Phönizisch-Punische Grammatik* (1970) § 95.

for the interchange between *šm* and *ʾšm* in the Phoenician theophorous names mentioned above.

Thus, in the Phoenician inscription of the Sidonian king Eshmunazar, dating from the beginning of the 5th Century B.C.[184], there occurs in 1.18: ... *wbt lʿštrt šm bʿl*..., "and a temple to Astarte, name of Baʿal"... In this text *šm*, "name", appears as an epithet of Astarte. The expression, however, is extremely difficult to explain. "Name" or "name of" in this connection seems to give expression to the relationship between the god and the goddess. Most probably it would be rendered better by "spouse" or "consort" in this particular instance. Or perhaps there was a goddess whose name, for some strange reason, really was *ʿštrt šm bʿl*. It may be of a certain interest that the same name for a goddess also occurs in the Ras Shamra texts[185]. The phenomenon may or may not be compared to the Punic *tnt pn bʿl*, "Tenith, Face of Baʿal"[186].

Thus, we have no absolute proof that our rendering of *ʾšm/šm* in relation to the god Ashim by "name" is correct. It may well be that here we have to do with a semantic value of *šm* that is totally unknown to us[187]. Still, as this etymology seems to represent the scholarly *opinio communis*, I have decided to accept it with the above reservations.

Quite another matter is it whether the etymology of the deity Ashim is of any great interest to this problem at all. Even if it could be proved that the etymology of Ashim was to be found in the common Semitic "name", this could hardly be said to be of any great interest as long as it does not provide any information about the nature of the deity. As is also the case with several other deities (*e.g.* the god Baʿal), the etymology is of purely historic interest and of no help when it comes to gaining a better understanding of the nature of the cult or the character of the deity. Admittedly, there are names of divinities whose etymology has a direct bearing on their function, or at least clearly had so in the early history of the deity. One only needs to think of a god like Resheph, the Canaanite god of pestilence. In general, however, I believe that a preoccupation with the etymology of the name of a deity may even lead to confusing the few facts that we do have about the deity in question. Thus, the fact that Baʿal means "lord", adds nothing of value towards the understanding of the nature and function of this deity in the Ancient Near East.

In addition to this are the problems mentioned above about the actual meaning of *šm/ʾšm* in this connection. In the above-mentioned example

---

[184] *KAI* nr. 14.

[185] R. E. W. Whitaker, *A Concordance* (1972) 510.

[186] *KAI* II (1973) 23. Cf. also J. C. L. Gibson, *Canaanite Myths and Legends* (1978) 4, n. 6.

[187] Cf. W. A. Ward, "Notes on some Semitic Loan-Words", *Or* 32 (1963) 425, n. 3, H. B. Huffmon, *Amorite Personal Names* (1965) 247-49.

we see that the word *šm* is best rendered "spouse", "consort". Obviously this is quite different from the rendering "name". And what about a name like the Biblical *šmwʾl*? Should this be understood as "Name of El", or perhaps "*šm* is god"? In this state of uncertainty we shall leave the problems connected to the etymology of the deity Ashim.

For the time being I think we should be content to accept that the original appellative "name" has become a proper name for a deity Ashim in the Ancient Near East. Any other conclusion to the evidence available will have to follow future, more comprehensive studies in the *ʾšm/šm* proper names. That the element *ʾšm/šm* was originally an appellative for the deity is more likely than that we have to do with a hypostatization here. On the whole, I find the problem of hypostatization very complicated[188].

How then should we explain the relationship of the deity Ashim, being male[189], to the deity Ashima mentioned in II Kings 17, 30 and Am 8, 14? According to the names of the deities it would seem that the Ashima of the Old Testament forms the female counterpart to the male deity Ashim attested in the Elephantine papyri. With regard to appellatives of deities, or names of deities that were originally appellatives, this phenomenon is well known from the history of religion of the Ancient Near East. I shall be content to mention only a few examples of such divine names known in a feminine as well as in a masculine form.

Corresponding to *bʿl*, there is the feminine *bʿlt*. This designation is not only known as an appellative of the goddess Anat in the Ras Shamra texts[190], but, as is also the case with Baʿal, is used as a proper name too. The most famous of the Baʿalats is the city-goddess of Byblos, Baʿalat Gebal[191]. We note with interest the similarity in the construction of this name and the Ashimat Shomron of Am 8, 14. A late Hellenistic attestation of the "same" goddess is the Palmyrean *blty*[192]. Another well known *Götterepithet* is *mlk*, "king"[193]. The female correspondent to masculine *mlk*

---

188 On this phenomenon, see in particular H. Ringgren, *Word and Wisdom* (1947) and "Hypostasen", *RGG*³ III (1959) 504-06, G. Pfeiffer, *Ursprung und Wesen der Hypostasenvorstellungen* (1967).

189 We cannot be too certain even of this. It *may* be that *ʾšm* is also feminine. It is often impossible to say whether Aramaic names are masculine or feminine (S. Segert, *Altaramäische Grammatik* (1975) § 4.8.1.1.6). The fact that we are most probably dealing with an appellative does not alter anything in this respect. Thus, one may find in personal names that the gender of the verbal element is masculine even if the deity referred to is feminine (cf. J. K. Stark, *Personal Names* (1971) 77 under *bltyḥn*). But even if it were *possible* that the name *ʾšm* represents a female deity, it is hardly probable.

190 *RS* 24.252, 1.6-8.

191 H.Gese, *Die Religionen Altsyriens* (1970) 45-46 and *passim.* Cf. also R. du Mesnil du Buisson, *Études sur les dieux phéniciens* (1970) 58-59.

192 J. Février, *La religion des palmyréniens* (1931) 64-65.

193 H. Gese, *Die Religionen Altsyriens* (1970) 97, F. Gröndahl. *Die Personennamen* (1967) 157-58, F. L. Benz, *Personal Names* (1972) 344. Cf. also above Chapter 4, n. 239.

is known to us from the Old Testament. In Jer 44, 17ff we read about the cult of *mlkt hšmym*, "Queen of Heaven". In this particular instance we are hardly justified in speaking of *mlkt* as a mere appellative. *mlkt hšmym* in Jer 44, 17ff is the proper name of a goddess. A goddess by the name *mlkt šmym* is also mentioned in the Aramaic papyri from Hermoupolis[194]. As an epithet of a goddess *mlkt* is probably best attested in Phoenician/Punic[195]. Lesser known is that also the famous goddess Anat had her male counterpart An(a)[196]. Another example from Ugarit is the female *pdry* corresponding to the male *pdr*[197]. Also the famous divine epithet *ʾdn* has its female counterpart in the form *ʾdt*[198]. No doubt these examples should demonstrate sufficiently the probability of a goddess Ashima forming the male counterpart of a god Ashim. This fact is supported also by late Hellenistic evidence.

6.3.2.3. The Hellenistic Evidence concerning the Goddess Simia

As mentioned above[199], an identification of the goddess Ashima in the Old Testament with the Semitic/Hellenistic goddess Simia has been suggested by several scholars[200]. No matter how one chooses to explain the etymological background of this divine name/appellative, I believe that this identification is correct. One should not, however, put too much into the word "identification" in this connection. In the same way that the name Ashima most certainly was used as a designation for various goddesses, the Hellenistic Simia (the name is spelt in a variety of ways) is used as a designation for several deities, most probably of the Astarte/Anath/Ashera type. Thus, even if we have no means of checking the assumption, we may assume that we have to do with the same goddess inasmuch as the many local variations of this deity most probably show the same main characteristics.

As earlier times knew of both a female *ʾšmt* and a male *ʾšm*, the Hellenistic age also has a female Simia corresponding to a male Simios.

---

194 E. Bresciani, M. Kamil, *Le lettere aramaiche di Hermopoli* (1966) 398. Cf. also J. T. Milik, "Les papyrus araméens d'Hermoupolis", *Bib* 48 (1967) index p. 605.

195 F. L. Benz, *Personal Names* (1972) 345-46.

196 H. Gese, *Die Religionen Altsyriens* (1970) 160.

197 F. Gröndahl, *Die Personennamen* (1967) 171-72.

198 O. Eissfeldt, "ʾadn", *TWAT* I (1973) 64.

199 See p. 167ff.

200 As far as I know, the first, systematic attempt to connect the two deities was made by S. Ronzevalle, "Inscription bilingue de Deir el-Qalaʿa", *RAr* 4. ser. t. 2 (1903) 35-37. Following H. Zimmern, ("Šīmat, Sīma, Tyche, Manāt," *Isl* 2 (1926) 574-84.), he later believes that the origin of this divine name is to be found in Akkadian *šimtu*, "destiny" ("Sîma - Athéna - Némésis", *Or* 3 (1934) 135). The same view was taken by A. Caquot, "Note sur le *Seimeion*", *Syr* 32 (1955) 66. On the different etymological explanations from common Semitic *šm*, "name", see above p. 175ff.

Unfortunately, the Hellenistic evidence of the goddess Simia, consisting for the most part of inscriptions, does not provide us with any detailed information on the nature of the goddess. The majority of the inscriptions relating to the goddess Simia (as well as the god Simios) have been found at the important cult centres of the Semitic/Hellenistic world: Edessa, Hatra, Hierapolis, Dura, Emesa, Palmyra, Berytus[201].

A major problem in connection with the Hellenistic attestations of Simia/Simios, besides the fact that they appear in several different languages (Greek, Latin, Aramaic, Syriac), is that the spelling of the name differs considerably, even within the same language[202].

Obviously this considerably reduces the possibility of extracting useful information from the Hellenistic evidence. Thus, we have no guarantee that all the references found in this bewildering collection of names with slightly different spellings are to the same Simia. Milik has attempted to bring some systematic order into the confusion by suggesting that we ought to differentiate between three Semitic roots in the Simia/Simios names[203]. Even if he may have a point here, I believe that Milik is far too optimistic with regard to the possibility of deciding which Semitic roots hide behind the different names. One can hardly expect a consistency in the spelling of the inscriptions of the Hellenistic age which would allow for any such strict distinctions. It would be particularly difficult, if not impossible, to reconstruct the original Semitic roots of the Greek and Latin names[204].

Still another problem connected to the Simia/Simios of Hellenism is that, in addition to the feminine and masculine forms, a neuter Semeion, being the designation for an apparent "sexless creature" is found.This Semeion, particularly famous for being described in Lucian's famous treatise on the Syrian goddess[205], has been the cause of much scholarly debate. How is the name Semeion to be explained? Is it a name for a deity, or is it a symbol or an image of a deity, or is it yet again something dif-

---

201 An excellent survey of the material, including the theophorous personal names, is provided by W. Fauth, "Simia", *PW* Suppl. B.14 (1974) 679-701. As this article is easily accessible, I do not give the evidence here. Among older surveys of the goddess Simia one may note T. Höfer, *ALGM* IV (1905-15) 660-62 (cf. also by the same author, "Seimios", *ibid.* 602), R. Dussaud, "Simea und Simios", *PRE* 2 R.3.B (1929) 137-40.

202 Cf. the survey by W. Fauth referred to in n. 201 above.

203 Cf. above n. 141.

204 As for Semitic personal names in Greek, most of the work that has been carried out has aimed at presenting the material rather than investigating methods of transcription (*e.g.* H. Wuthnow, *Die semitischen Menschennamen in griechischen Inschriften und Papyri* (1930), O. Masson, "Quelques noms sémitiques en transcription grecque", *Hommages à A. Dupont-Sommer* (1971) 61-73). Even a cursory glance at the material, however, raises serious doubts as to whether any exact retroversion is possible at all.

205 *Lucianus.* Ex. recens. C. Iacobitz. Vol. III (1839) 356ff.

ferent? Obviously I cannot take up the problem in this connection. Nevertheless, the discussion on Semeion must be taken into consideration if one wants to make the picture of the persistence of the Semitic Ashim/Ashima into the Hellenistic era complete[206].

The conclusion to be drawn from the late Hellenistic evidence of the goddess Ashima/Simia cannot be said to be impressive. Yet the evidence lends some support to our assumption given above concerning the parallel existence of a god Ashim and a goddess Ashima. Being relatively widespread, the Hellenistic evidence also bears witness to the great importance attached to the goddess Ashima/Simia in her late history. In the future, when more systematic work has been done on the Simia/Simios of the Hellenistic world, it may be hoped that this will throw some light upon the Ashima of the Old Testament too.

6.3.2.4. A Few Final Remarks on the Goddess Ashima of the Old Testament

As we have seen, it has been possible to establish as a fact that a goddess Ashima and a god Ashim have been worshipped over large parts of the Ancient Near East for several centuries.

With regard to the relationship between Ashim and Ashima we have no evidence that they have anything in common but the name. With this we may leave the god Ashim.

What then about the relationship of the Ashima of the Old Testament to the Simia of the Hellenistic world? We do know that the names of the goddesses are similar, but this does not allow us to believe that we have to do with the one and same deity. On the whole it is not possible to claim that where a deity X is mentioned in two different milieus, we are in fact dealing with the same deity. In the case of a name like Ashima, originally an appellative, we have to reckon with the possibility that several deities have been known by this name. Thus, an appellative like *bˁl* may have been used in widely different cults as designations for deities that had very little or nothing in common. Or, in cases where we are able to trace a certain cult back to an original source, spread through diffusion to other

---

[206] Of the theories put forward I would like to single out the ingenious proposition by H. Ingholt that Semeion was an image of the goddess Samia/Semaia, "Heavens". Ingholt was able to point to the iconography of the symbol as it was represented on contemporary Hierapolitan coins in support of his thesis, where he attached particular importance to the occurrence of the heavenly bodies on the image on the design of the coins (H. Ingholt, *Parthian Sculptures from Hatra* (1954) 17-46). After his theories had been criticized by Caquot, however, they did not get any further adherents (A. Caquot, "Note sur le *Semeion*", *Syr* 32 (1955) 59-69). The problem must still be considered unsolved. The most recent, thorough discussion of the problem of Semeion is that of R. A. Oden, *Studies in Lucian's De Syria Dea* (1977) 109-55.

cultures, we have no guarantee that differences in time and cultural environment have not changed the character of a particular deity. Gods are not, after all, static ideas but necessarily quite vulnerable to the local environment in which they are worshipped. Obviously this is a very complex field where we should not expect too much in the way of results.

One could object to the above remarks concerning the goddess Ashima and say that the religious cults of the Ancient Near East were extremely persistent and that this allows us to draw at least a few concrete conclusions.

I would not object to the fact that Ancient Near Eastern religion in many cases seems to show a remarkable persistency[207]. Yet I have the feeling that the evidence for the high degree of persistency which we do have has been widely overestimated and has led to the myth about the unchangeable Near East[208].

In addition to this the fact is that our evidence very often is far too meagre to allow for any conclusions at all. An example of such a case is the Ashima of the Old Testament.

Still, we are allowed to make guesses. From Am 8, 14, and from the very name of the goddess, *ʾšmt šmrwn*, we may assume that the cult of the deity in question was important at the time of the prophet Amos. Obviously the Ashimat Shomron is not to be counted among the many minor deities of the Ancient Near East. Accordingly with regard to the goddess's *Göttertypus*, we may think of her as a fertility goddess of the same kind as Astarte/Anath/Ashera[209]. In all likelihood Ashima was the city goddess of Samaria.

6.3.2.5. Samaria in the Book of Amos and in the Polemics of the Prophets

With the reference to the goddess Ashima of Samaria Amos has given us a small glimpse behind the scenes of religious life in the capital of the northern realm of Israel at the time of the prophet. Even if, according to the message of the prophet, the inhabitants of Samaria seemed to favour

---

[207] On the matter of the persistency of Canaanite religion in general, see in particular F. M. Cross, *Canaanite Myth and Hebrew Epic* (1973). That also other schools may accept a high degree of persistency may be seen *e.g.* from the remarks by M. Liverani in his review of *Ugaritica V*, *OrAnt* 8 (1969) 339-40. Cf. also R. A. Oden, "The Persistence of Canaanite Religion", *BA* 39 (1976) 31-36.

[208] Cf. my remarks in "De arabiske kilder og studiet av Det gamle Testamente", *NTT* 77 (1976) 172-73.

[209] In addition to the literature mentioned in this chapter, see also the more general works W. Helck, *Betrachtungen zur Grossen Göttin* (1971), and most recently M. Hörig, *Dea Syria* (1979).

cult places outside the city itself[210], the flourishing capital of the northern realm also had cults of its own. Yet the Book of Amos offers us no information about the cults of Samaria beyond the passages to which some consideration has already been given in this book[211]. Nevertheless we note with interest the harsh words of the prophet against Samaria in 3, 9-12:[212]

9. "Proclaim in the palaces in Ashdod
and in the palaces in the land of Egypt,
and say: Assemble on the mountains of Samaria
and see the great disorder in her centre,
the oppression in her midst.
10. They do not know how to do right, says Yahweh,
those who store up violence and devastation in their palaces,
11. Therefore says Yahweh Adonay thus:
An enemy shall surround the country,
and take your power away from you,
and your palaces shall be looted.
12. Thus says Yahweh:
As the shepherd rescues from the mouth of the lion two legs
or a piece of an ear, so shall the Israelites be rescued
that are sitting in Samaria, in the corner of a couch,
and on Damascus divans"[213].

As we see, this utterance against Samaria is mainly concerned with the moral and social behaviour of the Samaritans. Still, the reference in v. 12 to the luxurious seating arrangements *may*, on seeing the background of a text like Am 6, 4-7, reflect the *mrzḥ*[214]. This, however, remains uncertain. The reference may also imply criticism of the luxurious life of the upper class following their exploitation of the poor. Or we may have a combination of both of these motifs.

Amos is not the only one of the prophets to utter his words of doom against Samaria. Especially harsh are the words of Hosea against the capital. In Hos 8, 5-6 we read:

---

[210] Cf. above pp. 47-49.

[211] Above pp. 118-26, 143-80.

[212] The literature on this passage is limited. In addition to the current commentaries one may note among the more recent contributions L. A. Sinclair, "The Courtroom Motif in the Book of Amos", *JBL* 85 (1966) 351-53, M. O'Rourke Boyle, "The Covenant Lawsuit of the Prophet Amos", *VT* 21 (1971) 338-62.

[213] The translation of the two last expressions is complicated and their meaning somewhat uncertain. The reference is obviously to some kind of luxurious life led by the upper-class Samaritans. For a closer discussion of the couch/divan, see in particular H. Gese, "Kleine Beiträge zum Verständnis des Amosbuches", *VT* 12 (1962) 427-32, S. Mittman, "Amos 3, 12-15 und das Bett der Samaritaner", *ZDPV* 92 (1976) 149-67. It may well be that the description of the prophet in v. 12 relates to the *mrzḥ* institution (cf. above pp. 33-36, 42-44, 55, 127-42).

[214] Cf. above pp. 127-42.

> "I reject[215] your calf[216], Samaria. My anger burns against them[217]. For how long shall they be unable to behave innocently? V. 6. ...[218] a workman made it, and it is not a god. It shall become 'splinters'[219] the calf of Samaria."

And in 10, 5-8 Hosea refers to the worshipping of the inhabitants of Samaria of the calves[220] of Beth-Aven[221]. Most commentators on Israelite calf worship seem to believe that all references to calf worship in the Old Testament are to the bull-idols at Dan and Bethel. This is not necessary. In all probability there were bull/calf/cow idols at most of the main sanctuaries in ancient Israel, including Samaria[222].

Further, in his listing of all the sins of Israel in 6, 7 - 7, 16 we may read in Hos 7, 1a:

> "When I want to heal Israel, the sin of Ephraim,
> the wickedness of Samaria, is revealed."

The rest of this very important chapter deals with the religious and moral behaviour of the leaders of the northern realm and provides us with many valuable insights into the religious life of the time of the prophet. Unfortunately, the text is problematic and often difficult to understand.

The dissatisfaction of this prophet with the Samaritans is evident also from Hos 14, 1[223]. The description in this verse, however, is rather

---

215 The reading *znḥty* seems to fit the context better than the *znḥ* of MT.

216 *ʿgl*, "calf", "young bull" is in the Old Testament a common designation for an idol (Ex 32, 4.8.20.24.35, Dt 9, 16.21, I Kings 12, 28.32, II Kings 10, 29; 17, 16, 2 Chr 11, 15; 13, 8, Neh 9, 18, Ps 106, 19, Hos 13, 2 (on Hos 10, 5 cf. above p. 76). There is no reason to regard the word *ʿgl* as a "sarcastic diminutive" as is done by some scholars (cf. *e.g.* O. Michel *et al.*, "Der Tempel der goldenen Kuh", *ZNW* 49 (1958) 200-01).

217 The plural suffix may refer either to the people of Samaria or, which is more probable, to the "idols' (*ʿṣbym*) of the preceding verse.

218 MT has here *ky m yśrʾl*. Obviously the text is corrupt. I am unable to get any meaning out of it.

219 The meaning of Hebrew *šbbym* is uncertain. From the etymology of the word *šbbym* *may* have the meaning "splinters", or also "flames".

220 The text here curiously enough has *ʿglwt*, fem. pl. I have nevertheless rendered the word by the conventional "calves". Most of the commentators change the text to *ʿgl*, which is not necessary. Why should there be only *one* bull symbol at Beth-Aven? It is also possible that we should simply take MT as it stands and read "cows". As with the bull, also the cow was a widespread symbol of fertility in the Ancient Near East (cf. above pp. 44-47).

221 Beth-Aven is commonly regarded as a substitute name for Bethel. The biblical traditions, however, give reason to believe that Beth-Aven was a self-contained city. According to Jos 7, 2 Beth-Aven was situated east of Bethel (could this indicate the present Burǧ Bētīn?). Also Jos 18, 12-13 mentions Bethel and Beth-Aven as two different towns (cf. also 1 Sam 13, 5 and 14, 23). Cf. further above pp. 50-51.

222 Cf. above pp. 44, 50-51 and below 188-89.

223 This concluding pronouncement of doom against Samaria does not belong within the unity that starts in Chapter 14, but should rather be taken as the last verse of the preceding chapter.

general and does not provide us with any information on the religious cults of the city.

Also the prophet Micah utters harsh words against Samaria. In Mi 1, 5-7 [224] the prophet mentions in particular the images and the idols of the city [225].

And in Jer 23, 13 we read:

> "In the prophets of Samaria I have seen disgusting things.
> They prophesied by Baʿal and led my people Israel astray."

It is obvious that when the prophet Amos launches his attack on the moral and religious behaviour of the Samaritans, he behaves in accordance with a long prophetic tradition after him [226].

This negative attitude of the prophets towards the capital of the northern realm fits well into the picture of Samaria and her kings which we find in the Deuteronomists. In these authors the negative view of the city and its rulers goes hand in hand with references to the non-Yahwistic practices commonly to be found in Samaria [227].

Also the archaeological evidence which has been brought to the light of day as a result of the several excavations that have been carried out at the site of Samaria has contributed towards creating a picture of what life was like in this important city. As the capital of the North, founded by Omri [228], the city of Samaria was a prosperous city with an international atmosphere [229]. The excavations were also able to throw some light upon

---

224 The attempt by V. Fritz ("Das Wort gegen Samaria Mi 1, 2-7", *ZAW* 86 (1974) 316-31) to explain this oracle against Samaria as not genuine is unconvincing.

225 V. 7. On *ʾtnn zwnh*, "the prostitute's earning", in this verse, cf. above p. 27.

226 Cf. Is 7, 9; 8, 4; 9, 8; 10, 9-11; 36, 19, Jer 31, 5, Ez 16, 46-55; 23, 4.33, Ob 19.

227 See in particular I Kings 16, 26; 16, 32-33; 18, 1-46; 22, 52-53, II Kings 1, 1-4; 10, 18-29; 13, 6. Cf. also II Kings 17, 7ff (on this story cf. above p. 158ff).

228 I Kings 16, 23-24.

229 One may note the observations by Y. Aharoni and R. Amiran with regard to the sub-period "Israelite III" (840-587 B.C.) concerning the increasing differentiation between the cultures of Judah and Israel in this period. Particularly obvious is the increasing Assyrian influence in the northern realm ("A New Scheme for the Sub-Division of the Iron-Age in Palestine", *IEJ* 8 (1958) 184). The main excavation reports on Samaria are G. A. Reisner *et al.*, *Harvard Excavations at Samaria 1908-10*. Vols. 1-2 (1924), J. W. Crowfoot *et al.*, *The Buildings at Samaria* (1942), *id.*, *Early Ivories from Samaria* (1938), *id.*, *The Objects from Samaria* (1957), J. B. Hennessy, "Excavations at Samaria-Sebaste 1966", *Levant* 2 (1970) 1-21 (cf. further E. K. Vogel, "Bibliography", *HUCA* 42 (1971) 73-75 and the survey by H. Weippert, "Samaria", *BRL*² (1977) 265-69).

Of the vast literature on Samaria one may further mention A. Alt, "Der Stadtstaat Samaria", *KlSchr* 3 (1959) 258-302, *id.*, "Archäologische Fragen zur Baugeschichte von Jerusalem und Samaria", *ibid.* 303-25, A. Parrot, *Samarie* (1955), G. E. Wright, "Israelite Samaria and Iron Age Chronology", *BASOR* 155 (1959) 13-29, K. M. Kenyon, "Megiddo, Hazor, Samaria and Chronology", *BIAUL* 4 (1964) 143-56, P. R. Ackroyd, "Samaria", *Archaeology and the Old Testament* (1967) 343-54, *Eretz Shomron* (1973) *passim.*

the religious life of the city. The city of Samaria was at the height of its importance during the reign of King Jeroboam II, the time of the prophet Amos, and in particular the discoveries of the many different cult objects and figurines bear witness to the diversity of the cults that must have been practised in the city[230].

As for the goddess Ashima of Am 8, 14, one of the major goddesses of her time, no traces have been found. It may well be , however, that her cult survived in one of the many syncretistic cults of Hellenistic Samaria[231]. The answer to this we may probably never know.

6.3.3. The God of Dan

The next deity that is referred to in Am 8, 14 is not mentioned by name, but by the phrase "your god" + the local determination "Dan". It goes without saying that there is not much to be said about a deity of whom we do not even know the name.

The phenomenon, of which the expression *ʾlhym* + the suffix pronoun for 2nd pers. masc. represents one form, is well known in the Old Testament as well as in the rest of the Ancient Near East, and is most commonly referred to as the phenomenon of the "personal god"[232].

As there is no comprehensive work on the phenomenon "my/your, etc. god" based on Old Testament evidence, I cannot attempt any detailed treatment of the problem, but will be content to mention a few examples as illustrations of the occurrence of the phenomenon in Am 8, 14.

Roughly, there seem to be two different ways of using the expression "your god" in the Old Testament. It may be that the one has developed out of the other, but it is also clear that the two different usages existed side by side.

We may assume that the phrase "your god" reflects the geographical and personal constrictions of the local god or gods. An illustrative example of this is found in the Book of Ruth. Naomi, intending to go back to

---

[230] G. A. Reisner *et al.*, *Harvard Excavations*. Vol. 1 (1924) 384-85, J. W. Crowfoot *et al.*, *The Objects from Samaria* (1957) 76-82. Of particular interest are the many ivories that have been found (J. W. Crowfoot *et al.*, *Early Ivories from Samaria* (1938)). The relation of these ivories to the ivory palace of King Ahab (I Kings 23, 29) remains uncertain (cf. I. J. Winter, "Phoenician and North Syrian Ivory", *Iraq* 38 (1976) 1-22).

[231] Cf. D. Flusser, "The Great Goddess of Samaria", *IEJ* 25 (1975) 13-20, L.-H. Vincent, "Le culte d'Hélène à Samarie", *RB* 45 (1936) 221-32.

[232] For "my/your etc. god" in the Old Testament, see H. Ringgren, "*ʾlhym*", *TWAT* I (1973), W. H. Schmidt, "*ʾlhym*", *THAT* I[2] (1975) 162. For a survey of the Old Testament and Ancient Near Eastern material relating to the "personal god", see H. Vorländer, *Mein Gott* (1975), in particular 8-9, 121-22, 143, 149-50, 185, 294, 298-99. A thorough linguistic investigation of the phrase "my/your etc god" in the Old Testament remains a task of the future (cf., however, O. Eissfeldt, "Mein Gott" im Alten Testament", *ZAW* 61 (1945-48) 3-16).

Judah, tells Ruth to return to her own people, as Orphah, her sister-in-law, has done:

1, 15. "And she said: See, your sister-in-law has returned to her people and to her gods. Go[233] after your sister-in-law.
16. But Ruth said: Do not entreat me to leave you and go back, for where you go, I will go. Where you stay, I will stay. Your people shall be my people, and your gods shall be my gods."

And in the story of Jephthah's negotiation with the Ammonites in Jud 11, 12-28, we may read in v. 24:

"Is it not that what Chemosh your god gives you to possess, this you take possession of?
And all that Yahweh our god dispossesses in front of us, this we take possession of?"

Also in the prophet Micah we find similar thoughts expressed. We read in Mi 4, 5[234].

"For all the people walk each in the name of its god,
but we shall walk in the name of Yahweh our god,
always and for ever."

Most occurrences of the phrase "my god", "your god", etc., however, seem to have lost the original meaning of giving expression to the particular personal relationship to the deity, being simply a mere designation for the godhead. Thus, in 4, 12, after he has informed his fellow country-men of all the disasters which have befallen them as a result of their transgressions, Amos states on behalf of Yahweh:[235]

"Therefore I will do thus to you, Israel.
Because I will do this to you,
prepare yourself to meet your god, Israel!"

And in Am 9, 15, the very last words of the Book of Amos, we may read:

"I will plant them on their land,
and they shall never be uprooted from the land
that I have given to them, says Yahweh your god."[236]

---

[233] The Septuagint and the Peshitta have "Go also you..."

[234] The verse is probably an addition to the Book of Micah. It seems totally isolated in the context.

[235] Cf. above pp. 67-75.

[236] Most commentators take this verse to be a late addition to the Book of Amos. A typical representative of this view is U. Kellermann who sees vv. 8-15 as originating from Deuteronomic oriented circles in Judah at the time of the exile ("Der Amosschluss als Stimme deuteronomistischer Heilshoffnung", *EvTh* 29 (1969) 169-83). The assumption of Kellermann may find some support *inter alia* in the fact that the Book of Deuteronomy appears to be particularly fond of the expression "your god". The phrase occurs in the Book of Deuteronomy ca. 230 times with the suffix for masc. sing. and ca. 45 times with the plural suffix (H. Vorländer, *Mein Gott* (1975) 299).

In such and similar contexts where we find the expression "my/your, etc. god" it is very difficult to see that the phrase has the function of underlining the personal relationship of the deity to his people. Obviously it is not possible to say anything definitive on this before someone has examined the use of the formula more in detail. Even if the formula may seem to be used rather automatically as a common designation for the deity attached to the proper name, we note with interest that the Book of Deuteronomy seems particular fond of the expression[237]. This could be an indication that the authors of Deuteronomy, at least, use the expression "your god" in order to underline a personal relationship to the deity. But again, this is rather uncertain.

The conclusion, if we can call it that, to the rather vague reference to "your god, Dan" in Am 8, 14, cannot be said to be impressive. It is the character of the evidence that nothing can be said for certain. We may assume, however, that the reference is to the local Baᶜal, the city-god of Dan. Of the nature of this deity we know nothing. In all likelihood this deity represented a local variety of the ancient Canaanite Baᶜal type, a deity for whom the Old Testament gives ample evidence and who, for this reason, nevertheless can be said to represent a familiar figure[238].

A discussion on "the god of Dan" can hardly be said to be complete without also taking into account our general knowledge of the important cult centre at Dan. Only against this background shall we be able to appreciate fully the condemnation of the god of Dan by the prophet Amos. In fact, Amos is the only prophet to condemn the cult at Dan. None of the references to Dan in the prophetic literature[239] gives expression to a negative attitude towards the place. This fact may seem peculiar viewed against the background of what we learn of the cult place Dan from the biblical tradition.

6.3.3.1. Dan in the Biblical Tradition

Dan was the northern border city in the time of the monarchy, situated at the foot of the Anti-Lebanon range, under Mount Hermon. The biblical tradition preserved in Jud 18, 19 that the name of the city in earlier times was Laish is interesting in view of the attestation of a city by that name both in the Egyptian execration texts[240] and in the Mari

---

[237] Cf. n. 236 above. In addition to the Book of Deuteronomy, the formula "your god" is also particularly frequent in Deutero-Isaiah (all references are found in the book by Vorländer mentioned above n. 236.).

[238] Cf. M. J. Mulder, *Baᶜal in het Oude Testament* (1962). Cf. further J. C. de Moor, M. J. Mulder, "*bᶜl*", *TWAT* I (1973) 706-27.

[239] Jer 4, 15; 8, 16, Ez 48, 32.

[240] G. Posener, *Princes et pays* (1940) E 59, p. 92, J. Simons, *Handbook* (1937) I 31, II 26.

texts[241]. According to Jos 19, 47, however, the earlier name of the city was Leshem[242].

According to tradition, the name Dan for the earlier Laish follows the conquest of the city by the Danite tribe. The tradition is preserved in Jud 18. Besides the story of the tribe's search for a territory to live in, and its intent to take Laish (vv. 1-10), and its migration (vv. 11-26), we learn of its capture of the city and the foundation of the sanctuary (vv. 27-31)[243].

Dan is well known in the Bible from the expression "from Dan to Beersheba", currently used as a phrase denoting the whole of the territory of ancient Israel[244].

In the course of Israelite history the sanctuary at Dan would come to strengthen its position considerably.

Especially important was the event of the political and religious schism in Israel under Jeroboam I, the tradition of which is handed down in I Kings 12. Feeling the religious hegemony of Jerusalem as a threat to his newly established northern kingdom the king wanted to decrease the traditional pilgrimages to Jerusalem. Consequently, he established his own cult centres at Dan and Bethel where he set up a golden calf (I Kings 12, 29). Even if it is beyond doubt that Dan must have been an important cult centre even before this event, we must assume that the religious importance of the place increased with Jeroboam's re-establishment of the sanctuary, and in the Deuteronomic "history" there is hardly a royal undertaking that comes under more heavy attack than Jeroboam's making of the two golden calves at Dan and Bethel[245].

Even if there is a century and a half between the schism of Jeroboam and the prophet Amos, there is reason to believe that the major features

---

[241] G. Dossin, "La route de l'étain en Mésopotamie", *RA* 64 (1970) 98, 1.21 (cf. also p. 102), A. Malamat, "Northern Canaan and the Mari Texts", *Essays in Honor of Nelson Glueck* (1970) 170-72, *id.*, "Syro-Palestinian Destinations", *IEJ* 21 (1971) 35-36.

[242] This writing of the name of the town is easily understood in the light of the Akkadian spelling *la-yi-ši-im*^{ki} (cf. G. Dossin, *loc. cit.*).

[243] On this story and on the tribe of Dan, see A. Fernandez, "El santuario de Dan", *Bib* 15 (1934) 237-64, A. Murtonen, "Some Thoughts on Judges xvii sq.", *VT* 1 (1951) 223-24, C. Hauret, "Aux origines du sacerdoce danite", *Mélanges bibliques* (1957) 105-13, B. Mazar, "The Cities of the Territory of Dan", *IEJ* 10 (1960) 65-77, H.-J. Zobel, *Stammesspruch und Geschichte* (1965) 88-97, J. Strange, "The Inheritance of Dan", *StTh* 20 (1966) 120-39, A. Malamat, "The Danite Migration", *Bib* 51 (1970) 1-16, A. Globe, "The Muster of the Tribes in Judges 5, 11e-18", *ZAW* 87 (1975) 178-83.

[244] Cf. below n. 309.

[245] On Jeroboam, see M. Aberbach, L. Smolar, "Jeroboam", *IDBS* (1976) 473-75. On the schism, see R. de Vaux, "Le schism religieux de Jéroboam 1er", *Ang* 20 (1943) 77-91. On the calf cult at Dan, see S. B. Gurewicz, "When did the Cult associated with the "Golden Calves" fully develop in the Northern Kingdom", *ABR* 2 (1952) 41-44, O. Michel, O. Bauernfeind, O. Betz, "Der Tempel der goldenen Kuh", *ZNW* 49 (1958) 199-202, J. Dus, "Die Stierbilder von Bethel und Dan", *AION* 18 (1968) 105-37, H. Donner, "Hier sind deine Götter Israel", *Festschrift für Karl Elliger* (1973) 45-50.

of the cult at Dan did not undergo any radical changes in the course of this period. The golden calf set up by Jeroboam in Dan may well be the image of the local Baᶜal of Dan referred to by Amos in 8, 14.

Unfortunately we do not get any detailed information from the Old Testament concerning the cult at Dan. Even if much has been written on the tradition of the golden calves at Dan and Bethel, the bulk of it remains, and can only remain, theoretical. As is so often the case when it comes to religious practices of a controversial character, the Old Testament is unwilling to let us have any glimpse behind the scene.

One theory which might be worth mentioning is the one which sees the story of the golden calf in Ex 32 as a polemic attack on the bovine cult established by Jeroboam[246]. If this theory is correct, the tradition preserved in Ex 32 may throw considerable light upon the nature of the calf worship at Dan and Bethel. One should keep in mind, however, that the linking of the story contained in Ex 32 to the story about Jeroboam remains a theory. As far as I am able to judge, the theory is also very unlikely. There is no reason why Ex 32 should not represent a polemic attack on calf worship *in general*, not aiming at any particular cult. After all, we must assume that there were bull images at all the major "high places" in ancient Israel[247].

With regard to the persistence of the cult at Dan, the Old Testament traditions are able to offer us interesting information. From II Kings 10, 29 we learn that even if King Jehu (841-814(?)) was able to abolish the worship of Baᶜal in Israel, he was unable to get rid of the golden calves at Dan and Bethel. According to this information we are led to believe that the cult at Dan and Bethel after the reform of Jehu was a Yahwistic cult with bull images. From the preaching of Amos, however, we do not get the impression that the cult was Yahwistic. We are here touching upon an extremely difficult problem: of what nature were the cults denounced by the prophet Amos at Dan and Bethel? Were they really Yahwistic, but not sufficiently so according to the standards laid down by the prophets of Yahweh? Or were they Yahwistic/syncretistic? Or even Baᶜalistic? On the whole, what information is available does not allow any final answer to such questions. From the preaching of the prophets, from archaeology, and from extra-biblical texts[248], however, we may assume that the cults were strongly syncretistic. That these cults could have been Yahwistic is very unlikely when we read the severe polemics they are met with in the prophetic literature.

---

[246] See M. Aberbach, L. Smolar, "Calf, Golden", *IDBS* (1976) 123-24. On the story in Ex 32 see J. M. Sasson, "The Worship of the Golden Calf", *Essays Presented to Cyrus H. Gordon* (1973) 151-59.

[247] Cf. above n. 222.

[248] Cf. the remarks above pp. 6-7, 57-58, 68ff., 85, 117-18 and *passim*.

6.3.3.2. The Archaeology of Dan

Tel Dan (Arabic Tell el-Qāḍī) is generally accepted to be identical with the biblical city of Dan[249]. Since 1966 excavations have been carried out at the site by the Department of Antiquities and Museums in Israel under the directorship of A. Biran. Occasionally also other institutions have participated in the excavations[250].

Interesting discoveries have in particular been made in the north-western corner of the mound, in the area of the "high-place"[251]. It seems from the archaeological evidence that the zenith of the culture of the city was in the days of Jeroboam II. From the point of view of Am 8, 14 this is undoubtedly of great interest. There are also indications that the sanctuary at Dan existed for several centuries before the city was taken over by the Israelites. And as is so often the case with the old cult centres in the Ancient Near East, the cultic traditions of the site went on well into Hellenistic and Roman times. Several interesting objects were found from the Israelite period: oil lamps, clay figurines and figures of women.

During the 1974 excavations of the "high place" the archaeologists were able to distinguish three stages in the construction of the *bamah*: Stage A, dating to the 10th century, stage B from the mid 9th century, and finally stage C from the first half of the 8th century. In the same year the expedition also discovered a horned altar of limestone (travertine), measuring 40 × 40 cm and 35 cm high. Of particular interest is the assertion that traces of fire can be seen on the altar, indicating its being used for burnt-offerings. The dating of the altar is uncertain, but it may originate from the 9th century or earlier. Unlike the similar altar found at Beersheba[252], the Dan altar was found *in situ*[253].

Even if the results of the excavations carried out so far do not give us much information, what archaeological evidence we have got, combined

---

[249] On the basis of the identification, see H. Weippert, "Dan", *BRL*² (1977) 55. Even if one has to accept identifications of this kind on the basis of general consent, one should always bear in mind the problems involved in the identification of biblical sites (cf. H. J. Franken, "The Problem of Identification in Biblical Archaeology", *PEQ* 108 (1976) 3-11).

[250] Regular communications on the progress and findings of the excavations have been published by Biran in the following issues of *IEJ*: 19 (1969) 121-23, 239-41, 20 (1970) 118-19, 22 (1972) 164-66, 23 (1973) 110-12, 24 (1974) 262-64, 26 (1976) 54-55, 202-06. A more thorough survey of the excavations is given by Biran in "Tel Dan", *BA* 37 (1974) 26-51. Cf. also by the same author, "Dan, Tel", *EAE* I (1975) 313-21, "Dan (City)", *IDBS* (1976) 205, H. Weippert, "Dan", *BRL*² (1977) 55-56. For further literature, see E. K. Vogel, "Bibliography", *HUCA* 42 (1971) 25.

[251] A. Biran, *IEJ* 19 (1969) 240-41, 20 (1970) 118, 22 (1972) 165, 24 (1974) 262-64, *BA* 37 (1974) 40-43.

[252] Cf. below p. 200.

[253] A. Biran, "An Israelite Horned Altar at Dan", *BA* 37 (1974) 106-07 (cf. *IEJ* 24 (1974) 262).

with the biblical traditions, makes it clear that the cult centre at Dan was important enough to be attacked by the prophet Amos in the 8th century B.C.

6.3.4. The *drk* of Beersheba

The reading of MT in Am 8, 14 *wḥy drk bʾr-sbʿ* was always felt as to be a problem among the exegetes. From the context there can be little doubt that the phrase refers to some deity connected to the place Beersheba. The Hebrew phrase, however, seems to mean: "By the life of the road/way of Beersheba."

As in the case of the Ashima of Samaria, the commentators have been unable to agree on the meaning of the expression and have come out with quite a number of different explanations to the problem.

Several scholars who have commented on this difficult text change the consonantal text of MT from *drk* to *dwd*, which they take to be a designation for the tutelary god of Beersheba. Among the scholars who take this course we find Marti[254], Hoonacker[255], Sellin[256], Nowack[257], Robinson[258], Maag[259], Leahy[260], Kapelrud[261]. Also Hammershaimb[262] seems to think that a correction of the text from *drk* to *dwd*, *dwd* being a designation for the tutelary deity of Beersheba, *i.e.* Yahweh, represents the most probable solution to the problem. According to this scholar, a reading *hdrk*, "your honour", still referring to Yahweh, also represents a possible solution. Other scholars again retain the translation "way", but believe nevertheless that it would have been better to change the consonantal text to *dwd*[263].

Several scholars also retain MT and read *drk*, "way", taking the word to refer to the pilgrimages to Beersheba. Some of them even refer to the parallel Islamic usage of swearing by the pilgrimage to Mecca. In this group of scholars we find names like Harper[264] and Rudolph[265]. Also Neher[266] and Mays[266A] render *drk* with "way", but do not give any fur-

[254] K. Marti, *Das Dodekapropheton* (1904) 220, "Patron".
[255] A. V. Hoonacker, *Les douze petits prophètes* (1908) 277, "patron".
[256] E. Sellin, *Das Zwölfprophetenbuch* (1922) 216-17, "Schutzgott".
[257] W. Nowack, *Die kleinen Propheten* (1922) 163-64, "Patron".
[258] T. H. Robinson, *Die zwölf kleinen Propheten* (1938) 102 and 104, "Freund".
[259] V. Maag, *Text, Wortschatz und Begriffswelt* (1951) 56 (cf. also 139-40), "Liebling".
[260] M. Leahy, "The Popular Idea of God", *IThQ* 22 (1955) 69-70, "Patron-deity".
[261] A. S. Kapelrud, *Central Ideas* (1961).
[262] E. Hammershaimb, *The Book of Amos* (1970) 129-30.
[263] *E.g.* R. S. Cripps, *A Critical and Exegetical Commentary* (1929) 254 (cf. also 317-18), J. D. W. Watts, *Vision and Prophecy* (1958) 44.
[264] W. R. Harper, *A Critical and Exegetical Commentary* (1905) 184.
[265] W. Rudolph, *Joel, Amos, Obadja, Jona* (1971) 268 and 271.
[266] A. Neher, *Amos* (1950) 125 and 215.
[266A] J. L. Mays, *Amos* (1969) 148 and 150.

ther reasons for doing so. "Weg" is also the translation by Wolff[267] of *drk* in Am 8, 14. This scholar, however, admits that the translation is uncertain. In the commentary by Wolff one can find a fine survey of several of the attempts which have been made to solve the riddle of this *crux*.

In 1950, Neuberg came up with quite a new reading of the expression *drk bʾršbʿ*. Without making a change in the consonantal text he suggested the translation "By the life of thy Pantheon, Beer-Sheba". Neuberg partly builds his argument on Ugaritic[268]. His suggestion has later been taken up by Ackroyd[269].

Among the traditional commentators, Amsler is the only one who relates the *drk* of Am 8, 14 to Ugaritic *drkt*. His translation, accordingly, is: "Vive la puissance de Beer-Sheba"[270]. With his translation, Amsler has probably shown us the right way to start looking for a solution to the problem of *drk bʾrsbʿ*.

Of the different solutions which have been suggested for the problem of *drk* in Am 8, 14, I believe that changing the text from *drk* to *dwd* is the most unfounded. It should always be regarded as a sound principle not to emend the text as it stands. This does not mean, of course, that MT should be retained at all costs. There are instances where the text is obviously corrupt. In these cases one should not, as many scholars do today, go to extreme measures, using comparative philology, in order to retain an obviously obscure text. Even if such extremes are understandable as a reaction against an earlier school that was all too eager to emend the text whenever it suited, they cannot be tolerated.

When the emendation to *dwd* was first introduced on the scene, there hardly seemed to be any alternative explanation available: the word *drk* did seem impossible in the context. Today, this is not the case. As we shall see, it is quite possible to retain *drk* in this text.

The weakness of the reading *dwd* is further seen from the fact that even if a rather large group of scholars agree on the emendation from *drk* to *dwd*, there is no general agreement for the semantic value of the result of the emendation. As we have seen, we find different translations in different commentaries[271].

As for the possible existence of a deity *dwd*[272], it must be regarded as

---

[267] H. W. Wolff, *Dodekapropheton* 2 (1969) 371-72.

[268] F. J. Neuberg, "An Unrecognized Meaning of Hebrew *DÔR*", *JNES* 9 (1950) 215-17.

[269] P. R. Ackroyd, "The Meaning of Hebrew *dwr* Reconsidered", *JSS* 13 (1968) 4. Cf. also most recently D. N. Freedman, J. Lundbom, "*dôr*", *TWAT* II (1977) 187. Cf. also L. R. Fisher, *Ras Shamra Parallels* I (1972) 15 and 112.

[270] S. Amsler, *Amos* (1965) 237.

[271] Cf. above notes 254-63.

[272] A. S. Kapelrud, *Central Ideas* (1961) 59.

certain that we do not have any such deity attested[273]. There is some evidence that *dwd* has been used as an appellative for a deity, but even this is problematic[274]. With regard to the occurrence of the word *dwdh* in 1.12 of the Mesha inscription—referred to by several of the scholars who want to emend *drk* in Am 8, 14 to *dwd*—it should be kept in mind that the exact meaning of this word in the context is still an unsolved riddle[275].

Also the suggestion to retain MT and translate *drk* with "way", "road", I find unconvincing. As the context makes it quite clear that the reference in Am 8, 14 must be to some deity, there is hardly any reason why the phrase should be read as referring to swearing by the life of the "way of Beersheba". Not only is such a usage totally unknown in the Old Testament, but is also appears meaningless in a context like ours. As for the comparison with the Islamic usage of swearing by the pilgrimage to Mecca, it should be noted that the Muslims do not swear by the way to Mecca, but by the pilgrimage itself, which is different[276]. From more recent times, we know that the Arabs have the habit of swearing by all sorts of things[277], but it is hard to see that this should have any relevance for Am 8, 14.

Also the suggestion to translate "your pantheon" should be ruled out. Even if this may seem more acceptable than any of the suggestions presented above, it should not be forgotten that the context insists that we should look for a particular deity behind the word *drk*. As we know that the phraseology "your, etc" in such contexts as the present belongs to the phraseology of the personal god, the translation "your pantheon" seems even less appropriate.

This leaves us with the question whether *drk* of Am 8, 14 could be related to Ugaritic *drkt*, "dominion", etc., and appear as some sort of appellative for the deity of Beersheba.

The discussion of a relationship between Biblical Hebrew *drk* and Ugaritic *drkt* occupies a considerable place in recent Old Testament scholarship. The whole of this discussion concerns us only marginally.

It was for a long time felt among scholars that several of the occurrences of the root *drk* in the Old Testament could not have the semantic value "way", "road". This also applied when the traditional "way" was taken in the meaning "way" = "manner". Among the most notable passages, besides Am 8, 14, where this applies are Num 24, 17, Jer 3, 13, Hos 10, 13, Ps 110, 7; 138, 5, Prov 8, 22; 31, 3.

---

[273] Cf. J. Sanmartin-Ascaso, "*dwd*", *TWAT* II (1977) 157.
[274] *Ibid.* 164-67.
[275] *KAI* II (1973) 175, J. C. L. Gibson, *Textbook* I (1973) 79-80.
[276] See the remarks by S. Bartina, "Vivit Potentia Beer-Šeba", *VD* 34 (1956) 205.
[277] Cf. J. Pedersen, *Der Eid bei den Semiten* (1914) 164-65.

The first scholar to see a relation between Biblical Hebrew *drk* and Ugaritic *drkt*[278] was Albright[279]. The first, more systematic attempt was undertaken by Dahood in 1954[280]. This scholar has recently again and again stressed the relevance of Ugaritic *drkt* for Hebrew *drk*[281].

The first scholar to bring Ugaritic *drkt* to bear on the obscure occurrence of *drk* in Am 8, 14 was Bartina. Building on the previous identifications of Ugaritic *drkt* with Hebrew *drk*, Bartina attempts to demonstrate that *drk* in Am 8, 14 should be taken as the epithet of a divinity and translated "potentia". Bartina further adheres to the view advocated by Albright[282] that there is a connection between the Hellenistic goddess Derceto/Atargatis and the Canaanite deity mentioned in Am 8, 14[283].

After the first attempts to relate Hebrew *drk* to Ugaritic *drkt*, several scholars have entered the debate[284]. Obviously, it cannot be the task of the present investigation to treat the relationship between Biblical Hebrew *drk* and Ugaritic *drkt* in detail. On the whole, it seems that much of the research that has been done in this field has been superficial and unmethodical. It remains a fact, however, that several of the passages in the Bible which have the root *drk* cannot, on contextual evidence, bear a translation of the word with "way", "road", "manner", etc. From this point of view, there seems to be some value in the new approach we have

---

278 The references to *drkt* in the Ugaritic texts are found in R. E. Whitaker, *A. Concordance* (1972) 189.

279 W. F. Albright, "The Oracles of Balaam", *JBL* 63 (1944) 219, n. 82 (ad Num 24, 17). Already in 1934 Albright had pointed to a possible connection between Ugaritic *drkt* and the Hellenistic/Syriac goddess Derceto ("The North-Canaanite Poems", *JPOS* 14 (1934) 130, n. 153). Cf. further by the same author, "The Refrain 'And God saw *ki tob*' in Genesis", *Mélanges bibliques* (1957) 23, n. 6, and, "Some Canaanite-Phoenician Sources of Hebrew Wisdom", *Wisdom in Israel and in the Ancient Near East* (1955) 7, n. 6 (ad Prov 8, 22).

280 M. Dahood, "Ugaritic *drkt* and Biblical *derek*", *TS* 15 (1954) 627-31. In the article Dahood proposes several new readings in MT on the basis of Ugaritic *drkt.*

281 See in particular his *Ugaritic-Hebrew Philology* (1965) nr. 703, p. 55.

282 Cf. above n. 279.

283 S. Bartina, "Vivit Potentia Beer-Šeba", *VD* 34 (1956) 202-07.

284 See *i.a.* A. Jirku, "Eine Renaissance des Hebräischen", *FuF* 32 (1958) 211-12 (Prov 8, 22), J. B. Bauer, "Encore une fois Proverbes viii 22", *VT* 8 (1958) 91-92, C. H. Gordon, *UT* (1967) nr. 702, p. 387 (Hos 10, 13, Prov 31, 3). H. Zirker, on the other hand, finds the rendering by "dominion", which is the one currently suggested by those who have engaged themselves in this problem, dubious and prefers to translate the word with "Würde", "Rang" (des Herrschers), "Hoheit" ("derekh = potentia", *BZ* NF 2 (1958) 291-94). Zirker is critical towards the work that has been done concerning Hebrew *drk* and Ugaritic *drkt*. Even more critical is F. Nötscher (*Gotteswege und Menschenwege* (1958) 17-18, n. 20), who opposes any connection between the two words. More recently the relation between *drk* and *drkt* has become more official and has also appeared in dictionaries. Thus, *HAL*³ (1967) 223 gives several biblical passages where *drk may* signify "Stärke", "Macht". More sceptical about the whole matter is G. Sauer (*THAT* I (1975) 458), who believes that all occurrences of *drk* in the Bible may be understood without referring to any extra-biblical evidence (see also for further literature).

witnessed. One should not, however, too quickly resort to Ugaritic *drkt* and assume that the semantic value of Ugaritic *drkt* applies automatically to Hebrew *drk* in cases where the latter is not easily understood. After all, we are dealing with two different, even if strongly related, languages. It remains a task of the future to make a fresh comprehensive investigation of the relationship between Biblical Hebrew *drk* and Ugaritic *drkt* making use of proper linguistic methods.

With regard to *drk* in Am 8, 14, however, the problem is less complicated. There are no reasons why one should not adhere to the view advocated by Bartina[285] and take *drk* as an appellative "potentia" for the god of Beersheba.

The main reason why *drk* in Am 8, 14 should be understood in the light of Ugaritic *drkt* is, apart from the context itself, that the root *drk* also appears in an Ugaritic text as a designation for a deity. RS 24.252, an extremely important religious text, was first published by Virolleaud in 1968[286]. In lines 6-8 of this text the goddess Anat is referred to by a series of appellatives. One of these appellatives is *bʿlt drkt.* The expression could be translated "Lady of Might", or, if we choose to take the construction as being of the same kind as the so-called *genetivus epexegeticus* of classical Hebrew, "the Mighty Lady". Seen against the fact that the word *drk* in Am 8, 14 obviously does not yield any meaning when translated by the traditional "way", "road", we should not hesitate in making use of the Ugaritic parallel in this particular instance.

The facts that we may regard *drk* as an appellative of a deity and that we may translate the appellative/name "might", however, do not help us very much when it comes to the problems in relation to the nature of the "Might of Beersheba". With regard to the particular characteristics of the god of Beersheba mentioned in Am 8, 14, we remain basically ignorant. Seeing that *drk* in Am 8, 14 is masculine whereas the Ugaritic parallel is feminine, we may conclude that, in agreement with what we found with *ʾšm/ʾšmt(h)*[287], *drk/drkt* was used as an appellative/name for both male and female deities. With regard to the particular problems concerning the difficult relationship between appellatives and proper names we should have to assume that similar developments took place in the use of the original appellatives *drk/drkt* as was also the case with *ʾšm/ʾšmt(h)*[288].

---

[285] See above p. 194. Cf. also *inter alia* J. T. Milik, "Nouvelles inscriptions nabatéennes", *Syr* 35 (1958) 238-39, n. 6, J. Sanmartin-Ascaso, "*dwd*", *TWAT* II (1977) 166. Cf. also K. Koch, *ibid.* 294.

[286] *UG* V (1968) 551.

[287] Cf. above pp. 167-78.

[288] *Ibid.*

A further similarity between the divine appellatives/names *drk/drkt* and *ʾšm/ʾšmt(h)* is the probable reflection of *drk/t* in the late Hellenistic deity Derceto[289]. As mentioned above, several scholars have pointed to the obvious relevance of this Hellenistic deity for Am 8, 14[290]. Also Virolleaud, in his commentary to the first edition of RS 24.252, points to the relevance of the Hellenistic Derceto for a better understanding of the Ugaritic *bʿlt drkt*[291].

The name of the goddess Derceto occurs relatively frequently in the classical sources[292]. Even if the information offered by these sources is apparently rather confusing and, on several points even self-contradictory, there can be no doubt of their general value when used with caution.

On the whole, the Hellenistic Derceto seems to be another example of the persistence of the Canaanite/Syrian religion into the Hellenistic world[293]. Grossly simplified, we may say that the goddess represents a continuation and variant of the Semitic mother/fertility goddess known under such names as Anath, Astarte, Ashera, Ištar (and Ashima), etc. Of the Hellenistic appearances of this goddess, *the* Syrian goddess, Atargatis, is probably the one best known to us[294]. But as is the case with Atargatis and, for example, the Hellenistic goddess Simia[295], one should take care not to consider the many local variants of the goddess Derceto, witnessed to in such places as Hierapolis, Damascus, Ascalon, Dura, Palmyra, only to mention the more famous place-names, as appearances of one and the same goddess. What we *may* assume is that the major traits in the character of these different local appearances of the goddess are more or less similar, whereas her theology will have differed from place to place according to the local history of the goddess. Needless to say, our knowledge within this field is very limited.

One important fact which should be taken into account when considering the relationship between the *drk* of Beersheba in Am 8, 14 as a designation for the local Baʿal or city god and the Hellenistic deity Derceto, is the strong attestation of the name of the latter in relation to

[289] Cf. above pp. 178-80.
[290] See above p. 194.
[291] *UG* V (1968) 555.
[292] A survey of the occurrences of the name of the goddess Derceto, as well as a commentary on the literary sources, is found in P. L. van Berg, *Corpus cultus Deae Syriae* I-II (1972). A classic work containing much valuable information is F. J. Dölger, ΙΧΘΥΣ B.2 (1922). Cf. index p. 591 and notes 284 and 287.
[293] Cf. above p. 181.
[294] The most recent surveys on the Syrian goddess are W. Fauth, "Dea Syria", *KP* I (1964) 1400-03, F. R. Walton, "Atargatis", *RAC* I (1950) 854-60. Rich in information is also R. A. Oden, *Studies in Lucian's De Dea Syria* (1977). Cf. also n. 292 and n. 209 above.
[295] Cf. above pp. 178-80.

the city of Ascalon[296]. If we take a look at the map, we will find that Ascalon and Beersheba are situated not far apart. Thus, it may seem that the designation *drk/t* for the local deities was particularly favoured in this area. Whereas the *drk* of Beersheba is known to us only from Am 8, 14, the local usage of naming the deities *drk/t* persisted well into the Hellenistic age in the name of Derceto of Ascalon.

There is not much more to be said of the god *drk* of Beersheba. As the local Baᶜal of Beersheba, *drk bʾrsbᶜ* was one of the many Beᶜalim constantly referred to in the Old Testament[297]. From Am 8, 14 we may assume that the Baᶜal of Beersheba was counted among the more high-ranking of the many Canaanite Beᶜalim. This fact also corresponds to the great importance of the place Beersheba[298]. From a geographical point of view, however, it may seem strange that Amos, preaching in Samaria, should care about a deity worshipped as far away as in Beersheba. The denunciation of Ashima and the Baᶜal of Dan is more easily understood. But why distant Beersheba?

As far as I can see, there are two possible explanations why the prophet also mentions the god of Beersheba in his polemical attack on non-Yahwistic cults. From Am 5, 5 we have indications that the inhabitants of the northern realm went on pilgrimages to Beersheba[299]. Even if Amos is the only prophet to condemn the city of Beersheba[300], there is no reason why this should not have been the case. If we accept this, Am 8, 14 is easily understood in the light of the reference to pilgrimages in Am 5, 5. There is, however, also another possibility to be considered. If we take into consideration the rather direct and concrete accusations of the prophet in his attack on the cults of non-Yahwistic deities both in 5, 25-26 and in 8, 14 we get the impression that the prophet is attacking conditions in the actual city of Samaria rather than events taking place at remote cult places like Beersheba. And even if the cults at Bethel, Gilgal, Beersheba, etc. were indeed famous, they could hardly compete with the fame of the capital of Samaria. Thus, we may easily imagine that, when Amos mentions such a variety of different deities as we find in Am 5, 26 and Am 8, 14, this is a result of his being an eyewitness of these cults in the city of Samaria itself. From the Ancient Near Eastern history of religion we know the phenomenon of people

---

296 N. Glueck, "Explorations in Eastern Palestine III", *BASOR* 65 (1937) 19, n. 50, P.-L. van Berg, *Corpus cultus Deae Syriae* I-II (1972) *passim.*

297 Cf. above n. 238.

298 Cf. below p. 198ff.

299 Cf. also above p. 77f.

300 The introduction of *bbʾr šbᶜ* into the text of Hos 4, 15b, suggested by Wellhausen, Nowack, Budde, and Harper (cf. H. W. Wolff, *Dodekapropheton* I^2 (1965) 113) is unfounded.

carrying their local gods with them when making pilgrimage to one of the great religious centres[301]. And the language of 5, 26, at least, seems to indicate quite clearly that the gods in question were carried in procession[302]. It may well be, of course, that the deities mentioned in Am 5, 26 were worshipped in Samaria by the Samaritans. Considering the background of Am 8, 14, however, where the cults of such remote cult places as Beersheba are mentioned, we shall also have to consider the possibility that the deities from the surrounding villages and cities were carried into Samaria in procession on the days of the great festivals. Yet, the assumption that such a temporary import of different local gods took place remains less probable than that Amos is aiming at the pilgrimages of the Samaritans to the famous cult places of ancient Palestine, including Beersheba. The latter explanation to the problem has at least some support in the text of Amos itself[303].

6.3.4.1. Beersheba in the Bible and in Archaeology

The fact that the prophet Amos also mentions Beersheba in his attack on non-Yahwistic cults in Am 8, 14 indicates that the city must have been an important religious centre in the time of the monarchy. This is not surprising when we consider the role played by Beersheba in the biblical traditions. Yet one may find the words against Beersheba somewhat unexpected. The fact that Amos is the only prophet to condemn Beersheba is not surprising, for the prophetic condemnation of Dan is found only in Amos[304]. The problem is related rather to the geographical distance between Samaria and Beersheba. Situated in the remote southern part of Judah, biblical Beersheba was probably the administrative centre of the Negev. Why did the prophet not attack the cults of Bethel or Gilgal, religious centres mentioned by Amos on other occasions[305], rather than remote Beersheba? Problematic as it is, we shall have to be content with the attempts to provide an answer to this question made above.

Beersheba is, in addition to 8, 14, also mentioned by the prophet in 5, 5:

> ''Do not seek Bethel[306], do not go to Gilgal, nor cross over to Beersheba. For Gilgal shall go into exile and Bethel shall become nothing''[307].

---

[301] With regard to the Old Testament cf. W. R. Lane, ''Wallfahrt'', *BHH* III (1966) 2135. Cf. also the interesting information offered to us in Lucian's *De dea syria.* Ex recens. C. Iacobitz. Vol. III (1839) 360-61.

[302] Cf. above p. 119.

[303] Cf. above n. 299.

[304] Cf. above pp. 187-89.

[305] Cf. above pp. 47-58.

[306] Cf. above Chapter 4, n. 8.

[307] On this verse, see above p. 77ff. Cf. also pp. 54-58.

Beersheba holds an important place in the biblical traditions from the time of the patriarchs and is connected both with Abraham (Gen 21, 31-33), Isaac (Gen 26, 23-33), and Jacob (Gen 28, 10; 46, 1-5). Simply the fact that Beersheba is connected to all three of these patriarchal figures bears witness to its important role in the Bible[308].

Well known to readers of the Old Testament is the expression *mdn wᶜd-bʾr šbᶜ*, "from Dan to Beersheba", frequently used to indicate the whole of Israel from the border town Dan in the north to the border town Beersheba in the south[309].

With the exceptions of Am 5, 5 and 8, 14, however, none of the biblical passages containing references to Beersheba reveals anything of the city as a religious centre during the period of the monarchy. For this reason it is with the greatest interest that we turn our attention towards the excavations which have been carried out at Tel Beersheba, the site that has been identified with biblical Beersheba by the vast majority of scholars[310].

Tel Beersheba (Arabic Tell es-Sabaʾ) is situated east of the modern Israeli city of Beersheba. Several excavations have been carried out in the area, showing us that the place has a very ancient culture, going as far back as Chalcolithic times[311].

Of special interest in our connection are the excavations of the Institute of Archaeology at Tel Aviv University under the directorship of Professor Yohanan Aharoni from 1969 onwards[312]. From the start of the excavations it has been possible to follow their progress and the discoveries through the many short communications that have appeared in several learned journals[313].

---

[308] Cf. also Gen 21, 14 and 22, 19. On Beersheba in the biblical traditions, see W.Zimmerli, *Geschichte und Tradition von Beersheba* (1932), H. Haag, "Erwägungen über Beer-Šeba", *Sacra Pagina* I (1959) 335-45.

[309] Jud 20, 1, 1 Sam 3, 20, 2 Sam 3, 10; 17, 11; 24, 2.15, I Kings 5, 5 (MT). In 1 Chr 21, 2 (= 2 Sam 24, 2) and 2 Chr 30, 5 the names of the two towns have changed place to "from Beersheba to Dan" (on these expressions, see J. Boehmer, "Von Dan bis Beersheba", *ZAW* 29 (1909) 134-42). The name of Beersheba is mentioned also in other geographical expressions: Neh 11, 30, 2 Chr 19, 4, II Kings 23, 8, and occasionally in the "historical" books: Jos 15, 28; 19, 2 (1 Chr 4, 28), 1 Sam 8, 2, I Kings 19, 3, II Kings 12, 2 (2 Chr 24, 1), Neh 11, 27.

[310] Cf. M. Wüst, "Beersheba", *BRL*² (1977) 36.

[311] For a short survey of the "Beersheba culture", see J. Perrot, J. Gophna, "Beersheba", *EAE* I (1975) 153-59. Cf. further, E. K. Vogel, "Bibliography", *HUCA* 42 (1971) 15.

[312] Unfortunately, this eminent scholar died before he could finish the work.

[313] Suffice to mention the *IEJ* communications written by Aharoni himself, appearing in the following issues: 19 (1969) 245-47, 20 (1970) 227-29, 21 (1971) 239-32, 22 (1972) 164-66, 23 (1973) 254-56, 24 (1974) 270-72, 25 (1975) 169-71. Because of the unfortunate death of Aharoni, a full report has been published only for the first three seasons, 1969-71: Y. Aharoni (ed.), *Beer-Sheba* I (1973). Cf. further by the same author, "Excavations at Tel Beer-Sheba", *TA* 1 (1974) 34-42, "Excavations at Tel Beer-Sheba", *BA* 35 (1972)

Several interesting things relating to the religious life at Beersheba during the time of the monarchy have been brought to light as a result of the excavations. Even during the first season of 1969 important cult objects were discovered, and in the course of the following seasons several important objects were found[314]. A major discovery was made during the fifth season (24.6-24.8 1973) when a horned altar was found, clearly indicating that a temple must have existed in the area[315]. This remarkable altar, of the same kind as the one discovered at Dan[316], was not found *in situ*. The stones of the altar were re-used as a part of a repaired wall of a storehouse of stratum II, belonging to the 8th century. Of particular interest is the carving of a twisting snake found on the altar, the snake being a famous fertility symbol of the Ancient Near East[317]. The storehouse in which the altar was found seems to have been destroyed by conflagration towards the end of the 8th century, and it is believed that this is connected with the campaign of Sennacherib in 701 B.C. The city was not rebuilt in Israelite times. With regard to the altar itself, a possible connection between its dismantling and the religious reform carried out by king Hezekiah has been pointed to.

As a result of the discovery of the altar, the expedition concentrated in the following seasons upon an attempt to locate the temple. As no temple was found, the expedition was led to believe that the temple, like the altar, had been pulled down at some time. The discovery of a temple from Hellenistic times may indicate that it has been founded on the site of the earlier Israelite temple, thus preserving the ancient cultic traditions of the place[318].

The possibility that an Israelite temple has existed at the site is strong. This is not only suggested from the denunciation of Beersheba in the Book of Amos, but has also been confirmed by the discovery of a rich variety of cult objects from the time of the monarchy: Astarte figurines, zoomorphic vessels, etc. It is also remarkable that whereas a site such as neighbouring Arad shows very few "pagan" traits, the rich and unique group of cult objects found at Beersheba is basically "pagan" and shows strong Egyptian influence[319].

111-27, "Beer-Sheba, Tel", *EAE* I (1975) 160-68. Cf. further M. Wüst, "Beersheba", *BRL*² (1977) 36, B. Boyd, "Beer-Sheba", *IDBS* (1976), E. K. Vogel, "Bibliography", *HUCA* 42 (1971) 16.

[314] Y.Aharoni, *IEJ* 19 (1969) 246, 21 (1971) 231-32, *Beer-Sheba* I (1973) 56-70, "Excavations", *BA* 35 (1972) 126-27.

[315] Y. Aharoni, *IEJ* 23 (1973) 254-55, "The Horned Altar at Beersheba", *BA* 37 (1974) 2-6.

[316] Cf. above p. 190.

[317] Y. Aharoni, "The Horned Altar", *BA* 37 (1974) Fig. 2.

[318] Y. Aharoni, *IEJ* 24 (1974) 270-72.

[319] Y. Aharoni, "Excavations", *BA* 35 (1972) 127.

Archaeology, then, seems to confirm the picture given by Amos of Beersheba as a cult place of a strongly syncretistic or non-Yahwistic character. With regard to the deity *drk*[320] mentioned by the prophet in 8, 14 archaeology has been unable to reveal anything which could give any indication of the nature of the deity.

---

[320] I have preferred not to vocalize *drk*. Several suggestions have been made, but on the whole we should admit our ignorance on how the name/appellative of this deity was pronounced in ancient times. It *may* be that the suggestion of Milik (''Nouvelles inscriptions'', *Syr* 35 (1958) 238-39, n. 6), vocalizing *Durk*, is correct.

BIBLIOGRAPHY

Aalen, S., *Die Begriffe "Licht" und "Finsternis" im Alten Testament, im Spätjudentum und im Rabbinismus.* Oslo 1951 (*SNVAO.HF* No 1).

——, "*ʾwr*", *TWAT* I (1973) 160-82.

Aberbach, M., "Calf, Golden". [By] ... [and] L. Smolar, *IDBS* (1976) 123-24.

——, "Jeroboam". [By] ... [and] L. Smolar, *IDBS* (1976) 473-75.

Ackerman, J. S., "Prophecy and Warfare in Early Israel: A Study of the Deborah-Barak Story", *BASOR* 220 (1975) 5-13.

Ackroyd, P. R., "Samaria", *Archaeology and Old Testament Study. Jubilee Volume of the Society for Old Testament Study 1917-67.* Ed. by D. Winton Thomas. Oxford (1967) 343-54.

——, "The Meaning of Hebrew דור considered", *JSS* 13 (1968) 3-10.

Aharoni, Y., "A New Scheme for the Sub-Division of the Iron Age in Palestina". [By] ... and R. Amiran, *IEJ* 8 (1958) 171-84.

——, "Arad. Its Inscriptions and Temple", *BA* 31 (1968) 2-32.

——, "Tel Beersheba", *IEJ* 19 (1969) 245-47, 20 (1970) 227-29, 21 (1971) 230-32, 22 (1972) 164-66, 23 (1973) 254-56, 24 (1974) 270-72, 25 (1975) 169-71.

——, "Excavations at Tel Beer-Sheba", *BA* 35 (1972) 111-27.

——, (ed.), *Beer-Sheba I. Excavations at Tel Beer-sheba. 1969-71 Seasons*, Tel Aviv 1973 (*Tel Aviv University. Institute of Archaeology. Publications.* 2).

——, "The Horned Altar of Beer-Sheba", *BA* 37 (1974) 2-6.

——, "Excavations at Tel Beer-Sheba. Preliminary Report of the Fourth Season, 1972", *TA* 1 (1974) 34-42.

——, "Beersheba, Tel", *EAE* I (1975) 160-68.

Ahlström, G. W., *Aspects of Syncretism in Israelite Religion*, Lund 1963 (*HSoed* 5).

——, *Joel and the Temple Cult of Jerusalem*, Leiden 1971 (*SVT* XXI).

——, "Heaven on Earth - At Hazor and Arad", *Religious Syncretism in Antiquity.* Ed. by B. A. Pearson. Missoula, Mont. (1975) 67-83.

Aimé-Giron, N., *Textes araméens d'Égypte.* Le Caire 1931.

Albright, W. F., "The Evolution of the West-Semitic Divinity ʿAn-ʿAnat-ʿAttâ," *AJSL* 41 (1924-25) 73-101.

——, "The Syro-Mesopotamian God Šulmân-Ešmûn and Related Figures", *AfO* 7 (1931-32) 164-69.

——, "The North-Canaanite Poems of Alʾêyân Baʿal and the "Gracious Gods", "*JPOS* 14 (1934) 101-40.

——, "The Oracles of Balaam", *JBL* 63 (1944) 207-33.

——, *Archaeology and the Religion of Israel.* 3rd ed. Baltimore 1953.

——, "Some Canaanite-Phoenician Sources of Hebrew Wisdom", *Wisdom in Israel and in the Ancient Near East. Presented to H. H. Rowley ... in Celebration of his 65th Birthday, 24 March 1955.* Ed. by M. Noth and D. Winton Thomas. Leiden (1955) 1-15 (*SVT* III).

——, "The Refrain "And God Saw *ki tob*" in Genesis", *Mélanges bibliques rédigés en l'honneur de A. Robert.* Paris [1957] 22-26 (*TICP* 4).

——, *Yahweh and the Gods of Canaan. A Historical Analysis of two Contrasting Faiths.* London 1968 (*JLCR* 7).

Alt, A., "Die Syrische Staatenwelt vor dem Einbruch der Assyrer", *ZDMG* 88 (1934) 233-58.

——, "Das Gottesurteil auf dem Karmel", *KlSchr* 2 (1953) 135-49 (first published 1935).

——, "Der Stadtstaat Samaria", *KlSchr* 3 (1959) 258-302 (first published 1954).

——, "Archäologische Fragen zur Baugeschichte von Jerusalem und Samaria in der israelitischen Königzeit", *KlSchr* 3 (1959) 303-25 (first published 1955-56).

Amy, R., "Recherches dans la nécropole de Palmyre". Par ... et H. Seyrig, *Syr* 17 (1936) 229-66.

Amsler, S., "Amos, prophète de la onzième heure", *ThZ* 21 (1965) 318-28.
——, *Amos.* Neuchâtel 1965 (*CAT* 11A).
Asmussen, J. P., "Bemerkungen zur sakralen Prostitution im Alten Testament", *StTh* 11 (1957-58) 167-92.
Astour, M. C., "Some New Divine Names from Ugarit", *JAOS* 86 (1966) 277-84.
——, *Hellenosemitica. An Ethnic and Cultural Study in West Semitic Impact on Mycenaean Greece.* With a Foreword by C. H. Gordon. 2nd ed. Leiden 1967.
Avi-Yona, M. (ed.), *Encyclopedia of Archaeological Excavations in the Holy Land.* Vols. 1-4. Lond. 1975-78.
Avigad, N., "Excavations at Beth Sheᶜarim, 1955. Preliminary Report", *IEJ* 7 (1957) 239-55.
——, "An Unpublished Phoenician Seal", *Hommages à André Dupont-Sommer*, Paris (1971) 3-4.
Bach, R., "Gottesrecht und weltliches Recht in der Verkündigung des Propheten Amos", *Festschrift G. Dehn*, Neukirchen-Vluyn (1957) 23-34.
——, *Die Aufforderungen zur Flucht und zum Kampf im alttestamentlichen Prophetenspruch.* Neukirchen-Vluyn 1962 (*WMANT* 9.).
Bächli, O., "Zur Lage des alten Gilgal", *ZDPV* 83 (1967) 64-71.
Baena, G., "El vocabulario de II Reyes 17, 7-23. 35-39", *EstB* 32 (1973) 357-84.
——, "Carácter literario de II Reyes 17, 7-23", *EstB* 33 (1974) 5-29.
——, "Carácter literario de II Reyes 17, 13. 35-39", *EstB* 33 (1974) 157-79.
Baltzer, K., *Die Biographie der Propheten.* Neukirchen-Vluyn 1975.
Bammel, F., *Das heilige Mahl im Glauben der Völker. Eine religions-phänomenologische Untersuchung.* Gütersloh 1950.
Barr, J., "Hypostatization of Linguistic Phenomena in Modern Theological Interpretation", *JSS* 7 (1962) 85-94.
——, "Etymology and the Old Testament", *Language and Meaning. Studies in Hebrew Language and Biblical Exegesis. Papers Read at the Joint British-Dutch Old Testament Conference held at London, 1973*, Leiden (1974) 1-28 (*OTS* 19).
——, "Some Semantic Notes on the Covenant", *BeitrAltTheol* (1977) 23-38.
Barstad, H. M., "Die Basankühe in Amos iv 1", *VT* 25 (1975) 286-97.
——, "De arabiske kilder og studiet av Det gamle Testamente. Noen refleksjoner omkring en ny bok", *NTT* 77 (1976) 163-77.
——, ""Der rasende Zeus". Ein Beitrag zum Verständnis von Lukians "De dea Syria", Kap. 47", *Tem* 12 (1976) 163-73.
——, "*HBL* als Bezeichnung der fremden Götter im Alten Testament und der Gott Hubal", *StTh* 32 (1978) 57-65.
——, "Festmahl und Übersättigung. Der "Sitz im Leben" von RS 24.258", *AcOr* 39 (1978) 23-30.
Bartina, S., "Vivit Potentia Beer-Šeba! *VD* 34 (1956) 202-07.
Barton, J., *Amos's Oracles Against the Nations. A Study of Amos 1, 3-2, 5.* Cambridge 1980 (*MSSOTS*).
Baudissin, W. W., *Studien zur semitischen Religionsgeschichte. H. 1.* Berlin 1911.
——, *Adonis und Esmun. Eine Untersuchung zur Geschichte des Glaubens an Auferstehungsgötter und an Heilgötter.* Lpz. 1911.
Bauer, J. B., "Encore une fois Proverbes viii 22", *VT* 8 (1958) 91-92.
Baumgartner, W., "Herodots babylonische und assyrische Nachrichten", *Symbolae ad Studia Orientis pertinentes F. Hrozný dedicatae quas ed. V. Čihar, J. Klima, L. Matouš.* Praha (1950) 69-106 (*ArOr* 18).
Becker, J., *Gottesfurcht im Alten Testament.* Roma 1965 (*AnBib* 25).
Beek, M. A., "The Religious Background of Amos II 6-8", *OTS* 5 (1948) 132-41.
Beer, G., "[Review of] G. Dalman, *Neue Petraforschungen und der heilige Felsen von Jerusalem.* Lpz. 1912", *ZDMG* 67 (1913) 557-63.
Bennett, B. M., "The Search for Israelite Gilgal", *PEQ* 104 (1972) 111-22.
Bentzen, Aa., "The Ritual Background of Amos 1, 2-2, 16", *OTS* 8 (1950) 85-99.

Benz, F. L., *Personal Names in the Phoenician and Punic Inscriptions. A Catalog, Grammatical Study and Glossary of Elements.* Rome 1972 (*StP* 8).
Berg, P.-L. van, *Corpus cultus Deae Syriae* (*CCDS*). *I. Les sources littéraires. P. I. Répertoire des sources grecques et latines* (*sauf le De Dea Syria*). *P. 2. Étude critique des sources mythographiques grecques et latines* (*sauf le De Dea Syria*). Leiden 1972 (*EPRO* 28 [: 1-2]).
Berg, W., *Die sogenannten Hymnenfragmente im Amosbuch.* Bern 1974 (*EHS.T.* 45).
Bergman, J., "*zbḥ*", *TWAT* II (1977) 509-31. [Von] ..., H. Ringgren [und] B. Lang.
——, "Isis", *LÄ* III (1980) 186-203.
Berridge, J. M., "Zur Intention der Botschaft des Amos", *ThZ* 32 (1976) 321-40.
Beyerlin, W., *Herkunft und Geschichte der ältesten Sinaitraditionen.* Tübingen 1961.
Biblia Hebraica Stuttgartensia. Editio funditus renovata. Edd. K. Elliger et W. Rudolph. Textum Masoreticum curavit H. P. Rüger. Masoram elaboravit G. E. Weil. Stuttgart 1977.
Bibliotheca Geographorum Arabicorum. Ed. M. J. de Goeje. P. 7. 2nd ed. Leiden 1892.
Bič, M., *Das Buch Amos.* Berlin 1969.
Biran, A., "Tel Dan", *IEJ* 19 (1969) 121-23, 239-41, 20 (1970) 118-19, 22 (1972) 164-66, 23 (1973) 110-12, 24 (1974) 262-64, 26 (1976) 54-55, 202-06, 27 (1977) 242-46, 28 (1978) 268-71.
——, "Tel Dan", *BA* 37 (1974) 26-51.
——, "An Israelite Horned Altar at Dan", *BA* 37 (1974) 106-07.
——, "Dan, Tel", *EAE* I (1975) 313-21.
——, "Dan (City)", *IDBS* (1976) 205.
Blau, J., *A Grammar of Biblical Hebrew.* Wiesbaden 1976 (*PLO* N.S. 12).
Bleeker, C. J., "Some Remarks on the Religious Significance of Light", *The Gaster Festschrift* (1973) 23-34 (*JANES* 5).
Böhl, F. M. Th., "De maangod en de koe", *JEOL* 4 (1936) 202-04.
Boehmer, J., "Von Dan bis Beersheba", *ZAW* 29 (1909) 134-42.
Bonnet, H., *Reallexikon der ägyptischen Religionsgeschichte.* Berlin 1952.
Borger, R., *Die Inschriften Asarhaddons Königs von Assyrien.* Graz 1956 (*AfO.B* 9).
——, "Anath-Bethel", *VT* 7 (1957) 102-04.
——, *Handbuch der Keilschriftliteratur. B.1. Repertorium der sumerischen und akkadischen Texte.* Berlin 1967.
Botterweck, G. J., "Zur Authenzität des Buches Amos", *BZ* 2 (1958) 176-89.
——, *Theologisches Wörterbuch zum Alten Testament.* In Verbindung mit G. W. Anderson, H. Cazelles, D. N. Freedman, S. Talmon u. G. Wallis hg. v. ... u. H. Ringgren. B. I-Lief. 1- Stuttgart 1970-
—— ""Sie verkaufen den Unschuldigen um Geld". Zur sozialen Kritik des Propheten Amos", *BiLe* 12 (1971) 215-31.
——, "*ʾbywn*", *TWAT* I (1973) 28-43.
——, "ḥag̃". [Von] ... [und] B. Kedar-Kopfstein, *TWAT* II (1977) 730-44.
Bourke, J., "Le jour de Yahvé dans Joël", *RB* 66 (1959) 5-31, 191-212.
Boyd, B., "Beer-Sheba", *IDBS* (1976) 93-95.
Boyle, M. O'Rourke, "The Covenant Lawsuit of the Prophet Amos: III 1-IV 13", *VT* 21 (1971) 338-62.
Branden, A. van den, "Notes phéniciennes", *BMB* 13 (1956) 87-95.
Bresciani, E., "Nuovi documenti aramaici dall' Egitto", *ASAE* 55 (1958) 273-83. Tav. I-III.
——, *Le lettere aramaiche di Hermopoli.* [Di] ... e M. Kamil. Roma 1966 (*AANL.M* Ser 8. Vol. 12. Fasc. 5).
Breytenbach, A. P. B., "The Connection between the Concepts of Darkness and Drought as well as Light and Vegetation", *De fructu oris sui. Essays in Honour of A. van Selms.* Ed. by I. H. Eybers, F. C. Fensham, C. L. Labuschagne, W. C. van Wijk and A. H. van Zyl. Leiden (1971) 1-5 (*POS* 9).
Brichto, H. C., *The Problem of "Curse" in the Hebrew Bible.* Philadelphia, Pa. 1963 (*JBL.MS* 13).
Bright, J., *Covenant and Promise. The Prophetic Understanding of the Future in Pre-Exilic Israel.* Philadelphia, Pa. 1976.

Brockelmann, C., "Ein syrischer Regenzauber", *ARW* 9 (1906) 518-20.
——, *Lexicon Syriacum.* Ed. 2. aucta et emendata. Halis Saxonum 1928.
Brongers, H., "Fasting in Israel in Biblical and Post-Biblical Times", *OTS* 20 (1977) 1-21.
Brooks, B. A., "Fertility Cult Functionaries in the Old Testament", *JBL* 60 (1941) 227-53.
Brueggemann, W., "Amos iv 4-13 and Israel's Covenant Worship", *VT* 15 (1965) 1-15.
——, *Tradition for Crisis. A Study in Hosea.* Richmond, Va. 1968.
Bryan, D. B., *Texts Relating to the Marzeah: A Study of an Ancient Semitic Institution.* Unpubl. Diss. The John Hopkins University, 1973.
Buren, E. D. van, "The Sacred Marriage in Early Times in Mesopotamia", *Or* 13 (1944) 1-72.
——, *Symbols of the Gods in Mesopotamian Art.* Roma 1945 (*AnOr* 23).
Burrows, E., "Cuneiform and Old Testament: Three Notes, *JThS* 28 (1927) 184-85.
Buss, M. J., "The Meaning of "Cult" and the Interpretation of the Old Testament", *JBR* 32 (1964) 317-25.
——, "Prophecy in Ancient Israel", *IDBS* (1976) 694-97.
Buttenwieser, M., "*bkly ʿz lyhwh.* 2 Chronicles 30, 21. A Perfect Text", *JBL* 45 (1926) 156-58.
Campbell, E. F. jr., "W. F. Albright and Historical Reconstruction". [By] ... [and] J. Maxwell Miller, *BA* 42 (1979) 37-47.
Campbell, W. A., "Archaeological Notes. The Fourth and Fifth Seasons of Excavation at Antioch-on-the-Orontes 1935-1936", *AJA* 42 (1938) 205-18.
Cannon, W. W., "The Day of the Lord in Joel", *CQR* 103 (1926-27) 32-63.
Cantineau, J., "Inscriptions Palmyréniennes", *RA* 27 (1930) 27-51.
——, "Textes palmyréniens provenant de la fouille du temple de Bèl", *Syr* 12 (1931) 116-41.
——, "Tadmorea", *Syr* 17 (1936) 346-55.
Caquot, A., "Nouvelles inscriptions araméennes de Hatra (III)", *Syr* 32 (1955) 49-58.
——, "Note sur le SEMEION et les inscriptions araméennes de Hatra", *Syr* 32 (1955) 59-69.
——, "Problèmes d'histoire religieuse", *La Siria nel tardo bronzo.* Raccolti da M. Liverani. Roma (1969) 61-76 (*OAC* 9).
——, "[Review of] B. Porten, *Archives from Elephantine. The Life of an Ancient Jewish Military Colony.* Berkeley 1968", *Syr* 47 (1970) 176-79.
——, *Textes ougaritiques. T. I. Mythes et légendes.* Introd., trad., comm. par ..., M. Sznycer et A. Herdner. Paris 1974 (*LAPO*).
Carlson, R. A., "Profeten Amos och Davidsriket", *RoB* 25 (1966) 57-78.
Carmichael, C. M., "A Ceremonial Crux: Removing a Man's Sandal as a Female Gesture of Contempt", *JBL* 96 (1977) 321-36.
Carniti, C., "L'espressione "Il giorno di JHWH". Origine ed evoluzione semantica", *BeO* 12 (1970) 11-25.
Cassuto, U., *Hā-ʾĒla ʿĂnāth.* Jerusalem 1951.
Cathcart, K. J., "Weathering a Wake: A Cure for a Carousal. A Revised Translation of Ugaritica V Text 1". [By] ... and W. G. E. Watson, *PIBA* 4 (1980) 35-58.
Černy, L., *The Day of Yahweh and some Relevant Problems.* Praha 1948.
Christensen, D. L., "The Prosodic Structure of Am 1-2", *HThR* 67 (1974) 427-36.
——, *Transformations of the War Oracle in Old Testament Prophecy. Studies in the Oracles against the Nations.* Missoula, Mont. 1975 (*HDR* 3.).
Clemen, C., *Lukians Schrift über die syrische Göttin.* Übers. u. erläutert v.... Leipzig 1938 (*AO* 38: 3-4).
Clements, R. E., *Prophecy and Covenant.* London 1965 (*SBT* 43).
——, *Prophecy and Tradition.* Oxf. 1975 (*Growing Points in Theology*).
——, *A Century of Old Testament Study.* London 1976.
Clifford, R. J., "The Use of HÔY in the Prophets", *CBQ* 28 (1966) 458-64.
Clines, D. J. A., "New Year", *IDBS* (1976) 625-29.

Clermont-Ganneau, Ch., *Receuil d'archéologie orientale.* T. 1-8. Paris 1888-1924.
Coats, G. W., "Tradition Criticism, OT", *IDBS* (1976) 912-14.
Coggins, R. J., "The Old Testament and Samaritan Origins", *ASTI* 6 (1968) 35-48.
Colpe, C., "Zur mythologischen Struktur der Adonis-, Attis- und Osiris-Überlieferungen", *lišān mitḫurti. Festschrift W. Freiherr von Soden zum 19.VI.1968 gewidmet von Schülern und Mitarbeitern.* Unter Mitwirkung v. M. Dietrich hg. v. W. Röllig. Neukirchen-Vluyn (1969) 23-44 (*AOAT* 1).
Cooke, G. A., *A Text-Book of North-Semitic Inscriptions. Moabite, Hebrew, Phoenician, Aramaic, Nabatean, Palmyrene, Jewish.* Oxford 1903.
Coote, R. B., "Amos 1, 11 *RḤMYW*", *JBL* 90 (1971) 206-08.
——, "Tradition, Oral, OT", *IDBS* (1976) 914-16.
Corpus Inscriptionum Semiticarum ab Academia Inscriptionum et Litterarum Humaniorum conditum atque digestum. Paris 1881-.
Coulot, C., "Propositions pour une structuration du livre d'Amos au niveau rédactionnel", *RSR* 51 (1977) 169-86.
Cowley, A., *Aramaic Papyri of the Fifth Century B.C.* Ed., with Transl. and Notes by... Oxford 1923.
Craghan, J. F., "The Prophet Amos in Recent Literature", *BTB* 2 (1972) 242-61.
Cramer, K., *Amos. Versuch einer theologischen Interpretation.* Stuttgart 1930 (*BWANT* 51).
Crenshaw, J. L., "The Influence of the Wise upon Amos. The "Doxologies of Amos" and Job 5, 9-16; 9, 5-10", *ZAW* 79 (1967) 42-52.
——, "Methods in Determining Wisdom Influence upon "Historical" Literature", *JBL* 88 (1969) 129-42.
——, "A Liturgy of Wasted Opportunity (Am 4, 6-12, Isa 9, 7-10; 5, 25-29)", *Semitics* 1 (1970) 27-37.
——, "Prophecy, False", *IDBS* (1976) 701-02.
Cripps, R. S., *A Critical and Exegetical Commentary on the Book of Amos. The Text of the Revised Version ed. with Introd., Notes and Excursuses.* With a Foreword by R. H. Kennett. London 1929.
Cross, F. Moore jr., "The Divine Warrior in Israel's Early Cult", *Biblical Motifs. Origins and Transformations.* Ed. by A. Altmann. Cambridge, Mass. (1966) 11-30 (*STLi* 3).
——, *Canaanite Myth and Hebrew Epic. Essays in the History of the Religion of Israel.* Cambridge, Mass. 1973.
Crowfoot, J. M., *Early Ivories from Samaria.* [By] ... [and] G. M. Crowfoot. With a Note by E. L. Sukenik. London 1938 (*SaSe* 2).
——, *The Buildings at Samaria.* By ..., K. M. Kenyon [and] E. L. Sukenik. London 1942 (*SaSe* 1).
——, The Objects from Samaria. [By] ..., G. M. Crowfoot [and] K. M. Kenyon. With Contributions by S. A. Birnbaum, J. H. Iliffe, J. S. Kirkman, S. Lake, E. L. Sukenik. London 1957 (*SaSe* 3).
Crüsemann, F., "Kritik an Amos im Deuteronomistischen Geschichtswerk. Erwägungen zu 2. Könige 14, 27", *ProblBiblTheol* (1971) 57-63.
Curtiss, S. I., *Primitive Semitic Religion To-Day. A Record of Researches, Discoveries and Studies in Syria, Palestine and the Sinaitic Peninsula.* London 1902.
Cutler, B., "Identification of the *naʿar* in the Ugaritic Texts". [By] ... [and] J. MacDonald, *UF* 8 (1976) 27-35.
Dahood, M., "Ugaritic DRKT and Biblical DEREK", *TS* 15 (1954) 627-31.
——, "Ancient Semitic Deities in Syria and Palestine", *Le antiche divinità semitiche.* Studi di J. Bottéro, M. J. Dahood, W. Caskel, raccolti da S. Moscati. Roma (1958) 65-94 (*SS* 1).
——, "To Pawn one's cloak", *Bib* 42 (1961) 359-66.
——, *Ugaritic-Hebrew Philology. Marginal Notes on Recent Publications.* Rome 1965 (*BibOr* 17).
——, "Additional Notes on the *Mrzḥ* Text", *CRST* (1971) 51-54.
Dalman, G., *Neue Petra-Forschungen und der heilige Felsen von Jerusalem.* Leipzig 1912 (*Palästinische Forschungen zur Archäologie und Topographie* 2).

——, "Der Gilgal der Bibel und die Steinkreise Palästinas", *PJ* 15 (1919) 5-26.
——, *Arbeit und Sitte in Palästina.* B. 1-5. Gütersloh 1928-37.
Daumas, F., "Hathor", *LÄ* II (1977) 1024-33.
Degen, R., *Altaramäische Grammatik der Inschriften des 10.-8. Jh. v. Chr.* Wiesbaden 1969 (*AKM* 38: 3).
Deimel, A., *Pantheon Babylonicum.* Roma 1950 (*SL* IV T.B. 1).
Delavault, B., "Une stèle "molk" de Palestine dédiée à Eshmoun? RES 367 reconsidéré". [Par] ... [et] A. Lemaire, *RB* 83 (1976) 569-83.
Delcor, M., "Rites pour l'obtention de la pluie à Jérusalem et dans le Proche-Orient", *RHR* 178 (1970) 117-32.
——, "Repas cultuels esséniens et thérapeutes, thiases et ḥaburoth", *RdQ* 6 (1968) 401-25.
Delekat, L., "Zum hebräischen Wörterbuch", *VT* 14 (1964) 7-66.
Dietrich, E. K., *Die Umkehr (Bekehrung und Busse) im Alten Testament und im Judentum.* Stuttgart 1936.
Dietrich, W., *Prophetie und Geschichte. Eine redaktionsgeschichtliche Untersuchung zum deuteronomistischen Geschichtswerk.* Göttingen 1972 (*FRLANT* 108).
Dijk, J. van, "Une variante du thème de "l'Esclave de la lune"," *Or* 41 (1972) 339-48.
Dobbie, R., "Amos 5, 25", *TGUOS* 17 (1959) 62-64.
Dölger, F. J., ΙΧΘΥΣ. *B.2. Der Heilige Fisch in den antiken Religionen und im Christentum.* Münster in Westf. 1922.
Dommershausen, W., "*ḥll*", *TWAT* II (1977) 972-81.
Donner, H., *Kanaanäische und aramäische Inschriften.* [Von] ... [und] W. Röllig. Mit einem Beitrag von O. Rössler. B. I-III. Wiesbaden 1962-64. (B.I. 3. durchges. Aufl. 1971. B.II. 3. unveränd. Aufl. 1973. B.III. 3. unveränd. Aufl. 1976).
——, "Die soziale Botschaft der Propheten im Lichte der Gesellschaftsordnung in Israel", *OrAnt* 2 (1963) 230-45.
——, "Hier sind deine Götter, Israel", *Wort und Geschichte. Festschrift für K. Elliger zum 70. Geburtstag.* Hg. v. H. Gese u. H. P. Rüger. Neukirchen-Vluyn (1973) 45-50 (*AOAT* 18).
Dorson, R. M., "The Debate over the Trustworthiness of Oral Traditional History", *Volksüberlieferung. Festschrift für K. Ranke zur Vollendung des 60. Lebensjahres.* Hg. v. F. Harkort, K. C. Peeters und R. Wildhaber. Göttingen (1968) 19-35.
Dossin, G., "La route de l'étain en Mésopotamie au temps de Zimri-Lim", *RA* 64 (1970) 97-106.
Driver, G. R., *Canaanite Myths and Legends.* Edinburgh 1956 (*OTSt* 3).
Driver, S. R., *The Books of Joel and Amos.* Ed. by ... With Introd. and Notes. Cambridge 1907 (*CBSC*).
Du Mesnil du Buisson, R., *Les tessères et les monnaies de Palmyre. Un art, une culture et une philosophie grecs dans les moules d'une cité et d'une religion sémitique.* Paris 1962.
——, *Études sur les dieux phéniciens hérités par l'Empire Romain.* Leiden 1970 (*EPRO* 14).
Dürr, L., "Altorientalisches Recht bei den Propheten Amos und Hosea", *BZ* 23 (1935-36) 150-57.
Dumbrell, W. J., "The Role of Bethel in the Biblical Narratives from Jacob to Jeroboam I", *AJBA* 2 (1974-75) 65-76.
Dunant, C., "Nouvelles tessères de Palmyre", *Syr* 36 (1959) 102-10.
Dus, J., "Bethel und Mispa in Jdc. 19-21 und Jdc. 10-12", *OrAnt* 3 (1964) 227-43.
——, "Ein richterzeitliches Stierheiligtum zu Bethel? Die Aufeinanderfolge der frühisraelitischen Zentralkultstätten", *ZAW* 77 (1965) 268-86.
——, "Die Stierbilder von Bethel und Dan und das Problem der "Moseschar", "*AION* 18 (1968) 105-37.
Dussaud, R., *Les origines cananéennes du sacrifice israélite.* Paris 1921.
——, "Simea und Simios", *PRE* 2. R. 3. B (1929) 137-40.
Eakin, E. F., "Yahwism and Baalism Before the Exile", *JBL* 84 (1965) 407-14.
Ebach, J., "ADRMLK, "Moloch" und BAʿAL ADR". [Von] ... [und] U. Rütterswörden, *Festschrift für C. F. A. Schaeffer zum 80. Geburtstag am 6. März 1979*, Neukirchen-Vluym (1979) 219-26 (*UF* 11).

Ebeling, E., *Keilschrifttexte aus Assur religiösen Inhalts.* B.I. Leipzig 1915-19 (*WVDOG* 28). B.II. Leipzig 1920-23 (*WVDOG* 34).

——, "Keilschrifttexte medizinischen Inhalts. IV," *Archiv für Geschichte der Medizin* 14 (1923) 65-78.

Eggebrecht, G., *Die früheste Bedeutung und der Ursprung der Konzeption vom "Tage Jahwes".* Diss. Halle 1966.

Ehelof, H., "Das Motiv der Kindesunterschiebung in einer hethitischen Erzählung", *OLZ* 29 (1926) 766-69.

Ehrlich, A., *Randglossen zur hebräischen Bibel. Textkritisches, sprachliches u. sachliches. B.5. Ezechiel u. die kleinen Propheten.* Leipzig 1912.

Eilers, W. *Semiramis. Entstehung und Nachhall einer altorientalischen Sage. Mit 7 Abbildungen und einer Karte.* Wien 1971 (*Österr. Ak. d. Wiss. Phil. hist. Kl. Sitz. ber.* 274 B. 2. Abh.).

Eisenbeis, W., *Die Wurzel šlm im Alten Testament.* Berl. 1969 (*BZAW* 113).

Eissfeldt, O., "Vom Lebenswerk eines Religionshistorikers. Wolf Wilhelm Graf Baudissin am 6. Febr. 1926", *ZDMG* 80 (1926) 89-130.

——, "Der Gott Bethel", *ARW* 28 (1930) 1-30.

——, "Gott und Götzen im Alten Testament", *ThStKr* 103 (1931) 158-60.

——, "Mein Gott im Alten Testament", *ZAW* 61 (1945-48) 3-16.

——, "Etymologische und archäologische Erklärung alttestamentlicher Wörter", *OrAnt* 5 (1966) 165-76.

——, "marzeaḥ und marzēḥaʾ "Kultmahlgenossenschaft" im spätjüdischen Schrifttum", *Kleine Schriften* V. Tübingen (1973) 136-42.

——, "Kultvereine in Ugarit", *Ug* VI (1969) 187-95.

——, "Neue Belege für nabatäische Kultgenossenschaften", *MIOF* 15 (1969) 217-27.

——, "*ʾadn*", *TWAT* I (1973) 62-78.

——, "Gilgal oder Sichem (Dtn 11, 29-32; 27, 11-13; 27, 1-8, Jos 8, 30-35)", *Kleine Schriften* V (1973) 165-73.

Ellermeier, F., *Prophetie in Mari und Israel.* Herzberg am Harz 1968 (*TOA* 1.).

[Ephraem Syrus], *Sancti Ephraem Syri hymni et sermones.* Ed... T. J. Lamy. T. III. Mecheln 1889.

——, *Ephraemi Syrus opera omnia.* Ed. P. Benedictus. I-III. Roma 1732-46.

Epstein, J. N., "Jahu, AŠMbēthēl und ANTbēthēl", *ZAW* 32 (1912) 139-45.

Eppstein, V., "The Day of Yahweh in Jer 4, 23-28", *JBL* 87 (1968) 93-97.

Eretz Shomron. The 35th Archaeological Convention September 1972. Jerusalem 1973 (In Hebrew). [Ed.] Y. Aviram.

Erlandsson, S., "Amos 5, 25-27, ett crux interpretum", *SEÅ* 33 (1968) 76-82.

Erman, A., *Aegyptisches Handwörterbuch.* [Von] ... und H. Grapow. Berlin 1921.

Eschatologie im Alten Testament. Hg. v. H. D. Preuss. Darmstadt 1978 (*WdF* 480).

Evans-Pritchard, E. E., "Religion and the Anthropologists", *Bl* 41 (1960) 104-18.

——, *Theories of Primitive Religion.* London 1975 (Repr. from the corr. sheet of the 1965 ed.).

Everson, A. J., *The Day of Yahweh as Historical Event.* Unpubl. Diss. Union Theological Seminary 1969.

——, "The Days of Yahweh", *JBL* 93 (1974) 329-37.

——, "Day of the Lord", *IDBS* (1976) 209-10.

The Excavations at Dura-Europos conducted by the Yale University and the French Academy of Inscriptions and Letters. Preliminary Report of III Season of Work, Nov. 1929-March 1930. Ed. by P. V. C. Baur, M. I. Rostovtzeff and A. R. Bellinger. N. Haven 1932.

Fabry, H.-J., *Die Wurzel ŠÛB in der Qumran-Literatur. Zur Semantik eines Grundbegriffes.* Bonn 1975 (*BBB* 46).

——, "*dal*", *TWAT* II (1977) 221-44.

Fauth, W., "Dea Syria", *KP* I (1964) 1400-03.

——, "Simia", *PRESuppl* 14 (1974) 679-701.

Fendler, M., "Zur Sozialkritik des Amos. Versuch einer wirtschafts- und sozialgeschichtlichen Interpretation alttestamentlicher Texte", *EvTh* 33 (1973) 32-53.

Fensham, F. C., "Widow, Orphan and the Poor in Ancient Near Eastern Legal and Wisdom Literature", *JNES* 21 (1962) 129-39.

——, "Malediction and Benediction in Ancient Near Eastern Vassal-Treaties and the Old Testament", *ZAW* 74 (1962) 1-9.
——, "Common Trends in Curses of the Near Eastern Treaties and *Kudurru*-Inscriptions compared with Maledictions of Amos and Isaiah", *ZAW* 75 (1963) 155-75.
——, "A Possible Origin of the Concept of the Day of the Lord", *Biblical Essays. Proc. 9th Meeting of OTWSA Held at the University of Stellenbosch 26th-29th July 1966.* [Potchefstroom] (1966) 90-97.
——, "A Few Observations on the Polarisation Between Yahweh and Baal in 1. Kings 17-19", *ZAW* 92 (1980) 227-36.
Fernández, A., "El santuario de Dan. Estudio crítico-exegético sobre Jud 17-18", *Bib* 15 (1934) 237-64.
Feuchtwang, D., "Das Wasseropfer und die damit verbundenen Zeremonien", *MGWJ* 54 (1910) 535-52, 55 (1911) 43-63.
Février, J. G., *La religion des palmyréniens.* Paris 1931.
——, "Simia - Némésis", *JA* 224 (1934) 308-14.
——, "Remarques sur le grand tarif dit de Marseille", *CByrsa* 8 (1958-59) 35-43.
Ficker, R., "*šīr*", *THAT* II (1976) 895-98.
Fishbane, M., "The Treaty Background of Am 1, 11 and Related Matters", *JBL* 89 (1970) 313-18.
——, "Additional Remarks on *rḥmyw* (Am 1, 11)", *JBL* 91 (1972) 391-93.
Fisher, E. J., "Cultic Prostitution in the Ancient Near East? A Reassessment", *BTB* 6 (1976) 225-36.
Fisher, L. R., *Ras Shamra Parallels: Texts from Ugarit and the Hebrew Bible.* Vol. I. Roma 1972 (*AnOr* 49). Vol. II. Roma 1975 (*AnOr* 50).
Fitzmyer, J. A., *The Aramaic Inscriptions of Sefîre.* Rome 1967 (*BibOr* 19).
Floss, J. P., *Jahwe dienen - Göttern dienen.* Bonn 1975 (*BBB* 45).
Flusser, D., "The Great Goddess of Samaria", *IEJ* 25 (1975) 13-20.
Fohrer, G., "Remarks on Modern Interpretation of the Prophets", *JBL* 80 (1961) 309-19.
——, *Geschichte der israelitischen Religion.* Berlin 1969.
Frank, C., "Rm 155", *ZDMG* 68 (1914) 157-62.
Franken, H. J., "The Problem of Identification in Biblical Archaeology", *PEQ* 108 (1976) 3-11.
Frankena, R., *Tākultu. De sacrale maaltijd in het assyrische ritueel. Met een overzicht over de in Assur vereerde goden.* Leiden 1953.
Frazer, J. G., *The Dying God.* 3rd ed. London 1911 (*GB* 3).
——, *Adonis, Attis, Osiris.* 3rd ed. Vols. 1-2. London 1914 (*GB* 4: 1-2).
——, *The Golden Bough. A Study in Magic and Religion.* 3rd rev. enl. ed. Vol. 12. London 1915.
Freedman, D. N., "Harmon in Amos 4, 3". [By] ... and F. I. Andersen, *BASOR* 198 (1970) 41.
——, "*dôr*". [Von] ... [und] J. Lundbom, *TWAT* II (1977) 185-94.
Friedrich, J., "Churritische Märchen und Sagen in hethitischer Sprache", *ZA* 49 (1950) 224-33.
——, *Phönizisch-Punische Grammatik.* 2. völlig neu bearb. Aufl. [Von] ... [und] W. Röllig. Roma 1970 (*AnOr* 46).
Fritz, V., "Das Wort gegen Samaria Mi 1, 2-7", *ZAW* 86 (1974) 316-31.
Galling, K., "Bethel und Gilgal", *ZDPV* 66 (1943) 140-55, 67 (1945) 21-43.
——, "Der Gott Karmel und die Ächtung der fremden Götter", *Geschichte und Altes Testament. A. Alt zum 70. Geburtstag am 20. Sept. 1953... dargebracht.* Tübingen (1953) 105-25 (*BHTh* 16).
——, *Biblisches Reallexikon.* Tüb. 1937 (*HAT* 1. R. I).
——, *Biblisches Reallexikon.* Hrsg. v. ... 2., neugestaltete Aufl. Tüb. 1977 (*HAT* 1. R. I).
Gardiner, A., *Egyptian Grammar.* 2. rev. ed. Oxford 1950.
Gelb, I. J., *Computer-Aided Analysis of Amorite.* [By] ... With the Assistance of J. Bartels, S.-M. Vance, R. M. Whiting. Chicago 1980 (*AS* 2).
Gerleman, G., "*drš*". [Von] ... [und] E. Ruprecht, *THAT* I (1975) 460-67.

Gerstenberger, E., "The Woe-Oracles of the Prophets", *JBL* 81 (1962) 249-63.
Gese, H., "Kleine Beiträge zum Verständnis des Amosbuches", *VT* 12 (1962) 415-38.
——, "Die Religionen Altsyriens", *Die Religionen Altsyriens, Altarabiens und der Mandäer.* Von ..., M. Höfner, K. Rudolph. Stuttgart (1970) 1-232 (*RM* 10: 2).
Gesenius, W., *Hebräisches und aramäisches Handwörterbuch über das Alte Testament.* Bearb. v. F. Buhl. Unveränd. Neudruck der 1915 erschienen 17. Aufl. Berlin 1962.
——, *Gesenius' Hebrew Grammar as edited and enlarged by the late E. Kautzsch.* 2nd Engl. ed. (1910) by A. E. Cowley. Repr. Oxford 1963.
Geus, C. H. J. de, *The Tribes of Israel. An Investigation into some of the Presuppositions of Martin Noth's Amphictyony Hypothesis.* Assen 1976 (*SSN* 18.).
Gevirtz, S., "West-Semitic Curses and the Problem of the Origin of Hebrew Law", *VT* 11 (1961) 137-58.
——, "A New Look at an Old Crux: Amos 5, 26", *JBL* 87 (1968) 267-76.
Gibson, J. C. L., *Canaanite Myths and Legends.* 2nd ed. Edinburgh 1978 (1st ed. by G. R. Driver 1956. Cf. above).
——, *Textbook of Syrian Semitic Inscriptions. Vol. I. Hebrew and Moabite Inscriptions.* Oxford 1971. Repr. with corrections 1973. *Vol. II. Aramaic Inscriptions Including Inscriptions of the Dialect of Zenjirli.* Oxford 1975.
Globe, A., "The Muster of the Tribes in Judges 5, 11e-18", *ZAW* 87 (1975) 169-84.
Glueck, N., "Explorations in Eastern Palestine III", *BASOR* 65 (1937) 8-29.
——, *Deities and Dolphins. The Story of the Nabateans.* London 1966.
Gordon, C. H., *Homer and Bible. The Origin and Character of East Mediterranean Literature.* Ventnor, N.J. 1967 (Repr. from *HUCA* 26, 1955).
——, *Ugaritic Textbook.* Rome 1965 (*AnOr* 38).
Gottlieb, H., "Den tærskende Kvie - Mi 4, 11-13", *DTT* 26 (1963) 167-71.
——, "Amos und Jerusalem", *VT* 17 (1967) 430-63.
Gottwald, N. K., *All the Kingdoms of the Earth. Israelite Prophecy and International Relations in the Ancient Near East.* New York 1964.
——, "War, Holy", *IDBS* (1976) 942-44.
Gray, J., "Social Aspects of Canaanite Religion", *Volume du Congrès: Genève 1965.* Leiden (1966) 170-92 (*SVT* 15).
——, "The Day of Yahweh in Cultic Experience and Eschatological Prospect", *SEÅ* 39 (1974) 5-37.
——, "The Blood Bath of the Goddess Anat in the Ras Shamra Texts", *Festschrift für C. F. A. Schaeffer zum 80. Geburtstag am 6. März 1979.* Neukirchen-Vluyn (1979) 315-24 (*UF* 11).
Green, A. R. W. *The Role of Human Sacrifice in the Ancient Near East.* Missoula Mont. 1975 (*ASORDS* 1).
Greenberg, M., "The Hebrew Oath Particle ḤAY/ḤE", *JBL* 76 (1957) 34-39.
Greenewalt, C. H., *Ritual Dinners in Early Historic Sardis.* With a Contribution by S. Payne. L.A. 1978 (*UCP.CS* 17).
Greenfield, J. C., "Un rite religieux araméen et ses parallèles", *RB* 80 (1973) 46-52.
Grelot, P., *Documents araméens d'Égypte.* Introd., trad., presentation de ... Paris 1972.
Gressmann, H., *Der Ursprung der israelitisch-jüdischen Eschatologie.* Göttingen 1905 (*FRLANT* 6).
——, "Η ΚΟΙΝΩΝΙΑ ΤΩΝ ΔΑΙΜΟΝΙΩΝ", *ZNW* 20 (1921) 224-30.
——, *Altorientalische Texte zum Alten Testament.* In Verb. mit E. Ebeling, H. Ranke, N. Rhodokanakis hrsg. v. ... 2. völlig neugest. u. stark vermehrte Aufl. Berlin 1926.
Griffith, F. L., "Notes on Mythology", *PSBA* 21 (1899) 277-79.
Grimes, J. E., "Narrative Studies in Oral Texts", *Current Trends in Textlinguistics.* Ed. by W. U. Dressler (1978) 123-32 (*Research in Text Theory* 2).
Grimm, D., "Erwägungen zu Hos 12, 12 "In Gilgal opfern sie Stiere"," *ZAW* 85 (1973) 339-47.
Grimme, H., "Die Jahotriade von Elephantine", *OLZ* 15 (1912) 11-17.
Grintz, J. M., "'ʿAi which is Beside Beth-Aven'. A Re-Examination of the Identity of ʿAi", *Bib* 42 (1961) 201-16.

Grönbæk, J. H., "Zur Frage der Eschatologie in der Verkündigung der Gerichtspropheten", *SEÅ* 24 (1959) 5-21.
Gröndahl, F., *Die Personennamen der Texte aus Ugarit.* Roma 1967 (*StP* 1).
Güterbock, H. G., *Kumarbi. Mythen vom churritischen Kronos aus den hethitischen Fragmenten zusammengestellt, übers. u. erkl.* [Leiden] 1946 (*IstSchr* 16).
Gunneweg, A. H. J., *Leviten und Priester. Hauptlinien der Traditionsbildung und Geschichte des israelitisch-jüdischen Kultpersonals.* Göttingen 1965 (*FRLANT* 89).
Gunkel, H., *Einleitung in die Psalmen. Die Gattungen der religiösen Lyrik Israels.* Von ... Zu Ende geführt von J. Begrich. Göttingen 1933 (*HK* Erg. b. zur II: Abt).
Gurewicz, S. B., "When did the Cult associated with the "Golden Calves" fully develop in the Northern Kingdom?", *ABR* 2 (1952) 41-44.
Gurney, O. R., "Tammuz Reconsidered: Some Recent Developments", *JSS* 7 (1962) 147-60.
——, *Some Aspects of Hittite Religion.* Oxford 1977 (*SchL* 1976).
Guzzo, M. G. Amadasi, *Le iscrizioni feniche e puniche delle colonie in Occidente.* Roma 1967 (*SS* 28).
Haag, E., "Der Tag Jahwes im Alten Testament", *BiLe* 13 (1972) 238-48.
Haag, H., "Erwägungen über Beer-Šeba", *Sacra Pagina.* (1959) 335-45.
Habel, N. C., *Yahweh Versus Baal. A Conflict of Religious Cultures.* New York 1964.
Haenchen, E., *Die Apostelgeschichte.* 1969 (*KEK* III).
Hahn, H. F., *Old Testament in Modern Research.* Philadelphia PA. 1954.
Hammershaimb, E., "On the Ethics of the Old Testament Prophets", *Congress Volume: Oxford 1959.* Leiden (1960) 75-101 (*SVT* VII).
——, *Amos.* 3. udg. Copenhagen 1967.
——, *The Book of Amos. A Commentary.* Transl. by J. Sturdy. Oxford 1970. (English transl. of the book in Danish mentioned above).
Haran, M., "Observations on the Historical Background of Amos 1, 2-2, 6", *IEJ* 18 (1968) 201-12.
——, *Temples and Temple-Service in Ancient Israel. An Inquiry into the Character of Cult Phenomena and the Historical Setting of the Priestly School.* Oxford 1978.
Harding, G. L., *An Index and Concordance of Pre-islamic Arabian Names and Inscriptions.* Toronto 1971 (*NMES* 8).
Harper, W. R., *A Critical and Exegetical Commentary on Amos and Hosea.* Edinburgh 1905 (*ICC*).
Harvey, J., "Le "rîb-Pattern", réquisitoire prophétique sur la rupture de l'alliance", *Bib* 43 (1962) 172-96.
Hauret, C., "Aux origines du sacerdoce danite. À propos de Jud 18, 30-31", *Mélanges bibliques rédigés en l'honneur de André Robert.* Paris [1957] 105-13 (*TICP* 4).
Hawkins, J. D., "Hamath", *RLA* 4 (1972-75) 67-70.
Hayes, J. H., "The Usage of Oracles against Foreign Nations in Ancient Israel", *JBL* 87(1968) 81-92.
Helck, W., *Betrachtungen zur Grossen Göttin und den ihr verbundenen Gottheiten.* München 1971 (*Religion und Kultur der alten Mittelmeerwelt in Parallelforschungen* 2).
Hélewa, F. J., "L'origine du concept prophétique du "Jour de Yahvé", " *ECarm* 15 (1964) 3-36.
Helfmeyer, F. J., *Die Nachfolge Gottes im Alten Testament.* Bonn 1968 (*BBB* 29).
Hempel, J., "Die Lichtsymbolik im Alten Testament", *StGen* 13 (1960) 352-68.
——, "Licht, Heil und Heilung im biblischen Denken", *Antaios* 2 (1961) 375-88.
——, "Die israelitischen Anschauungen von Segen und Fluch im Lichte altorientalischer Parallelen", *Apoxysmata. Vorarbeiten zu einer Religionsgeschichte und Theologie des Alten Testaments. Festgabe zum 30. Juli 1961.* Berlin (1961) 30-113 (*BZAW* 81).
Hennessy, J. B., "Excavations at Samaria-Sebaste 1966", *Levant* 2 (1970) 1-21.
Hentschke, R., *Die Stellung der vorexilischen Schriftpropheten zum Kultus.* Berlin 1957 (*BZAW* 75).
Hermisson, H.-J., *Sprache und Ritus im altisraelitischen Kult. Zur "Spiritualisierung" der Kultbegriffe im Alten Testament.* Neukirchen-Vluyn 1965 (*WMANT* 19).
Herodotos. Für den Schulgebrauch erkl. v. K. Abicht. B.1. 4. Aufl. Leipzig 1884.

Herrmann, S., *Urprung und Funktion der Prophetie im Alten Israel.* Opladen 1976 (*Rheinisch-Westfälische Ak. d. Wiss. Geisteswissenschaften. Vorträge* G. 208).
Herter, H., "Die Soziologie der antiken Prostitution im Lichte des heidnischen und christlichen Schrifttums", *JAC* 3 (1960) 70-111.
Hesse, F., "Amos 5, 4-6.14f.", *ZAW* 68 (1965) 1-17.
Hild, J. A., "Saturnus", *Saglio* 4 (1911) 1083-90.
Hillers, D. R., *Treaty-Curses and the Old Testament Prophets.* Rome 1964 (*BibOr* 16.).
——, *Covenant: The History of a Biblical Idea.* Baltimore 1969 (*Seminars in the History of Ideas*).
Hobbs, T. R., "Amos 3, 1b and 2, 10", *ZAW* 81 (1969) 384-87.
Höfer, T., "Semea", *ALGM* B.4. Leipzig (1905-15) 660-62.
——, "Seimios', *Ibid.* 602.
Hölscher, G., *Die Propheten. Untersuchungen zur Religionsgeschichte Israels.* Lpz. 1914.
——, "Sigmund Mowinckel som gammeltestamentlig forsker", *NTT* 24 (1923) 73-138.
——, *Die Ursprünge der jüdischen Eschatologie.* Giessen 1925 (*VTKG* 41. Folge).
Hörig, M., *Dea Syria. Studien zur religiösen Tradition der Fruchtbarkeitsgöttin in Vorderasien.* Neukirchen-Vluyn 1979 (*AOAT* 208).
Hoffmann, G., "Versuche zu Amos", *ZAW* 3 (1883) 87-126.
Holladay, J. S., "Assyrian Statecraft and the Prophets of Israel", *HThR* 63 (1970) 29-51.
Holladay, W. L., *The Root ŠÛBH in the Old Testament. With Particular Reference to its Usages in Convenantal Contexts.* Leiden 1958.
——, "On Every High Hill and Under Every Green Tree", *VT* 11 (1961) 170-76.
Holm-Nielsen, S., "Die Sozialkritik der Propheten", *Denkender Glaube. Festschrift Carl Heinz Ratschow zur Vollendung seines 65. Lebensjahres am 22. Juli 1976 gewidmet.* Hg. v. O. Kaiser. Berlin (1976) 7-23.
Hoonacker, A. van, *Les douze petits prophètes.* Trad. et commentés par ... Paris 1908 (*EtB*).
——, *Une Communauté Judéo-Araméenne à Éléphantine, en Égypte, aux VIe et Ve siècles av. J.C.* London 1915 (*SchL* 1914).
Horst, F., "Der Eid im Alten Testament", *EvTh* 17 (1957) 366-84.
——, "Eid. II. Im AT", *RGG*³ B.2 (1958) 349-50.
——, *Gottes Recht. Gesammelte Studien zum Recht im Alten Testament.* Hg. v. H. W. Wolff. München 1961 (*TB* 12).
Hrozný, B., "L'inscription "hittite"-hiéroglyphique d'Apamée", *Syr* 20 (1939) 134-35.
Huber, E., *Die Personennamen in den Keilschrifturkunden aus der Zeit der Könige von Ur und Nisin.* Leipzig 1907 (*AB* 21).
Huffmon, H. B., "The Covenant Lawsuit in the Prophets", *JBL* 78 (1959) 285-95.
——, *Amorite Personal names in the Mari Texts. A Structural and Lexical Study.* Baltimore 1965.
——, "Prophecy in the Ancient Near East", *IDBS* (1976) 697-700.
Hvidberg-Hansen, F. O., *La déesse TNT. Une étude sur la religion canaanéo-punique. I. Texte. II. Notes.* Copenhagen 1979.
Hyatt, J. P., "The Deity Bethel and the Old Testament", *JAOS* 59 (1939) 81-98.
Ingholt, H., "Un nouveau Thiase à Palmyre", *Syr* 7 (1926) 128-41.
——, "Five Dated Tombs from Palmyra", *Ber* 2 (1935) 57-120.
——, "Inscriptions and Sculptures from Palmyra II", *Ber* 5 (1938) 93-140.
——, *Parthian Sculptures from Hatra. Orient and Hellas in Art and Religion.* New Haven, Conn. 1954 (*Memoirs of the Conn. Ac. of Arts and Sciences* 12).
——, *Recueil des tessères de Palmyre.* Par ..., H. Seyrig, J. Starcky, suivi de remarques linguistiques par A. Caquot. Paris 1955 (*BAH* 58).
Isbell, C. D., "Another Look at Amos 5, 26", *JBL* 97 (1978) 97-99.
Jacobsen, T., *The Treasures of Darkness. A History of Mesopotamian Religion.* New Haven, CT. 1976.
——, *Toward the Image of Tammuz and Other Essays on Mesopotamian History and Culture.* Ed. by W. L. Moran. Cambridge Mass. 1970.
Jalabert, L., *Inscriptions grecques et latines de la Syrie.* Par ... et R. Mouterde. T.2. *Chalcidique et Antiochène* (*Nos. 257-698*). Paris 1939. T.5. Avec la collobaration de C. Mondésert, *Émésène* (*Nos. 1998-2710*). Paris 1959.
Janzen, W., *Mourning Cry and Woe Oracle.* Berlin 1972 (*BZAW* 125).

Jastrow, M., *A Dictionary of the Targumim, the Talmud Babli and Yerushalmi, and the Midrashic Literature.* B.II. London and New York 1903.
Jean, C.-F., *Dictionnaire des inscriptions sémitiques de l'Ouest.* Éd. nouv. [Par] ... [et] J. Hoftijzer. Leiden 1965.
Jenni, E., *Theologisches Handwörterbuch zum Alten Testament.* Hg. v. ... unter Mitarbeit v. C. Westermann. B.I-II. München 1971-76. (B.I. 2. durchges. Aufl. 1975).
——, "*yôm*", *THAT* I² (1975) 707-26.
Jensen, J., *The Use of tôrâ by Isaiah. His Debate with the Wisdom Tradition.* Washington, D.C. 1973 (*CBQ Monograph Series* 3).
Jeremias, J., *Theophanie. Die Geschichte einer alttestamentlichen Gattung.* Neukirchen-Vluyn 1965 (*WMANT* 10).
Jirku, A., "Eine Renaissance des Hebräischen", *FuF* 32 (1958) 211-12.
Johnson, A. R., *The Cultic Prophet and Israel's Psalmody.* Cardiff 1979.
Kaiser, O., *Einleitung in das Alte Testament. Eine Einführung in ihre Ergebnisse und Probleme.* Gütersloh 1969.
Kapelrud, A. S., *Joel Studies.* Uppsala 1948 (*UUÅ* 1948: 4).
——, "Cult and Prophetic Words", *StTh* 4 (1950) 5-12.
——, *Baal in the Ras Shamra Texts.* Copenhagen 1952.
——, *Central Ideas in Amos.* Repr. Oslo 1961.
——, "Israel's Prophets and their Confrontation with the Canaanite Religion", *Syncretism. Based on Papers read at the Symposium on Cultural Contact, Meeting of Religions, Syncretism, held at Åbo on the 8th-10th of September, 1966.* Stockholm (1969) 162-70 (*SIDA* 3).
——, *The Violent Goddess. Anat in the Ras Shamra Texts.* Oslo 1969.
——, "*ʾbyr*", *TWAT* I (1973) 43-46.
——, *The Message of the Prophet Zephaniah. Morphology and Ideas.* Oslo 1975.
Kaplony, P., "Eid", *LÄ* I (1975) 1188-1200.
Keel, O., "Rechttun oder Annahme des drohenden Gerichts? (Erwägungen zu Amos, dem frühen Jesaja und Micha)", *BZ* NF 21 (1977) 200-18.
Keilschrifttexte aus Assur verschiedenen Inhalts. Ed. O. Schroeder. Leipzig 1920 (*WVDOG* 35).
Keller, C. A., "Über einige alttestamentliche Heiligtumslegenden. I." *ZAW* 67 (1955) 141-68.
——, *Nahoum, Habacuc, Sophonie.* Neuchâtel 1971 (*CAT* 11B).
——, "*šbʿ* ni.", *THAT* II (1976) 855-63.
Kellermann, D., "ʾāšām in Ugarit?" *ZAW* 76 (1964) 319-22.
——, "*ʾšm*", *TWAT* I (1973) 463-72.
——, "*ḥmṣ*", *TWAT* II (1977) 1061-68.
Kellermann, U., "Der Amosschluss als Stimme deuteronomistischer Heilshoffnung", *EvTh* 29 (1969) 169-83.
Kelso, J. L., *The Excavation of Bethel (1934-1960). (Joint Expedition of the Pittsburgh Theological Seminary and the American School of Oriental Research in Jerusalem).* Cambridge Mass. 1968 (*AASOR* 39).
Kenyon, K. M., "Megiddo, Hazor, Samaria and Chronology", *BIAUL* 4 (1964) 143-56.
Kingston Soper, B., "For Three Transgressions and for Four. A New Interpretation of Amos 1, 3 etc.," *ET* 71 (1959) 86-87.
Kirk, G. S., *Myth. Its Meaning and Functions in Ancient and Other Cultures.* Cambridge 1970.
Kittel, R., "Der Gott Betʾel", *JBL* 44 (1925) 123-53.
Klein, R. W., "The Day of the Lord", *CTM* 39 (1968) 517-25.
Klinz, A., "*hieròs gámos*", *PRE* Suppl. B.6 (1935) 107-13.
Knierim, R., *Die Hauptbegriffe für Sünde im Alten Testament.* Gütersloh 1965.
——, "*pšʿ*", *THAT* II (1976) 488-95.
Knight, D. A., *The Traditions of Israel. The Development of the Traditio-Historical Research of the Old Testament, with Special Consideration of Scandinavian Contributions.* Missoula, Mont. 1973 (*SBLDS* 9).
Knudtzon, J. A., *Die El-Amarna-Tafeln.* Mit Einl. u. Erläuterungen hg. v. ... Anm. u. Reg. bearb. v. O. Weber u. E. Ebeling. T. I-II. Neudruck d. Ausg. Leipzig 1915. Aalen 1964.

Koch, K., "Die Entstehung der sozialen Kritik bei den Propheten", *ProblBiblTheol* (1971) 236-57.
——, *Amos. Untersucht mit den Methoden einer strukturalen Formgeschichte.* Von ... und Mitarbeitern. B. I-III. Neukirchen-Vluyn 1976 (*AOAT* 30).
——, "*ṣdq*", *THAT* II (1976) 507-30.
——, "*dæræk*", *TWAT* II (1977) 263-312.
Köcher, F., *Die babylonisch-assyrische Medizin in Texte und Untersuchungen.* B. III. *Keilschrifttexte aus Assur* 3. Berlin 1964.
Köhler, L., *Lexicon in Veteris Testamenti Libros.* Ed.... [Cum] W. Baumgartner: *Wörterbuch zum Aramäischen Teil des Alten Testaments...* Ed. photomech. iterata cui adjectum est supplementum... Leiden 1958.
——, *Hebräisches und aramäisches Lexikon zum Alten Testament.* Von ... u. W. Baumgartner. 3. Aufl. neu bearb. v. W. Baumgartner unter Mitarb. v. B. Hartmann u. E. Y. Kutscher. Leiden 1967-.
König, E., *Historisch-comparative Syntax der hebräischen Sprache. Schlusstheil des historisch-kritischen Lehrgebäudes des hebräischen.* Leipzig 1897.
——, "Die Gottheit Aschima", *ZAW* 34 (1914) 16-30.
Kornfeld, W., "L'adultère dans l'Orient antique", *RB* 57 (1960) 92-109.
——, "Fruchtbarkeitskulte im Alten Testament", *WBTh* 10 (1965) 109-17.
Kraeling, E. G., *Aram and Israel, or the Arameans in Syria and Mesopotamia.* New York 1918 (*OSCU* 13).
——, *The Brooklyn Museum Aramaic Papyri. New Documents of the Fifth Century B.C. from the Jewish Colony at Elephantine.* Ed. with a historical Introduction by ... New Haven, Conn. 1953.
——, *The Old Testament since the Reformation.* London 1955.
Kramer, S. N., "Cuneiform Studies and the History of Literature: The Sumerian Sacred Marriage Texts", *PAPS* 107 (1963) 485-516.
——, "The Sacred Marriage. A Panoramic View of the Sumerian Evidence", *Proceedings of the 26. International Congress of Orientalists.* Vol. 2. New Delhi (1968) 28-32.
——, *The Sacred Marriage Rite. Aspects of Faith, Myth, and Ritual in Ancient Sumer.* Bloomington 1969.
Kraus, H.-J., "Gilgal. Ein Beitrag zur Kultusgeschichte Israels", *VT* 1 (1951) 181-99.
——, "Die prophetische Botschaft gegen das soziale Unrecht Israels", *EvTh* 15 (1955).
——, *Psalmen*, B.1. 3. unveränderte Aufl. Neukirchen-Vluyn 1966 (*BKAT* 15: 1).
——, "Der lebendige Gott. Ein Kapitel biblischer Theologie", *EvTh* 27 (1967) 169-200.
——, *Geschichte der historisch-kritischen Erforschung des Alten Testaments.* 2. Aufl. Neukirchen-Vluyn 1969.
Kutsch, E., "Die Wurzel *ʿṣr* im Hebräischen", *VT* 2 (1952) 57-69.
——, *Verheissung und Gesetz. Untersuchungen zum sogenannten "Bund" im Alten Testament.* Berl. 1973 (*BZAW* 131).
Labuschagne, J., *The Incomparability of Yahweh in the Old Testament.* Leiden 1966 (*POS* 5).
Lambert, W. G., *Babylonian Wisdom Literature.* Oxford 1960.
——, "A Middle Assyrian Tablet of Incantation", *Studies in Honor of B. Landsberger on his Seventy-Fifth Birthday.* Chicago (1965) 283-88 (*AS* 16).
——, "A Middle Assyrian Medical Text", *Iraq* 31 (1969) 28-39.
Landsberger, B., *Der kultische Kalender der Babylonier und Assyrer.* Leipzig 1917 (*LSSt* 6).
Langdon, S., *Babylonian Liturgies. Sumerian Texts from the Early Period and from the Library of Ashurbanipal, for the Most Part Transliterated and Transl., with Introd. and Index.* Paris 1913.
——, "A Fragment of a Series of Ritualistic Prayers to Astral Deities in the Ceremonies of Divination", *RA* 12 (1915) 189-92.
——, *Sumerian Liturgies and Psalms.* Philadelphia, PA. 1919 (*PBS* 10: 4).
——, *Babylonian Penitential Psalms to which are added Fragments of the Epic of Creation from Kish in the Weld Collection of the Ashmolean Museum Excavated by the Oxford-Field Museum Expedition.* Paris 1927 (*OECT* 6).
Langhe, R. de, *Les textes de Ras Shamra-Ugarit et leurs rapport avec le milieu biblique de l'Ancien*

Testament. I. Paris 1945 (*Universitas Catholica Lovaniensis. Diss. ad gradum magistri in Facultate Theologica vel in Facultate Iuris Canonici.* Ser. II. T.35).
Langlamet, F., *Gilgal et les récits de la traversée du Jourdain* (*Jos III-IV*). Paris 1969 (*CRB* 11).
Largement, R., "Le jour de Yahweh dans le contexte orientale". [Par] ... [et] H. Lemaitre, *Sacra Pagina* (1959) 259-66.
Leahy, M., "The Popular Idea of God in Amos", *IThQ* 22 (1955) 68-73.
Lécrivain, C., "Thiasos", *Saglio* t. 5 (1912-19) 257-66.
Leeuwen, C. van, "The Prophecy of the YÔM YHWH in Amos V 18-20", *OTS* 19 (1974) 113-34.
Leglay, M., *Saturne Africain. Monuments.* I-II. Paris 1961-66.
——, *Saturne Africain. Histoire.* Paris 1966 (*BEFAR* 205).
Lehmann, M. R., "Biblical Oaths", *ZAW* 81 (1969) 74-92.
Lemaire, A., "Les inscriptions de Khirbet el-Qôm et l'Ashéra de YHWH", *RB* 84 (1977) 595-608.
Lemche, N. P., *Israel i dommertiden. En oversigt over diskussionen om Martin Noths "Das System der zwölf Stämme Israels"*. Copenhagen 1972 (*Tekst og Tolkning* 4).
——, "The Manumission of Slaves - The Fallow Year - The Sabbatical Year - The Yobel Year", *VT* 26 (1976) 38-59.
——, "The Greek "Amphictyony" - Could it be a Prototype for the Israelite Society in the Period of the Judges?" *JSOT* 4 (1977) 48-59.
Lemonnyer, A., "Achima", *RSPhTh* 8 (1914) 289-96.
Levy, J., *Wörterbuch über die Talmudim und Midraschim, nebst Beiträgen v. H. L. Fleischer.* 2. Aufl. mit Nachträgen u. Berichtigungen von L. Goldschmidt. B. III. Berlin 1924.
Lidzbarski, M., *Ephemeris für semitische Epigrafik.* I-III. Giessen 1902-15.
——, *Altsemitische Texte. H. I. Kanaanäische Inschriften.* Giessen 1907.
Limburg, J., "The Prophets in Recent Study: 1967-77", *Interp* 32 (1978) 56-68.
Lindblom, J., "Gibt es eine Eschatologie bei den alttestamentlichen Propheten?" *StTh* 6 (1952) 79-114.
——, *Prophecy in Ancient Israel.* Oxford 1962.
Lindhagen, S., *Den profetiska samhällskritiken i Israel och Juda under 700-talet f. Kr.* Stockholm 1978.
Lipiński, E., "The Goddess Aṯirat in Ancient Arabia, in Babylon, and in Israel", *OLoP* 3 (1972) 100-119.
——, "Eshmun, "Healer"," *AION* 23 (1973) 161-83.
Littmann, M. E., "Deux inscriptions religieuses de Palmyre", *JA* (1901) 374-381.
Liverani, M., "[Review of] J. Nougayrol, E. Laroche, C. Virolleaud, C. F. A. Schaeffer, *Ugaritica V.* Paris 1968 (*MRS* 16.) (*BAH* 80.)," *OrAnt* 8 (1969) 338-40.
Löhr, M., *Das Räucheropfer im Alten Testament. Eine archäologische Untersuchung.* Halle (1927) 155-91 (*SKG.G* 4. J. H. 4).
Loewenstamm, S. E., "A Remark on the Typology of the Prophetic Vision (Amos 8, 1-3)", *Tarb* 34 (1965) 319-22 (in Hebrew).
Loretz, O., "Die prophetische Kritik des Rentenkapitalismus. Grundlagen-Probleme der Prophetenforschung", *UF* 7 (1975) 271-78.
Luciani Samosatensis opera. Ex rec. C. Jacobitz. Vol. 3. Lipsiae 1872.
Luria, B. Z., "The Propecies Unto the Nations in the Book of Amos from the Point of view of History", *BetM* 54 (1973) 287-301 (in Hebrew).
Luther, M., *Deutsche Bibel.* 4.B. *Bibelrevisionen (Schluss) und Einträgungen in Handexemplaren.* Weimar 1923. 11. B. 2. H. *Die Übersetzung des Prophetenteils des Alten Testaments* (*Daniel bis Maleachi*). Weimar 1960.
Lutz, H.-M., *Jahwe, Jerusalem und die Völker. Zur Vorgeschichte von Sach 12, 1-8 und 14, 1-5.* Neukirchen-Vluyn 1968 (*WMANT* 27).
Læssøe, J., "A Prayer to Ea, Shamash, and Marduk from Hama", *Iraq* 18 (1956) 60-67.
Maag, V., *Text, Wortschatz und Begriffswelt des Buches Amos.* Leiden 1951.
——, "Zum Hieros Logos von Beth-El", *Kultur, Kulturkontakt und Religion. Gesammelte Studien zur allgemeinen und alttestamentlichen Religionsgeschichte.* Zum 70. Geburtstag hg. v. H. H. Schmid u. O. H. Steck. Göttingen (1980) 29-37.

Maass, F., "ḥll", *THAT* I (1975) 570-75.
McCarthy, D. J., *Treaty and Covenant. A Study in Form in the Ancient Oriental Documents and in the Old Testament.* New ed. completely rewritten. Rome 1978 (*AnBib* 21A).
——, *Treaty and Covenant. A Study in Form in the Ancient Oriental Documents and in the Old Testament.* Rome 1963 (*AnBib* 21).
——, *Old Testament Covenant. A Survey of Current Opinions.* Oxford 1973 (*Growing Points in Theology*).
MacDonald, J., "The Structure of II Kings xvii", *TGUOS* 23 (1969-70) 29-41.
——, "The Status and Role of the naʿar in Israelite Society", *JNES* 35 (1976) 147-70.
Maigret, A. de, *La citadella aramaica di Hama. Attività, funzioni e comportamento.* Rome 1979 (*OAC* 15).
Malamat, A., "Am 1, 5 in the Light of the Barsip Inscriptions", *BASOR* 129 (1953) 25-26.
——, "Prophetic Revelations in New Documents from Mari and the Bible", *Volume du Congrès: Genève 1965.* Leiden (1966) 207-27 (*SVT* 15).
——, "Northern Canaan and the Mari Texts", *Essays in Honor of Nelson Glueck. Near Eastern Archaeology in the Twentieth Century.* Ed. by J. A. Sanders. Garden City, N.Y. (1970) 164-77.
——, "The Danite Migration and the Pan-Israelite Exodus-Conquest: A Biblical Narrative Pattern", *Bib* 51 (1970) 1-16.
——, "Syro-Palestinian Destinations in a Mari Tin Inventory", *IEJ* 21 (1971) 31-38.
Malefijt, A. de Waal, *Religion and Culture. An Introduction to Anthropology of Religion.* 3rd Printing London 1970.
March, W. E., "*Lākēn*: Its Functions and Meanings", *Rhetorical Criticism. Essays in Honor of James Muilenburg.* Ed. by J. J. Jackson and M. Kessler. Pittsburgh, PA (1974) 256-84 (*PTMS* 1).
Marcus, D., "Civil Liberties under Israelite and Mesopotamian Kings", *JANES* 10 (1978) 53-60.
Markert, L., *Struktur und Bezeichnung des Scheltworts. Eine gattungskritische Studie anhand des Amosbuches.* Berlin 1977 (*BZAW* 140).
Marti, K., *Das Dodekapropheton.* Erkl. v.... Tübingen 1904 (*KHC* Abt. 13).
Martin-Achard, R., "Trois ouvrages sur l'alliance dans l'Ancien Testament", *RThPh* 110 (1978) 299-303.
Masson, O., "Recherches sur les phéniciens dans le monde hellénistique", *BCH* 93 (1969) 679-700.
——, "Quelques noms sémitiques en transcription grecque à Délos et à Phénée', *Hommages à A. Dupont-Sommer.* Paris (1971) 61-73.
Matthiae, P., "Il motivo della vacca che allatta nell'iconografia del Vicino Oriente antico," *RSO* 37 (1962) 1-31.
Mayes, A. D. H., *Israel in the Period of the Judges.* London 1974 (*SBT* 2nd Ser. 29.).
Mays, J. L., "Words about the Words of Amos. Recent Study of the Book of Amos", *Interp* 12 (1959) 260-72.
——, *Amos. A Commentary.* London 1969 (*OTL*).
——, *Micah. A Commentary.* London 1976 (*OTL*).
Mazar, B., "The Cities of the Territory of Dan", *IEJ* 10 (1960) 65-77.
Meier, G., *Die assyrische Beschwörungssammlung Maqlû.* Berlin 1937 (*AfO.B.* 2).
Meissner, B., *Die Bauinschriften Asarhaddons.* [Von] ... [und] P. Rost, Leipzig 1898 (*BASS* 3 189-362).
Meloni, G., "Testi assiri del British Museum", *RSO* 4 (1911-12) 559-98.
Mendenhall, G. E., "Ancient Oriental and Biblical Law", *BA* 17 (1954) 26-46.
——, "Covenant Forms in Israelite Tradition", *BA* 17 (1954) 50-76.
Meyer, E., *Der Papyrusfund von Elephantine. Dokumente einer jüdischen Gemeinde aus der Perserzeit und das älteste erhaltene Buch der Weltliteratur.* 2. Aufl. Leipzig 1912.
Meyer, R., "Gegensinn und Mehrdeutigkeit in der althebräischen Wort- und Begriffsbildung", *Festschrift für C. F. A. Schaeffer zum 80. Geburtstag am 6. März 1979.* Neukirchen-Vluyn (1979) 601-12 (*UF* 11).

Michel, O., "Der Tempel der goldenen Kuh (Bemerkungen zur Polemik im Spätjudentum)". [Von] ..., O. Bauernfeind [und] O. Betz, *ZNW* 49 (1958) 197-212.
Milik, J. T., "Nouvelles inscriptions nabatéennes", *Syr* 35 (1958) 227-51.
——, "Les papyrus araméens d'Hermoupolis et les cultes syrophéniciens en Égypte perse", *Bib* 48 (1967) 546-622.
——, *Recherches d'épigraphie proche-orientale. I. Dédicaces faites par des dieux (Palmyre, Hatra, Tyr) et des thiases sémitiques à l'époque romaine.* Paris 1972 (*BAH* 92).
Miller, P. D., "The *Mrzḥ* Text", *CRST* (1971) 37-48.
Mittmann, S., "Amos 3, 12-15 und das Bett der Samarier", *ZDPV* 92 (1976) 149-67.
Moor, J. C. de, *The seasonal Pattern in the Ugaritic Myth of Baᶜalu according to the Version of Ilimulku.* Neukirchen-Vluyn 1971 (*AOAT* 16).
——, "*ᵓšrh*", *TWAT* I (1973) 473-81.
——, "Ugarit", *IDBS* (1976) 928-31.
Moran, W. L., "New Evidence from Mari on the History of Prophecy", *Bib* 50 (1969) 15-56.
Morgenstern, J., "Amos Studies I-III", *HUCA* 11 (1936) 19-140, 12-13 (1937-38) 1-53, 15 (1940) 59-304.
Morin, P. J., *The Cult of the Dea Syria in the Greek World.* Unpubl. Diss. The Ohio State University. 1960.
Moscati, S., *An Introduction to the Comparative Grammar of the Semitic Languages.* By ..., A. Spitaler, E. Ullendorf, W. v. Soden. Ed. by S. Moscati. Wiesbaden 1969 (*PLO NS* 6).
Motzki, H., "Ein Beitrag zum Problem des Stierkultes in der Religionsgeschichte Israels", *VT* 25 (1975) 470-85.
Mowinckel, S., *Psalmenstudien II. Das Thronbesteigungsfest Jahwäs und der Ursprung der Eschatologie.* Kristiania 1922 (*SVSK.HF* 1921 No. 6).
——, *Psalmenstudien V. Segen und Fluch in Israels Kult und Psalmdichtung.* Kristiania 1924 (*SVSK.HF* 1923 No. 3).
——, *Jesajadisiplene. Profetien fra Jesaja til Jeremia.* Oslo 1926.
——, *Religion og kultus.* Oslo 1950.
——, *Offersang og sangoffer. Salmediktningen i Bibelen.* Oslo 1951.
——, "Jahves dag", *NTT* 59 (1958) 1-56, 209-29.
Muilenburg, J., "The Site of Ancient Gilgal", *BASOR* 140 (1955) 11-27.
Mulder, M. J., *Baᶜal in het Oude Testament.* Den Haag 1962.
——, *Kanaänitische goden in het Oude Testament.* Den Haag 1965 (*Ex* 4. R. Deel 4-5).
——, *De naam van de afwezige god op de Karmel. Onderzoek naar de naam van de Baäl van de Karmel in I Koningen 18.* Rede ... aan de Rijksuniversiteit te Leiden op vrijdag 28 september 1979. Leiden 1979.
Munch, P. A., *The Expression bajjôm hāhūᵓ. Is it an eschatological terminus technicus?* Oslo 1936 (*ANVA.HF* 1936. No. 2).
Murtonen, A., "Some Thoughts on Judges xvii sq.", *VT* 1 (1951) 223-24.
Naveh, J., "Aramaica Dubiosa", *JNES* 27 (1968) 317-25.
Negev, A., "Nabatean Inscriptions from ᶜAvdat (Oboda)", *IEJ* 1 (1961) 127-38, 13 (1963) 113-24.
Neher, A., *Amos. Contribution à l'étude du prophétisme.* Paris 1950.
Neubauer, K. W., "Erwägungen zu Amos 5, 4-15", *ZAW* 78 (1966) 292-316.
Neuberg, F. J., "An Unrecognized Meaning of Hebrew DÔR", *JNES* 9 (1950) 215-17.
Newlands, D. L., "Sacrificial Blood at Bethel?" *PEQ* 104 (1972) 155.
Nötscher, F., *Zwölfprophetenbuch oder kleinen Propheten.* Würzburg 1948 (*EB.AT*).
——, *Gotteswege und Menschenwege in der Bibel und in Qumran.* Bonn 1958 (*BBB* 15).
Noort, E., *Untersuchungen zum Gottesbescheid in Mari. Die "Mariprophetie" in der alttestamentlichen Forschung.* Neukirchen-Vluyn 1977 (*AOAT* 202).
Noth, M., *Die israelitischen Personennamen im Rahmen der gemeinsemitischen Namengebung.* Stuttgart 1928 (*BWANT* 46).
——, *Das System der Zwölf Stämme Israels.* Stuttgart 1930 (*BWANT* 52).
——, "Bethel und Ai", *PJ* 31 (1935) 7-29.
Nougayrol, J., "Einführende Bemerkungen zur babylonischen Religion" *Theologie und*

Religionswissenschaft. Der gegenwärtige Stand ihrer Forschungsergebnisse und Aufgaben in Hinblick auf ihr gegenseitiges Verhältnis. Hg. v. U. Mann. Darmstadt (1973) 28-46.

Nowack, W., *Die kleinen Propheten.* Übers. u. erkl. v.... 3. neu bearb. Aufl. Göttingen 1922 (*HK* 3. Abt. 4. B).

Nyberg, H. S., *Studien zum Hoseabuche. Zugleich ein Beitrag zur Klärung des Problems der alttestamentlichen Text-Kritik.* Uppsala 1935 (*UUÅ* 1935: 6).

Oden, R. A., "The Persistence of Canaanite Religion", *BA* 39 (1976) 31-36.

——, *Studies in Lucian's De Syria Dea.* Missoula, Mont. 1977 (*HSM* 15).

——, "Theoretical Assumptions in the Study of Ugaritic Myths", *MAARAV* 2 (1979-80) 43-63.

Oesterley, W. O. E., "Messianic Prophecy and Extra-Israelite Beliefs", *CQR* 119 (1934-35) 1-11.

Oral Tradition and Old Testament Study. Ed. R. C. Culley. Missoula, Mont. 1976 (*Semeia* 5).

Otzen, B., *Studien über Deuterosacharja.* Copenhagen 1964 (*AThD* 6).

Östborn, G., *Yahweh and Baal. Studies in the Book of Hosea and Related Documents.* Lund 1956 (*AULT* 1955: 6).

Le Palais Royal d'Ugarit. Publ. sous la direction de C. F. A. Schaeffer. III. *Textes accadiens et hourrites des archives Est, Ouest et Centrales.* Par J. Nougayrol, avec des études de G. Boyer et E. Laroche. [T. 1-2]. Paris 1955 (*MRS* 6.). IV. *Textes accadiens des archives Sud (Archives International).* Par J. Nougayrol. [T. 1-2]. Paris 1956 (*MRS* 9). V. *Textes en cunéiformes alphabétiques des archives Sud, Sud-Ouest et du Petit Palais.* Par C. Virolleaud. Paris 1965 (*MRS* 11).

Parker, E. A., "A Note on the Chronology of II Kings 17, 1", *AUSS* 6 (1968) 129-33.

Parrot, A., *Maledictions et violations de tombes.* Paris 1939.

——, *Samarie. Capitale du royaume d'Israël.* Neuchâtel 1955 (*CAB* 7).

Paul, S. M., "Sargon's Administrative Diction in II Kings 17, 27", *JBL* 88 (1969) 77-74.

——, "Amos 1, 3-2, 3. A Concatenous Literary Pattern", *JBL* 90 (1971) 397-403.

Pedersen, J., *Der Eid bei den Semiten. In seinem Verhältnis zu verwandten Erscheinungen sowie die Stellung des Eides im Islam.* Strassburg 1914 (*SGKIO* 3).

Perlitt, L., *Bundestheologie im Alten Testament.* Neukirchen-Vluyn 1969 (*WMANT* 36).

Perrot, J., "Beersheba". [By] ... [and] R. Gophna, *EAE* I (1975) 153-59.

Petersen, D. L., "Northwest Semitic Religion: A Study of Relational Structures". [By] ... [and] M. Woodward, *UF* 9 (1977) 233-48.

Pfeiffer, G., *Ursprung und Wesen der Hypostasenvorstellungen im Judentum.* Stuttgart 1967 (*AzTh* 1. R. H. 31).

——, "Denkformenanalyse als exegetische Methode, erläutert an Amos 1, 2-2, 16", *ZAW* 88 (1976) 56-71.

Plataroti, D., "Zum Gebrauch des Wortes *mlk* in Alten Testament", *VT* 28 (1968) 286-300.

Pope, M. H., *Song of Songs. A New Translation with Introduction and Commentary.* Garden City, N.Y. 1977 (*AncB* 7C).

Porten, B., *Archives from Elephantine. The Life of an Ancient Jewish Military Colony.* Berkeley 1968.

——, "The Religion of the Jews of Elephantine in Light of the Hermopolis Papyri", *JNES* 28 (1969) 116-21.

Posener, G., *Princes et pays d'Asie et de Nubie. Textes hieratiques sur des figurines d'envoûtement du Moyen Empire, suivis de remarques paléographiques sur les textes similaires de Berlin par B. van de Walle.* Bruxelles 1940.

Preuss, H. D., *Verspottung fremder Religionen im Alten Testament.* Stuttgart 1971 (*BWANT* 5. F. H. 12).

——, "*glwlym*", *TWAT* II (1977) 1-5.

Priest, J., "The Covenant of Brothers", *JBL* 84 (1965) 400-06.

Pritchard, J. B., "Tell Es-Saʿidiyeh", *RB* 73 (1966) 574-76.

Rad, G. v., "The Origin of the Concept of the Day of Yahweh", *JSS* 4 (1959) 97-108.

——, *Theologie des Alten Testaments. B. II. Die Theologie der prophetischen Überlieferungen Israels.* 2. Aufl. München 1961.

——, *Der Heilige Krieg im alten Israel.* 5. Aufl. Göttingen 1969.
Rahtjen, B. D., "A Critical Note on Am 8, 1-2", *JBL* 83 (1964) 416-17.
Rainey, A. F., "Dust and Ashes", *TA* 1 (1974) 77-83.
Raitt, T. M., "The Prophetic Summons to Repentance", *ZAW* 83 (1971) 30-49.
Ramlot, L., "Prophétisme. La Bible. Rapports avec la culte. Le devoir d'intercession prophétique", *DBS* 8 (1967-72) 1162-66.
Randellini, L., "Ricchi e poveri nel libro del profeta Amos", *SBFLA* 2 (1951-52) 5-86.
Ranke, H., *Die Personennamen in den Urkunden der Hammurabi-dynastie. Ein Beitrag zur Kenntnis der semitischen Namenbildung.* München 1902.
——, *Early Babylonian Personal Names from the Published Tablets of the so-called Hammurabi Dynasti (B.C. 2000).* Philadelphia PA. 1905 (*The Babylonian Expedition of the University of Pennsylvania. Series D. Researches and Treatises.* Ed. by H. V. Hilprecht. Vol. 3).
——, *Die Aegyptischen Personennamen.* Hamburg 1932-52.
Reichert, A., "Altar", *BRL*² (1977) 5-10.
——, "Massebe", *BRL*² (1977) 206-09.
Reiner, E., *Šurpu. A Collection of Sumerian and Akkadian Incantations.* Graz 1958 (*AfO.B* 11).
Reisner, G. A., *Harvard Excavations at Samaria 1908-1910.* [By] ..., C. S. Fisher [and] D. G. Lyon. Vol. I. *Text.* Vol. II. *Plans and Plates.* Cambridge, Mass. 1924 (*HSS*).
Renan, E., "[The presentation and first translation of *RES* 1215]", *CRAI* 4. sér. t. 16 (1889) 12-13.
Rendtorff, R., *Studien zur Geschichte des Opfers im Alten Testament.* Neukirchen-Vluyn 1967 (*WMANT* 24).
Renger, J., "Untersuchungen zum Priestertum in der altbabylonischen Zeit", 1. Teil," *ZA* 58 (1967) 110-88.
——, "Heilige Hochzeit. A. Philologisch", *RLA* 4 (1972-75) 251-59.
Repértoire d'épigraphie sémitique. Publ. par la Commission du Corpus Inscriptionum Semiticarum. Paris 1900-.
Reventlow, H., *Das Amt des Propheten bei Amos.* Göttingen 1962 (*FRLANT* 80).
Reymond, P., *L'eau, sa vie, et sa signification dans l'Ancien Testament.* Leiden 1958 (*SVT* 6).
Rhodes, A. B., "Israel's Prophets as Intercessors", *Scripture in History and Theology: Essays in Honor of J. C. Rylaarsdam.* Ed. by A. L. Merrill and T. W. Overholt. Pittsburgh. PA. (1977) 107-130 (*PTMS* 17).
Ribichini, S., "Per una riconsiderazione di Adonis", *RSF* 7 (1979) 163-74.
Ringgren, H., *Word and Wisdom. Studies in the Hypostatization of Divine Qualities and Functions in the Ancient Near East.* Lund 1947.
——, "Hypostasen", *RGG*³ III (1959) 504-06.
——, "Hieros gamos i Egypten, Sumer och Israel", *RoB* 18 (1959) 23-51.
——, *Israelitische Religion.* Stuttgart 1963 (*RM* 26).
——, "Light and Darkness in Ancient Egyptian Religion", *Liber Amicorum. Studies in Honour of C. J. Bleeker.* Leiden (1969) 140-50 (*SHR* 17).
——, "*ʾb*", *TWAT* I (1973) 1-19.
——, "*ʾlhym*", *TWAT* I (1973) 299-300.
Robinson, T. H., *Die zwölf kleinen Propheten. Hosea bis Micha.* Von ..., *Nahum bis Maleachi* v. F. Horst. Tübingen 1938 (*HAT* 1. R. 14).
——, *Die zwölf kleinen Propheten. Hosea bis Micha.* 3. Aufl. Tübingen 1964 (*HAT* 1. R. 14).
Ronzevalle, S., "Inscription bilingue de Deir el-Qalaʿa dans le Liban, près de Béryte", *RAr* 4. sér. t. 2 (1903) 29-49.
——, "Sîma - Athéna - Némésis", *Or* 3 (1934) 121-46.
Rose, M., *Der Ausschliesslichkeitsanspruch Jahwes. Deuteronomistische Schultheologie und die Volksfrömmigkeit in der späten Königszeit.* Stuttgart 1975 (*BWANT* 106).
Rosenthal, F., "Canaanite and Aramaic Inscriptions", *ANET.* Ed. by J. B. Pritchard. 2nd ed. Princeton, N.J. (1955) 499-505.
——, *A Grammar of Biblical Aramaic.* Wiesbaden 1961 (*PLO* N.S. 5).
Ross, J. F., "Prophecy in Hamath, Israel, and Mari", *HThR* 63 (1970) 1-28.
Rost, L., "Erwägungen zu Hos 4, 13f." *Festschrift A. Bertholet zum 80. Geburtstag gewidmet von Kollegen und Freunden.* Hg. v. W. Baumgartner, O. Eissfeldt, K. Elliger, L. Rost. Tübingen (1950) 451-60.

Rostovtzeff, M., *Caravan Cities.* Transl. by T. T. Rice. Oxford 1932.

Rowley, H. H., *The Aramaic of the Old Testament. A Grammatical and Lexical Study of its Relations with other Early Aramaic Dialects.* Oxford 1929.

——, "Ritual and the Hebrew Prophets", *JSS* 1 (1956) 338-60.

——, "Elijah on Mount Carmel", *BJRL* 43 (1960) 190-219.

——, "The Samaritan Schism in Legend and History", *Israel's Prophetic Heritage. Essays in Honor of James Muilenburg.* Ed. by B. W. Anderson and W. Harrelson. New York (1962) 208-22.

Rudolph, W., "Präparierte Jungfrauen? (Zu Hosea 1)", *ZAW* 75 (1963) 65-73.

——, *Jeremia.* 3., verbess. Aufl. Tübingen 1968 (*HAT* 1. R. 12).

——, "Amos 4, 6-13", *Wort, Gebot, Glaube. Beiträge zur Theologie des Alten Testaments. Walther Eichrodt zu 80. Geburtstag.* Zusammen mit J. J. Stamm u. E. Jenni hg. v. H. J. Stoebe. Zürich (1970) 27-38 (*ATANT* 59).

——, "Die angefochtenen Völkersprüche in Amos 1 und 2", *Schalom. Studien zur Glaube und Geschichte Israels.* Alfred Jepsen zum 70. Geburtstag dargebracht von Freunden, Schülern und Kollegen. Hg. v. K.-H. Bernhardt. Stuttgart (1971) 45-49 (*AzTh* 1. R. H. 46).

——, *Joel, Amos, Obadja, Jona.* Mit einer Zeittafel von A. Jepsen. Gütersloh 1971 (*KAT* 13: 2).

——, "Schwierige Amosstellen", *Wort und Geschichte. Festschrift für K. Elliger zum 70. Geburtstag.* Hg. v. H. Gese u. H. P. Rüger. Neukirchen-Vluyn (1973) 157-62 (*AOAT* 18).

Ryckmans, J., "Le repas rituel dans la religion sud-arabe," *Symbolae Biblicae et Mesopotamicae F. M. T. de Liagre Böhl dedicatae.* Ed. M. H. Beek *et al.* Leiden (1973) 327-34 (*Nederlands instituut voor het nabije Oosten. Studia Francisci Scholten memoriae dicata.* 4).

Sachau, E., *Aramäische Papyrus und Ostraka aus einer jüdischen Militärkolonie zu Elephantine.* Leipzig 1911.

Safar, F., "Inscriptions of Hatra", *Sumer* 9 (1953) 7-20.

Sanmartin-Ascaso, J., "*dwd*", *TWAT* 2 (1977) 152-67.

San Nicolò, M., "Eid", *RLA* II (1938) 305-15.

Sasson, J. M., "The Worship of the Golden Calf", *Orient and Occident. Essays Presented to Cyrus H. Gordon on the Occasion of his Sixty-fifth Birthday.* Ed. by H. A. Hoffner Jr. Neukirchen-Vluyn (1973) 151-59 (*AOAT* 22).

——, "On M. H. Pope's Song of Songs [AB7c]", *MAARAV* 1 (1978-79) 177-96.

Sauer, G., "*dæræk*", *THAT* I (1975) 456-60.

Savignac, R., "Notes de voyage de Suez au Sinai et à Pétra", *RB* 10 (1913) 429-42.

Sayce, A. H., "An Aramaic Ostracon from Elephantine," *PSBA* 31 (1909) 154-55.

Scharbert, J., *Solidarität in Segen und Fluch im Alten Testament und in seiner Umwelt. I. Väterfluch und Vätersegen.* Bonn 1958 (*BBB* 14).

Scheil, V., *Textes élamites-sémitiques.* 4. sér. Avec la collaboration de J. E. Gautier. Paris 1908 (*MDP* 10).

Schlumberger, D., "Neue Ausgrabungen in der syrischen Wüste nordwestlich von Palmyra", *AA* 50 (1935) 595-633.

——, *La Palmyrène du Nord-Ouest. Villages et lieux de culte de l'époque impériale. Recherches archéologiques sur la mise en valeur d'une région du désert par les Palmyréniens. Suivie du recuil des inscriptions sémitiques de cette région par H. Ingholt et J. Starcky, avec une contribution de G. Ryckmans.* Paris 1951.

Schmid, H. H., "Amos. Zur Frage des "geistigen Heimat" des Propheten", *WuD* N.F. 10 (1969) 85-103.

Schmidt, H., *Die Grossen Propheten.* Übers. u. erkl. v... Mit Einleitungen versehen v. H. Gunkel. Göttingen 1915 (*SAT* 2. Abt. 2. B).

Schmidt, N., "On the Text and Interpretation of Amos 5, 25-27", *JBL* 13 (1894) 1-15.

Schmidt, W., "Baals Tod und Auferstehung", *ZRGG* 15 (1963) 1-13.

Schmidt, W. H., "Die deuteronomistische Redaktion des Amosbuches. Zu den theologischen Unterschieden zwischen dem Prophetenwort und seinem Sammler", *ZAW* 77 (1965) 168-93.

——, "Die prophetische "Grundgewissheit". Erwägungen zur Einheit prophetischer Verkündigung", *EvTh* 31 (1971) 630-50.
——, "Suchet den Herrn, so werdet ihr leben", *Ex Orbe Religionum. Studia Geo Widengren ... Oblata.* Ed. C. J. Bleeker, S. G. F. Brandon, M. Simon. Pars Prior. Leiden (1972) 127-40 (*SHR* 21).
——, *Zukunftsgewissheit und Gegenwartskritik. Grundzüge prophetischer Verkündigung.* Neukirchen-Vluyn 1973 (*BSt* 64).
——, "*ʾlhym*", *THAT* I² (1975) 162.
Schollmeyer, A., *Sumerisch-babylonische Hymnen und Gebete an Šamaš.* Zusammengestellt u. bearb. v.... Paderborn 1912 (*SGKA.E* 1).
Schoville, K. N., "A Note on the Oracles of Amos Against Gaza, Tyre, and Edom", *Studies on Prophecy. A Collection of Twelve Papers.* Leiden (1974) 55-63 (*SVT* 26).
Schrader, E., "Assyrisch-Biblisches. 1. Kewan und Sakkuth (Amos 5, 26)", *ThStKr* 47 (1874) 324-35.
Schroeder, O., "Eine Götterliste für den Schulgebrauch", *Orientalische Studien F. Hommel zum 60. Geburtstag am 31. Juli gew. v. Freunden, Kollegen und Schülern.* B. 1. Leipzig (1917) 175-81 (*MVÄG* 21).
——, *Keilschrifttexte aus Assur verschiedenen Inhalts.* Leipzig 1920 (*WVDOG* 35).
Schüngel-Straumann, H., *Gottesbild und Kultkritik vorexilischer Propheten.* Stuttgart 1972 (*SBS* 60).
Schunck, K.-D., "Strukturlinien in der Entwicklung der Vorstellungen vom "Tag Jahwes"," *VT* 14 (1964) 319-30.
——, "Der "Tag Jahwes" in der Verkündigung der Propheten", *Kairos* 11 (1969) 14-21.
——, "*bmh*", *TWAT* 1 (1973) 662-67.
Schwantes, S. J., "Note on Amos 4, 2b", *ZAW* 79 (1967) 82-83.
Seebass, H., "Elia und Ahab auf dem Karmel", *ZThK* 70 (1973) 121-36.
Segert, S., *Altaramäische Grammatik. Mit Bibliographie, Chrestomathie und Glossar.* Leipzig 1975.
Sekine, M., "Das Problem der Kultpolemik bei den Propheten", *EvTh* 28 (1968) 605-09.
Sellin, E., *Der alttestamentliche Prophetismus. Drei Studien.* Leipzig 1912.
——, *Das Zwölfprophetenbuch.* Übers. u. erkl. v.... Leipzig 1922 (*KAT* 12).
Seters, J. van, *Abraham in History and Tradition.* New Haven, Conn. 1975.
Seux, M. J., *Épithètes royales akkadiennes et sumériennes.* Paris 1967.
——, *Hymnes et prières aux dieux de Babylonie et d'Assyrie.* Introd., trad. et notes de ... Paris 1976 (*LAPO* 8).
Seyrig, H., "Altar Dedicated to Zeus Betylos", *The Excavations at Dura-Europos Conducted by Yale University and the French Academy of Inscriptions and Letters. Preliminary Report of Fourth Season of Work Oct. 1930-March 1931.* Ed. by P. V. C. Baur, M. I. Rostovtzeff and H. R. Bellinger. New Haven, Conn. (1933) 68-71.
——, "Les tessères palmyréniennes et le banquet rituel", *Mémorial Lagrange. Cinquantenaire de l'École biblique et archéologique française de Jérusalem.* Paris (1940) 51-58.
——, "Antiquités syriennes. 78. Les dieux de Hiérapolis", *Syr* 37 (1960) 233-52.
Silvermann, M. H., *Jewish Personal Names in the Elephantine Documents: A Study in Onomastic Development.* Unpubl. Diss. Brandeis University (Mass.) 1967.
——, "Aramean Name-types in the Elephantine Documents", *JAOS* 89 (1969) 691-709.
——, "Onomastic Notes to "Aramaica Dubiosa", *JNES* 28 (1969) 192-96.
Simons, J., *Handbook for the Study of Egyptian Topographical Lists Relating to Western Asia.* Leiden 1937.
Sinclair, L. A., "The Courtroom Motif in the Book of Amos", *JBL* 85 (1966) 351-53.
Sjöberg, Å. W., *The Collection of the Sumerian Temple Hymns.* [By] ... and E. Bergman. New York 1969 (*TCS* 3).
Smend, R., *Jahwekrieg und Stämmebund. Erwägungen zur ältesten Geschichte Israels.* Göttingen 1963 (*FRLANT* 84).
——, "Das Nein des Amos", *EvTh* 23 (1963) 404-23.
Smith, J. M. P., "The Day of Yahweh", *AJT* 5 (1901) 505-33 [Note: Incorr. pag. Cf. pp. 512 and 529].
Sobernheim, M., *Palmyrenische Inschriften.* Berlin 1905 (*MVAG* 10: 2).

Soden, W. v., "Gibt es ein Zeugnis dafür, dass die Babylonier an die Wiederaufstehung Marduks geglaubt haben?" *ZA* 51 (1955) 130-66.
——, "Ein neues Bruchstück des assyrischen Kommentar zum Marduk-Ordal", *ZA* 52 (1957) 224-34.
——, "Licht und Finsternis in der sumerischen und babylonisch-assyrischen Religion", *StGen* 13 (1960) 647-53.
——, "Stierdienst", *RGG*³ VI (1962) 372-73.
——, *Akkadisches Handwörterbuch.* Unter Benutzung d. lexikalischen Nachlasses v. B. Meissner bearb. v.... B. I-. Wiesbaden 1965-
——, "Zur Stellung des 'Geweihten' (*qdš*) in Ugarit", *UF* 2 (1970) 329-30.
Soggin, J. A., "Der prophetische Gedanke über den Heiligen Krieg als Gericht gegen Israel", *VT* 10 (1960) 79-83.
——, "Das Erdbeben von Am 1, 1 und die Chronologie der Könige Ussia und Jotham von Juda", *ZAW* 82 (1970) 117-21.
——, "*mælæk*", *THAT* I (1971) 908-20.
——, "*šub*", *THAT* II (1976) 884-91.
——, *Introduction to the Old Testament. From its Origins to the Closing of the Alexandrian Canon.* Transl. by J. Bowden from the 2nd rev. Italian ed. 1974. London 1976.
Speier, S., "Bemerkungen zu Amos", *VT* 3 (1953) 305-10.
Speiser, E. A., "Note on Am 5, 26", *BASOR* 108 (1947) 5-6.
——, *Genesis.* Introd., Transl., and Notes by ... Garden City, N.Y. 1964 (*AncB* 1).
Starcky, J., "Autour d'une dédicace palmyrénienne à Šadrafa et à Duʿanat", *Syr* 26 (1949) 43-85.
——, "Pétra et la Nabatène", *DBS* VIII (1966) 886-1017.
Stark, J. K., *Personal Names in Palmyrene Inscriptions.* Oxford 1971.
Stolz, F., *Jahwes und Israels Kriege. Kriegstheorien und Kriegserfahrungen im Glauben des alten Israels.* Zürich 1972 (*AThANT* 60).
Strabonis Geographica. Rec. A. Meineke. Vol. III. Lipsiae 1877.
Strange, J., "The Inheritance of Dan", *StTh* 20 (1966) 120-39.
Stroete, G. Te, "Sünde im Alten Testament. Die Wiedergabe einiger hebräischen Ausdrücke für "Sünde" in fünf gangbaren west-europäischer Bibelübersetzungen", *Übersetzung und Deutung. Studien zu dem Alten Testament und seiner Umwelt A. R. Hulst gewidmet von Freunden und Kollegen.* Nijkerk (1977) 164-76.
Ström, Å., "Abendmahl I", *TRE* I (1977) 43-47.
Stuart, D., "The Sovereign's Day of Conquest", *BASOR* 221 (1976) 159-64.
Syrie Centrale. Inscriptions sémitiques publiées par Le Cte de Vogüe. Paris 1868-77.
Sæbø, M., "*ṣlḥ*", *THAT* II (1976) 551-56.
——, "*yom*". [Von] ..., W. v. Soden [und] J. Bergman, *TWAT* III, Lief. 4/5 (1980) 559-86.
Søgaard, H., "Gilde", [Av] ..., S. Ljung, V. Niitemaa, G. A. Blom, *KLNM*(*N*) V (1960) 299-313.
Taber, C. R., "Marriage", *IDBS* (1976) 573-76.
——, "Sex, Sexual Behaviour", *IDBS* (1976) 817-20.
Tallqvist, K. L., *Die assyrische Beschwörungsserie maqlû.* Nach den Originalen im British Museum hg. v.... I. *Einleitung, Umschrift, Übersetzung, Erläuterungen u. Wörterverzeichnis.* [1894?] (*Acta Societatis Scientiarum Fennicæ* 20: 6).
——, *Akkadische Götterepitheta. Mit einem Götterverzeichnis und einer Liste der prädikativen Elemente der sumerischen Götternamen.* Helsingfors 1938 (*StOr* 7).
Talmon, S., "The "Desert Motif" in the Bible and in Qumran Literature", *Biblical Motifs. Origins and Transformation.* Ed. by A. Altmann. Cambridge, Mass. (1966) 31-63 (*STLi* 3).
——, "*har*", *TWAT* II (1977) 459-483.
Teixidor, J., "Bulletin d'épigraphie sémitique", *Syr* 46 (1969) 319-58.
——, "Bulletin d'épigraphie sémitique 1970", *Syr* 47 (1970) 357-89.
——, *The Pagan God. Popular Religion in the Greco-Roman Near East.* Princeton, N.J. 1977.

Terrien, S., "Amos and Wisdom", *Israel's Prophetic Heritage. Essays in Honor of J. Muilenburg*. Ed. by B. W. Anderson and W. Harrelson. London and New York (1962) 108-15.
Thomas, D. Winton, "*KELEBH* 'Dog': Its Origin and some Usages of it in the Old Testament", *VT* 10 (1960) 410-27.
Thompson, T. L., *The Historicity of the Patriarchal Narratives: The Quest for the Historical Abraham*. Berlin 1974 (*BZAW* 133).
Thureau-Dangin, F., *Tablettes d'Uruk à l'usage des prêtres du Temple d'Anu au temps des Séleucides*. Publ. par ... Paris 1922 (*TCL* 6).
——, "Les fêtes d'Akitu d'après un texte divinatoire", *RA* 19 (1922) 141-48.
Torrey, C. C., "On the Text of Amos 5, 26, 6, 1, 7, 2", *JBL* 13 (1894) 61-63.
Trapiello, J. G., "La noción del "Día de Yahve" en el Antiguo Testamento", *CuBi* 26 (1969) 331-36.
Trible, P., "Woman in the O.T.", *IDBS* (1976) 963-66.
Tångberg, K. A., "Var Israels "klassiske" profeter botspredikanter? Oversikt over en del synsmåter hos kristne og jødiske bibelforskere i nyere tid", *TTK* 50 (1979) 93-105.
Ungern-Sternberg, R. v., "Die Bezeichnungen "Licht" und "Finsternis" im Alten Testament", *DtPfrBl* 65 (1965) 642-46.
Ungnad, A., *Aramäische Papyrus aus Elephantine. Kleine Ausgabe unter Zugrundelegung von E. Sachau's Erstausgabe*, bearb. v.... Leipzig 1911.
Vaux, R. de, "Sur quelques rapports entre Adonis et Osiris", *RB* 42 (1933) 31-56.
——, "Les prophètes de Baal sur le mont Carmel", *BMB* 5 (1941) 7-20.
——, "Le schisme religieux de Jeroboam 1er", *Mélanges Vosté* (1943) 77-91 (*Ang* 20).
——, *Les sacrifices de l'Ancien Testament*. Paris 1964.
——, *Ancient Israel. Its Life and Institutions*. Transl. by J. McHugh. 3rd paperback impr. London 1976.
Vawter, B., "Prophecy and the Redactional Question", *No Famine in The Land. Studies in Honor of John L. McKenzie*. Ed. by J. W. Flanagan and A. Weisbrod Robinson. Missoula, Mont. (1975) 127-39.
Vincent, L.-H., "Le culte d'Hélène à Samarie", *RB* 45 (1936) 221-32.
——, *La religion des Judéo-araméens d'Éléphantine*. Paris 1937.
Virolleaud, C., "Textes pour servir à l'histoire de la religion assyro-babylonienne", *RSEHA* 12 (1904) 269-75.
——, "Nouveaux fragments inédits du Musée Britannique", *Babyloniaca* 1 (1907) 185-209.
——, *La déesse ʿAnat. Poème de Ras Shamra*. Publ., trad. et commenté [par] ... Paris 1938 (*MRS* 4).
——, "Les nouveaux textes mythologiques et liturgiques de Ras Shamra (24e campagne, 1961). 1. RS 24.258", *Ug* V (1968) 545-51 (*MRS* 16).
Vogel, E. K., "Bibliography of Holy Land Sites", *HUCA* 42 (1971) 1-96.
Volz, P., *Das Neujahrsfest Jahwes (Laubhüttenfest)*. Tübingen 1912 (*SGV* 67).
——, "Die radikale Ablehnung der Kultreligion durch die alttestamentlichen Propheten", *ZSTh* 14 (1937) 63-85.
Vorderasiatische Schriftdenkmäler der königlichen Museen zu Berlin. Hg. v. d. Vorderasiatischen Abteilung. H.5. Leipzig 1908.
Vorländer, H., *Mein Gott. Die Vorstellungen vom persönlichen Gott im Alten Orient und im Alten Testament*. Neukirchen-Vluyn 1975 (*AOAT* 23).
Vuilleumier-Bessard, R., *La tradition cultuelle d'Israël dans la prophetie d'Amos et d'Osée*. Neuchâtel 1960 (*CTh* 45).
Waard, J. de, "The Chiastic Structure of Amos V 1-17", *VT* 27 (1977) 170-77.
Waardenburg, J., *Classical Approaches to the Study of Religion. Aims, Methods and Theories of Research*. Vol. 1. 's-Gravenhage 1973 (*RaR* 3).
Wagner, S., "Überlegungen zur Frage nach den Beziehungen des Propheten Amos zum Südreich", *ThLZ* 96 (1971) 653-70.
——, "*drš*", *TWAT* II (1977) 313-29.
Walton, F. R., "Atargatis", *RAC* I (1950) 854-60.

Wanke, G., "ʾwy and hwy", *ZAW* 78 (1966) 215-18.
Ward, J. M., *Amos and Isaiah. Prophets of the Word of God.* Nashville 1969.
Ward, W. A., "Notes on Some Semitic Loan-Words and Personal Names in Late Egyptian", *Or* 32 (1963) 413-36.
Watts, J. D. W., "Note on the Text of Amos V 7", *VT* 4 (1954) 215-16.
——, *Vision and Prophecy in Amos. 1955 Faculty Lectures Baptist Theological Seminary, Rüschlikon/Zürich., Switzerland.* Leiden 1958.
——, "A Critical Analysis of Am 4, 1ff.", *Society of Biblical Literature. 108. Annual Meeting. Proceedings.* Vol. II. Missoula, Mont. (1972) 489-500.
Weidner, E. F., "Der Tag des Stadtgottes", *AfO* 14 (1941-44) 340-42.
Weinfeld, M., *Deuteronomy and the Deuteronomic School.* Oxford 1972.
——, "Burning Babies in Ancient Israel. A Rejoinder to Morton Smith's Article in *JAOS* 95 (1975), pp. 477-79", *UF* 10 (1978) 411-13.
Weippert, H., "Jahwekrieg und Bundesfluch in Jer 21, 1-7", *ZAW* 82 (1970) 396-409.
——, "Die "deuteronomistiche" Beurteilungen der Könige von Israel und Juda und das Problem der Redaktion der Königsbücher", *Bib* 53 (1972) 301-39.
——, "Dan", *BRL*² (1977) 55-56.
——, "Samaria", *BRL*² (1977) 265-69.
Weippert, M., "Gott und Stier. Bemerkungen zu einer Terrakotte aus jāfa", *ZDPV* 77 (1961) 93-117.
——, "'Heiliger Krieg' in Israel und Assyrien. Kritische Anmerkungen zu Gerhard von Rads Konzept des 'Heiligen Krieges im alten Israel'," *ZAW* 84 (1972) 460-93.
Weiser, A., *Die Prophetie des Amos.* Giessen 1929 (*BZAW* 53.).
——, *Das Buch der zwölf kleinen Propheten. I. Die Propheten Hosea, Joel, Amos, Obadja, Jona, Micha.* Übers. u. erkl. v... 2. neubearb. Aufl. Göttingen 1956 (*ATD* 24: 1).
Weiss, H.-F., "Zehnte", *BHH* III (1966) 2208-09.
Weiss, M., "The Origin of the "Day of the Lord" - Reconsidered", *HUCA* 37 (1966) 29-60.
——, "The Pattern of Numerical Sequence in Amos 1-2. A Re-Examination", *JBL* 86 (1967) 416-23.
Wellhausen, J., *Israelitische u. jüdische Geschichte.* 3. Ausg. Berlin 1897.
——, *Die kleinen Propheten.* Übers. u. erkl. v... 3. Ausg. Berlin 1898. 4. unveränd. Aufl. Berlin 1963.
Welten, P., "Salbe und Salbgefässe", *BRL*² (1977) 260-64.
——, "Götterbild, männliches," *ibid.* 99-111.
——, "Götterbild, weibliches," *ibid.* 111-119.
——, "Göttergruppe", *ibid.* 119-122.
Wensinck, A. J., "The Semitic New Year and the Origin of Eschatology" *AcOr* 1 (1923) 158-99.
Westermann, C., *Grundformen prophetischer Rede.* München 1960 (*BEvTh* 31).
——, "Propheten", *BHH* 3 (1966) 1496-1512.
——, *Der Psalter.* 2. Aufl. Stuttgart 1969.
——, *Lob und Klage in den Psalmen.* 5. erw. Aufl. Göttingen 1977.
Whedbee, J. W., *Isaiah and Wisdom.* Nashville 1971.
Whitaker, R. E., *A Concordance of the Ugaritic Literature.* Cambridge, Mass. 1972.
Widengren, G., "Konungens vistelse i dödsriket. En studie till Psalm 88", *SEÅ* 10 (1945) 66-81.
——, "Hieros gamos och underjordsvistelse. Studier till det sakrala kungadömet i Israel", *RoB* 7 (1948) 17-46.
——, *Sakrales Königtum im Alten Testament und im Judentum.* Stuttgart 1955 (*FDV* 1952).
Wilch, J. R., *Time and Event. An Exegetical Study of the Use of ʿēth in the Old Testament in Comparison to Other Temporal Expressions in Clarification of the Concept of Time.* Leiden 1969.
Will, E., "Le rituel des Adonies", *Syr* 52 (1975) 93-105.
Williams, A. J., "A Further Suggestion about Amos iv 1-3", *VT* 29 (1979) 206-11.

Wilson, J. A., "The Oath in Ancient Egypt", *JNES* 7 (1948) 129-56.
Wilson, R. R., *Prophecy and Society in Ancient Israel.* Philadelphia Pa. 1980.
Wörterbuch der Mythologie. Abt. 1. B. 1. *Götter und Mythen im Vorderen Orient.* Unter Mitarbeit v. D. O. Edzard, W. Helck, M. Höfner, M. H. Pope, W. Röllig, E. v. Schuler hg. v. H. W. Haussig. Stuttgart 1965.
Wolff, H. W., *Dodekapropheton I. Hosea.* Neukirchen-Vluyn 1961 (*BK. AT* 14: 1).
——, "Der Aufruf zur Volksklage", *ZAW* 76 (1964) 48-56.
——, "Das Thema "Umkehr" in der alttestamentlichen Prophetie", *Gesammelte Studien zum Alten Testament.* München (1964) 130-50 (*TB* 22).
——, *Amos' geistige Heimat.* Neukirchen-Vluyn 1964 (*WMANT* 19).
——, *Dodekapropheton 2. Joel und Amos.* Neukirchen-Vluyn 1969 (*BK.AT* 14: 2).
——, "Das Ende des Heiligtums in Bethel", *Archäologie und Altes Testament. Festschrift für Kurt Galling.* Hg. v. A. Kuschke und E. Kutsch. Tübingen (1970) 287-98.
——, "Die eigentliche Botschaft der klassischen Propheten", *BeitrAltTheol* (1977) 547-57.
——, "Wie verstand Micha von Morechet sein prophetisches Amt?", *Congress Volume: Göttingen 1977.* Leiden (1978) 403-17. (*SVT* 29).
Woude, A. S. van, "*ṣābāʾ*", *THAT* II (1976) 498-507.
Wright, G. E., "Israelite Samaria and Iron Age Chronology", *BASOR* 155 (1959) 13-29.
——, "The Lawsuit of God: A Form-Critical Study of Deuteronomy 32", *Israel's Prophetic Heritage. Essays in Honor of James Muilenburg.* Ed. by B. W. Anderson and W. Harrelson. London and New York (1962) 26-67.
Würthwein, E., "Amos 5, 21-27", *ThLZ* 72 (1947) 143-52.
——, "Amos-Studien", *ZAW* 62 (1949-50) 10-52.
——, "Kultpolemik oder Kultbescheid?" Beobachtungen zu dem Thema "Prophetie und Kult"," *Tradition und Situation. Studien zur alttestamentlichen Prophetie. Arthur Weiser zum 70. Geburtstag... dargebracht...* Hg. v. E. Würthwein u. O. Kaiser. Göttingen (1963) 115-31.
Wüst, M., "Bethel", *BRL*[2] (1977) 44-45.
Wuthnow, H., *Die semitischen Menschennamen in griechischen Inschriften und Papyri des vorderen Orients.* Leipzig 1930 (*Studien zur Epigraphik und Papyruskunde* 1: 4).
Xella, P., *Il mito di Šhr e Šlm. Saggio sulla mitologia ugaritica.* Roma 1973 (*SS* 44).
——, *Problemi del mito nel Vicino Oriente antico.* Napoli 1976 (*AION Suppl.* 7).
Yahuda, A. S., "Bagdadische Sprichwörter", *Orientalische Studien Theodor Nöldeke zum 70. Geburtstag gewidmet.* B. I. Giessen (1906) 399-416.
Yamauchi, E. M., "Cultic Prostitution. A Case Study in Cultural Diffusion", *Orient and Occident. Essays Presented to Cyrus H. Gordon on the Occasion of his 65. Birthday.* Ed. by H. A. Hoffner Jr. Neukirchen-Vluyn (1973) 213-22 (*AOAT* 22).
Zadok, R., "Geographical and Onomastic Notes", *JANES* 8 (1976) 113-26.
Zakovitch, Y., "*For Three... and for Four". The Pattern of the Numerical Sequence Three-Four in the Bible: The Adaption of a Common Oral Pattern to the Literature of the Bible.* [Vols I-II]. Jerusalem 1979 (in Hebrew).
Zenger, E., "Jahwe und die Götter. Die Frühgeschichte der Religion Israels als eine theologische Wertung nichtisraelitischer Religionen," *ThPh* 43 (1968) 338-59.
Ziegler, J., "Die Hilfe Gottes "am Morgen"," *Alttestamentliche Studien Friedrich Nötscher zum 60. Geburtstag gewidmet.* Dargeb. v. H. Junker u. J. Botterweck. Bonn (1950) 281-88 (*BBB 1).*
Zimmerli, W., *Geschichte und Tradition von Beersheba im Alten Testament.* Giessen 1932.
——, *Ezechiel.* Neukirchen-Vluyn 1969. (*BK.AT* 13).
Zimmern, H., *Der babylonische Gott Tamūz.* Leipzig 1909 (*ASGW.PH* 28).
——, *Zum babylonischen Neujarhsfest.* 2. Beitrag. Leipzig 1918 (*BVSAW.PH* 70: 5).
——, "Šīmat, Sīma, Tyche, Manāt", *Isl* 2 (1926) 574-84.
Zirker, H., "derekh = potentia?" *BZ* NF 2 (1958) 291-94.
Zobel, H.-J., *Stammesspruch und Geschichte. Die Angaben der Stammessprüche von Gen 49, Dtn 33 und Jdc 5 über die politischen und kultischen Zustände im damaligen "Israel"*, Berlin 1965 (*BZAW* 95).
——, "*hwy*", *TWAT* II (1977) 382-88.

ADDENDA

Borger, R., "Keilschrifttexte verschiedenen Inhalts", *Symbolae Biblicae et Mesopotamicae F. M. T. de Liagre Böhl dedicatae*. Ed. M. H. Beek *et al.* Leiden (1973) 38-55 (*Nederlands instituut voor het nabije Oosten. Studia Francisci Scholten memoriae dicata.* 4).

Bright, J., *Jeremiah*. Introd., transl., and notes by ... 2nd ed. New York 1965 (*AncB.* 21).

Eissfeldt, O., *Molk als Opferbegriff im Punischen und Hebräischen und das Ende des Gottes Moloch.* Halle (Saale) 1935 (*BRGA* 3).

Jahnow, H., *Das hebräische Leichenlied im Rahmen der Völkerdichtung*. Giessen 1923 (*BZAW* 36).

Jenni, E., "*ʾāb*", *THAT* I (1971) 1-18.

Lane, W. R., "Wallfahrt", *BHH* III (1966) 2135.

Loewenstamm, S. E., "Eine lehrhafte ugaritische Trinkburleske", *UF* 1 (1969) 71-77.

Montgomery, J. A., "Notes from the Samaritan", *JBL* 25 (1906) 49-54.

Moor, J. C. de, "Studies in the New Alphabetic Texts from Ras Shamra I", *UF* 1 (1969) 167-88.

——, "*bʿl*". [Von] ... [und] M. J. Mulder, *TWAT* I (1973) 706-727.

Rendtorff, R., "El, Baʿal und Jahwe. Erwägungen zum Verhältnis von kanaanäischen und israelitischen Religion", *ZAW* 78 (1966) 277-92.

Rüger, H. P., "Zu RŠ 24.258", *UF* 1 (1969) 203-06.

Virolleaud, C., "Les Rephaïm. Fragments de poèmes de Ras-Shamra", *Syr* 22 (1941) 1-30.

——, "Six textes de Ras Shamra provenant de la XIVe campagne (1950)", *Syr* 28 (1951) 163-79.

Waddington, W. H., *Voyage archéologique en Grèce et en Asie Mineure* ... [3] P. 3 *Inscriptions grecques et latines recueillies en Grèce et en Asie Mineure*. Par Philippe Le Bas et ... Paris 1870.

Winter, I. J., "Phoenician and North Syrian Ivory Carving in Historical Context: Questions of Style and Distribution", *Iraq* 38 (1976) 1-22.

Wüst, M., "Beerseba", *BRL*² (1977) 36.

AUTHOR INDEX

SCRIPTURE REFERENCES

JOSHUA

EZEKIEL

SUBJECT INDEX

SELECT

(References are to pages only)